AVRORA.

That is, the

Day-Spring.

Or

Dawning of the Day in the Orient

Or

𝔐𝔬𝔯𝔫𝔦𝔫𝔤=𝔎𝔢𝔡𝔫𝔢𝔰𝔰𝔢

in the Rifing of the

S V N.

That is

The Root or Mother of

Philofophie, Aftrologie & Theologie

from the true Ground.

Or

A Defcription of Nature.

I. How All was, and came to be in the Beginning.
II. How Nature and the Elements are become Creaturely.
III. Alfo of the Two Qualities Evill and Good.
IIII. From whence all things had their Original.
V. And how all ftand and work at prefent.
VI. Alfo how all will be at the End of this Time.
VII. Alfo what is the Condition of the Kingdom of God, and of the Kingdom of Hell.
VIII. And how men work and act creaturely in Each of them.

All this fet down diligently from a true Ground in the Knowledge of the Spirit, and in the impnlfe of God.

By

Jacob Behme

Teutonick Philofopher.

Being his FIRST BOOK.

Written in *Gerlitz* in *Germany* Anno Chrifti M. DC. XII. on Tuefday after the Day of Pentecoft or Whitfunday *Ætatis fuæ* 37.

London, Printed by *John Streater,* for *Giles Calvert,* and are be fold at his Shop at the *Black-fpread-Eagle* at the Weft-End of *Pauls,* 1656.

Kessinger Publishing's Rare Reprints
Thousands of Scarce and Hard-to-Find Books!

DEDICATED

TO THE MEMORY OF

THAT DEVOUT, GOD-FEARING MAN

CARL VON ENDERN

Esai 9. 2.
Math 4. 16.

W Hollar fecit.

Photogravure 1914.

Rev. 1. 4.

Rev. 4. 5.

Rev. 5. 6. & 10.

THE BRIEF CONTENTS OF THE TWENTY-SIX CHAPTERS OF THE FIRST BOOK OF THE AUTHOR, CALLED THE *AURORA*.

CONTENTS xlv

J. B. PREFACE FOR THE *AURORA*

To the Courteous Reader

1. COURTEOUS Reader, I compare the whole *Philosophy, Astrology*, and *Theology*, together with their mother, to a goodly tree which groweth in a fair garden of pleasure.

2. Now the earth in which the tree standeth affords sap continually to the tree, whereby the tree hath its living *quality*: But the tree in itself groweth from the *sap* of the earth, becomes large, and spreadeth itself abroad with its branches: And then, as the earth worketh with its power* upon the tree, to make it grow and increase, so the tree also worketh continually with its *branches*, with all its strength, that it might still bear good fruit abundantly.

3. But when the tree beareth few fruit, and

---

* "power" (*Kraft*), "virtue." In the great majority of cases where Sparrow uses the word "power," the original, *Kraft*, is best rendered by the word "virtue," as St Martin has done.

those but small, shrivelled, *rotten*, and worm-eaten, the fault doth not lie in the will of the tree, as if it desired *purposely* to bear evil fruit, because it is a goodly tree of good *quality*. But here lieth the fault: because there is often great cold, great heat, and mildew, caterpillars and other worms happen to it; for the *quality* in the deep, from the influence of the stars, spoileth it, and that maketh it bear but few good fruit.

4. Now the tree is of this condition, that the bigger and older it is, the sweeter fruit it beareth: In its younger years it beareth few fruit, which the crude and wild nature of the ground or earth causeth, and the *superfluous* moisture in the tree: And though it beareth many fair blossoms, yet the most of its apples fall off whilst they are growing; unless it standeth in a very good soil or mould. Now this tree also hath a good sweet quality; but there are *three* others, which are contrary to it, namely, the bitter, the sour, and the astringent.

5. As the tree is, so will its fruit be, till the sun worketh on them and maketh them sweet; so that they become of a pleasant taste, and its fruit must also *hold out* in rain, wind and tempest.

6. But when the tree groweth old, that its branches wither and the sap ascendeth *no more*, then below the stem or stock there grow many suckers; at last from the root twigs grow also, and transfigure the old tree, shewing that *it* also

was once a green twig and young tree, and is now become old. For nature, or the sap, struggleth * so long till the stock groweth quite dry; and then it is to be cut down and burnt in the fire.

7. Now observe what I have signified by this *similitude:* The garden of this tree signifieth the *world*; the soil or mould signifieth *nature*; the stock of the tree signifies the *stars*; by the *branches* are meant the *elements*; the fruit which grow on this tree signify *men*; the sap in the tree denoteth the pure *Deity.* Now men were made out of nature,† the *stars*, and *elements*; but *God* the Creator reigneth in all: even as the *sap* doth in the whole tree.

8. But there are two *qualities in nature*, even until the *Judgment* of God: The one is pleasant, heavenly and holy; the other is fierce, wrathful, hellish and thirsty.

9. Now the good one qualifieth and worketh continually with all industry to bring forth *good* fruit, and the *Holy Ghost* reigneth therein, and affords thereunto sap and life: the bad one springeth and driveth with all its endeavour to bring forth *bad* fruit continually, to which the devil affordeth sap and *hellish* flame. Now both

---

* "struggleth" (*wehret sich*), "resisteth" or "persisteth"; the real meaning implies both renderings. St M. has, "*se conserve.*"

† "men were made out of nature," etc. Note by St Martin: "The author does not invariably use the word 'nature,' as applying to the actual and visible world."

are in the tree of nature, and *men* are made out of *that* tree, and live in this world, in this garden, *between* both, in great danger; suddenly the sun shineth on them; by and by, winds, rain, and snow fall on them.

10. That is, if man elevateth his spirit into the *Deity*, then the Holy Ghost moveth, springeth and qualifieth in him: But if he permit his spirit to sink into the world, in lust towards *evil*, then the devil and hellish sap stir and reign in him.

11. Even as the apple on the tree becometh corrupt, rotten and worm-eaten, when frost, heat, and mildew fall on it, and easily falls off and perisheth: So doth man also when he suffers the devil to rule in him with his *poison*.

12. Now as in nature there are, spring up and reign, good and bad; even so in man: But man is the *child of God*, whom God hath made out of the best kernel of nature, to reign in the good, and to overcome the bad: Though evil sticketh unto man, even as in *nature* the evil hangeth on the good, yet he can overcome the evil if he elevateth his spirit in God; for then the *Holy Ghost* stirs and moveth in him, and helps him to overcome.

13. As the good quality in nature is potent to overcome the evil, for the good quality is and cometh from God, and the Holy Ghost is the *Ruler* therein, even so is the fierce wrathful

quality powerful to overcome in a *malicious* wicked soul : For the devil is a potent *ruler* in the wrath * or fierceness, and is an eternal prince of the same.

14. But man, through the fall of Adam and Eve, hath cast himself into fierce wrathfulness, so that the evil hangeth on him; otherwise his moving and driving † would be *only* in the good. But now his moving and driving are in *both*. And it is as St *Paul* saith, [1] *Know ye not, that to* [1] Rom. vi. 16. *whom you yield yourselves servants in obedience, his servants ye are, to whom ye obey, either to sin unto death, or to the obedience of God unto righteousness.*

15. But because man hath an *impulse* or inclination to both good and evil, he may lay hold on which he pleaseth; for he liveth in this world between *both*, and both *qualities*, the good and the bad, are in him; in whichsoever man moveth, with that he is endued, either with a holy, or with a hellish power. For Christ saith, [2] *My Father will give the Holy Ghost to those that* [2] Luke xi. 13. *ask Him.*

* "in the wrath," etc. Note by St Martin: "By the word 'wrath,' the author understands the eternal power itself, as separated from love, justice and light."

† "his moving and driving" (*sein Quell und Trieb*), "his source and motive power." St M. has "*son impulsion,*" "his impelling power." In the next par. and in several which follow, Sparrow renders the word *Trieb*, "impulse," or "inclination"; of these, the former is the better of the two.

16. Besides, God commanded man to do good, and forbad him to do evil; and now doth daily call and cry aloud, preach and exhort man unto good; whereby we see well enough that God *willeth not evil*, but his will is, That *his kingdom* should *come*, and *his will be done, on earth as it is in heaven.* But now man is poisoned through sin, that the fierce wrathful quality, as well as the good, reigneth in him, and he is now *half* dead, and in his gross ignorance can no more know God his Creator, nor nature and its operation: Yet hath nature used its best endeavours from the beginning till now, to which God hath given his Holy Ghost, so that it [nature] hath at all times generated * wise, holy, and *understanding* men, who learned to know nature, and their Creator, and who always in their writings and teachings have been a *light* to the world, whereby God hath raised his Church on earth, to his eternal praise. Against which the devil hath *raged*, and spoiled many a noble twig, through the wrathful fierceness in nature, whose *prince* and god he is.

17. For nature hath many times prepared and fitted a learned judicious man with good gifts, and then the devil hath done his utmost to seduce that man, and bring him into *carnal pleasures*, into pride, into a desire to be rich, and

---

* "generated," lit., "generated and prepared," *i.e.* guided and instructed.

to be in authority and power. Thereby the devil hath ruled in him, and the fierce wrathful *quality* hath overcome the good; his understanding and his knowledge and wisdom have been turned into *heresy* and error, and he hath made a mock of the truth, and been the author of great errors on earth, and a good leader of the devil's host.

18. For, ever since the beginning, the bad quality in nature hath wrestled with the good, and doth still wrestle, and hath elevated itself, and spoiled many a noble fruit even in the mother's *womb*, as it plainly appeareth, first by *Cain* and *Abel*, who came from one womb. From his mother's womb *Cain* was a despiser of God, and proud; but *Abel*, on the contrary, was a humble man, and one that feared God.

19. The same is seen also in the *three* sons of *Noah*; as also by *Abraham's* sons, *Isaac*, and *Ismael*, especially by *Isaac's* in *Esau* and *Jacob*, who struggled and wrestled even in the mother's womb: therefore said God, [1] *Jacob have I loved, and Esau have I hated*; which is nothing else but that both qualities in nature have vehemently wrestled the one with the other.

[1] Mal. i. 2, 3. Rom. ix. 13.

20. For when God at that time moved in nature, and would *reveal* himself unto the world through righteous *Abraham*, *Isaac*, and *Jacob*, and would raise a Church to himself on earth for his glory, then in nature malice also moved, and its prince *Lucifer*. Seeing there was good and bad

in man, therefore both *qualities* could reign in him, and therefore there was born at *once* in one womb an evil man and a good man.

21. Also it is clearly seen by the *first* world, as also by the *second*, even unto the end of our time, how the heavenly and the hellish kingdoms in nature have always wrestled the one with the other, and stood in great travail, even as a woman in the birth. This doth most clearly appear by *Adam* and *Eve*. For in Paradise there grew up a tree of both *qualities*, of good and bad, wherewith *Adam* and *Eve* were to be tempted, to try whether they would hold out in the *good quality* in the angelical kind and form. For the *Creator forbad* Adam *and* Eve *to eat of the fruit:* But the evil quality in nature wrestled with the good, and brought *Adam* and *Eve* into a lust and longing to eat of both. Thereupon they presently came to be of a bestial form and kind, and did eat of good and bad, and must increase and live in a *bestial* manner; and so many a noble twig begotten or born of them perished.

22. Afterwards it is seen how God wrought in nature, when the holy fathers in the first world were born: As *Abel, Seth, Enos, Kenan, Mahalaleel, Jared, Henoch, Methusalah, Lamech,* and holy *Noah.* These made the name of the Lord known to the world, and preached *Repentance:* For the Holy Ghost wrought *in* them.

23. On the contrary, the hellish god also

wrought *in* nature, and begot mockers and despisers, first *Cain* and his posterity : And it was with the first world as with a young tree, which groweth, is green, and blossometh fairly, but bringeth little good fruit, by reason of its *wild* kind. So nature in the first world brought forth but little good fruit, though it blossomed fair in *worldly* knowledge, and luxury or wantonness, *which* could not apprehend the Holy Spirit, who wrought in nature then, as well as now.

24. Therefore said God, [1] *It repents me, that I have made man,* and he stirred up nature so, that all flesh which lived on dry land died, excepting the root and stock, that remained in virtue : and so he hath hereby *dunged* the wild tree, and manured it, that it should bear *better* fruit. But when the same sprang up again, it brought forth good and bad fruit again : Among the sons of *Noah* there were found again mockers and despisers of God, and there grew *hardly* any good branch on the tree, which brought forth any *holy* and good fruit : The other branches were bearing also, and brought forth wild Heathen.

25. But when God saw that man was thus dead in his knowledge, he moved nature again, and *shewed* unto *man* how there was *good and bad* therein, that man should *avoid evil,* and *live unto the good* ; and he caused fire to fall down out of nature, and fired *Sodom* and *Gomorrah,*

[1] Gen. vi. 6.

for a terrible example to the world. But when the blindness of men grew predominant, and they refused to be taught by the spirit of God, he gave *laws* and *precepts* unto them, shewing how they should behave themselves, and confirmed the laws and precepts with *wonders*, and with signs, lest the knowledge of the true God should be quite extinct. But for all this, the light did *not* manifest itself, for the darkness and wrathful fierceness in nature struggled against it, and the prince of darkness ruled powerfully.

26. But when the tree of nature came to its middle age, then it began to bear some *mild* and sweet fruit, to shew that it would henceforth bear pleasant fruit. Then were born the *holy prophets*, out of the sweet branch of the tree, who taught and preached of the *light*, which hereafter should overcome the wrathful fierceness in nature. And then there arose a light in nature among the Heathen, so that they knew nature, and her operation, although this was a light in the *wild* nature *only*, and was not yet the *holy* light.

27. For the wild nature was not yet overcome, and light and darkness wrestled so long the one with the other, till the *sun* arose, and with its heat forced this tree, so that it did bear pleasant sweet fruit; that is, till there came the Prince of Light, out of the heart of God, and *became man* in nature, and wrestled in his human body, in the power of the divine light, in the wild nature.

That same Prince and *Royal* Twig grew up in
nature, and became a tree in nature, and spread
its branches abroad from the east to the west;
and encompassed the whole nature, and wrestled
and fought with the fierce wrath which was in
nature, and with the prince thereof, till he overcame and triumphed, as a king in nature, and
took the *prince of wrath* or fierceness *captive*
in his own [1] house.   [1] Psal. lxviii.

28. This being done, there grew out of the
Royal Tree, which was grown in nature, many
thousand *legions* of precious sweet twigs, all
which had the scent and taste of that precious
tree. Though there fell upon them rain, snow,
hail and tempestuous storms, so that many a twig
was *torn* and beaten off from the tree, yet still
others grew in their places. For the wrath or
fierceness in nature, and the prince thereof, raised
great *tempests*, with hail, thunder, lightning and
rain, so that many glorious twigs were torn from
the sweet and good tree.

29. But these twigs were of such a pleasant,
sweet and delightful taste, that no human nor
angelical tongue is able to express it: For there
was great *power* and virtue in them, so that they
were good to *heal* the wild Heathen. Whatever
Heathen did eat of the twig of this tree was
delivered from the wild nature in which he was
born, and became a sweet branch in this precious
tree, and sprang in that tree, and bore precious

fruit, like the Royal Tree. Therefore many Heathen hastened to the precious tree, where the precious twigs lay, which the prince of darkness, by his storms and tempestuous winds, had torn off; and whatever Heathen did smell at the twig so torn off was healed of his wild wrath or fierceness, which he had brought from his mother into the world.

30. But when the prince of darkness saw that the Heathen *strove* and contended about these *twigs*, and not about the *tree*, therein he found great loss and damage, and then he ceased with his storms toward the east and south, and placed a merchant under the tree, who gathered up the twigs which were fallen from the precious tree: And when the Heathen came, and enquired after the good and virtuous twigs, then the merchant presented and offered them for money, to make gain of the precious *tree*. For this the prince of wrath or fierceness required at the hands of his merchant, because the tree was grown upon his ground and land, and spoiled his soil.

31. So when the *Heathen* saw that the fruit of the precious tree was put to *sale*, they flocked to the merchant, and bought of the *fruit* of the tree; and they came to buy also from foreign islands, even from the ends of the world. Now when the merchant saw that his wares were in request and esteem, he plotted how he might gather a great treasure to his *master*, and so sent *factors* abroad

everywhere, to offer his wares to sell, praising them highly : But he *sophisticated* the wares, and sold other fruit instead of the good, which were not grown on the good tree ; this he did to increase his master's treasure.

32. But the Heathen, and all the islands and nations which dwelt on the earth, were all grown on the *wild* tree, which was good and bad, and therefore were half blind, and did not discern the good tree (which, however, spread its branches from the east to the west) else they would *not* have bought of the *false* wares.

33. But because they knew not the precious tree, which spread its branches over them all, *all of them ran after and to the factors*, and bought of them *mixed* false wares instead of good, and supposed they served for health : But because *all* of them *longed* after the good tree, (which, however, moved over them all), many of them were healed, because of their great desire they had to the tree. For the fragrancy of the tree, which moved over them, healed them of their wrath or fierceness and *wild* nature, and not the false wares of the factors : this continued a long time.

34. Now when the prince in the darkness, who is the source of wrath or fierceness, malice and perdition, *perceived* that men were healed of their poison and wild nature by the fragrancy of the precious tree, he was enraged, and planted a wild tree towards the north, which sprang up and

grew in the fierceness or wrath of nature, and made proclamation, saying: *This is the Tree of Life; he that eateth of it, shall be healed and live eternally.*

35. For in that place, where the wild tree grew, was a wild place, and the people there had the true light of God from the beginning, even unto that time, and to this day, though unknown: and the tree grew on the mount *Hagar* in the house of *Ismael* the mocker. But when proclamation was made of the tree, *Behold, this is the Tree of Life!* then the wild people, who were *not* born of God, but of the wild nature, *flocked* unto the tree, and *loved* the wild tree, and did eat of its fruit.

36. And the tree grew to a mighty bigness, by the sap of *wrath* or fierceness in nature, and spread abroad its branches, from the north to the east and west: But the tree had its source and root from the wild nature, which was good and bad; and as the tree was, so were its fruits. But though the men of this place were grown out of the wild nature, yet the tree grew over them all, and grew so huge, that it reached with its branches even unto the esteemed *precious land* or country under the holy tree.

37. But the cause that the wild tree grew to such a huge bigness, was because the nations under the good tree all ran after the *factors* who sold the *false* wares, and did eat of the false

fruits, which were good and bad, and supposed they were healed thereby, and meddled *not* with the holy, good, effectual tree.

38. In the meanwhile they grew more blind, weak and impotent, and were *disabled* to suppress the growing of the wild tree towards the north: For they were too weak and impotent, and they saw well enough that the tree was wild, and bad; but they wanted strength, and could not suppress the growing of the tree.

39. Yet if they had not run after the false wares those factors *sold*, and had not eaten of the *false* fruits, but rather eaten of the precious tree, then they might have gotten strength to oppose the wild tree. But because they ran a whoring after the wild nature in human *conceits* and opinions, in the lusts of their hearts, in a hypocritical way, therefore the wild nature did predominate over them, and the wild tree grew high and large over them, and spoiled them with its wild *rankness*.

40. For the prince of wrath or fierceness in nature gave his power to the tree, to spoil men that did eat of the wild fruits of the factors: Because they forsook the Tree of Life, and sought after their own cleverness, as mother *Eve* did in Paradise, therefore their own *innate quality* predominated in them, *and brought them into strong delusions*, as St *Paul* saith.[1] And the prince of wrath or fierceness raised *wars* and tempests

[1] 2 Thess. ii. 11.

from the wild tree towards the north, against the
people and nations that were *not* born of the wild
tree; and the tempest that came from the wild
tree overthrew them in their weakness and
faintness.

41. And the *merchant* under the good tree
dissembled with the nations of the south and
west, and towards the north, and commended his
wares hugely, and cunningly deceived the simple
ones; and those that were witty, he made them
his factors, that they also might have their
livelihood or livings out of it, and he brought it
so far that nobody saw or knew the holy tree any
more, and so he got all the land to himself, and
then made proclamation, [1] *I am the stock of the
good tree, and stand on the root of the good tree,
and am engrafted into the Tree of Life, buy my
wares which I sell*: and then you shall be *healed*
of your wild birth, and live for ever.

[1] 2 Thess. ii.

42. I am grown out of the root of the good
tree, and the fruit of the holy tree is in my
power, and I sit on the *throne* of the divine
power; I have power in heaven and on earth,
Come unto me, and buy for money the fruit of
life.

43. Whereupon all nations flocked to him, and
did buy and eat, even till they fainted: All the
kings of the south, the west, and towards the
north, did eat the fruits of the *factor*, and lived
under a great impotence; for the wild tree of the

north grew more and more over them, and made *waste* of them a long time. And there was a miserable time upon earth, such as never was since the world stood; but men thought that time to be *good*, so terribly had the merchant under the good tree *blinded* them.

44. But in the *evening* God in his mercy took *pity* on man's misery and blindness, and stirred up the good tree again, even that glorious *divine* tree, which did bear the fruit of life; then there grew a twig *nigh* unto the root, out of that precious tree, and was green, and to it was given the *sap* and spirit of the tree, and it spoke with the tongue of man, and *shewed* to every one the precious tree, and its voice was heard in many countries.

45. Then men resorted thither to see and to hear what was the matter, and there was shewn unto them the precious and vigorous Tree of Life, of which men had eaten at the beginning, and were *delivered* of their wild nature. And they were mightily rejoiced, and did eat of the Tree of Life with great joy and refreshing, and so got new strength from the Tree of Life, and sang a new song concerning the true *real Tree of Life*, and so were delivered from their wild birth, and then hated the merchant and his factors, as also their false wares.

46. But all those came that did hunger and thirst after the Tree of Life, and those that sat

in the *dust*, and they did eat of the holy tree, and were healed of their *impure* birth and wrath, or fierceness of nature, in which they lived; and so were *engrafted* into the Tree of Life. But only the factors of the merchant *came not*, and his and their dissemblers, and those that made their gains with false wares, and had gathered treasure together, for they were drowned and quite dead in the gain of the merchant's whoredom, and lived in the wild nature; and so their anguish and shame (which was discovered) *kept* them back, because they went a whoring so long with the merchant, and seduced the souls of men; notwithstanding they gloried that they were engrafted into the Tree of Life, and lived in sanctity by a divine power, and hawked about the fruit of life.

47. Now because their shame, deceit, covetousness, knavery and wickedness were discovered, they waxed dumb, and stayed behind; they were ashamed,* and repented not of their abominations and *idolatry*, and so went not with the hungry and thirsty to the Fountain of Eternal Life; and therefore they grew faint in their thirst, and their torment riseth up from eternity to eternity, and they are gnawed in their conscience.

48. Now the merchant, seeing that the deceit

---

* "they were ashamed," etc., lit., "they were ashamed to repent." St M. has, "*ils n'osaient pas faire pénitence*," "they did not dare [or venture] to repent."

of his false wares was *discovered*, grew very wroth, and despaired, and bent his bow against the holy people, who would buy no more of his wares, and so destroyed many of the *holy* people, and blasphemed the *green twig that was grown up out of the Tree of Life*. But then the *great prince MICHAEL*, who *standeth before God*, came and fought for the *holy* people, and overcame.

49. But the prince of darkness perceiving that his merchant had a fall, and that his deceit was discovered, raised a *tempest* from the north out of the wild tree against the holy people, and the merchant of the south made an assault upon *them* : then the holy people grew hugely in their blossom, even as it was in the beginning, when the holy and precious tree grew, and that overcame the wrath or fierceness in nature and its prince ; thus it was at that time.

50. Now when the noble and holy tree was revealed to *all* nations, so that they saw how it moved over them and spread its fragrancy over all people, and that any one that pleased might eat of it, then the people grew weary of eating its *fruit*, which grew on the tree, and longed to eat of the root of the tree ; and the cunning and wise people sought after the *root*, and contended about the same : so the strife was great about the root of the tree, insomuch that they *forgot* to eat of the fruit of the sweet tree, by reason of the controversy about the root of the tree.

51. Now they minded *neither* the root nor the tree, but the prince of darkness had another design, intending something else; when he saw that they would eat no more of the good tree, but contended about the root, he perceived that they were grown *very weak* and faint, and that the wild nature predominated in them again.

52. Therefore he stirred them up to pride, so that every one supposed that he had the root at hand, every one must look after and hear him and reverence him : Whereby they built their palaces and great houses, and served in secrecy their idol, *Mammon*; whereby the lay people were troubled and caused to offend, and so lived in carnal pleasures, in the desire of the *wild* nature, and served their belly in wantonness, though they fell into misery, relying upon the fruit of the tree, which moved over them all, that *thereby* they might be *healed*.

53. In the meanwhile they served the prince of darkness according to the impulse of the wild nature, and the precious tree stood there only for a May-game or mocking-stock, and many lived like *wild beasts*, and led a wicked life, in pride, pomp, stateliness and lasciviousness, and the rich consumed the labour and sweat of the poor, and oppressed him in addition.

54. All evil actions were approved of for bribery: The *laws* issued forth out of the *evil quality* in nature, and every one strove after *riches* and

goods, after pride, pomp and stateliness; there was no deliverer for the poor; scolding, railing, cursing and swearing were *not* disapproved nor held vicious, and so they defiled themselves in the wrathful or fierce *quality*, even as a swine tumbleth in the dirt and mire.

55. Thus did the shepherds with the sheep: they retained no more than the bare *name* of the noble tree; its fruit, virtue and life were only a *cover* to their *sins*. Thus the world lived at that time, saving a small remnant or number, which were generated in the midst among the thorns in great *tribulation* and contempt, out of all nations upon the earth, from the east to the west.

56. There was no difference, they all lived upon the impulse of the wild nature, in impotence, even to a small number, which were delivered out of all nations, as it was before the *deluge*, and before the growing of the noble tree in nature; and thus it was also at that time.

57. But why men, in the end, did long so eagerly after the *root* of the tree, is a *mystery*,* and hitherto it was concealed from the wise and prudent; neither will it rise up to the height, but in the deep, in great simplicity.

58. As indeed the noble tree with its kernel

* "a mystery, and hitherto," etc. A free but correct rendering would be: "a mystery which hitherto was concealed from the wise and prudent; neither will it be made manifest openly to the high-minded, but open out in the depth of humility in great simplicity."

and heart hath *always* been concealed from the worldly wise, though they supposed they stood, some at the root, and some at the very top of the tree; yet this was no more than a shining mist before their eyes.

59. But the noble tree, from the beginning till now, strove in nature to its utmost, that it might be revealed to *all people*, [of all] tongues, and languages, against which the devil in the wild nature raged, and fought like a fierce lion.

60. But the noble tree bore the more and the sweeter fruit, and revealed itself more and more against all the fury and madness of the devil, even to the end : and *then it was light. For there grew at the root of the noble tree a green twig*, which gat the sap and life of the root, to which was given the *spirit* of the *tree*; so that it transfigured or made clearly manifest the noble tree in its glorious virtue and power, and nature also, in which it grew.

61. Now when this was done, then *both the gates* of nature, the knowledge of the *two qualities* of good and bad, were opened, and so the *Heavenly Jerusalem* was manifested, and the *kingdom of hell* also, to all men upon earth. And the light and voice was heard in the *four winds*, and the false merchant in the south was quite revealed, and his *own* hated him, and rooted him out from the whole earth.

62. This being done, the wild tree towards the

north *withered*, and all people beheld with wonder or great astonishment the holy tree, even in *foreign* islands. And the prince in the darkness was revealed, and his mysteries were discovered, and his shame, ignominy and perdition the men upon earth did *see* and *know*, for it was *light*.

63. This lasted but a short time; for men forsook that light, and lived in carnal pleasures, to their own perdition: For as the gate of light had opened itself, so did the gate of darkness also; and from them both went forth all manner of powers and arts that were therein.

64. For as men had lived from the beginning in the growth of the wild nature, and hunted after earthly things only, so in the end things were not mended, but rather grew worse.

65. In the middle of this time were raised many great stormy winds from the west towards the east and north: But from the north there went forth a *great stream of water* towards the holy tree, and spoiled many twigs in the holy tree, and in the *midst* of the stream it was light, and so the wild tree towards the north withered.

66. Then the prince in the darkness was enraged in the great motion of nature. For the *holy tree* moved in nature, as one that would by and by be elevated and kindled in the *glorification* of the holy divine *Majesty*, and cast the wrath or fierceness from it, which had so long stood against it, and had wrestled with it.

67. In like manner the tree of darkness, wrath, fierceness and perdition moved furiously, as one that would be kindled by and by, and therein the prince with his *legions* went forth to spoil the noble fruit of the good tree.

68. And it stood horribly in nature in the fierce quality, in that quality wherein the prince of darkness dwelleth, to speak after the manner of men; even as when men see terrible and cruel weather coming on, which maketh a horrible appearance, with lightning and tempestuous winds, at which men stand terrified.

69. On the other side, in the good quality in which the *holy tree of life* stood, all was pleasant, sweet and delightful, like a heavenly joyfulness. These two moved furiously the one against the other, till the whole nature was kindled of both qualities in one moment.

70. The tree of life was kindled in its own quality by the fire of the *Holy Ghost*, and its quality burnt in the fire of heavenly joyfulness, in an unsearchable light and glory.

71. All *voices* of the heavenly joyfulness, which have been from eternity in the good quality, qualified, mixed or harmonized in this fire; and the light of the Holy Trinity shone into the tree of life, and replenished or filled the whole quality in which it stood.

72. The tree of the fierce quality, which is the other part in nature, was kindled also, and burnt

in the fire of *God's wrath* in a hellish flame; and the fierce source rose up into eternity, and the prince of darkness with his legions abode in the fierce wrathful quality, as in his own kingdom.

73. In this fire were consumed the *earth*, the *stars*, and the *elements*, for all were on fire at once, each in the fire of its own quality, and all became separable.* For the Ancient of Days moved himself in it, wherein every power, and all the creatures, and whatsoever can be *named*, even the powers of heaven, of the stars, and of the elements, became thin again, and were fashioned according to that form which they were in from the beginning of the creation.†

74. Only the *two qualities*, good and bad, which have been in nature the one in the other, were separated, and the bad one was given to the prince of malice and wrath, or fierceness, for an eternal habitation; and that is called *Hell*, or a *Rejection*, which in eternity no more apprehends or toucheth the good quality, but is an oblivion of all good, and that to its eternity.

75. In the other quality stood the Tree of eternal Life, and its source and offspring de-

---

* "all became separable": St M. has, "*dissolved.*"

† "For the Ancient of Days," etc., lit., "For the Ancient of Days moved himself, in whom are all powers [virtues], all creatures and all that can be named; and the powers of heaven, of the stars and of the elements became thin again," etc. The word "*dünne,*" "thin," is rendered "simple" by St M.

scended from the Holy *Trinity*, and the Holy
Ghost shone into the same. And all men came
forth which descended from the loins of *Adam*,
who was the first man, each in his virtue, and in
that quality in which each did grow on earth.

76. Those that on earth had eaten of the good
tree, which is called *JESUS CHRIST*, *in them*
flowed the *mercy* of God unto eternal joy; they
had in them the power of the good quality, they
were received into the good and holy quality, and
they sang the song of their *Bridegroom*, each in
his voice, according to his own holiness.

77. But those that were born in the *light of
nature*, and of the Holy Ghost, and on earth
never *fully* knew the Tree of Life, but were
grown in its power, which overshadowed all men
upon earth, as very many nations, heathen, and
babes, which were also received into the same
power wherein they were grown, and wherewith
their spirit was clothed, they sang the song
according to their power and measure in the
noble Tree of eternal Life; for every one was
glorified according to his power, virtue, measure
and proportion.

78. The holy nature generated joyful, heavenly
fruit, even as on earth it had generated fruit
in both the qualities, which were both good
and bad, so now it generated heavenly fulness
of joy.

79. Those men who were now like angels, did

each eat the fruit of his *quality*, and they sang the song of God, and the song of *the Tree* of eternal *Life*.

80. And that was in the Father as a holy play, a triumphing joy; for to that end all things at the beginning were made out of the Father, and now they abide so to all eternity.

81. But those who were grown on earth in the power of the *tree of wrath*, that is, those whom the fierce quality had overcome, and who were withered in the wickedness of their spirit, in their *sins*, all those came forth also, each in his power or faculty; and they were received into *the kingdom of darkness*, and each was invested in that power in which he was grown up; and their king is called *Lucifer*, viz. one expelled or driven forth from the light.

82. The hellish quality brought forth fruit also, as it had done upon earth; only, the good was severed or parted from it, and therefore now it brought forth fruit in its *own* quality. And these men (who were now like the spirits), did each eat the fruit of his quality, and so did the devils also.

83. For as there is a difference in men upon earth in their qualities, and all are not of one quality, condition or disposition, even so among the rejected reprobate spirits; and so also in the heavenly pomp in angels and men; and that lasteth unto its eternity. *AMEN*.

84. *Courteous Reader,* This is a short information concerning the *two qualities* in nature from the beginning to the end, how there arose from thence *two kingdoms,* a heavenly and a hellish, and how they stir in this time and strive the one against the other, and what the issue of it will be in the time to come.

THE CONTENTS OF THIS BOOK

By Way of Introduction

*T*O this book I have given this name,
The ROOT or MOTHER of *Philosophy, Astrology*, and *Theology*.

And that you may know what it doth treat of, *Observe,*

I.

1. In the *Philosophy* it treateth of the divine power.

I. *What God is.*

II. *How in the being of God, is created nature, the stars and the elements.*

III. *From whence every thing hath its original.*

IV. *How heaven and earth were created.*

V. *How angels, men, and devils were created.*

VI. *How heaven and hell, and whatever is creaturely, were created, and what the* Two Qualities *are in nature.*

All out of a true ground in the knowledge of the spirit, by the impulse and motion of God.

29

II.

2. In the *Astrology* it treateth,

I. *Of the powers of nature, of the stars and of the elements.*

II. *How all creatures proceeded from thence.*

III. *How the same do impel and rule all.*

IV. *And work in all, and how good and bad are wrought by them in men and beasts.*

V. *Whence it cometh that good and bad are, and reign in this world.*

VI. *And how the kingdoms of heaven and of hell consist therein.*

3. My purpose is not to describe the course, place and name of all stars, and what is their annual conjunction, opposition, quadrate, or the like, and what they yearly and hourly operate, which, by a long process of time, and by diligent contemplation, observation, deep sense, calculation and computation, hath been observed by wise, skilful and expert men, who were rich and large in spirit.

4. Neither have I studied or learned the same, and I leave that to the learned to discourse of; my intention is to write according to the spirit and sense, and not according to speculation.

III.

5. In the *Theology* it treateth,

I. *Of the kingdom of Christ, what constituteth the same.*

II. *How it is set in opposition to the kingdom of hell.*

III. *How* in nature *it fighteth and striveth against the kingdom of hell.*

IV. *How men, through* faith *and* spirit, *are able to overcome the kingdom of hell, and triumph in divine power and obtain eternal blessedness, and all this as a victory in the battle.*

V. *How man, through the operation or working in the hellish quality, casts himself into perdition.*

VI. *And what the issue of both will be at last.*

6. The supreme title is AURORA, that is, *The Dawning of the Day in the East*, or *Morning Redness in the rising of the* SUN.

It is a secret Mystery, concealed from the wise and prudent of this world, of which they themselves shall shortly be sensible: But to those who read this book in singleness of heart, with a desire after the Holy Spirit, who place their hope in God only, it will *not* be a hidden secret, but a manifest knowledge.

7. I will not explain this title, but commit it to the judgment of the *impartial* Reader, who wrestleth in the good quality of this world.

8. Now if Mr Critic, who qualifieth or worketh with his wit in the fierce quality, gets this book into his hand, he will oppose it, as there is always a stirring and opposition between the kingdom of heaven and the kingdom of hell.

I. First, he will say that I ascend too *high* into the Deity, which is not a meet thing for me to do.

II. Then, secondly, he will say that I boast of the Holy Spirit, and that I had more need to live accordingly, and make demonstration of it by wondrous works or miracles.

III. Thirdly, he will say that I am not learned *enough*.

IV. Fourthly, he will say that I do it in a vainglorious way.

V. Fifthly, he will be much offended at the *simplicity* of the author; for in the world it is usual [or customary] to be mindful only of high things, and to be irritated by simplicity.

9. To these partial, worldly critics I set in opposition the *patriarchs* of the first world, who were mean despised men, against whom the world and the devil raged, as in the time of *Henoch*. When the holy fathers first preached [or when they began to preach] powerfully of the name of the Lord, they did not ascend with their bodies into heaven, and behold all with their *eyes*: yet the Holy Ghost revealed himself in *their spirits*.

10. Afterwards, it is seen in the next world among the holy patriarchs and *prophets*, who were all mean simple men, and some of them were *herdsmen*.

11. And when the *MESSIAH, CHRIST*, the

Champion in the battle in nature, assumed the humanity, though he was the King and Prince of men, yet in this world he kept himself in a low estate and condition, and was a stranger to the world. And his *Apostles* were poor despised *fishermen.*

12. Nay, Christ himself returneth [1]*thanks to* [1] Matt. xi. 25. *his heavenly Father, that he hath concealed these things from the worldly wise men, and revealed them unto babes.*

13. Besides, it is seen how they also were *poor sinners*, having the impulses both of good and of bad in nature. And yet they reproved and preached against the sins of the world, yea, against their own sins, which they did by the impulse of the Holy Spirit, and not in vainglory.

14. Neither had they any ability from their own strength and power to teach of God's Mysteries in that kind, but all was by the impulse of God.

15. So neither can I say anything of myself, nor boast or write of anything, save this : that I am a *simple* man, and, besides, a *poor sinner*, and have need to pray daily, *Lord, forgive us our sins* ; and to say with the Apostle, *O Lord, thou hast redeemed us with thy blood.*

16. Neither did I ascend into heaven, and behold all the works and creatures of God ; but the same heaven is *revealed* in my spirit, so that in the spirit I know the works and creatures of God.

17. Besides, the will to that is not my natural will, but it is the *impulse* of the spirit; and for it I have endured many an assault of the devil.

18. The spirit of man is descended not only from the stars and elements, but there is hidden therein a spark of the light and power of God.

19. It is *not* an empty word which is set down in *Genesis*, [1] *God created man in his own image, in the image of God created he him.* For it hath this sense and meaning, *viz.* that he is created out of the *whole being* of the Deity.

[1] Gen. i. 27.

20. The *body* is from the elements: therefore it must have elemental food.

21. The *soul* hath its original, not only from the body, though it taketh its rise in the body, and hath its first beginning in the body; yet in it it hath also its source from without, by and from the air; and so the Holy Ghost ruleth in it, in that manner as he replenisheth and filleth all things, and as all things are in God; and so God himself is all.

22. Seeing then in the soul the Holy Spirit is creaturely, *viz.* the propriety or portion of the soul, therefore it searcheth even into the *Deity*, and also into *nature*; for it hath its source and descent from the *being* of the whole Deity.

23. When it is kindled or enlightened by the Holy Ghost, then it beholdeth what God its Father doth, as a son beholdeth what his father doth at home in his house.

24. It is a *member* or child in the house of the heavenly Father.

25. As the eye of man seeth even unto the stars, from whence it hath a *finite* original and beginning, so also the soul seeth even *into* the divine being wherein it liveth.

26. But the soul having its source also out of nature, and that in nature there is good and bad, and that man hath cast himself, through sin, into the fierceness or wrath of nature, so that the soul is daily and hourly defiled with *sins*, therefore it knoweth but in part.

27. For the wrath or fierceness in nature *reigneth* now also in the soul. The Holy Ghost doth not go into the wrath or fierceness, but reigneth in the *source* of the soul, which *is* in the light of God, and fighteth against the wrath or fierceness in the soul.

28. Therefore the soul *cannot* attain unto any *perfect* knowledge in this life, till at the end, when light and darkness are separated, and wrath or fierceness is, with the body, consumed in the earth, then the soul seeth clearly and perfectly in God its Father.

29. But when the soul is kindled or enlightened by the Holy Ghost, then it *triumpheth* in the body, like a huge fire, which maketh the heart and reins tremble for joy.

30. There is not presently a great and deep knowledge in God its Father, but its love towards

God its Father triumpheth thus in the fire of the Holy Spirit.

31. The knowledge of God is sown in the fire of the Holy Ghost, and at first is as small *as a grain of mustard-seed*, as Christ makes the [1] comparison. *Afterwards it groweth large like a tree, and spreadeth itself abroad* in God its Creator.

32. Just as a drop of water in the ocean cannot avail much; but if a great river runneth into it, that maketh a great commotion.

33. Time past, present, and to come, as also depth and height, near and afar off, are all *one* in God, one comprehensibility.

34. The holy soul of man seeth the same also, but in this world in part only. It happeneth *sometimes* that it seeth nothing at all, for the devil doth assault it furiously in the fierce wrathful source that is in the soul, and oftentimes covereth the noble mustard-seed; therefore man must always be at strife [or in conflict].

35. In this manner, and in this knowledge of the spirit, I will write in this book concerning God our Father, in whom are all things, and who himself is all; and will handle how all is become separable and creaturely, and how all is impelled and moveth in the *whole* tree of life.

36. Here you shall see, 1. The true ground of the Deity; 2. How all was *one* being, essence or substance before the time of this world; 3. How

the *holy angels* were created, and out of what;
4. How the terrible fall happened, of *Lucifer*,
together with his *legions*; 5. How heaven, earth,
stars and the elements were made; 6. How
metals, stones and the creatures in the earth are
generated; 7. How the birth of life is, and the
corporeity of all things; 8. What the true *heaven*
is, in which God and his saints do dwell; 9.
What the *wrath* of God is, and the *hellish* fire;
10. And how all is become kindled and inflamed.* In brief, *how, and what, the essence
of all being is.*

37. The first seven chapters treat very plainly
and comprehensibly of the being of God, and
of angels, by *similitudes*, that the Reader may,
from one step to another, at last come to the
deep sense and true ground.

38. In the *eighth* chapter beginneth the depth
in the divine being, and so on, the further the
deeper.

39. Special points are often repeated, and
described still more deeply, for the Reader's
sake, and by reason of my slow and dull apprehension.†

40. That which you do not find sufficiently
explained in this book, you will find more clearly
in the [1]second and [2]third books.

41. For corruption is the cause why we know

[1] *Of the Three Principles.*
[2] *Of the Three-fold Life of Man.*

* "kindled and inflamed" (*anzündlich*), "inflammable."

† See Ch. X. par. 41 *et seq.*, and Ch. XXI. par. 66.

but in part, and have not perfect knowledge at once.

42. Yet this book is THE WONDER OF THE WORLD, which the holy soul will understand well enough. Thus I commit the Reader into the meek and holy love of God.

THE FIRST CHAPTER

*Of Searching out the Divine Being in Nature:
Of both the Qualities, the* Good *and the* Evil.

1. THOUGH flesh and blood cannot conceive or apprehend the being of God, but the spirit only when enlightened and kindled from God:

2. Yet if a man will speak of God, and say what God is, then,

I. A man must diligently consider the *powers* in nature.

II. Also the whole creation, heaven and earth.

III. The stars, the elements, and the creatures that are proceeded from them. As also the holy angels, devils, and men; moreover, heaven and hell.

Of the Two Qualities in One.

3. In this consideration are found *two qualities*, a *good* one and an *evil* one, which are in each other as one thing in this world, in all powers, in the stars and the elements, as also in all the creatures; and no creature in the flesh, in the

39

natural life, can subsist, unless it hath the two qualities.

What a Quality is.*

4. Now here a man must consider what the word quality meaneth or is. A quality is the mobility, boiling, springing and driving of a thing.

Of Heat.

5. As for example, *heat*, which burneth, *con-sumeth* and driveth forth all whatsoever that cometh into it which is not of the same property; and again, it *enlighteneth* and warmeth all cold, wet and dark things; it compacteth and hardeneth soft things.

Of Light and Fierceness.

6. Heat containeth likewise two other kinds in it, namely, (1) Light, and (2) Fierceness; of which

---

* The *understanding* of the thing here called *quality* is the foundation of that whole revelation of Jacob Behme's, and of all *Mysteries* of which his writings are only a description. For all along, the seven qualities are called sometimes seven sources, seven species, kinds, manners, circumstances, conditions, powers, operations or faculties of a thing. Also [the seven qualities are sometimes called] the qualifying or fountain spirits, which give, model, image or frame the power, virtue, colour, taste, figure, shape, constitution, substance, essence and distinct being of all things, whichever were, are, shall be or can be, in, from and to *all* eternity, in God and in all creatures, in heaven, in hell or in this world; also the forms or properties of nature, which is the *Salitter* or power of God. And so they are the seven spirits of God, as in the *Revelation of John* i. 4; iii. 1; iv. 5; v. 6. [J. Sparrow.]

take notice in this manner. The light, or the heart of the heat, is in itself a pleasant, joyful glance or lustre,* a power of *life*, an enlightening and glance of a thing which is afar off, which light is a piece or source of the heavenly kingdom of joy.

7. For it maketh *living* and moving all things in this world. All flesh, trees, leaves and grass grow in this world in the power of the light, and have their life therein, *viz.* in the good.

8. Again, heat containeth also a fierceness or *wrath*, which burneth, consumeth and spoileth; this wrath or fierceness springeth, driveth and elevateth itself in the light, and maketh the light moveable.

9. Heat wrestleth and fighteth together in its twofold source as one thing: It is also one thing, but it hath a double source: the *light* subsisteth in God without heat, but it doth not subsist so in nature.

10. For all qualities in nature are one in another as one *quality*, in that manner as God is all, and as all things descend and come forth from him: For God is the *heart* or fountain of nature,† from him cometh all.

* "glance or lustre" (*Anblick*), "sight."

† "God is the heart or fountain of nature," etc. Note by St M.: "Here, by the word 'nature,' must be understood, not actual nature, but an anterior nature. The author holds as a fundamental principle that there is a perfectly harmonized and eternal nature, out of which has arisen, violently, the temporal,

11. Now the *heat* reigneth and predomin-
ateth in all powers in nature, and warmeth all,
and is *one* source or spring in *all*; for if it
were not so the water would be too cold, and
the earth would be congealed, and there would
be no air.

12. The heat is *predominant* in all, in trees,
herbs and grass, and maketh the water moveable,
so that through the springing of the waters, herbs
and grass grow out of the earth. Heat is therefore called a quality, because it operateth, moveth
and boileth (or welleth up) in all, and elevateth
all.

13. But the *light* in the heat giveth power to
all qualities, so that all grow *pleasant* and joyful:
Heat without light availeth not the other qualities, but is a *perdition* to the good, an evil source
or spring; for all is spoiled in the fierceness or
wrath of the heat. Thus the light in the heat is
a quick spring or living fountain, into which the
Holy Ghost entereth, but the Holy Ghost entereth
not into the fierceness or wrath.

14. Yet the heat maketh the light moveable,
fugitive and disordered nature wherein we live. At times he
uses a qualifying expression to indicate the distinction; but
often, as in the present case, he suppresses the qualificative.
Again, he refers in turns, but without warning, to eternal and
then to actual nature, as can be seen in the next par.,
and the reader is left in uncertainty as to his meaning. A
little attention, however, will prevent error. This work cannot
be read lightly; it must be devotedly studied if it is to be
understood."

so that it springeth and driveth forth ; as is seen in winter, when the light of the sun is *likewise* upon the earth, but the *hot* rays of the sun cannot reach into the earth, and that is the reason why no fruit groweth in winter.

Of the Qualification of the Cold Quality.

15. *Cold* is a quality also, as well as *heat* ; it qualifieth or operateth in all creatures whatsoever that come forth in *nature*, and in all whatsoever that move therein, in men, beasts, fowls, fishes, worms, leaves and grass.

16. Heat is set in *opposition* unto it, and qualifieth therein, as if it were one and the same thing ; but cold opposeth the fierceness or rage of the heat, and *allayeth* the heat.

17. Cold containeth also two sorts or species * in it, which are to be observed, *viz.* It *mitigateth* the heat, maketh all things pleasant, and is in all creatures a quality of life ; for no creature can subsist without *cold* ; for it is a springing, driving mobility in every thing.

18. The other kind or species is *fierceness* ; for where this getteth power it suppresseth all, and spoileth all, even as the heat doth ; no life could subsist in it if the heat did not hinder that. The fierceness of cold is a destruction to every life, and the house of death, even as the hot fierceness also is.

* " species." St M. uses the word "*characteristics.*"

Of the Qualification of the Air and the Water.

19. *Air* hath its original from heat and cold; for heat and cold work powerfully* and replenish all, whereby is caused a lively and *stirring* motion; but when cold allayeth or *mitigateth* the heat, then both their qualities are rarefied and made thin; and the *bitter* quality attracteth or concreteth them together, so that they become dewy.

20. But the air hath its original and greatest motion from *heat*, and the water hath its original and greatest motion from *cold*.

21. Now these two qualities wrestle continually the one with the other, the *heat* consumeth the water, and the cold condenseth or crowdeth the air.   Now air is the cause and spirit of every *life* and motion in the world, be it in flesh or in any of the vegetables; all whatever is hath its *life* from the air, and nothing whatsoever that moveth and is in this world can subsist without air.

22. *Water* also springeth in every living and moving creature in this world.   In the water consisteth the body of everything, as the spirit

¹ Or in flesh.   consisteth in the air, be it ¹in animals or in vegetables.

23. These two [air and water] are caused by

* "work powerfully" (*treiben gewaltig von sich*), *i.e.* "produce an out-going impelling force."

heat and cold, and qualify or mix* and operate
together as one thing.

24. Now in these two qualities two other
species or kinds are to be observed, *viz.* a *living*
operation and a *dead* operation. The air is a
living quality, if it be temperate or moderate in a
thing, and the Holy Ghost reigneth in the calmness
or *meekness* of the air; and all the creatures
rejoice therein.

25.† But there is a *fierceness* or wrath also in it,
so that it killeth and destroyeth by its terrible
disturbance. But the qualification taketh its
original from the fierce disturbance or elevation,
so that it moveth and driveth in every creature;
from whence *life* hath its originals and doth exist;
and therefore both of them must be in this life.

26. The water also hath a fierce *deadly* spring,
for it killeth and consumeth; and so all things
that have a life and being must *rot* and perish in
the water.

27. Thus heat and cold are the cause and
original of water and air, in which everything
acteth and *standeth*; every life and mobility

* "qualify or mix" (*qualificiret unter einander*), "qualify
between themselves." The idea is that of interaction.

† "But the air also containeth a fierceness or wrath, so
that it killeth and destroyeth by its violence" [St M. has
"furious impetus"]. "Nevertheless the qualification ariseth
from this furious impetus; and thus in all things there is a
motion and a stimulus whence life ariseth and wherein it
consisteth, therefore both qualities must be in this life."

standeth therein. Of this I shall write plainly, concerning the creation of the stars.

Of the Influences of the other Qualities in the Three Elements, Fire, Air, and Water.

Of the Bitter Quality.

28. The *bitter* quality is the heart in every life; for as it attracteth together the water in the air, and also dissipateth the same, so that it [the water] becometh *separable*; so also in other creatures, and in the vegetables of the earth. For leaves and grass have their *green colour* from the bitter quality.

29. Now if the bitter quality dwelleth meekly and gently in any creature, then is it the *heart* or joy therein; for it dissipateth all other evil influences, and is the beginning or cause of joy or of *laughing*.

30.* For the bitter quality, when stirred, causeth the creature to tremble and be joyful, and to be lifted up in its whole body; for the stirring of the bitter quality is, as it were, a glimpse or ray of or from the heavenly kingdom of joy, an exaltation of the spirit, a spirit and virtue in all plants of the earth, a mother of life.

31. The Holy Ghost springeth, moveth and

* A new translation of this par. has been substituted for Sparrow's rendering.

driveth vehemently in this quality, for this quality is a part of the heavenly joyfulness, as I shall demonstrate afterwards.

32. But it hath also in it another species or kind, namely, the fierceness or wrath, which is the very house of death, a corruption of all good, a perdition and destruction of the life in the flesh.

33. For if it be too much elevated or too preponderant in any creature, and be inflamed in the heat, then flesh and spirit separate, and the creature loseth its life and must die; for then it moveth and kindleth the element fire; and in the great heat and bitterness no flesh can subsist. But if it be kindled in the element water, and springeth [becometh active] therein, it causeth debility and sickness* in the flesh, and finally death.†

Of the Sweet Quality.

34. The *sweet* quality is set opposite to the *bitter*, and is a *gracious*, amiable, blessed and pleasant quality, a refreshing of the life, an allaying of the fierceness. It maketh all pleasant and *friendly* in every creature; it maketh the vegetables of the earth fragrant and of good taste, affording fair, yellow, white and ruddy *colours*.

* The German word *Siechtage*, translated "debility and sickness," implies lingering sickness, and is aptly rendered *des langueurs* by St M.

† The last clause of this par. does not appear in Sparrow's translation. It is in the German eds. of 1682, 1715, and 1730, but not in 1656, nor in Schiebler's ed.

35. It is a glimpse and source of meekness, a pleasant habitation of heavenly joyfulness, a house or mansion of the Holy Ghost, a qualification of love and *mercy*, a joy of the life.

36. But, on the other side, it hath also a fierce or wrathful source, a source of death and corruption. For if it be *kindled* in the bitter quality in the element water, then it breedeth diseases, and the blotchy plague * or pestilence, and corruption of the flesh.

37. But if it be kindled in the heat and bitterness, then it infecteth the element air, whereby is engendered a sudden spreading plague and sudden death.

Of the Sour Quality.

38. The *sour* quality is set opposite to the bitter and the sweet, and is a good temper to all, a *refreshing* and cooling when the bitter and the sweet qualities are too much elevated or too preponderant. It is a longing delight in the taste, a pleasure of life, a stirring, boiling, flowing joy † in everything; a desire, longing and lust of joyfulness, a still joy or habitation of the *spirit*. Thus it is a temperature to all living and moving creatures.

---

* "blotchy plague" (*aufgeschwollene Pestilentz*), lit., "swollen plague." St M. renders this, "*des enflures et des maladies pestilentielles*," "swellings and plague-like [*i.e.* infectious] sicknesses."

† "a stirring, boiling, flowing joy" (*eine quellende Freude*), "a welling-up joy."

39. It containeth also a source of evil and corruption : For if it predominate too much, or stirreth too much *in anything*, so that it be *inflamed*, then it engendereth *sadness* and melancholy.

40. In the water it causeth a stink, putridness and rankness,* a forgetfulness of all good things, a melancholy or sadness of life, a house of death, a beginning of sorrow and an end of joy.

Of the Astringent or Saltish Quality.

41. The *saltish* quality is a good [1] temperature [1] Or temper. in the bitter, the sweet and the sour, making every thing pleasant; it opposeth the *rising* of the bitter quality, as also of the sweet and the sour, *lest* they should be inflamed : it is a sharp quality, a delight in the taste, a source of life and joy.

42. It containeth also fierceness and corruption : Being inflamed in the *fire* it engendereth a hard, tearing and stony nature, a fierce, wrathful source, a *destruction* of life, whereby the stone or gravel is engendered in the flesh, causing great pain and torment to the flesh.

43. But if it be inflamed in the *water*, then it engendereth in the flesh, scabs, sores, pox, leprosy, and is a *mourning* house of death, a misery and a forgetting of all good things.

---

* "putridness and rankness" (*rühricht und brüchicht*), "active and swamp-like." The idea is that of fermentation.

THE SECOND CHAPTER

An Introduction, shewing how men may come to apprehend The Divine, and the Natural, Being.   And further of the two Qualities.

1. ALL whatsoever that hath been mentioned above is called *quality*, because it qualifieth, operateth or frameth all in the deep above the earth, also upon the earth and in the earth, in one another, as *ONE* thing, and yet hath several distinct virtues and operations, and but one mother, from whence descend and spring all things.

2. All the creatures are made and descended from *these qualities*, and live therein as in their mother; and the earth and stones descend or proceed from thence also; and all that groweth out of the earth liveth and springeth forth out of the virtue of these qualities; no *rational man* can deny it.

3. Now this twofold source, good and evil, in everything, is caused by the stars; for as the creatures in the earth are, in their qualities, so also are the stars.

4. For from its twofold source, * everything hath its great mobility, running, springing, driving and growing.† For meekness in nature is a still *rest*, but the fierceness in every power maketh all things moveable, running and generative.

5. For the driving qualities cause a lust ‡ in all creatures unto evil and good, so that all [things] are *desirous* one of another, to copulate and increase, decrease, grow fair, perish, love and hate.

6. In every creature in this world there is a *good* and *evil* will and source; in men, beasts, fowls, fishes, worms, and in all that is upon the earth; in gold, silver, copper, tin, iron, steel; wood, herbs, leaves and grass; as also in the earth, in stones, in the water, and in all whatsoever that can be thought of.

7. There is nothing in nature wherein there is not good and evil; everything moveth and liveth in this double impulse, working or operation, be it what it will.

8. But the holy angels, and the fierce wrathful devils, are here to be excepted; for these are

---

* "from its twofold source," St M. further brings out the meaning by the following rendering: " *de sa double impulsion particulière*," "from its particular twofold impulse."

† "its great mobility, running . . . driving." St M. has: " *sa grande activité, son cours . . . son stimulant*," "its great activity, its course . . . its stimulus."

‡ "a lust." In the sense of desire: the German " *Lust* " implies no evil or excessive desire.

severed apart: Each of these liveth, qualifieth
and ruleth in his own peculiar quality.

9. The holy angels live and qualify in the
light, in the *good* quality wherein the Holy Ghost
reigneth. The devils live and reign in the *fierce*
wrathful quality, in the quality of fierceness and
wrath, destruction or perdition.

10. Yet both of these, the good and the evil
angels, were made out of the qualities of nature
from whence all things existed, only they differ
in their qualifying, or in their condition.

11. The holy *angels* live in the power of
meekness, of the light and joyfulness: The
devils live in the power of the rising or elevating
quality of fierceness, terror and darkness, and
cannot comprehend the light, into which condition they precipitated and cast themselves through
their pride and elevation of themselves; as I
shall shew afterwards, when I shall write of the
creation.

12. If thou wilt not believe that in this world
all descendeth or cometh from the stars, I will
demonstrate it to thee, if thou art not a block-
head, but hast some little reason and understanding left; therefore take notice of that which
followeth.

13. First behold the *sun*; it is the heart or
king of all stars, and giveth *light* to all stars
from the east to the west; it enlighteneth and
warmeth all, all liveth and groweth by its power;

besides, the joy of all creatures consisteth in its virtue.

14. If that should be taken away or become extinct, then all would be dark and cold; neither would there grow any fruit, and neither man nor beast could *propagate* and increase, because their heat would be extinguished and their *seed* would be cold and torpid.

Of the Quality of the Sun.

15. If thou wilt be a philosopher and *naturalist*, and search into *God's being in nature*, and discern how all is come to pass, then pray to God for the Holy Spirit, to enlighten thee with it.

16. For in thy flesh and blood thou art not able to apprehend it, and though thou dost read it, yet it is but as a fume or mist before thine eyes.

17. In the Holy Ghost alone, who is in God, and also in the whole nature,* out of which all things were made, in him alone canst thou search into the whole body or corporeity of God, which is *nature*; as also into the Holy Trinity itself.

18. For the Holy Ghost goeth forth from the Holy Trinity, and reigneth and ruleth in the *whole body* or *corpus* of God; that is, in the whole nature.

* "the whole nature." This expression is, in this and most other instances, rendered by St M.: "*la nature universelle*," "universal nature."

19. Even as the spirit of man ruleth and reigneth in the whole body, in all the veins, and replenisheth the *whole man*; even so the Holy Ghost replenisheth the whole nature, and is the *heart* of nature, and reigneth in the good qualities of everything.

20. Now, if thou hast that spirit in thee, so that it enlighteneth, *filleth* and replenisheth thy spirit, then thou wilt understand what followeth in this writing.

21. But if not, then it will be with thee as it was with the *wise* Heathen, who gazed and stared on the creation,* and would search and sift it out by their *own reason*; and though with their fictions and conceits † they came before God's countenance or face, yet they were not able to see it, but were stark *blind* in the knowledge of God.

22. As the Children of *Israel* in the desert could not behold the countenance of *Moses*, and therefore, when he drew near to the people, he must put a veil before his face.

23. The cause of this was, that they neither understood nor knew the true God and his will, who, *notwithstanding*, walked among them; and therefore that veil was a sign and type of their blindness and misunderstanding.

* "gazed and stared on the creation" (*sich in der Schöpfung vergafften*), "became enamoured with the creation," *i.e.* fell under the spell of the creation.

† "fictions and conceits" (*Dichten*), "romance" or "allegories"; the word is by no means used in an abusive sense.

24. As little as a piece of work can apprehend him that made it, so little also can *man* apprehend and know God his Creator, unless the Holy Ghost *enlighten* him; which happeneth only to those that rely not upon themselves, but set their *hope*, will and desires upon God alone, and move in the Holy Ghost, and these are *one spirit* with God.

25. Now if we consider rightly of the sun and stars, with their *corpus* or body, operations and qualities, then the very divine being may be found therein, and we may find that the virtues of the stars are nature itself.

26. If the whole wheel, *circumference* or sphere of the stars be well considered, then it is soon found that the same is the mother of all things, or the nature out of which all things are come, and wherein all things stand and live, and whereby everything moveth; all things are made of these powers, and therein they all abide *eternally*.

27. Though indeed *they shall be changed* at the end of this time, when good and evil shall be separated. So in like manner angels and men, *in the* [particular] *virtue of nature*, out of which they had gotten their first beginning, shall subsist in God eternally.

28. But here thou must elevate thy mind in the *spirit*, and consider how the *whole nature*, with all the powers which are in nature, also

the wideness, depth and height, also heaven and earth, and all whatsoever is therein, and all that is above the heavens, is together the *body* or corporeity of God; and the powers of the stars are the fountain veins in the natural body of God *in this world.*

29. Thou must not conceive that in the body of the stars is the *triumphing* Holy Trinity, God the Father, Son, and Holy Ghost, in which there is no evil, for it is the light-holy, eternal fountain of joy, which is indivisible and unchangeable, which no creature can sufficiently apprehend or express; which dwelleth and is above the body of the stars in itself, whose depth no creature is able to measure or fathom.

30. But we must not so conceive as if God were not at all in the *corpus* or body of the stars, and in this world: For when we say, *ALL*, or *from eternity to eternity*, or *All in All*, then we understand the entire *GOD*.

31. For a similitude or example take man, *who is made after the image or similitude of God,* as it is [1] written.

32. *The interior or hollowness in the body of man* is, and signifieth, the deep between the stars and the earth.

33. *The whole body with all its parts* signifieth heaven and earth.

34. *The flesh* signifieth the earth, and is also from earth.

35. *The blood* signifieth the water, and is from the water.

36. *The breath* signifieth the air, and is also air.

37. *The windpipe and arteries,** wherein the air qualifieth or operateth, signify the deep between the stars and the earth, wherein fire, air and water qualify in an elementary manner, and so the warmth, the air, and water, qualify also in the *windpipe and arteries*, as they do in the deep above the earth.

38. *The veins* signify the powerful flowings out † from the stars, and are also the powerful outgoings of the stars; for the stars with their powers reign in the veins, and drive forth the form, shape and condition in men.

39. *The entrails* or *guts* signify the operation of the stars, or their consuming of all that which is proceeded from their power, for whatsoever they *themselves* have made that they consume again, and remain still in their virtue and power; and so the guts also are the consuming of all that which man thrusteth and stuffeth into his

---

* "The windpipe and arteries." Curiously enough, the original has here the word "*Blase*," bladder, which St M. has rendered literally. It is, however, clear from the context that J. B. meant the breathing organs, and used the word *Blase* on account of its likeness to the verb "*blasen*," to blow.

† "powerful flowings out" (*Kraftgänge*), or "powerful currents," or again, "passages." The German word applies both to the "flowing" and to the channel for the same.

guts, even all whatsoever groweth from the power of the stars.

40. *The heart* in man signifieth the heat or the element of fire, and it is also the heat; for the heat in the whole body hath its original in the *heart*.

41. The *windpipe* and *arteries* signify the element of air, and the air ruleth also therein.

42. *The liver* signifieth the element of water, and it is also the water; for from the liver cometh the blood in the whole body into all the members. The liver is the mother of the blood.

43. *The lungs* signify the earth, and are also of the same quality.

44. *The feet* signify near and afar off; for near and afar off are all one in God: And so man by means of his feet can come and go *near* and *far off*; let him be where he will, he is in nature neither near nor *afar off*; for in God these are *one* thing.

45. *The hands* signify God's omnipotence; for as God in nature can *change* all things, and make of them what he pleaseth, so man also can with his hands *change* all things which grow in or proceed from nature, and can make with his hands out of them what he pleaseth: He ruleth with his hands the *work* and being of the whole nature, and so they very well signify the omnipotence of God.

Now observe here further,

46. *The whole body to the neck* signifieth and is the round circle or sphere of the stars, as also the deep within or between the stars, wherein the *planets* and *elements* reign.

47. *The flesh* signifieth the earth, which is congealed, and hath no motion; and so the flesh in itself hath no reason, comprehensibility or mobility, but is moved only by the power of the *stars*, which reign in the flesh and veins.

48. No more could the earth bring forth any fruit, nor could there grow any metals, as gold, silver, copper, iron or stones, if the *stars* did not work in them; nor could there grow any grass without the operation of the stars.

49. The *head* signifieth heaven; the same is grown on the body, by the veins, passages and going forth of powers; and so all the powers come again from the head and *brain* into the body, into the fountain-veins or arteries of the flesh.

50. Now heaven is a pleasant palace of joy, wherein all the powers are, as they are in the whole nature in the stars and elements, but not *so hard* working and springing. For every *power of heaven* hath but one species, kind or form of power, springing very *bright and meek*, not promiscuously evil and good one in another, as in the stars and elements in the whole nature, but very *pure.*

51. It is made out of the midst of the *waters*, but not qualifying in such a manner as the *water* in the *elements*, for fierceness or wrath is not therein. However, heaven belongeth to nature, because the stars and elements have their original and power from the *heaven*.

52. For heaven is the *heart* of the water. Likewise, in all creatures, and in all that is in this world the water is the *heart* thereof, and nothing can subsist without water, be it in the flesh or out of the flesh, in the vegetables of the earth or in metals and stones, in everything the water is the kernel or the heart.

53. So heaven is the heart in nature, wherein all the powers are, as in the stars and elements, and it is a soft, supple and meek matter of all powers, as the brain in man's head is.

54. Now heaven kindleth with its power the stars and elements, so that they move and work: And so the *head* of man is also like heaven.

55. For as in heaven all powers are meek and full of joy,* and as heaven hath a *closure* or *firmament* above the stars, and yet all powers go forth from heaven into the stars, so the brain also hath a closure or firmament between it and the body, and yet all the powers go forth from the brain into the body, and into the whole man.

56. *The head containeth the five senses*, viz.

---

* "full of joy" (*freudenreich . . . und qualificiren*), "full of joy and qualify," *i.e.* qualify [operate] in joy.

seeing, hearing, smelling, tasting and feeling, wherein the stars and elements qualify, and therein existeth the sidereal or heavenly, starry or astral and natural spirit in men and beasts; in this flow forth good and evil, for it is the *house* of the stars.

57. Such power the stars borrow from heaven, that they can make in the flesh a living and moving *spirit* in man and beast. The moving of the heaven maketh the stars moveable, and so the head also maketh the body moveable.

58. *Now open here the eyes of thy spirit, and behold God thy Creator.*

Question.

Here now the question is, From whence hath heaven, or whence borroweth it, this power, that it causeth such *mobility* in nature?

Answer.

59. Here you must lift up your eyes beyond nature, into the light-holy triumphing divine power, into the unchangeable Holy Trinity, which is a triumphing, springing, moveable being, and all powers are therein, as in nature.

60. For this is *the eternal mother of nature*, of which heaven, earth, stars, elements, angels, devils, men, beasts, and all have their being; and therein *ALL* standeth.

61. When we nominate heaven and earth, stars

and elements, and all that is therein, and all whatsoever is above the heaven, then thereby is nominated the *total God*, who hath made himself *creaturely* in these above-mentioned beings, in his power which goeth forth from him.

62. But *GOD* in his TRINITY is unchangeable, and whatever there is in heaven and upon earth and above the earth, hath its spring, source and original from the *power* which proceedeth from God.

63. Yet you must *not* therefore conceive that in God there is good and evil, for God himself is the *good*, and hath the *name* from good, which is the triumphing eternal joy : Only *all* the *powers* which you can search out in nature, and which are in *all* things, proceed from him.

Question.

64. Now perhaps you may say, *Is there not good and evil in nature?* And *seeing everything cometh from God, must not then the evil also come from God?*

Answer.

65. Behold, there is a *gall* in man's body, which is *poison*, and man cannot live without this gall ; for the gall maketh the *astral spirits* moveable, joyous, triumphing or laughing, for it is the source of joy.

66. But if it be inflamed or kindled in one of

the elements, then it *spoileth* the whole man, for the wrath in the astral spirits cometh from the gall.

67. That is, when the gall overfloweth and runneth to the heart, then it kindleth the element of *fire*, and the fire kindleth the astral *spirits* which *reign* in the *blood* in the veins and in the element of *water*; and then the whole body trembleth by reason of the wrath and the poison of the gall.

68. Such a source hath *joy*, and from the same substance also as the *wrath*. That is, when the gall in the *loving* or sweet quality is inflamed, in that which man is in love withal, then the whole body trembleth for the joy; in which many times the *astral* spirits are affected also, when the gall is overflown, and is kindled in the *sweet* quality.

69. *But it hath no such substance in God, for he hath not flesh and blood, but he is a* [1] *Spirit, in whom all powers are*; as we pray in the Lord's prayer, [2] *Thine is the power.*

70. As it is written of him, [3] *He is Wonderful, Counsel, Power, Champion, Eternal Father, Prince of Peace.*

71. The *bitter* quality is in God also, but not in that manner as the gall is in man, but it is an *everlasting* power, in an elevating, triumphing spring or source of joy.

72. And though it is written in *Moses*, [4] *I am an angry, zealous God*, yet the meaning of it is

[1] John iv. 24.

[2] Matt. vi. 13.

[3] Isaiah ix. 6.

[4] Exod. xx. 5. Deut. iv. 24.

not that God is angry *in himself*, and that there ariseth a fire of anger in the *Holy Trinity*.

73. No; that cannot be, for it is written, *against those that hate me*,* in that same creature, *the fire of anger riseth up*.

74. If God should be angry in himself, then the *whole nature* would be on fire, which will come once to pass *on the last day*, in *nature*, but *not* in *God, in God the triumphing joy will burn*; it was never otherwise from eternity, nor will it ever be otherwise.

75. The elevating, springing, triumphing joy in God maketh heaven triumphing and *moveable*, and *heaven* maketh the *stars* and *elements* moveable, and the stars and elements make the *creatures* moveable.

76. Out of the *powers* of God are the heavens proceeded; out of the *heaven* are the stars; out of the *stars* are the elements; out of the *elements* are the *earth* and the *creatures* come to be.

77. Thus all had its beginning, even to the angels and devils, which, before the creation of heaven, stars and the earth, were produced from the same power from which the heaven, the stars and the earth were produced.

78. This is a short entrance or introduction, shewing how one must consider the divine and

---

* "against those that hate me," etc. Sparrow has given a literal translation of the German. St M. has, "as to them that hate me, it is in them that the fire of anger riseth up."

the natural being.   Henceforth I will describe the true ground and depth concerning what God is, and how all things are framed in God's being.

79. This indeed hath been partly concealed from the beginning of the world to this time, and man with his *reason* could not comprehend it.

80. But seeing God is pleased to reveal himself in simplicity in this last time, I shall give way to his impulse and will; I am but a very little spark of light. *AMEN.*

THE THIRD CHAPTER

Of the most blessed Triumphing, Holy, Holy, Holy Trinity, GOD the Father, Son, and Holy Ghost, ONE only God.

1. COURTEOUS Reader, here I would have you faithfully *admonished* to let go your opinion and conceit, and not yield to the spell of the *Heathenish* wisdom, nor be offended at the simplicity of the author : for this work comes not from *his reason*, but from the impulse of the spirit.

2. Only be thou careful to get into thy spirit the Holy *Ghost*, who issueth forth from God, and he will lead thee into all truth, and reveal *himself* unto thee.

3. Then thou wilt see well enough in his light and power; even into the holy *Trinity*, and understand those things which are written hereafter following.

Of GOD the FATHER.

4. When our Saviour JESUS CHRIST taught [1] Matt. vi. 9. his disciples to pray, he said; [1] *When ye pray, say thus : Our Father, which art in heaven.*

5. The meaning is not as if heaven could comprehend, encompass or contain God the *Father*; for heaven *itself* is made by the divine power: for *Christ* saith, [1] *My Father is greater than all.*

[1] John x. 29.

6. And God saith in the Prophet, [2] *Heaven is my throne, and the earth is* [3] *my footstool. What house would you build for me?* [4] *I compass the heaven with a span, and the earth with three fingers.* Also, [5] *I will dwell in Jacob, and Israel shall be my tabernacle.*

[2] Isaiah lxvi. 1.

[3] the dirt under my feet.

[4] Isaiah xl. 12.

[5] Psal. cxxxv. 4.
Syrac xxv. 13.

7. But in that Christ calls his Father a *heavenly* Father, his meaning is that his Father's *lustre* and power appear and shine very *bright* and pure in heaven; and that *above* the circle or enclosure which we behold with our eyes, and which we call *heaven*, doth appear the totally *triumphing* Holy Trinity, *The Father, Son, and Holy Ghost.*

8. Thereby Christ also distinguisheth his *heavenly* Father from the father of *nature*, which is indeed the stars and the elements; these are our natural father, out of which we are made, and by whose impulse we live here in this world, and from whence we have our food and nourishment.

9. *Therefore* God is our heavenly Father, in that our *soul* continually longeth after him, and is desirous of him, yea it thirsteth and hungereth continually after him.

10. The *body* hungereth and thirsteth after the father of nature, *viz.* the stars and the elements,

and *that father* feedeth and nourisheth the body.

11. But the soul thirsteth after the heavenly holy Father, and he giveth meat and drink to it, feeding it with his holy Spirit, and the spring, source or fountain of joy.

12. Yet we have *not two* fathers, but *one* only : For heaven is made by his power, and the stars are made out of his wisdom which is *in him*, and which proceedeth forth *from him*.

Of the Substance and Property of the Father.

13. When we consider the whole nature and its property, then we see the Father.

14. When we behold heaven and the stars, then we behold his eternal *power* and wisdom : So many stars stand in the whole heaven that they are innumerable and incomprehensible to *reason*, and some of them are not visible, so manifold and [so] *various* is the power and wisdom of God the Father.

15. But every star in heaven differeth in its power and *quality*, which also maketh so many distinctions in and among the creatures upon the earth, and in the whole creation.

16. All the *powers* which are in *nature* proceed from God the Father; all light, heat, cold, air, water; and all the powers of the earth, bitter, sour, sweet, astringent, hard and soft, and more than can be reckoned; all have their *beginning* from the Father.

17. Therefore if a man would liken the Father to anything, he should liken him to the round globe of heaven.

18. Thou must not conceive here that every power which is in the Father standeth in a peculiar severed or divided part and *place* in the Father, as the stars do in heaven.

19. No, the spirit sheweth that *all* the powers in the Father are one in another as one power.

20. A resemblance, image or figure whereof we have in the Prophet [1] *Ezekiel*, who seeth the Lord [1] Chap. i. in the spirit and resemblance like a wheel, having *four other wheels* one in another, the four being like one another; and when they moved they went straight forward, which way soever the wind did sit or blow, and that way they all went forward, having no cause of returning.

21. Thus it is with God the Father; for all the powers are in the Father, one in another, *as one power*; and all powers consist in the Father, in an unsearchable light and clarity or brightness and glory.

22. Yet thou must not think that God, who is in heaven and above heaven, doth there stand and hover, like a power and quality which hath in it *neither* reason nor knowledge.

23. As the sun which turneth round in its circle, and poureth forth from itself heat and *light*, whether it be for benefit or hurt to the earth and creatures, which indeed would be for

hurt if the other planets and stars did not hinder.

24. No, the Father is *not so*, but he is an all-mighty, all-wise, all-knowing, all-seeing, all-hearing, all-smelling, all-feeling, all-tasting God, who in himself is meek, friendly, gracious, merciful and full of joy, yea joy itself.

25. And he is thus from eternity to eternity unchangeable: He never changed himself in his *being*, neither will he change himself in all *eternity*.

26. He is proceeded or born of nothing, but he *himself* is all, in eternity; and all whatsoever is, is come from his power, which from eternity goeth forth from *him*.

27. His immensity, height and depth, *no creature*, no nor any angel in heaven, can search into, but the angels live in the *power* of the Father, very meekly and full of joy, and they always *sing* in the power of the Father.

Of GOD *the* SON.

28. If a man will see *God* the *Son*, he must once more look upon natural things, otherwise I *cannot* write of the Son: The spirit indeed beholdeth him, but that can neither be spoken nor *written*; for the divine being consisteth in power, which can neither be written nor spoken.

29. Therefore, if we intend to speak of God, we must use *similitudes*. For we live in this world

as men who know *but in part*, and are made of
that which is but in part. Therefore I cite the
Reader into *the life to come*, where and when I
shall speak more properly and more clearly of
this high article.

30. In the meanwhile the loving Reader is to
attend to the sense and *meaning of the spirit*, and
then, if he hath but any *hunger* in him, he will
not fail to get a little refreshing.

Now observe,

31. The Turks and Heathen say, *God hath no
Son* : Set wide open your eyes here ; and do not
make yourselves stark blind, and you will see the
Son.

32. The Father is all, and all power subsisteth in the Father : He is the beginning and
the end of all things ; and besides and beyond
him is nothing ; and whatever is, is from the
Father.

33. For *before* the beginning of the creation
of the creatures there was nothing but GOD only ;
and where there is nothing, out of that, nothing
will be. All things must have a cause or root, or
else nothing will be.

34. Yet you are not to think that the Son is
another God than the Father. Neither should
you think that the Son is without or apart from
the Father, and that he is a severed part or
divided piece, as when two men stand the one by

the other, where one comprehendeth not the other.

35. No, the Father and the Son are not of *such* a substance, or such a kind of thing; for the Father is not an *image*, to be likened to anything; the Father is the *fountain* of all powers, and all the powers are one in another as one power, and therefore he is said to be ONE only GOD.

36. Otherwise, if his powers were *divided*, then he were not all-mighty, but now he is the self-subsisting, all-mighty and all-powerful God.

37. And the *Son* is the *Heart* in the Father; all the powers which are in the Father are the *propriety* of the Father; and the Son is the *Heart*, or the kernel or pith in all the powers in the whole Father, and he is the *cause* of the springing joy in all powers in the whole Father.

38. From the Son, who is the Father's Heart in all his powers, the eternal joy ariseth and springeth in all the powers of the Father; such a joy *as no eye hath seen, nor ear heard, neither hath ever entered into the heart of any man*, as St *Paul* [1] saith.

[1] 1 Cor. ii. 9.

39. But if a man here on earth is enlightened with the Holy Ghost from the fountain of JESUS CHRIST, so that the spirits of nature, which signify the Father, are kindled in him, then there ariseth such a joy in his *heart*, and it goeth forth into all his *veins*, so that the whole body trembleth, and the soulish, animal spirit triumpheth, as if it

were in the holy Trinity, which is understood
only by those who have been guests in that
place.

40. This is but a [1]type or glimpse of *the Son* [1] See Ch. 4, *of God* in man, whereby *faith* is strengthened and v. 15.
preserved: For the joy cannot be so great in an
earthen *vessel* as in a heavenly, wherein the
perfect power of God is, fully.

Now here I must write a Similitude.

41. I will shew thee a similitude in nature,
signifying how the holy being in the holy
Trinity is.

42. Consider heaven, which is a round *globe*,
having neither beginning nor end, for its beginning and end are everywhere, which way soever
you look upon it: So is *God*, who is in and
above the heaven, he hath neither beginning nor
end.

43. Now consider further the circle or sphere
of the stars, they denote the *various* powers and
wisdom of the Father, and they also are made by
the power and wisdom of the Father.

44. Now the heaven, the *stars*, and the whole
deep between the stars, together with the *earth*,
signify the Father.

45. And the *seven planets* signify the seven
spirits of God, or the princes of the angels,
among which also lord L U C I F E R was one before
his fall; all [these] were made out of the Father

in the beginning of the creation of angels, before the time of this world.*

46. *Now observe* : The sun stirreth in the midst, in the deep between the stars, in a round circle, and is the heart of the stars, and giveth light and power to all the stars, so *tempering* the power of the stars that all becometh pleasant and joyful.

47. It *enlighteneth* also the heaven, the stars, and the deep above the earth, working in all things that are in this world, and is the king and the heart of all things of this world, and so rightly signifieth the *Son* of God.

48. For as the sun standeth in the midst, between the stars and the earth, enlightening all powers, and is the light and *heart* of all the powers, and is all the joy in this world, besides, all beauty and pleasantness standeth in the light and power of the sun.

49. Even so the Son of God *in* the Father is the Heart of the Father, and shineth in all the powers of the Father; his power is the moving *springing joy* in all the powers of the Father,

* "before the time of this world." At the end of this par. St M. has the following note: "The author was imbued with the ideas which were prevalent until the time of Herschel, in relation to the seven planets. Many assert that up to that astronomer's discovery, only six were known. But others declare that even in the event of many other planets being discovered, they would nevertheless, as a whole, remain the organ of seven powers which rule temporal (*actuelle*) nature as well as eternal nature, and that the only error would consist in the application made of this number seven."

and shineth in the whole Father, as the sun doth in the whole world.

50. If the earth should be taken away, which signifieth the *house* of misery, of trouble, or of hell, then the whole deep would be light in one place as well as in another: as indeed, from the *lustre* of the Son of God, the whole deep in the Father is as light* in one place as in another.

51. As the sun is a self-subsisting creature, power and light, which shineth not *forth from* or out of all creatures, but *in* and into all creatures, and all creatures rejoice in its power.

52. So the Son in the Father is a self-subsisting Person, and enlighteneth all the powers in the Father, and is the Father's joy *or Heart* in his centre, or in the midst of him.

Observe here the great Mystery of God.

53. Further, the sun is made or generated from all the stars, and is a light taken from the whole nature, and shineth again into the whole nature of this world; it is *united* with the other stars, as if itself together with all the stars were but *one* star.

54. So the Son of God is continually generated from all the powers of his Father from eternity,

---

* "light ... light." The German *gar lichte* is adjectival, and is rendered by St M., "luminous." In the *New Testament*, "full of light" renders exactly the meaning implied here: "Thy whole body shall be full of light," *Matt.* vi. 22.

and is not made, but is the heart and *lustre* shining forth from the powers of his heavenly Father ; a self-subsisting Person, the centre or body of the lustre in the deep.

55. For the Father's power generateth the Son continually from eternity to eternity ; but if the Father should *cease to generate*, then the Son would be no more : Also, if the Son should shine no more in the Father, then the Father would be a dark valley : And then the Father's power would not rise from eternity to eternity, and so the divine being would not *subsist*.

56. Thus the Father is the *self-subsisting* being * of all powers, and the Son is the Heart in the Father, which is generated continually out of all the powers of the Father, who again *enlighteneth* the powers of the Father.

57. Do not conceive that the Son in the Father is so mixed that his *Person* can neither be seen nor known : No ; for if it were so then it were but one Person.†

58. For as the *sun* shineth not from or out of the *other* stars, though it had its original from the *other* stars, so also the Son shineth not from

---

* "the self-subsisting being" (*das selbständige Wesen*). St M.'s rendering is, " *l'essence radicale*," "the root-essence."

† At the end of this par., and referring to pars. 56 and 57, St M. adds : "This passage, as well as others on the divine Persons, has been developed to a considerable extent, elucidated and greatly improved upon in other works of the author. It must be looked upon as provisional."

or out of the powers of the Father, as to his
body or *corporeity*.

59. Though he is generated continually out of
the powers of the Father; yet he shineth back
again into the powers of the Father, for he is
another Person than the Father, but *not* another
God.

60. He is eternally *in* the Father, and the
Father generateth him continually from eternity
to eternity, and the Father and the Son are O N E
God, of an equal being in power and omnipotence.

61. The Son seeth, tasteth, heareth, feeleth,
smelleth and comprehendeth *all*, as the Father
doth; in *his* power all liveth and is, whatsoever
is good, as in the Father; but that which is bad
or evil is *not* in *him*.

Of GOD *the* HOLY GHOST.

62. *God the Holy Ghost* is the third Person in
the triumphing holy Deity, and proceedeth from
the Father and the Son, and is the holy moving
spring or *fountain* of joy in the whole Father.

63. He is a pleasant, meek, quiet wind, or
whispering breath, or *still voice*, out of all the
powers of the Father and of the Son; as [1] *on*
mount Horeb with the prophet *Elijah*, and on
[2] *Whitsunday* or the Day of Pentecost with the
Apostles, may be perceived.

[1] 1 Kings xix. 12.

[2] Acts ii.

64. Therefore if we would describe his Person,
substance and property from the true ground, it

must be represented in a *similitude*. For the spirit cannot be written down, being no creature, but the moving, flowing, boiling power of God.

65. Consider the sun and stars again : The *stars* being many and several, inexpressible and innumerable, signify the Father : out of the stars the *sun* is come to be ; for God hath made it out of *them*, and it signifieth the Son of God.

66. From the sun and stars proceed the *four elements*, fire, air, water and earth, as hereafter I shall demonstrate plainly, when I shall write of the *creation*.

Now observe :

67. *The three elements*, fire, air and water, have a *threefold* moving or qualification, but proceed from one body ; and consider, the fire or heat swells and flies aloft from the sun and stars ; and [1] from the heat the air [1] swells and flies * aloft ; and from the air comes the water.

[1] Or expandeth itself.

68. And in *this* motion or qualification consisteth the life and spirit of all creatures, and whatever can be named in this world ; and *that* signifieth the Holy Ghost.

69. And as the three elements, fire, air and water, proceed from the sun and stars, and are *one body* in one another, and cause the *living*

* "swells and flies" (*empöret sich*), "rises aloft." In the 1715 and 1730 eds. there is added—presumably from Gichtel's MS. notes to his 1682 ed.—("gebäret"), "generateth itself forth." Thus, "empöret (gebäret) sich."

motion, and the spirit of all the creatures of this world,

70. So the Holy Ghost proceedeth from the Father and the Son, and causeth the *living motion* in all the powers of the Father.

71. And as the three elements move in the deep, as a *self-subsisting* spirit, and cause heat, cold and clouds, and flow forth from the power of all the stars; and as all the powers of the sun and stars are in the three elements, as if they *themselves were* the sun and stars, from whence is the life and spirit of all creatures, and doth consist therein; just so the Holy Ghost proceedeth from the Father and the Son, and moveth in the whole Father, and is the spirit and life of all the powers of the whole Father.

Observe here the deep Mystery.

72. *All* the *stars* which men see, and those which they do not see, they all signify the *power* of God the Father; and out of these stars is generated the *sun*, which is the *heart* of all the stars.

73. Also there goeth forth into the deep from all the stars the *power* which is in every star: And the power, heat and shining of the sun goeth likewise into the deep.

74. In the deep the power of all stars, together with the heat and lustre of the sun, are all but *one thing*, a moving, boiling, *hovering*, like a

spirit or matter; * only it hath not reason, for it is not the Holy Spirit. And thus also the fourth element must adhere or belong to a natural spirit, or it is not capable of reason.

[75. "*Thus God the* Father *goeth forth in his* "*deep out of all his powers, and generateth the* "*splendour, the Heart, or the Son of God in his* "*centre.*"]

76. Which may be likened to the round *globe* of the *sun*, which shineth upwards, downwards, and on every side; and so the splendour, together with all the powers, goeth forth from the Son of God in the whole Father.

77. Now in the whole deep of the Father, externally, without the Son, there is nothing but the manifold and unmeasurable or unsearchable *power* of the Father.

78. And the unsearchable power and *light* of the Son is, in the deep of the Father, a living, all-powerful, all-knowing, all-hearing, all-seeing, all-smelling, all-tasting, all-feeling *spirit*, wherein is all power, splendour and wisdom, as in the Father and the Son.

79. And as in the four elements there is the power and splendour of the sun and *all* the stars, so it is in the whole deep of the Father, and that

* "a moving, boiling, hovering, like a spirit or matter" (*eine bewegende Wallung gleich eines Geistes oder einer Materia*), "a moving undulation [*i.e.* a wave-like motion] like that of a spirit, or of a substance."

is, and is rightly called, the *Holy Ghost*, which is the third self-subsisting Person in the Deity.

Of the Holy TRINITY.

80. Now when we speak or write of the *three Persons* in the Deity, you must *not conceive* that therefore there are three Gods, each reigning and ruling by himself, like temporal kings on the earth.

81. No : [1] such a substance and being is not in God ; for the divine being consisteth in power, and not in body or flesh.

[1] Or the Trinity hath no such substance and being in God.

82. The Father is the whole divine power, whence *all creatures* have proceeded, and hath been always, from eternity : He hath neither beginning nor end.

83. The Son is in the Father, being the Father's Heart or light, and the Father generateth the Son continually, from eternity to eternity ; and the Son's *power* and splendour shine back again in the whole Father, as the sun doth in the *whole* world.

84. The Son is also *another* Person than the Father, but not externally, without or severed from the Father, *nor* is he any other God than the Father is ; his power, splendour, and omnipotence, are *no less* than the whole Father.

85. The Holy Ghost *proceedeth* from the Father and the Son, and is the *third* self-subsisting Person in the Deity. As the *elements* in this

world go forth from the sun and the stars, and
are the moving spirit which is in everything in
this world,

86. So the Holy Ghost is the moving spirit in
the whole Father, and proceedeth or goeth forth
from eternity to eternity *continually* from the
Father and the Son, and replenisheth the whole
Father; he is nothing less or greater than the
Father and the Son; his *moving power* is in the
whole Father.

87. *All things* in this world are according to
the similitude of this *Ternary*. Ye blind Jews,
Turks and Heathen, open wide the eyes of your
mind: in your body, and in every natural thing,
in men, beasts, fowls and worms, also in wood,
stone, leaves and grass, I will shew you the likeness of the Holy Ternary in God.

Objection.

88. Ye say, There is but *one* being in God, and
that God hath no Son.

Answer.

89. Open your eyes, and consider yourselves:
Man is made according to the similitude, and out
of the power, of God in his Ternary. Behold
thy inward man, and then thou wilt see it most
plainly and clearly; if hou art *not* a fool and an
irrational beast; therefore observe,

90. In thy heart, in thy veins, and in thy

brain, thou hast thy spirit; and all the powers which move in thy heart, in thy veins, and in thy brain, wherein thy life consisteth, signify God the Father.

91. From that power springeth up thy *light*, so that thou seest, understandest and knowest in the same power what thou art to do; for that light glimmereth in thy whole body; and the whole body moveth in the power and knowledge of the *light*, which signifieth God the Son; for the body helpeth all the members in the knowledge of the light.

92. For as the *Father* generateth the *Son* out of his power, and as the Son shineth back in the whole Father; so in like manner the *power* of thy heart, of thy veins, and of thy brain generateth a *light* which shineth in all thy powers in thy whole body. Open the eyes of thy mind, consider it, and you will find it so.

93. *Now observe*: As from the Father and the Son there *goeth forth* the Holy Ghost, who is a self-subsisting Person in the Deity, and moveth in the whole Father, so also out of the powers of thy heart, veins and of thy brain, goeth forth the *power* which moveth in thy *whole* body; and out of thy *light*, in the same power, goeth forth reason, understanding, skill and wisdom to govern the whole body, and to distinguish all whatsoever is externally [1] without the body.

[1] *extra corporem.*

94. And both these * are but one, in the government of thy mind,† *viz.* [they are] thy *spirit*, which [spirit] signifieth God the Holy Ghost. And the Holy Ghost from God *ruleth in* this spirit in thee, if thou art a child of *light*, and not a child of *darkness.*

95. For in respect of *this* light, understanding and government, is man *distinguished* from the beasts, and is an angel of God; as I shall clearly shew when I write of the creation of man.

96. Therefore observe exactly, and take notice of the order of this book, and then thou wilt find *whatsoever thy heart desireth or ever longed for.*

97. Thus you find in man *three* fountain-springs. First, the *power* in thy whole mind,‡ which signifieth God the Father. Then secondly, the *light* in thy whole mind, enlightening the whole mind, which signifieth God the Son. Then thirdly, there goeth forth out of all thy powers, and out of thy light also, a *spirit* which hath understanding.

98. For all the veins, together with the light in thee, as also thy heart and thy brain, and all whatsoever is in thee, make or constitute *that*

---

* "both these," *i.e.* the two "powers" of par. 93—"the power which moveth in thy whole body," and "reason, understanding, skill," etc.

† The German substantive rendered by Sparrow "mind" in this par. is *Gemüthe*, mind, soul, heart, feeling, disposition. The word is specifically applicable to the organ of feeling, rather than to mind, as "mind" is ordinarily understood.

‡ "whole mind" (*gantzen Gemüthe*). See par. 94 above.

spirit; and that is thy *soul*; and it well signifieth the Holy Ghost, which goeth forth from the Father and the Son, and reigneth in the whole Father; for the *soul* of man reigneth in the *whole* body.

99. But the body or the bestial flesh in man signifieth the *dead* corrupted earth, which man through his *fall* hath so framed to himself; of which more shall be spoken in its due place.

100. [" *The* soul *containeth the first principle;* " *and the* soul's spirit *the second principle* " in Ternario sancto, *in the holy Ternary; and* " *the* outward spirit, *viz. the astral, containeth* " *the third Principle of this world."*]*

101. Thus you find also the Ternary of the Deity in beasts; for as the spirit of a man is, and existeth, so is it also in a beast, and therein is no difference.†

102. But the difference lieth in *this*, that **man** is made by God himself out of the best kernel or *pith* of nature, to be his angel and similitude, **and** *God ruleth* in man with his holy spirit; so that

---

* In Sparrow's translation this par. is not marked as one of the additions by J. B. himself in 1620. In the German ed. of 1656 the par. is treated as an addition, and no alteration was made by Gichtel in the ed. of 1682.

† "for as the spirit of a man is," etc. Sparrow has given a literal translation of the German. The par. could be rendered thus: "for the spirit ariseth and existeth in a beast just in the same manner as in a man."

man can speak, discourse, distinguish and understand all things.

103. But a beast is made of the *wild* nature of this world; the *stars* and *elements* have generated beasts through their motion, according to the will of God.

104. So existeth the spirit in birds, fowls and worms also; and *all* hath its threefold source in *similitude* to the Ternary in the Deity.

105. You see also the Ternary of the Deity in wood and stones, as also in herbs, in leaves and in grass, only *these* are *all* earthly.

106. However, nature generateth nothing in this world, be it what it will, and though perhaps it should stand or continue but scarce a minute, yet it is all generated in the Ternary, or according to the similitude of God.

107. *Now observe*: In wood, stone or herbs there are three things contained, nor can anything be generated or grow if but one of the three should be left out.

108. I. First, there is the *power*, from which a *body* comes to be, whether wood, stone or herbs.

II. After that, there is a *sap* in that thing, which is the *heart* of the thing.

III. Thirdly, there is in it a *springing*, flowing power, smell or taste, which is the *spirit* of the thing, whereby it groweth and increaseth. Now if any of these three fail, the thing cannot *subsist*.

109. *Thus* you find in everything a similitude

of the *Ternary* in the divine being, look upon
what you will; let no man make himself so stark
blind as to think *otherwise*, or to think that God
hath no Son and no Holy Ghost.

110. I shall make this *more* plain and clear
when I come to write of the *creation*; for I do
not borrow of other men in my writings: And
though indeed I quote many examples and testimonies of God's saints, yet all is written by God
in my mind, so that I *absolutely* and infallibly
believe, know and see it; yet not in the flesh, but
in the spirit, in the impulse and motion of God.

111. It is not so to be understood that my reason
is greater or higher than that of all other men
living; but I am the Lord's *twig* or branch, and
am a very mean and little spark of his; he may
set me where he pleaseth, I cannot hinder him
in that.

112. Nor is this my *natural will*, that I could
do it by my own small ability; for if the spirit
were withdrawn from me, then I could neither
know nor understand *my own writings*; and I
must on every side fight and struggle with the
devil, and lie open to temptation and affliction as
well as other men.

113. But in the following chapters you will
soon see the devil and his kingdom *laid naked*;
his pride and reproach shall suddenly *be discovered.*

THE FOURTH CHAPTER

Of the creation of the Holy Angels. An Instruction or open Gate of Heaven.

1. THE learned, and almost all writers, have very much *encumbered* and mightily troubled their heads, to *search*, contrive and conceive in nature (and have brought forth many and sundry *opinions*) concerning how and of what the holy angels were created: And on the other side, what was that horrible *fall* of the great prince *Lucifer*, or how he became so *base* a wicked and fierce wrathful devil, from whence that *evil quality* should spring, or what drove him to it.

2. And though this ground and great mystery hath remained hidden from the beginning of the world, and that human flesh and blood is *not able* to conceive or apprehend it,

3. Yet God, who created the world, will reveal himself *now* at the end; and all great mysteries will be manifested or revealed, to intimate that the great Day of Revelation and final Judgment is *near*, and *daily* to be expected.

4. On which will be restored again all that which hath been lost through *Adam*, and in which the kingdom of heaven, and the kingdom of the devil, in this world, shall be *severed asunder*.

5. But *how* all this will be done God will reveal in the highest plainness and simplicity, so that no man will be able to oppose him.

6. Therefore every one should lift up his eyes, for his redemption draweth near, and not *seek after* riotous living and vain show, supposing it to be the best life here; whereas in their arrogance they *sit* in the midst of hell, to wait upon Lucifer as *his guard*.

7. Which they themselves shall suddenly be *sure* to *see*, with great terror, anguish and eternal despair, as also to their shame and scorn: of which the devils are a *terrible* example, who were once the fairest and *brightest* angels in heaven, as I shall reveal, write and *manifest* here following. I will suffer God's impulse, I am not able to withstand it.

Of the Divine Quality.

8. Since thou hast perceived, in the *third* chapter, the ground of the Ternary in the divine being, I shall here shew plainly the *power* and operation, as also the qualities or qualification, in the divine being; or *from what* the angels were properly and peculiarly created, or what their *body* and power are.

9. As I said before,* all the powers or virtues are in God the Father, and no man with his sense and thoughts can *reach* to apprehend it. But in the stars and the elements, as also by all the creatures in the whole creation of this world, a man may *clearly know* it.

10. All power and virtue is in God the Father; and proceedeth also forth from him, as light, heat, cold, soft, gentle, sweet, bitter, sour, astringent or harsh, sound or noise, and much more that is not possible to be spoken or apprehended. *All these* are in God the Father, one in another as one power, and yet all these powers move in his *exit* or going forth.

11. But the powers in God do not operate or qualify in the same *manner* as in nature in the stars and elements, or in the creatures.

12. No, you must *not* conceive it so: For lord *Lucifer* by his elevation made the powers of impure nature *thus* burning, bitter, cold, astringent, sour, dark and unclean.

13. But in the Father all powers are mild and

---

* Lit., "as I said before, all virtue is in God the Father, which [virtue] no man can, with his senses, reach to apprehend. But in the stars . . . this can be clearly known [or recognized]," or "one may clearly know [or recognize this]." In the original the two "its" do not appear to refer to the same antecedent. The first is a feminine, and refers to "virtue" (*Kraft*); the second a neuter, which grammatically must refer to the whole statement, "all virtue is in God the Father." St M., too, takes *Kraft* to imply a plural meaning, "powers"; and then, for Sparrow's "it," "it," writes "them."

soft, like heaven, and very full of joy, for all the powers triumph in one another, and their voice or sound riseth up from eternity to eternity.

14. There is nothing in them but love, meekness, mercy, friendliness or courtesy ; even such a triumphing, rising source or fountain of joy, wherein all the voices of heavenly joyfulness *sound* forth, so that no man is able to express it, nor can it be likened to anything.

15. But if a man *will* liken it to anything, it may *nearest* be [1]likened to the soul of man, when *kindled* or enlightened by the Holy Ghost.

[1] See Chap. 3, v. 40.

16. For then it is thus joyful and triumphing, and all powers rise up in it and triumph, and so raise the bestial body that it trembleth : This is a true glimpse of the *divine* quality, as the quality is in God. But in God all is spirit.

17. In God the quality of water is not of *such* a running and qualifying condition or manner as it is in *this* world, but is a spirit, very bright, clear and thin, wherein the Holy Ghost riseth up, a *mere power*.

18. The bitter quality qualifieth in the sweet, and in the astringent (or harsh and sour) quality, and the *love* riseth up therein from eternity to eternity.

19. For the love in the light and clarity or glorious brightness goeth forth from the *Heart* or Son of God, in all the powers of the Father, and the Holy Ghost moveth in them all.

20. And this, in the deep of the Father, is like a divine [1]SALITTER, which I must needs liken to the *earth*, which before its corruption was even such a *Salitter*.

21. But not so hard, cold, bitter, sour and dark, but like the deep, or like heaven, very clear and pure, wherein all powers were *good*, fair and heavenly; but that prince Lucifer thus *spoiled* them, as you will perceive here following.

22. This heavenly Salitter or powers one in another generate heavenly joyful fruits and colours; all manner of trees and plants, on which *grow* the fair, pleasant and lovely fruits of *life*.

23. There spring up also in these powers and virtues all manner of blossoms and *flowers*, with fair heavenly colours and smells.

24. They are of *several* tastes, each according to its quality and kind, very *holy*, *divine* and full of joy.

25. For every quality beareth its own fruit: *as* in the corrupted murderous den or dark valley and dungeon of the earth there spring up all manner of earthly trees, plants, flowers and fruits,

26. Also *within the earth grow* curious precious stones, silver and gold; and these are a *type* of the heavenly generating or production.

27. Nature *laboureth* with its utmost diligence upon this corrupted dead earth, that it might generate heavenly forms and species or kinds;

but it generateth *only* dead, dark and hard fruits, which are no more than a mere shadow or type of the heavenly.

28. Moreover, its fruits are *altogether* fierce or biting, bitter, sour, astringent or harsh and hot, also cold, hard and naught; they have *scarce* any spark or spice of goodness in them.

29. Their sap and spirit is *mixed* with hellish quality, their scent or smell is a very *stink.* Thus hath lord *Lucifer* caused them to be; as I shall clearly shew hereafter.

30. Now when I write of trees, plants and fruits, you must *not* understand them to be *earthly*, like those that are in this world; for it is *not* my meaning that there shall grow in heaven such dead, hard trees of wood, or *such* stones as consist of an earthly quality.

31. No, but my meaning is heavenly and spiritual, yet *truly* and *properly such*: I mean no other thing than what I set down in the letter.

32. In the divine pomp and state *two* things are especially to be considered : *First*, the *Salitter* or the divine powers, which are moving, springing powers.

33. In that same power groweth up and is generated fruit according to every quality and species or kind, viz. *heavenly* trees and plants, which without ceasing bear fruit, blossom fairly, and grow in divine power, so joyfully that I can neither speak it nor write it down ;

34. But stammer it like a *child* that is learning to speak, and can by *no means* rightly call it forth to be known as the spirit giveth it.

35. The *second* form or property of heaven in the divine pomp or state is *Mercurius* or the sound, as in the *Salitter* of the earth there is the sound, whence there groweth gold, silver, copper, iron and the like; of which men make all manner *of musical instruments* for sounding or for mirth, as bells, organ-pipes and other *things* that make a sound: There is likewise a sound in all the creatures upon earth, else all would be in stillness and *silence*.

36. By that sound all powers are moved in *heaven*, so that all things grow joyfully, and generate very beautifully: And as the divine power is manifold and various, so also the sound or *Mercurius* is manifold and various.

37. For when the powers spring up in God they *touch* and stir one another, and move one in another, and so there is a constant harmony, *mixing* or concert, from whence go forth all manner of colours.

38. In those colours grow all manner of *fruits*, which rise or spring up in the *Salitter*, and the *Mercurius* or sound mingleth itself therewith, and riseth up in all the powers of the Father, and then sounding and *tunes* rise up in the heavenly joyfulness.

39. If you should in this world bring many

thousand sorts of musical instruments together, and all should be tuned in the best manner, most artificially, and the most skilful masters of music should play on them in concert together, all would be no more than the *howlings* and barkings of dogs, in *comparison* with the *divine music*, which riseth up through the divine sound and tunes from eternity to eternity.

40. Further, if thou wilt consider the heavenly divine pomp, state and *glory*, and conceive how it is, and what manner of sprouting, branching, delight and joy there is in it,

41. View this world diligently, and *consider* what manner of fruit, sprouts, and branches grow out of the *Salitter* of the earth, from trees, plants, herbs, roots, flowers, oils, wine, corn and whatever else there is that thy *heart* can find out; *all* is a *type* of the heavenly pomp.

42. *For* the *earthly* and corrupt nature hath continually laboured from the beginning of its creation to this day to bring forth *heavenly* forms or shapes in the earth, as also in man and beasts; as men very well see that every year *new arts* are invented and brought to light, which hath been constantly so from the beginning to this time.

43. But yet nature hath *not* been *able* to bring forth heavenly power, virtue and qualities, therefore its fruit is half dead, corrupt and impure.

44. You must *not think* that in the divine pomp

there come forth beasts, worms and other creatures in flesh, as in this world they do: No; but I mean only the *wonderful* proportion, power, virtue and comeliness of feature in them.

45. Nature laboureth with the utmost diligence in its power to produce *heavenly* figures, shapes or forms; as we see, in men, beasts, fowls and worms, as also in the increase or growth of the earth, that all things are done, shew and appear most perfectly and ingeniously.

46. *For Nature would fain be delivered from this vanity, that it might procreate heavenly forms in the holy power.*

47. For in the divine pomp go forth likewise *all manner* of sprouting and vegetation of trees, plants and all manner of fruit; and every one beareth *its own* fruit, yet not in an earthly quality and kind, but in a *divine* quality, form and kind.

48. Those fruits are not of so dead, hard, bitter, sour and astringent a relish for *food*; nor do they *rot* and grow stinking, as those in this world do, but all consist in holy divine power.

49. Their constitution or *composition* is from divine power, from the *Salitter* and *Mercurius* of the divine pomp, and they are the food of the holy angels.

50. If man's *abominable* fall had not spoiled it he would have been feasted in *such* a manner in this world, and would have eaten in a twofold

manner such fruits as indeed were presented to
him in Paradise.

51. But the infectious *lust*, evil attraction or
impulse of the devil, who had infected and spoiled
the *Salitter* of which *Adam* was made, *that* brought
man into an *evil longing* or lust *to eat* of both the
qualities, the *evil* and the *good*, whereof I will
write clearly here following, and demonstrate it.

Of the Creation of Angels.

52. The spirit sheweth plainly and clearly that,
before the creation of angels, the divine being,
with its rising and qualifying, was from eternity,
and remained so *in* the creation of angels, as it is
also at *this day*, and will so continue *in* and *to*
eternity.

53. The space, room or *place* of this *world*,
together with the creaturely heaven, which we
behold with our eyes, as also the space or place
of the *earth* and stars, together with the deep,
was in such a form as still at *this* day it *is* in,
aloft, above the heavens, in the divine pomp.

54. But it *was* [or became] in the creation of
the angels, the kingdom of the great prince
Lucifer : [" *Understand according to the* second
" Principle, *out of which he was thrust forth into*
" *the outermost, which also is the very innermost*
" *of all.*"]

55. Who, by his proud elevation in his kingdom,
kindled the qualities or the divine *Salitter* out of

which he was made; [" *Understand the* centre *of*
" *his* nature, *or the* first Principle;"] and set it
on fire.

56. Supposing thereby he would grow hugely
and highly *light* and qualifying above the Son of
God. But he became a fool; therefore *this place*
or space, in its burning quality, could *not* subsist
in God, whereupon the creation of this world
ensued.

57. But this world at the end, in *God's*
appointed time, will be *set* again into its first
place, as it was before the creation of angels;
and lord *Lucifer* will have a *hole* * or dungeon
for his eternal habitation therein, and he will
remain eternally in his kindled quality, which
will be an eternal, base, filthy, reproachful habitation, an empty, void dark valley or dungeon, a
hole of fierceness or *wrath.*

Now observe,

58. God in his moving created the holy angels
at once, not out of a strange *matter*, but out of
himself, out of his *own* power and eternal wisdom.

59. But the philosophers had *this opinion*: as
if God had made the angels out of the light only;
but they *erred therein*, for the angels were made
not only out of the light, but out of *all* the powers
of God.

60. As I have shewn *before*, there are *two*

* " a hole " (*eine Höle*), " a hollow place," " a cavern."

things especially to be observed in the deep of God the Father; first, that the power, or all the powers of God the Father, of the Son, and of the Holy Ghost, are very lovely, pleasant and various, and yet are all *one in another* as one power.

61. As the powers of all the stars *rule* in the air, so also in God; But with its operation every power in God *sheweth* itself severally and distinctly.

62. Then afterwards, that the sound is in every power, and the tone or tune of the sound is according to the quality of every power; and therein consisteth the total heavenly kingdom of joy. From this divine *Salitter* and *Mercurius* all angels are made, *viz.* out of the body of nature.

Question.

63. But thou mayest here ask, *How* are they made or generated, or in what way and manner?

Answer.

64. If I had the *tongue* of an angel, and thou hadst an angelical *understanding*, we might very finely discourse of it. But the spirit only seeth it, and the tongue cannot advance towards it. For I can use *no other* words than the words of this world; but now the Holy Ghost being in thee, thy *soul* will well apprehend it.

65. For behold, the total holy Trinity hath with its moving composed, *compacted* or figured

a body or image out of itself, like a *little* god, but not so fully or *strongly* going forth as the whole Trinity, yet in some measure according to the *extent* and capacity of the creatures.

66. For in God there is *neither* beginning nor end; but the angels *have* a beginning and end,* but not circumscriptive, apprehensive, palpable or *conclusive* †; for an angel can sometimes be great, and suddenly little again; their alteration is as swift as man's thoughts are. All *qualities* and powers are in an angel, *as* they are in the whole Deity.

67. But thou must rightly understand this: They are made and compacted together, or figured, out of the *Salitter* and *Mercurius*, that is, out of the *exit* or excrescence.‡

68. Consider this *similitude:* Out of the sun and stars go forth the elements, and they make in the *Salitter* of the earth a *living* spirit, and the stars remain in their circle or sphere, and *that* spirit likewise getteth the quality of the stars.

69. But now the spirit, after its compaction, is a severed *distinct* thing, and hath a substance of

---

* "the angels have a beginning and end." Note by St M.: "that is to say, an origin and a scope of operation."

† "circumscriptive, apprehensive, palpable or conclusive" (*abmesslich oder begreiflich*), "measurable or palpable." St M. translates: "*que l'on ne peut mesurer ni circonscrire,*" "which cannot be measured nor circumscribed."

‡ "the exit or excrescence" (*der Ausgang*), "the efflux." St M. has, "*l'effluve,*" the effluence.

its own, as all the stars have ; and the stars also are and remain severed and distinct things, each of them is free to itself.

70. Nevertheless the quality of the stars *reigneth* in the spirit ; yet the spirit can and may raise or demerse itself * in its own qualities, or may live in the *influences* of the stars, as it pleaseth : It is free, for it hath got for its *own* the qualities which it hath in itself.

71. And though it *had them* at the beginning from the stars, yet they are now its proper *own* : Just as a mother when she hath the seed in herself, as long as she hath it in her, and that it is a *seed*, it is hers ; but when the seed is become a *child*, then it is no more the mother's, but is the child's proper own.

72. And though the child be in the mother's *house*, and the mother *nourish* the child with her food, and the child could *not* live without the mother, yet both the body and the spirit, which are generated out of the seed of the mother, are the *child's* proper own, and it retaineth its corporeal right to itself.

73. And in this *manner* it is with the angels, they also are all composed, framed or figured out of the *divine seed*, but every one hath its own *body* to itself. Though they are in God's

* "raise or demerse itself," or "assert or sink itself." St M. renders this, "*se corroborer ou s'affoiblir*," "assert itself or weaken."

house, and feed on the *fruit* of their mother, out of which they were made, yet the bodies are their *proper* own.

74. But the quality *externally* without them, or externally without their bodies, *viz.* their mother, is *not* their propriety, as also their mother is not the child's propriety; also the *mother's* food is not the *child's* propriety; but the mother giveth it to the child out of love, seeing she hath generated the child.

75. She may *well* also thrust the child out of her house, when the child is stubborn, and will not be obedient, and may *withdraw* her food from it, which also thus befell the *principality* of Lucifer.

76. Thus God may withdraw his divine power, which is externally without the angels, when they elevate themselves against him; but when that is done, a *spirit* must pine away and perish.

77. As when the air, which also is man's mother, is withdrawn from a man, he must needs die; so also the *angels* cannot live without their mother.

THE FIFTH CHAPTER

Of the Corporeal Substance, Being and
Propriety of an Angel.

Question.

1. NOW here the question is, What manner of *body, form* or *shape* hath an angel, or what figure is it of?

Answer.

2. As man is created to be the image and similitude of God, *so also* are the angels, for they are the *brethren of men,* and *men in the resurrection will have no other form* or image *than the angels have,* as our King CHRIST himself [1] testifieth.

3. Besides, the angels *never* shewed themselves in any *other* form or shape to men here on earth, than in a *human* form and shape.

4. Therefore seeing that in the resurrection we shall be like the angels, the angels must needs be shaped and figured like us, or else we must assume to ourselves *another* image or shape

[1] Matt. xxii. 30.

103

in the resurrection, which would be against and *contrary* to the first creation.

5. Thus also, [1]*on mount Tabor, Moses and Elias appeared,* in their own form and shape, *to the disciples of Christ,* though they had been a long time in heaven before.

6. And [2]*Elias was taken up into heaven* alive, *with his living body,* and yet had now *no* other form or shape than he had when he was on earth.

7. Also *when Christ went to heaven, two angels hovered in the clouds,* [3]*and said to the disciples, Ye men of Israel, what do you look after? This JESUS shall come again, as you have seen HIM go away to heaven.*

8. Thus it is plain and clear enough that he will come again in the same form at the last day, with a *divine* and glorified body, as a Prince of the holy angels, which will be the men-angels.

9. The spirit also testifieth clearly that angels and men have one and the *same* image; for out of the same place wherein Lucifer sat, and *out of* which he was made, God hath made *another angel* instead of expulsed Lucifer and his legions, which angel was ADAM, if he had but persevered in his clarity, brightness or glory.

10. But there is yet a sure hope of resurrection, and then we shall get the angelical clarity or glory and purity again.

11. *Now thou wilt ask, How then are the angels created according to the image of God?*

Answer.

12. First, the compacted, figured body is indivisible and incorruptible, and not to be *felt* by man's hands; for it is constituted or composed out of the *divine power*, and that power is so knit and *bound* together that it can never be destroyed again.

13. For as *none*, no *not* anything, can destroy the whole Deity, *so* also there is *not* anything that can destroy an angel; for every angel is formed, figured, set together or composed out of *all* the powers of God, not with flesh and blood, but out of the *divine* power.

14. First, the body is out of all the *powers* of the Father, and in those powers is the *light* of God the Son; now the powers of the Father and of the Son, which are in an angel creaturely, generate an understanding *spirit*, which riseth up in that angel.

15. First of all, the powers of the Father generate a light, whereby an angel seeth into the *whole* Father, whereby he can see the *outward* power and operation of God, which is externally without its own body, and thereby can *see* its fellow-brethren, and can see and *enjoy*

the glorious fruit of God, and therein consisteth its joy.

16. At *first* that light came out of the Son of God in the powers of the Father, into the angelical body creaturely, and is the *body's* proper own, which cannot be withdrawn from it by anything, *unless* itself extinguisheth it, as *Lucifer* did.

17. Now all the powers, which are in the whole angel, generate that light; and as God the Father generateth his Son to be his *Heart*, so the power of the angel also generateth *its* son and heart in itself, and that *again* enlighteneth all powers in the whole angel.

18. After that there goeth forth out of all the powers of the angel, and also out of the light of the angel, a fountain, which springeth or welleth up in the whole angel; and that is its spirit, which riseth up into all eternity; for in this same spirit is all perception and all knowledge [*i.e.* understanding] of all powers and of all types and modes [of life] which are in the whole [universal] God.

19. For that spirit springeth up out of all the powers of the angel, and goeth up into the *mind*, where it hath *five* open doors; there it can look round about and *see* whatsoever is in God, and also whatsoever is in itself.

20. And so it goeth forth from all the powers of the angel, as also from the light of the angel; *as the Holy Ghost* goeth forth from the Father

and the Son, and *filleth* the whole *corpus* or body.

Now observe the great Mystery.

21. There are *two* things to be observed in God; the *first* is the *Salitter*, or the divine powers, out of which is the body or corporeity; and the *second* is the *Mercurius*, tone, tune or sound : thus also it is, in *like manner* and form, in an angel.

22. First there is the power, and in the power is the tone or tune, which, in the spirit, riseth up into the head, into the mind,* as in man in the brain ; and in the mind it [the tone] hath its open doors or gates ; but in the heart it hath its seat and its origin, where it springeth [or ariseth] from all the powers.

23. For the fountain of all powers floweth [1] in [1] Or to. the heart, as it doth also in man, and in the head it hath its *princely* seat, where it seeth all, smelleth all, and feeleth all.

24. And now when it seeth and heareth the *divine* tone, tune and sound rise up, which is externally without it, then is its spirit *affected* and kindled with joy, and elevateth itself in its princely seat, and *singeth* and ringeth forth very joyful words concerning God's holiness, and concerning the fruit and vegetation of the *eternal life.*

* "into the head, into the mind." J. B. does not here use *Kopf,* the usual word for head, but *Haupt.* "Mind" = *Gemüthe.* See Ch. 3, par. 94.

25. Also concerning the ornament, colours and beauty of the eternal *joy*, and concerning the amiable blessed glance or gracious *aspect* and countenance of God the Father, Son, and Holy Ghost; also concerning the excellent fraternity, fellowship and *communion* of angels, concerning the continual everlasting joyfulness, concerning the holiness of God, and concerning the *angels' own* princely government.

26. In brief, concerning *all powers*, and that which proceedeth *from* all God's powers; which, in regard of the untowardness of my corruption in the flesh, I *cannot* write, I would much rather be there present myself.

27. But what I cannot write here I will commit to *thy soul* to consider further of it, and at the Day of the *Resurrection* you shall see it most plainly and clearly.

28. You should not here scorn my spirit, for it is *not* sprung forth from the wild beast, but is generated from my power and virtue, and *enlightened* by the Holy Ghost.

29. Here I write not without knowledge; but if thou, like an *epicure* and fatted swine of the devil, from the devil's instigation, shouldst *mock* at these things and say:

30. The fool surely hath *not* gone up to heaven and seen or heard them, *these* are mere fables; then, in the power of my knowledge, I would have you warned, and *cited* before the severe judgment of God.

31. And though in my body I am powerless to bring thee there, yet *That* from which I have my knowledge is mighty and potent enough to cast thee even into the abyss of hell.

32. *Therefore* take warning, and consider that thou also belongest to the angelical choir, and read the following *hymn* with longing delight, and then the Holy Ghost will be awakened and stirred up in thee, and thou also wilt get a desire and longing after the heavenly *chorus* and choir of dancing. *Amen.*

33. The musician hath wound up his pegs, and tuned his strings; the Bridegroom cometh. When the round beginneth take *heed* thou dost not get the *hellish* [1] *gout* in thy feet; lest thou be found incapable or *unfit* for the angelical dance, and so be thrust out from the *wedding*, seeing thou hast on no *angelical garment*.

[1] Podagra.

34. Surely the gate will be locked upon thee, and so thou wilt not enter in any more, but wilt *dance* with the *hellish wolves* in the hellish fire; truly thou wilt then forget to mock, and sorrow will *gnaw* thee.

Of the Qualification of an Angel.

Question.

35. The question now is, What manner of *qualification* hath an angel?

Answer

36. The *holy soul* of a man, and the spirit of an angel, are and have one and the same substance and being, and there is no difference therein, but only in the *quality* itself, or in their corporeal government; that which qualifieth *outwardly*, or from without, in man by the air hath a *corrupt earthly* quality, yet on the other side, hidden from the creatures, it hath also a *divine* and *heavenly* quality.

37. But the *holy* soul understandeth it well, as the kingly prophet *David* saith, [1] *The Lord rideth on the wings of the wind.* In the angel the divine property qualifies only in perfect holiness, divinity and purity.*

[1] Psalm civ. 3.

Question.

38. But a simple man may ask, What do you mean by the word *qualifying*, or what is that?

Answer.

39. I mean thereby the power, which in the body of the angel *entereth in* from without, and cometh forth again; as in a similitude, when a man fetcheth breath and breatheth it forth again; for *therein* standeth the life both of the body and of the spirit.

* The last clause of this par. does not appear in Sparrow's translation. It is in all the German eds. *except* 1656 and Schiebler's ed.

40. The quality from without *kindleth* the spirit in the heart, in the first fountain, whereby all the powers in the whole body become stirring, and then that quality in the corporeal spirit, which is the *natural spirit* of an angel or a man, riseth up into the head, where it hath its princely seat or throne and government, and there it hath its *counsellors*, whose advice it taketh.

41. The *first* counsellor is the *eyes*; they are affected with everything they look upon, for they are the *light*.

42. For as the light goeth forth from the Son of God in the whole Father into all the powers, and affecteth all the powers of the Father, and on the other side all the powers of the Father affect the light of the Son of God *wherefrom ariseth the Holy Spirit*: *

43. So do the eyes work in the thing they look upon, and the thing worketh again in the eyes, and the counsellor, the eyes, bringeth it into the head before the princely seat or throne; and there it is to be approved of.

44. Now if the spirit is *pleased* therewith, then it bringeth the same to the heart, and the heart giveth it to the passages or *issuings* forth of the powers or fountain-veins in the whole body; and then the mouth and hands and feet fall to work.

* The words printed in italics are not in Sparrow's translation, nor in the German ed. of 1656, nor in Schiebler's ed. They are in all other German eds.

45. The *second* counsellor is the *ears*, which have their rise also from all the powers in the whole body through the spirit; their fountain is *Mercurius* or the *sound*, which ariseth from all the powers.

46.* And as in all the powers of God the *Mercurius* riseth and soundeth, wherein the heavenly tone, tune or joy consisteth, and the tone or tune goeth forth out of all the powers, and so in the *attraction* of the spirit in God is *elevated* or raised up:

47. And when one power toucheth or stirreth the other, and tuneth or soundeth, then the tune or sound *goeth forth*, and riseth up *again* in all the powers of the Father; and so all the powers of the Father are *again* affected therewith, whereby they are always impregnated with the tune, and *continually* generate it again in every power:

48. Thus the second counsellor in the head is the *ears*, they stand open, and in all that soundeth the *sound* goes forth through them.

49. Now where the *Mercurius* soundeth and is

* "Likewise it is from all the powers of God that the Mercurius riseth and soundeth, wherein the heavenly tone or joy consisteth. The tone or tune goeth forth from all the powers, and riseth up in the attraction (*Zusammenfügung*) of the spirit in God; and when one power stirreth the other and soundeth, then the tone or tune goeth forth and riseth up again in all the powers of the Father, and all the powers of the Father are again affected therewith, whereby they are always impregnated with the tone and continually generate it again in every power" (St Martin).

elevated or predominant, there the *Mercurius* of the spirit goeth also in, and is thereby affected, and *bringeth it* [the sound] before the princely throne in the head, where it is to be approved by the *other* four counsellors.

50. And if the spirit is pleased therewith, then it [the spirit] bringeth the same before its mother into the heart, and the heart, or the fountain of the heart, *giveth it* [the sound] to all the powers in the whole body; and then the mouth and hands lay hold on it.

51. But if the *whole* princely council in the head be *not* pleased, so that it [the sound] is approved, then it [the princely council] lets that go again, and bringeth it [the sound] not to the mother, the heart.

52. The *third* princely counsellor is the *nose*; there the fountain riseth up from the body in the spirit into the nose, and there it hath two open doors or gates.

53. As the excellent, precious and amiable *blessed* savour or smell goeth forth from all the powers of the Father and of the Son, and *tempereth* itself with all the powers of the Holy Ghost, whence the *Holy Spirit* and most precious savour riseth up from the fountain of the Holy Ghost; and floweth or boileth in all the powers of the Father, and *kindleth* all the powers of the Father, whereby they are impregnated *again* with the amiable blessed savour or *saving*

smell, and so generate it in the Son and Holy Ghost:

54. *So also* in angels and men, the power of the smell riseth up out of all the powers of the *body* by and through the *spirit*, and cometh forth at the *nostrils* of the nose, and is affected with all smells or savours, and bringeth them through the nostrils of the nose, which is the third counsellor, into the head, before the princely seat or throne.

55. And there it is to be proved *whether* the smell be a good smell or savour, pleasing to man's constitution and complexion, or no: If it be *good*, then the counsellor bringeth the same to its mother, that the smell may be brought to effect; if it be not good, then is it expelled and thrust away.

56. And *this* counsellor of the smell, which is generated out of the *Salitter*, is also mixed with *Mercurius*, and so belongeth to the heavenly joyfulness, and is a glorious, *excellent* and fair fountain in God.

57. The *fourth* princely counsellor is the *taste* on the *tongue*, which also ariseth from all the powers of the body through the spirit into the tongue: for all *fountain-veins* of the whole body go into the tongue, and the tongue is the sharpness or *taste* of all the powers:

58. Just as the Holy Ghost goeth forth from the Father and the Son, and is the sharpness or

proof of all powers, and in his moving or rising up bringeth all that which is good *again* into all the powers of the Father, whereby the powers of the Father are *impregnated* again, and so continually generate the taste.

59. But that which is *not good* the Holy Ghost *speweth out*, as a loathsome *abomination*, as it is written in the [1] *Apocalypse* ; and as he spewed out the great prince *Lucifer* in his pride and perdition ; for the Holy Ghost could no more endure to taste the fiery proud *stinking* quality. And thus it happens to all proud stinking men.

[1] Rev. iii. 16.

60. O man, let this be told thee, for the spirit is earnestly *jealous* in this thing especially : *Desist* from pride ; or else it will be with you as it befell the devils. There is no jesting or *trifling* herein ; the time is very short, thou wilt suddenly taste it, I mean the hellish fire.

61. Now as the Holy Ghost proveth all, so the *tongue* also proveth all tastes : and if the same pleaseth the spirit, then the spirit bringeth the same into the head, to the *other four* counsellors before the princely seat, and there it is proved whether it be profitable or wholesome for the qualities of the body.

62. If so, then is it brought to the mother, the *heart*, which giveth it to all the *veins* or powers of the body, and then the mouth and hands lay hold of it.

63. But if it be *not* good, then the tongue *sptis*

or speweth it out, before it comes to the princely council.

64. But *though* the taste be pleasant to the tongue, and is a good taste, but yet is not *serviceable* and useful for the whole body, then it is *rejected* nevertheless, when it comes before the council, and the tongue must spit or *spew* it out, and touch it no more.

65. The *fifth* princely counsellor is the *feeling*; which fifth counsellor ariseth also from all the powers of the body in the spirit, into the head.

66. As *all powers* go forth from God the Father and Son, in the Holy Ghost, so one toucheth another, from whence existeth the *tune* or *Mercurius*, so that all the powers sound and move themselves.

67. Else if one did not touch another, nothing would stir *at all*, and so this touching maketh the Holy Ghost *stir*, so that he riseth up in all the powers, and toucheth all the powers of the Father, wherein then existeth the heavenly joyfulness or *triumphing*, as also tuning, sounding, generating, blossoming and vegetation or springing, *all* which hath its rising from this, that one power *toucheth* another.

¹ John v. 17.   68. For Christ saith in the Gospel, ¹*I work, and my Father worketh also.* And he meaneth this very touching and working, in that every power goeth forth from him, and generateth the Holy Ghost, and in the Holy Ghost all the powers

are *already* clearly *stirred*, by the going forth of the Father.

69. Therefore the Holy Ghost floweth, *boileth* and riseth up from eternity to eternity, and kindleth again all the powers of the Father, and maketh them stirring, so that they are always impregnated.

70. In such manner it is *also* in angels and men : for all powers in the body (Corpus) arise, and *touch* one another, or else angels and men could feel nothing.

71. But if one member be too much *stirred*, it crieth to the whole body for help, and the whole body *stirs*, as if it were in a great commotion or *uproar*, as if the *enemy* were at hand, and cometh to help that member, and to deliver and release it from the pain.

72. This you may see if a *finger* be but hurt, crushed or wounded, or any other member of the body, be it which it will ; presently the spirit in that place *runneth* suddenly to the mother, the heart, and complaineth to the mother ; and if the pain do but a little *exceed*, then the mother rouseth up and awakeneth all the members of the body, and *all* must come to help *that* member.

Now observe,

73. Thus *one* power continually toucheth and stirreth another in the whole body, and all the powers rise up into the head before the princely

council, which princely council proveth the stirring of all the powers.

74. Now if one member stirreth *too much*, and at any time *hurteth* a princely counsellor; (as by *seeing*, it would be in love with that which it *ought not* to be in love withal):

75. As lord Lucifer did, who saw the Son of God, and fell in love with that *high light*, and moved and stirred himself so very much, intending to be *equal* with him, or indeed to be *higher* and brighter than he; such stirring or meddling the counsellors reject.

76. Or if one member would stir and move too vehemently by *hearing*, and would fain hear false and wicked tongues in talking lies and fictions, and bring that to the *heart*, this also is rejected by the counsellors.

77. Or if it would by the *smelling* get a longing or lusting after that which is none of its own. As lord *Lucifer* did also, who longed after the *holy* savour or *sweet smell* of the Son of God, and intended in his elevation and kindling to smell and savour yet *more pleasantly*.

78. In that manner he also deceived our mother *Eve*, saying, [1] *If she did but eat of the forbidden tree*, then *she should be wise* or witty, *and be like God*; but this smelling or *stirring* the council likewise rejecteth.

[1] Gen. iii. 5.

79. Or if by *tasting* it should fall into a desire and longing to *eat* that which is *not* of the

quality of the body, or is none of its own; as mother *Eve* in Paradise fell a longing to eat of the devil's crab-apples, and *did* eat thereof; such stirring in lust the council also rejecteth.

80. In short, there are therefore *five* in the princely council, that one should *advise* another, and every one is of a peculiar *sundry* quality; and that compacted or concreted spirit which is *generated* out of all the powers is their king or prince, and he sitteth in the *head* in the brain of a man, and in an angel in that power which is instead of the brain of a man, and in the head also, upon his princely throne, and executeth everything which was concluded and decreed by the whole princely council.*

* "and he sitteth in the head in the brain of a man," etc. "In man, he sitteth in the head, in the brain; and in an angel he sitteth also in the head, upon his princely throne, in that power which is instead of the brain of a man, and executeth everything," etc. (St Martin).

THE SIXTH CHAPTER

How an Angel, and how a Man, is the Similitude and Image of God.

1. BEHOLD! as the *being* or *essence* in God is, so also is the being in *man* and in *angels*; and as the divine body is, so also is the angelical and the human body or corporeity.

2. But with this difference alone, that an angel, and a man, is a *creature*, and *not* the *whole* being, but a son of the whole being, whom the whole being hath generated; and therefore it is fit that it should be in *subjection* to the whole being, seeing that it is the *son* of the body of the whole being.

3. Now if the son resist and *oppose* the father, it is but right that the father should cast him away out of the house, seeing the *son* sets himself against him that hath generated him, and from whose power he is *become* a creature.

4. For if any one make somewhat out of that which is his own, he may, if it doth *not* prove according to his will, do with it what he pleaseth, *and make it either a vessel of honour or of dishonour*; which was done even so to *Lucifer.*

Now observe:

5. From all qualities the *whole* divine power of the Father speaketh forth the W O R D; that is, the Son of God.

6. Now that voice, or *that* W O R D which the Father speaketh, goeth forth from the Father's *Salitter* or powers, and from the Father's *Mercurius*, sound or tune: This the Father speaketh forth in himself, and *that* W O R D is the very splendour or glance proceeding from all his powers.

7. But when it is spoken forth it stayeth or sticketh *no more* in the powers of the Father, but soundeth or tuneth back again in the whole Father in *all* powers.

8. Now that W O R D which the Father *pronounceth* or speaketh forth hath such a *sharpness*, that the tone of the W O R D goeth swiftly in a moment through the whole *deep* of the Father, and that sharpness is the *Holy Ghost.*

9. For the W O R D which is spoken forth or outspoken abideth as a splendour or glorious [1] *edict* before the king.

[1] Or *proclamation.*

10. But the tone or sound, which goeth forth through the *Word, executeth* the edict of the Father, which he had outspoken through the Word; and that is the *birth* or geniture of *the holy Trinity.*

11. Now behold! An angel, and a man also, is

thus: The power in the whole body hath all the *qualities*, as it is in God the Father.

12. And as all the powers in God the Father rise up from eternity to eternity, so all the powers rise up also in an angel, and in a man, into the *head*; for higher they cannot rise; for they are but creatures that have a beginning and end.

13. And in the head is the *divine* council-seat or throne, and [the throne] signifieth God the Father, and the *five senses* or qualities are the counsellors, which have their influences out of the *whole* body, out of all the powers.

14.* The five senses always hold counsel in the power of the whole body, and when a conclusion is formed, the same is uttered [or pronounced] by the united council [lit. judge] in its [the council's] centre, or in the midst of the body, as a word, in the heart; for the heart is the fountain-spring of all powers, whence the word itself taketh its rise [or ariseth].

15.* Then the word standeth in the heart as a self-subsisting person, compacted from all the powers [combined]; it is a word and representeth or denoteth God the Son. Then [also] it riseth up from the heart into the mouth and upon the tongue, which [latter] is the sharpness, and sharpeneth the word, so that it soundeth, and differentiateth it according to the five senses.

* In this par. a new translation has been substituted for Sparrow's original rendering.

16. From what quality soever the word taketh its original, in that quality it is thrust forth upon the tongue, and the power of the *distinction* or difference goeth forth from the *tongue*; and that signifieth the Holy Ghost.

17. For as the Holy Ghost goeth forth from the Father and the Son, and *distinguisheth* and sharpeneth all, and effecteth or produceth that which the Father speaketh through the Word:

18. So also the tongue sharpeneth, *articulateth* and distinguisheth all that which the *five senses* in the head bring through the heart on to the tongue; and the spirit goeth forth from the tongue through the *Mercurius* or tone in *that* place, as it was decreed or concluded by the council of the *five senses*, and executeth it all.

Of the Mouth.

19. The *mouth* signifieth that thou art an un-almighty son of thy Father, whether thou art an angel or a man. For through the mouth thou *must* draw into thee the power of thy Father, if thou wilt *live*.

20. An angel must do so, *as well* as a man, though indeed he needs not to use the element of *air* in that manner *as* a man doth; yet he must attract into himself, through the mouth, *the spirit* from which the *air* in this world existeth.

21. For in heaven there is *no* such air, but the qualities are very meek and joyful, like a pleasant

cheering *breath* of wind, and the Holy Ghost is among all the qualities in the *Salitter* and *Mercurius*.

22. This the angel *also* must make use of, or else he cannot be a *moveable* creature, for he must also eat of the heavenly fruit through the mouth.

23. Thou must *not* understand this in an *earthly* manner; for an angel hath no guts, neither flesh nor bones, but is constituted or composed by the divine power in the shape, *form* and manner of a man, and hath all members like man, *except* the members of generation, and the fundament or *going out of the draff*, neither hath an angel need of them.

24. For man first gat his members of generation and fundament in his doleful and *lamentable* fall. An angel sendeth forth nothing but the *divine* power, which he taketh in at his mouth, wherewith he kindleth his heart, and the heart kindleth all the *members*, and *that* he sendeth forth from himself again at the mouth, when he speaketh and praiseth God.

25. But the heavenly fruits which he eateth are *not* earthly; and though they are in such a *form* and shape as the earthly, yet they are mere *divine* power, and have such a pleasant lovely taste and smell that I cannot liken it to anything in this world; for they *taste* and *smell* of the *Holy Trinity*.

26. Thou must not think that they are there only as it were a type or *shadow* of things; *no*; for the spirit sheweth plainly that in the heavenly pomp, in the heavenly *Salitter* and *Mercurius*, grow *divine* trees, plants, flowers, and all *sorts* of whatever is in this world but as a type and resemblance: As the angels are, so are the vegetation and fruits, all *from* the divine power.

27. These heavenly sprouts and springings thou must *not wholly* liken to this world: For there are two qualities *in this world*, a *good* and an *evil*; and many things grow through the power of the evil quality, which doth *not* so in heaven.

28. For heaven hath but *one* form or manner: nothing groweth there which is *not good*.   Lord *Lucifer* alone hath deformed and dressed this world in that manner: Therefore was mother *Eve ashamed*, *when she had eaten* of that which was dressed by the *evil* quality; in like manner also she was ashamed of her members of generation, which she had caused by the biting of *this apple*.

29. The angelical and heavenly fruit hath *not* such [an evil quality or] substance: Indeed it is most certain and true *that there* are all manner of fruits in *heaven*, and *not* types and shadows merely: Also that the angels *pluck* them with their hands, and eat them, as we that are men do, but they need *not* any teeth to do it withal, *neither* have they any, for the fruit is of a divine power.

30. Now all this, whatsoever an angel maketh use of, which is externally *without* him, for the supporting his life, is *not* his corporeal propriety, as if he had it by a natural right, but the *heavenly* Father giveth it to the angels in love.

31. True it is that their body is their own propriety, for God hath given it to them for a propriety. Now whatsoever is given to any one for his *own*, or for propriety, that is his by *right* of *nature*, and he doth not deal righteously who taketh it from him again, unless [he doth so] upon condition and agreement; and thus neither doth God [take things away again]. Therefore an angel is an eternal incorruptible creature, which standeth or subsisteth in all eternity.

32. But what would the body *profit* him, if God did *not feed* it, for then it would have no mobility, and would lie still like a dead block. Now, *therefore*, the angels are obedient to God, and humble themselves before the *powerful* God; they honour, laud and praise him in his great deeds and works of *wonder*, and sing continually of God's *holiness*, *because* he feedeth them.

Of the Gracious, Blessed, and Joyful Love of the Angels towards God, from a true Ground.

33. The right *love* in the *divine* nature cometh from the *fountain* of the Son of God. Behold, thou child of man, let this be told thee: The

angels know *already* what is the right love toward God, but thou needest it in thy *cold heart*.

34. Observe, when the gracious, *amiable*, blessed, joyful glance and light, together with the *sweet* power out of the Son of God, shineth into all powers in the whole Father, then *all* the powers are kindled by the gracious, amiable, blessed, lovely *light* and sweet power, in a triumphing and joyful manner.

35. So also when the gracious, amiable, blessed and joyful light of the Son of God *shineth* on the loving angels, and casteth its beams into their heart, then all the powers in *their* body are kindled, and there riseth up such a *joyful* love-fire, that for great joy they sing and ring forth praises, and [there riseth up] that which neither I nor *any* other creature is able to express.

36. With this *song* I would have the Reader *cited* into the other life, where he will have *experience* thereof: I am not able to set it down in writing.

37. But if thou wilt have experience of it in *this* world, *give over* thy hypocrisy, bribery and deceit, and thy scorning; and turn thy heart in all seriousness to God: *Repent* thee of thy sins, with a true intention and resolution to live holily, and pray to God for his holy spirit.

38. *Wrestle* with him, as the holy patriarch *Jacob* did, [1] *who wrestled with him all the night,* [1] Gen. xxii. 24.

till the dawning of the day, or morning *redness* broke forth, *and would not give over till God had blessed him.* Do thou so likewise with him, and the Holy Ghost will get a form in thee.

39. If thou holdest on in thy earnestness, and wilt not give over, then will *this* fire come suddenly upon thee, like lightning, and shine into thee; and then thou wilt well *experience* that which I have here written, and wilt *easily* believe that which is in my book.

40. Thou wilt also become quite *another* man, and wilt think thereon all the days of thy life; thy delight will be *more* in heaven than on earth.

41. For the *conversation* of the holy soul *is in heaven*, and though indeed it converseth in the body on earth, yet it is always *continually* with its Redeemer JESUS CHRIST, and eateth as a guest with him. Note this!

THE SEVENTH CHAPTER

Of the Court, Place and Dwelling, also of the Government of Angels, how these things stood at the Beginning, after the Creation, and how they became as they are.

1. HERE the devil will *oppose* like a snarling dog, for his shame will be discovered; and he will give the Reader many a sore stroke, and always put him in *doubt* that these things are not so.

2. For nothing doth torment the devil more than when his glory is *upbraided* to him, by signifying what a glorious king and prince he hath been: When this is objected to him, then he is in a *rage* and madness, as if he would storm and overflow all the world.

3. If this chapter should be lighted upon by a Reader in whom the fire of the Holy Spirit should be somewhat *weak*, I fear the devil would be very busy to set upon him, tempting him to *doubt* whether the things set down here be so or no, that the devil's kingdom might not stand so very naked, nor his shame be so *quite* discovered.

4. Now if he can but suppose that he will bring it to pass to be doubted of in any heart, he will not *fail* to use his *utmost* skill, pains and labour therein.   Already I see very well that he hath it in his purpose.

5. Therefore I would have the Reader warned that he be *diligent* in the reading hereof, and patient so long till he cometh to the reading of the *creation* and of the *government* of this world, then he will find it plainly and clearly demonstrated from *nature*.

Now observe:

6. When God Almighty had *decreed* in his council that he would make angels or creatures out of himself, then he made them out of his eternal power and *wisdom*, according to the form and manner of the Ternary in his Deity, and according to the *qualities* in his divine being.

7. At first he made three kingly governments or dominions, answerable to the *number* of the Holy Trinity, and each kingdom had the order or ordinance, power and *quality* of the divine being.

8. Now elevate thy sense, thoughts and spirit into the deep of the Deity, for here a gate is *opened*.   The place or space of this world, the deep of the earth, and above the earth even to heaven, as also the created *heaven*, which was made *out of the* [1]*midst of the waters*, which moveth above the stars, and which we behold

[1] Or centre.

with our eyes, whose depth we cannot sound or reach with our sense, *all* this place or room together was one kingdom, and *Lucifer* was king therein, *before* his being thrust out.

9. The other two kingdoms, that of *Michael* and that of *Uriel*, are *above* the created heaven, and are like that other kingdom.

10. These three kingdoms together contain such a deep as is not of any *human* number, nor can they be measured by anything.

11. Yet you must know that these *three* kingdoms *have* a beginning and an end; but that God, who hath made these three kingdoms out of himself, is infinite, and hath no end.

12. Yet without and beyond and besides these three kingdoms there is likewise the *power* of the Holy Trinity, for God the Father hath *no end*.

13. But thou art to know this Mystery: that in the centre or *midst* of these three kingdoms is generated the splendour or Son of God.

[14. "*This needs explanation: Read the [1]second* "*and the [2]third part of these writings, where it is* "*described more fundamentally: for nothing that* "*is divisible, measurable or circumscriptive is* "*here meant or understood, only it was in* "*simplicity and plainness so set down at the first,* "*because of the slow and dull apprehension.*"]

[1] *The Three Principles.*
[2] *The Three-fold Life.*

15. And the three kingdoms are *circular* round about the Son of God, *neither* of them is farther from or nearer to the Son of God,

for one is equally as near about the Son of God as another.

16. From *this* ¹ fountain, and from all the powers of the Father, goeth forth the Holy Ghost, together with the light and power of the Son of God, in and through all *angelical* kingdoms or dominions, and without, *beyond* and besides all the angelical kingdoms; which no angel or man is able to dive or search into.

17. Neither have I any purpose to consider of it *further*, much less to write; but *my revelation* reacheth even into the three kingdoms, like an angelical knowledge.

18. But *not* in my reason or apprehension, nor in *perfection* like an angel, but *in part*, and so long only as the spirit tarrieth in me, further I know it not.

19. When he parteth from me I know nothing but the elementary and earthly things of this world: but the spirit seeth even into the *depth* of Deity.

Question.

20. Now one may ask, What manner of substance or thing is it, that the Son of God is [thus] generated in the centre or *midst* of these three kingdoms? *Surely* one angelical host must needs be nearer unto him than another, seeing their kingdom hath so great a deep?

21. Then, also, the glory, clarity or *brightness*

and power of the Son of God would not be so great without, *beyond* or besides those kingdoms, as in, with and *among* those that are near him, and as in the angelical circuit or court.

Answer.

22. The holy angels were made to be creatures from God, that they should *praise, sing,* ring forth and jubilate before the Heart of God, (which is the Son of God), and *increase* the heavenly joy.

23. *Where* else then should the Father place them, than before the gate of his Heart? Doth not all joy of man, which is in the *whole* man, arise from the fountain of the heart? So then in God also there ariseth the great joy out of the fountain of his Heart.

24. Therefore hath he created the holy angels out of himself, which are as it were *little* gods, answerable to the being and qualities of the whole God, that in the divine power they should act *forth* the praise, and sing and ring forth in the power, and *increase* the arising joy from the Heart of God.

25. But the splendour and the power of the Son of God, or Heart of God, which is the *light* or source and fountain of joy, taketh up his *fairest* and most joyful original in the centre or *midst* of these kingdoms, and shineth into and *through* all the angelical gates.

26. Thou must understand this *properly*, what

the meaning of it is: For when I speak by way of similitude, and *liken* the Son of God to the sun, or to a round globe, it hath not that meaning as if he were a circumscriptive fountain, which can be *measured*, or whose depth, beginning or end could be fathomed. I write so by way of similitude only, till the *Reader* can come to the true understanding.

27. For the meaning here is not that the Son of God should be generated in the centre or midst of these angelical gates only, and nowhere else without, beyond or *besides* these angelical gates.

28. For the powers of the Father are *everywhere*, from and out of which the Son is generated, and from which the Holy Ghost goeth forth; *how* then should he be generated in the centre of these angelical gates only?

29. This therefore is the only ground and *meaning*, that the holy Father, who is ALL, would *have* in these angelical gates his most joyful and most richly loving qualities, out of which is generated the most joyful and most *richly loving* light, word, heart, or fountain of powers; and therefore hath he created his holy angels in *this* place for his joy, honour and glory.

["30. *In the abyssal or bottomless eternity* " *indeed, it is* [*the same*] *in one place as in another;* " *but where there are no creatures nothing can be* " *known, except by the spirit in its wonders.*"]

31. And this is the *select* place of the glory of

God, which God the Father, in himself, hath made choice of, *wherein* his holy WORD or Heart is generated in *highest* glory, clarity or brightness, power and triumphing joy.

32. For observe this mystery : The light, which is generated out of the powers of the Father, who is the true fountain of the Son of God, is generated *also* in an angel, and in a holy man, so that in the same light and knowledge he [the Son of God] triumpheth in *great* joy.

33. How then is it that the light should *not* be generated everywhere, in the *whole* Father? For its power is ALL, and everywhere, even there, where our heart and senses or thoughts cannot reach.

34. So now, *where* the Father is, *there* also is the Son and the Holy Ghost; for the Father everywhere *generateth* the Son, his holy WORD, power, light and sound, and the Holy Ghost goeth everywhere forth from the Father and the Son, even *within* all the angelical gates, and also *without*, beside * or beyond the angelical gates.

35. Now if a man likeneth the Son of God to the *globe* of the sun, as I have often done in the foregoing chapters, that is spoken in the way and manner of natural similitudes; and I was *constrained* to write so, because of the lack of understanding of the Reader, that so he might raise his sense or thoughts in these natural things,

* "beside." See note to par. 46.

and climb from step to step, from one *degree* to another, till he might come into the high Mysteries.

36. But it hath not this meaning, that the Son of God is a circumscribed, compacted, figured image, like the sun.

37. For if it were so, then *must* the Son of God have a beginning, and the Father must have generated him in time, and then he could *not* be the eternal, almighty Son of the Father; but the Son would be like a king, who had yet a *greater* king *above* him, who had generated him in time, and in whose power it was to alter and *change him.*

38. This would be such a Son as had a beginning, and his power and splendour would be like the power of the sun which goeth forth from the sun, the body or globe of the sun standing still in its place: If this were so, then indeed one angelical [1]gate would be *nearer* to the Son of God than another.

¹ Oɪ *port.*

39. But here I will shew to thee the highest gate of the divine Mystery, and thou needest seek no higher; for there is no higher.

Observe:

40. The Father's power is all, in and above all heavens, and the same power everywhere generateth the light. Now this UNIVERSAL POWER is, and is called, the *universal power* of

the Father; and the light which is generated out of that universal power is, and is called, the Son.

41. But it is therefore called the Son, in that it is generated out of the Father, so that it is the *Heart* of the Father in his powers.

42. And being *generated*, it is another person than the Father is; for the Father is the *power* and the kingdom, and the Son is the *light* and the splendour in the Father, and the Holy Ghost is the *moving* or *exit* * out of the powers of the Father and of the Son, and formeth, figureth, *frameth* and imageth all.

43. As the *air* goeth forth from the power of the sun and stars, and moveth in this world, and causeth that all creatures are generated, and that the grass, herbs and trees spring and grow, and causeth *all* whatsoever is in this world to be:

44. So the Holy Ghost goeth forth from the Father and the Son, and moveth or acteth, formeth or frameth and imageth all that is in the *whole God*.

45. All growing or vegetation and forms in the Father arise and spring up in the moving of the Holy Ghost; therefore there is but ONE only GOD, and *three* distinct *Persons* in one divine being, essence or substance.

46. Now if a man should say the Son of God

* "exit" (*Ausgang*), "effluence"; rendered by St M., "expansion."

were an image, circumscriptive or measurable
like the sun, then the three Persons would be
only in that place where the Son is, and his
splendour or *shining* would be without or beyond
him, and as gone forth from the Son; and the
Father would be one, only externally, without
or beside * the Son, and then the power of the
Father, which would be afar off and wide distant
from the Son, *would not* generate the Son
and Holy Ghost, externally, without and beyond
the angelical gates; and so there would be
an un-almighty being, externally, without or
beside this place of the Son; and, moreover, the
Father would be a circumscribed or measurable
being.

47. Which is *not* so: But the Father everywhere generateth the Son out of all his powers,
and the Holy Ghost goeth everywhere forth from
the Father and the Son, and so *there is* but
ONE only God in one being, with three distinct
persons.

48. Of which you have a similitude in the
precious gold ore, or a gold-stone unseparated.
First there is the matter, that is, the *Salitter* and
Mercurius, which is the *mother* or the whole
stone, which generateth the gold everywhere in

---

* "beside." In par. 34 the word used in the original is
"*ausser*," "without," *i.e.* out of. In par. 46, "*ausserhalb*,"
"without," *i.e.* outside of. The latter term St M. translates,
"*détaché*," "apart from."

the whole *stone*; and in the gold is the glorious power or virtue of the stone.

49. Now the *Salitter* and *Mercurius* signify the Father, the gold signifieth the Son, and the power or virtue signifies the Holy Ghost: In such a manner also is the *Ternary* in the holy Trinity, only that all moveth and goeth forth therein universally.

50. In a gold-stone men find also a little piece of it in some place, wherein there is more and *purer* gold, than in another not discerned, though there is gold in the *whole* stone or ore.

51. Thus also is the place or space in the *centre* or midst of the angelical gates a more pleasant, more gracious, amiable and blessed place to the Father, wherein his Son and Heart is generated in the most richly and fully loving manner, and wherein the Holy Ghost goeth forth from the Father and the Son in the most richly and fully loving manner.

52. Thus you have the right ground of this Mystery, and you *ought not* to think that the Son of God was generated of the Father at *once*, at a *certain time*, as one that hath a beginning, and that he standeth now as a *king*, and would be worshipped.

53. No; this would *not* be an eternal Son, but one that had a beginning, and was under, beneath or *inferior* to the Father that had generated him.

54. *Neither* would he be all-knowing, for he could not know how it was before his Father had generated him.

55. But the Son is generated *continually* from eternity unto eternity, and shineth continually from eternity into the powers of the Father again, whereby the powers of the Father are always from eternity to eternity *continually* impregnated with the Son, and generate him continually.

56. Out of which the Holy Ghost *continually* existeth from eternity to eternity, and so continually from eternity to eternity goeth forth from the Father and the Son, and hath neither beginning nor end.

57. And *this* being is not so in *one* place only of the Father, but *everywhere* in the whole Father, who hath neither beginning nor end; into which no creature can reach with its *senses* or thoughts.

Of the Nativities *or* Genitures of the *Angelical Kings, and how they came to be.*

[58. " *This also is more fundamentally de-* " *scribed in the* [1] second *and in the* [2] *third book.*"]

[1] *Three Principles.*
[2] *Threefold Life.*

59. The person or the *body* of a king of angels is generated out of all the qualities, and out of all the powers of his *whole* kingdom, through the moving, welling-up spirit of God; and therefore such a one is their king, in that his power

reacheth into all the angels of his whole kingdom, and he is the head and general or leader, the most beautiful and most powerful Cherubim or *throne angel.* Such a one was lord Lucifer also before his fall.

[60. "*This also is more fundamentally de-*"*scribed in our* second *and* third *books; viz. in*"*the Three Principles of the Divine Being, and*"*in the Threefold Life of Man.*"]

Of the Ground or Foundation, and Mystery.

61. If a man would find out the Mystery, and the deepest ground, he must diligently and *exactly* view and consider the creation of this world, the government or dominion, and rule or order, as also the qualities of the stars and the elements.

62. Although these are of a *corrupted* and twofold being, which is not living, nor hath understanding; for it is but the corrupt *Salitter* and *Mercurius*, in which king Lucifer kept house, wherein is both evil and good; though it be indeed the *real* power of God, which before its corruption was bright and pure, as now it is, in heaven.

63.* These powers of the stars and elements, did the Creator, after the horrible fall of Lucifer's kingdom, bring together again into the same order as that in which the kingdom of the angels stood in the divine pomp before this fall.

* A new translation of this par. has been substituted for Sparrow's original rendering.

64. Only thou must *not think* that the angelical kingdom with its creatures was so rolled, wheeled and turned round about, as now the stars are, which are only powers, and *in regard* of the birth or geniture of this world are thus wheeled or turned about, whose birth or geniture standeth in the moving, *boiling anguish* in evil and good, in corruption and redemption, till the end of this enumeration, or till the last day.

Now observe:

65. The sun *standeth* in the centre or *midst* of the deep, and is the light or heart which proceeded out of all stars: For when, in the kingdom of Lucifer, before the creation of the world, the *Salitter* and *Mercurius* was thin or dim, and had qualified the one with the other, *then* God extracted the heart out of all the powers, and made the sun thereof.

66. Therefore the sun is the most shining and the brightest of all, and re-enlighteneth all the stars again; all the stars *work* in its power, and it itself hath the power of all the stars; it *kindleth* all the powers of the stars with its splendour and heat, and so every star receiveth from the sun, according to its power and condition or *kind*.

67. *Thus* also is the frame and constitution of the angelical kingdom: The sun signifieth the supreme throne-angel, the *Cherubim* or king in an angelical kingdom: Such a one as lord Lucifer

was before his fall : He had his *seat* in the centre
or midst of his kingdom, and reigned by his power
in all his angels.

68. Just as, in the *Salitter* and *Mercurius*, the
sun ruleth in all the powers of this world, that is,
in softness and hardness, in sweetness and sourness,
in bitterness and astringency, in heat and cold,
in air and water.

69. As is *apparent* in winter, when there is so
hard cold or frost that the water becometh ice ;
though the sun shineth somewhat warm through
all the cold frost, yet for all its beams, by which
it shineth on them, water *freezeth* into snow and
ice.

70. But *here* I will shew thee the right Mystery.
Behold, the sun is the heart of all powers in this
world, and is compacted, framed or composed out
of all the powers of the stars, it *re-enlighteneth*
·all the stars, and all the powers in this world,
and all powers grow *active*, operative or qualifying in its power.

[71. "*Understand it* magically : *For it is a*
" *mirror, looking-glass, or similitude of the eternal*
" *world.*"]

72. As the Father generateth his Son, *that is*,
his heart or light out of all his powers, and that
light which is the Son generateth the *life* in all
the powers of the Father, so that in the same
light, in the Father's powers, goeth forth all
manner of growing, vegetation, springing, orna-

ments and joy; so is the kingdom of angels also constituted, all according to the *similitude* and being of God.

73. A Cherubim or *leader* of a kingdom of angels is the *fountain* or heart of his whole kingdom, and is made out of all the powers out of which his angels are made, and is the most powerful and the brightest of them *all*.

[74. " *The angelical king is the centre or foun-*
" *tain; as Adam's soul is the beginning and centre*
" *of all souls. And, as from the place of the sun*
" *was created and generated the planetic wheel*
" *or sphere, wherein each star is desirous of the*
" *splendour and power of the sun, so the angels*
" *are desirous of their Cherubim or prince; all*
" *according to God, and to his similitude.*"]

75. For the Creator hath extracted the heart out of the *Salitter* and *Mercurius* of the divine powers; [" *Understand he hath composed it by*
" *the* Fiat, *viz. the centre of nature.*"]

76. And the Creator hath formed out of that the Cherubim or *king*, that the Cherubim or king might press or penetrate again with his power into all the angels, and *affect* them all with his power.

77. Just as the sun with its power presseth into all the stars, and affecteth them all; or as the power of God the Son presseth into all the powers of God the Father, whereby they are *all* affected, wherein the birth or geniture of the heavenly joyfulness springeth up.

78. In this form, condition and *manner* it is with the angels also. All the angels of one kingdom signify the many and *various powers* of God the Father; the angelical king signifieth the Son of the Father, or the *heart* out of the powers of the Father, out of which the angels are made; the *exit* out of the king of angels, or his going forth into his angels,* or his *affecting* of his angels, signifieth God the Holy Ghost.

79. As the Holy Ghost goeth forth from the Father and the Son, and affecteth all the powers of the Father, as also all heavenly *fruits* and *forms*, from whence all hath its rising, and wherein the heavenly joyfulness doth consist:

80. Just in such a manner is the *operation* or power of a Cherubim or throne-angel, which worketh or operateth in all his angels, as the Son and Holy Ghost *operate* in all the powers of the Father; or as the sun operateth in all the powers of the stars.

81. Whereby all angels *obtain* the will of the throne-angel, and are all *obedient* to him; for they all work in his power which is *in them* all.

82. For they are the *members* of his body; as all the powers of the Father are *members* of the Son, and he is their heart; and as all heavenly

* "the exit out of the king of angels, or his going forth into his angels." "The exit" (*Ausgang*) is rendered by St M., "*l'expansion*," and "going forth into," "*l'imprégnation*." The original has, "*Ausgang . . . Inficirung*," "going out . . . going into." See Ch. 8, par. 65.

forms and fruits are members of the Holy Ghost, and he is *their* heart, in whom they rise up.

83. Or as the sun is the heart of all the stars, and as all stars are members of the sun, and work one *among* another as one star, and yet the sun is the heart *therein*; though indeed there are many and various powers, yet all work in the power of the sun, and all hath its *life* fróm the power of the sun; look on what you please, be it in animals, in metals or in vegetables of the *earth*.

THE EIGHTH CHAPTER

Of the whole Corpus *or* Body *of an*
Angelical Kingdom.

The Great Mystery.

1. THE angelical kingdoms are *throughout* formed according to the Divine Being, and they have no other form or condition than the *Divine* Being hath in its Trinity.

2. This only is the difference : that their bodies are *creatures*, which have a beginning and an end, and that the kingdom where their locality, *habitation* or court is, is not their corporeal propriety, or proper own, having it for their natural right, as they have their bodies for a *natural right*.

3. But the kingdom belongs to God the Father, who hath made it out of his powers, and he **may** set it and *dispose* it which way he pleaseth; otherwise their body is made according to all, **and** out of all, the *powers* of the Father.

4. Their power generateth the light and know-

ledge *in them.*   As God generateth his Son out
of *all* his powers; and as the Holy Ghost goeth
forth out of *all* the powers of the Father and the
Son; so also in an angel: the spirit goeth forth
from their heart, from their light and from *all*
their powers.

Now observe:

5. As the condition and *constitution* of an angel
is, in his *corporeal* body, with all the members
thereof, such also is the condition of a whole
kingdom, which together is as it were but one
angel.

6. If a man rightly considereth all circumstances, he will find that the whole government
in its locality, circumference or *region* in a
kingdom, is of the same condition or constitution as the body (Corpus) of an angel, or as is
the *Holy Trinity.*

Observe here the Depth.

7. *All power* is in God the Father, and he is
the *fountain* of all powers in his deep; in *him*
are light and darkness,* air and water, heat and
cold, hard and soft, thick and thin, sound and
tone, sweet and sour, bitter and astringent, and
that which I *cannot* number or rehearse.

* "light and darkness."   Here St M. refers the reader to
pars. 9–16 of Ch. 4 for a better understanding of this statement.

8. I *conceive* of it only in my body,* for that is originally, from *Adam* to this time, made out of *all powers*, and *according to the image of God*.

9. But here thou must *not* think that the powers in God the Father are in such wise, or qualify in such a *corrupt* manner and kind, as in man, which lord Lucifer hath so brought to pass; no, it is all very lovely, pleasant, *delicious* and joyful, very gentle, and meek or mild.

10. First there is the light (as I may *naturally* compare or resemble it) like the light of the sun, but not so *intolerable* as the light of the sun is to our corrupted perished eyes, but very lovely, pleasant and delightful, an *aspect* or glance of love.

11. But the darkness is *hidden* in the centre of the light, that is, when a creature, who is made out of the power of the light, would move and boil *higher* and faster in that light than God Himself doth, then in that creature that light would go out and be *extinguished*.

[12. " *Understand, the creature kindleth the* " *fire, if its spirit elevateth itself beyond the* " humility that is from *love: Read the* second " *and* third *books, viz. The Three Principles*, and " *The Threefold Life of Man*."]

---

* "I conceive of it only in my body" (*allein an meinem Leibe nehme ichs ab*), *i.e.* "from [a consideration of] my body alone [as apart from any other consideration] I take it to be so."

13. And instead of light it hath *darkness*, and therein the creature is *sensible*, by experience, that there is a darkness hidden in the centre.

14. As when a man kindleth a wax *candle* it giveth light, but when it is put out, then is the snuff or candle darkness: *Thus* also the light shineth from all the powers of the Father; but when the powers are perished or *corrupted*, then the light is extinguished, and the powers would remain in darkness, as is apparent by *Lucifer*.

15. In God the air also is not of such a kind, but is a lovely, pleasant, still breath or voice, blowing or moving; that is, the *exit*, going forth or moving of the powers is the *original* of the air, in which the Holy Ghost riseth up.

16. Neither is the water of such a kind in God, but it is the *source* or fountain in the powers, *not* of an elementary kind, as in this world; if I should liken it to anything, I must liken it to the sap or *juice* in an apple, but very bright and *lightsome*, like heaven, which is the spirit of all powers.

17. It is lord Lucifer who hath thus *spoiled* it, that it rageth and raveth so in this world, which so runneth and floweth, and is so thick and dark, and moreover *if it runneth not*, it becometh stinking; of which I shall treat more largely when I shall write of *the creation*.

18. In God the heat is a most lovely, pleasant, soft, gentle, mild, meek warmth, an effluence

or going forth of light, which expandeth itself, rising up *from* the light, wherein the source or fountain of love springeth up.

19. The cold also in God is not of such a kind, but is a cooling or refreshing of the heat, a mollifying or allaying of the spirit, a rising up, boiling or moving of the spirit.

Note here the Depth.

20. In *Moses* God saith, when he gave the *Law* to the Children of *Israel*, [1] *I am an angry jealous God to those that hate me* ; afterwards he also calls himself *a merciful God to them that fear him.*

[1] Exod. xx. 5, 6.
Deut. v. 9, 10.

Question.

21. Now the question is, What in heaven is the wrath of God? And whether God be angry in himself; or how is God moved to anger?

Answer.

Here there are chiefly *seven* sorts of qualities or circumstances to be observed.

I. *Of the First Species or Circumstance.*

22. First: In the divine power there is, hidden in secret, the astringent quality, which is a quality of the *kernel*, pith or hidden being, a sharp compaction or penetration in the *Salitter*, very sharp and harsh or astringent, which *generates* hardness, and also coldness; and when the astringent

quality is *kindled* it generateth a sharpness like unto *salt*.

23. This astringent quality is one *species* or source of wrath in the divine *Salitter*; and when this source is kindled, which may be done by *great motion* or elevation, touching or stirring, then the astringent causeth, or qualifieth in, great *coldness*, which is very sharp, like unto salt, very hard, binding, knitting and *attracting* together like a stone.

24. But in the heavenly pomp or state it is not so elevating; * for it doth *not elevate* itself, neither doth it kindle itself; king *Lucifer* alone hath kindled this quality in his kingdom, through his elevation and *pride*, whence this quality is *burning* even till the last day.

25. And by this now, in the creation of this world, the stars and the elements, as also the creatures, *tremble* and burn; out of it existeth also the house of death and of hell, also an eternal, base, loathsome habitation for the kingdom of *Lucifer*, and for all Godless men.

26. In the heavenly pomp this quality generateth the *sharpness* of the spirit, out of which, and whereby, the creaturely being is so formed or constituted that a heavenly *body* may be framed, as also all manner of colours, forms and sprouts or vegetation.

* "it is not so elevating" (*erheblich*) or "predominant." St M. has: "*elle ne s'exalte pas,*" "it does not exalt itself."

27. For it is the contraction, *compacting* or imaging of a thing, and therefore it is the first quality, and a *beginning* of the angelical creatures, and of all images or likenesses which are in heaven, and all which are in this world, and all *whatsoever* that can be named or expressed.

28. But if it be kindled through exaltation, which those creatures that are created out of the *divine Salitter* alone can do (and *only* in their own kingdom), then it is a burning source-vein of the wrath of God.

29. For it is one of the *seven spirits of God*, in whose power standeth the divine being or essence in the whole divine power and heavenly pomp.

30. So if it be kindled, then it is a *fierce* source of wrath, and a beginning of hell, and a torment and woe of the hellish fire, also a quality of *darkness*; for therein are extinguished the divine love, and also the divine light.

[31. "*It is a key which locketh in to the* "*chamber of* death, *and generateth death, from* "*whence proceed earth, stones and all hard* "*things.*"]

II. *Of the Second Species or Circumstance.*

32. The Second quality, or second spirit of God in the divine *Salitter*, or in the divine power, is the *sweet* quality, which worketh in the astringent, and mitigateth the astringent, so that it is altogether lovely, pleasant and mild or meek.

33. For it is the *overcoming* of the astringent quality, and is the very source or *fountain* of the mercy of God, which overcometh the wrath, whereby the astringent harsh source is *mollified*, and God's mercy riseth up.

34. Of this you have a *similitude* in an apple, which at first is astringent, *harsh* or chokey, but when the sweet quality forceth and overcometh it, then it is very soft, lovely and pleasant to *eat* : Thus it is in the divine power also.

35. For when men speak of the mercy of God the Father, they speak of his *power*, of his *fountain* spirits, of the qualities which are in the *Salitter*, out of which his most richly loving *Heart* or Son is generated.

Observe here:

36. The astringent or harsh quality is the heart, pith or *kernel* in the divine power, the contraction, compaction or imaging, forming or impression ; for it is the sharpness and *cold*, as it is seen that the harsh astringent cold *drieth* the water, and maketh it sharp ice.

37. The sweet quality is the *allaying* or warming, whereby the harsh or astringent and cold quality becometh thin and *soft*, whence the water taketh its original.

38. Thus the astringent quality *is* and *is called* the heart ; and the sweet is called *barm* or *warm*,

or softening or *mitigating*[1]: they are the two
qualities out of which the Heart or Son of God
is generated.

[1] In German, Barm-Hertz-igkeit. Warm-heart-edness, mercy.

39. For the astringent or *harsh* quality, in its
stock or kernel, when it qualifieth or operateth in
its own power, is a darkness: The sweet quality,
in its own power, is a moving, boiling, warming
and rising light, a source or *fountain* of meekness
and well-doing.

40. But while both of them qualify or operate
the one in the other, in the divine power, as if
they were but *one* power, they are a meek, mild,
lovely, pleasant, *merciful* qualifying.

41. These two qualities are *two* of the spirits
of God, among the *seven* qualifying or fountain-
spirits in the divine power.

42. Whereof you have an image in the Revelation of *John*, where he seeth [1] *seven golden candle-
sticks* or lights *before the Son of God*, which
signify *the seven spirits of God*, which shine in
great clarity, brightness or lustre before the Son
of God, out of which the Son of God is continually
generated from eternity to eternity, and is the
Heart of the seven spirits of God, and which I
will here describe in *order* one after another.

[1] Rev. i.

43. You must here elevate your sense or
mind in the *spirit*, if you intend to understand
and *apprehend* it; or else in your own sense
or mind you will be an astringent, hard, blind
stock.

III. *Of the Third Circumstance or Species.*

44. The Third quality, or the third spirit of God in the Father's power, is the bitter quality; which is a penetrating or *forcing* of the sweet and the astringent or harsh qualities, and which is *trembling*,* penetrating and rising up.

Observe here:

45. The astringent or harsh quality is the kernel or stock, and is sour or *attractive*; and the sweet is the light, *mollifying* and softening; and the bitter is *penetrating* or triumphing, which riseth up and triumpheth in the astringent or harsh quality, and in the sweet.

46. This is the source of joy, or the cause of the *laughing*, elevating joy, whereby a thing trembleth and jubilateth for joy; whence the heavenly joy existeth.

47. Moreover, it is the imaging or forming of all sorts of *red* colours in its own quality; in the sweet it imageth or formeth all sorts of *white* and *blue*; in the astringent, or harsh and sour, it formeth all sorts of *green*, *dusky* and mixed colours, with all manner of forms or *figures* and *smells*.

48. The bitter quality is the first spirit from whence mobility taketh its original, whence the

---

* "trembling," rendered by St M., "*vibrante*," "vibrating" or "tense."

life becometh stirring, and is well called *Cor* or the heart, for it is the trembling, shivering, elevating, penetrating spirit, a triumphing or joy, an elevating source of *laughing*; in the sweet quality the bitter is mollified, so that it becometh very richly loving and joyful.

49. But if it be moved, elevated and kindled too much, then it kindleth the sweet and the astringent or harsh qualities, and is like a tearing, stinging and *burning* poison, as when a man is tormented with a raging plague-sore, which maketh him *cry out* for woe and misery.

50. In the divine power this quality, when it is kindled, is the spirit of the zealous or jealous and bitter *wrath* of God, which is unquenchable, as may be seen by the legions of *Lucifer*.

51. Yet further: this quality, when it is kindled, is the bitter hellish fire, which putteth out the light, turning the sweet quality into a *stink*, causing a sharpness and tearing, a hardness and coldness in the astringent or harsh quality.

52. In the sour quality it causeth a *rankness* and brittleness, a stink, a misery, a house of mourning, a house of darkness, of death and of hell; an end of joy, which therein can no more be thought upon: For it cannot be quieted or *stilled* by anything, nor can it be enlightened again by anything; but the dark, astringent or harsh, stinking, sour, torn, bitter, *fierce* quality riseth up to all eternity.

Now observe :

53. In these three species or qualities standeth the corporeal being, or the *creatural* being of all creatures in heaven and in this world, whether it be angel or man, beast or fowl or vegetable, of a heavenly or of an earthly form, quality and kind, as also *all* colours and forms.

54. Briefly, whatsoever imageth itself, standeth in the power and authority of these three *head qualities*, and is formed by them, and also is formed out of their own power.

55. First, the astringent and sour quality is a *body* or source which attracteth the sweet power, and the cold in the astringent or harsh quality maketh it *dry*.

56. For the sweet quality is the heart of the water, for it is thin and light or bright, and is like heaven : and the bitter quality maketh it separable or *distinct*, so that the powers form themselves into *members*, and cause mobility in the body.

57. And when the sweet quality is dried, then it is a *corpus* or body, which is perfect, but wanting reason.

58. And the bitter quality penetrateth into the *body*, into the astringent or sour and into the sweet qualities, and frameth all sorts of colours according to that quality to which the body is *most eagerly* inclined, or according to that quality

which is strongest in the body, according to that [strongest quality] the bitter quality frameth the body, with its *colours*, and according to that [same] quality the creature hath its greatest impulse and inclination, motion, boiling and will.

IV. *Of the Fourth Circumstance or Species.*

59. The Fourth quality, or the fourth fountain-spirit in the divine power of God the Father, is the heat, which is the true *beginning* of life, and also the true *spirit* of life.

60. The astringent or harsh and sour quality, and the sweet, are the *Salitter*, which belongeth to the *body*, out of which the body is framed.

61. For coldness and hardness stand in the astringent quality, and are a *contraction* and drying ; and in the *sweet* quality stand the water, and the light or shining-ness, and the whole matter of the body.

62. And the bitter quality is the *separation* and forming, and the heat is the spirit, or the kindling of the life, whereby the spirit existeth in the body, which [spirit] springeth or moveth in the whole body, and shineth out from the body, and also maketh the *living motion* in all the qualities of the body.

63. Two things chiefly are to be eyed in *all the qualities* : If you look upon a body you first see the stock or pith, or the kernel of all the qualities, which is framed or *composed* out of all the quali-

ties; for to the body belong the astringent or harsh, sour, sweet, bitter and hot qualities; these qualities being *dried together*, make the body or stock.

The Great Mystery of the Spirit.

64. Now in the body these qualities are *mixed*, as if they all were but *one* quality; yet each quality moveth or boileth in its own power, and so goeth forth.

65. *Each* quality goeth forth from itself into the others, and *toucheth* or stirreth the others, that is, it *affecteth** the others, whereby the other qualities get the will of this quality; that is, they prove the sharpness and spirit of this, as to what *is in it*, and always mix with it continually.

66. Now the astringent or harsh quality (together with the sour), always *contracteth* or attracteth the other qualities together, and so apprehendeth and retaineth the body and drieth it.

67. For it drieth all the other powers, and *retaineth* them all through its infection or *influence*; and the sweet softeneth and moisteneth all the others, and so blendeth and tempereth itself with all the others, whereby they become daintily pleasant and mild or soft.

* "affecteth" (*inficiret*), "infecteth," implying interaction. This graphic expression of J. B. is, in most cases, translated by Sparrow in the above manner, though in a very few instances he uses "qualify" and "influence." St M. has "*inqualifter*," which is apparently of his own coining.

68. The bitter maketh all the others *stirring* and moveable, and parteth or distinguisheth them into members; so that every member in this tempering obtaineth the *fountain* of all the powers, whence mobility existeth.

69. The heat kindleth all the qualities, out of which the light riseth up and expandeth itself* aloft in *all* the qualities, so that they see one another: For when the *heat* worketh in the sweet moisture, then it generateth the light in all the qualities, so that one quality seeth the others.

70. From whence the senses and thoughts exist, so that one quality seeth the others, which are also in it, and *tempered* with itself, and *proveth* them with its sharpness, so that there cometh to be but one will; which in the body riseth up in the first fountain-source or well-spring in the *astringent* or harsh quality.

71. There the bitter quality penetrateth in the heat through the astringent, and the sweet in the water letteth it *easily* or gently through; and there the bitter in the heat goeth *through* the sweet water forth from the body and maketh *two* open *gates*, which are the eyes, the first sense or sensibility.

72. You have an example and type or *resemblance* of this, if *you* behold and consider this world, especially the earth, which is of the *kind*

* "riseth up and expandeth itself"—*empiret (gebäret) sich.* See Ch. 3, par. 67.

and *condition* of all qualities, and all *manner* of figures or shapes are formed and imaged therein.

73. First the astringent quality is therein, which attracteth the *Salitter* together, and *fixeth* or maketh the earth firm and compact, so that it cometh to be a solid *body*, which holds together and doth not break asunder, and [the astringent quality] imageth, frameth or formeth therein *all manner* of bodies, according to the kind of each quality, *viz.* all manner of stones and ores of minerals, and all manner of roots, according to the *condition* or kind of each quality.

74. Now when these are imaged or formed, there it [the astringent quality] lieth as a *corporeal*, springing, boiling mobility, for it moveth or boileth *through* and *in* the bitter quality in itself, as in its own imaged, formed or framed body; but *without* the heat, which is the [1]*spirit* of nature, it hath *as yet* no life to growing, vegetation, springing or spreading abroad.

[1] Or nature-spirit.

75. But when the heat of the sun *shineth* upon the earth, then there spring and grow in the earth all manner of images or figures of ores or minerals, herbs, roots and worms, and *all whatsoever* is therein.

Understand this aright.

76. In the earth the heat of the sun kindleth the sweet quality of water, in all imaged or framed *figures*; and then through the heat the

light cometh to be in the sweet water, and that *enlighteneth* the astringent or sour quality, and the bitter, so that they see *in* or *by* the light; and in that seeing the one riseth up into the other, and *proveth* the other, that is, in that seeing the one tasteth of the other's sharpness, from whence cometh the taste.

77. When the sweet quality perceiveth the *taste* of the bitter quality, it [1] caggs * at it, and giveth back; even as a man, when he tasteth astringent, harsh or bitter *gall*, openeth both the [2] gums of his *palate* in his mouth in his [3] cagging, and wideneth his palate more than it is of itself; and just so doth the sweet quality against the bitter.

[1] checks or stops it.

[2] throat or jaws.

[3] Or checking.

78. When the sweet quality thus stretcheth or *wideneth* itself, and retireth from the bitter, then the astringent always presseth after it, and *would* also fain taste of the sweet: and always maketh the body, that is behind it, and *in* it, to be dry; for the sweet quality is the mother of the water, and is very meek, mild, soft and gentle.

79. Now when the astringent or harsh and the bitter qualities get *their* light from the heat, then they *see* the sweet quality, and taste of its sweet water, and then they continually make *haste after* the sweet water, and drink it up, for

* "caggs . . . cagging" (*flend sich*). The German verb, *sich flennen*, means, to make a wry face.

they are very hard, rough and thirsty, and the heat drieth them *quite up*.

80. And the sweet quality always flieth from the bitter and the astringent, and always stretcheth its [1] palate *wider*, and the bitter and the astringent continually hasten after the sweet, and *refresh* themselves from the sweet, and dry up the body.

[1] throat or jaws.

81. Thus is the true springing or *vegetation* in nature, be it in man, beast, wood, herbs or stones.

Now observe the End of Nature in this World.

82. When the sweet quality thus flieth from the bitter, and from the sour and astringent, then the astringent and the bitter make *all the haste they can* after it, as their best treasure ; and the sweet presseth vehemently from them, and striveth so much that it *driveth* and penetrateth through the astringent or harsh quality, and *rends* the body, and goeth forth from the body, out above the earth, and hasteneth so fast, till a long *stalk* groweth up.

83. Then the heat above the earth presseth upon the stalk, and so the bitter quality is then kindled by the heat, and [1] it receiveth a *repulse* from the heat, so that it is terrified, and the astringent quality drieth it.

[1] the stalk.

84. Therein the astringent, the sweet, the bitter and the heat *struggle* together, and the astringent quality in its coldness continually

maketh their dryness, and so the sweet withdraweth on the *sides*, and the others hasten after it.

85. But when it seeth that it is *like* to be taken or captivated (the bitter quality from *within* pressing so hard upon it, and the heat from *without* pressing upon it also), it maketh the bitter fervent or burning, and inflameth it, and there it [the sweet quality] *leapeth*, springing up through the astringent quality, and riseth up again aloft; so there cometh to be a hard *knot* behind it in that place where the struggling was, and the knot gets a hole or *orifice*.

86. But when the sweet quality leapeth or springeth up through the knot, then the bitter quality had so much *affected* or wrought upon it that it was all in a trembling; and as soon as it cometh *above* the knot it suddenly stretcheth itself forth on *all* sides, striving to fly from the bitter quality; and in that stretching forth its body keepeth hollow in the middle, and in the trembling, leaping or *springing up* through the knot, it still gets more stalk or leaves, and now is frolick or cheerly that it hath escaped the *battle*.

87. So when the heat from without thus presseth upon the stalk, then the qualities become *kindled* in the stalk, and press through the stalk, and so become affected or wrought upon in the external light of the sun, and generate *colours* in the stalk, according to the kind of its quality.

88. But so long as the sweet water is in the stalk, the stalk *retaineth* its greenish colour according to the kind of the sweet quality.

89. Such substance the qualities always bring to pass with the heat in the stalk, and the stalk always groweth *farther*, and always one *storm* or assault is held after another, whereby the stalk always getteth *more* knots, and still spreadeth forth its branches farther and farther.

90. In the meanwhile the heat from without always drieth the sweet water in the stalk, and the stalk is always *smaller* at the top ; the higher it groweth the smaller it is, *growing on* so long till it can escape or run *no* farther.

91. And then the sweet quality yieldeth to be taken *captive*, and so the bitter, the sour, the sweet and the astringent reign jointly together, and the sweet stretcheth itself a little forth, but it can *escape* no more, for it is captivated or caught.

92. And then from all the qualities which are in the body, there groweth a *bud* or head, and there is a new body in the bud or head, which is formed or figured *answerable* or like to the first root in the earth, only now it gets another more subtile * form.

93. And then the sweet quality extends itself gently or mildly, and there grow little *subtile* *

---

* "subtile" (*subtile*), "delicate" or "fine," and implying the idea of their underlying positions.

leaves in the head, which are of the kind of all the qualities, and then the sweet water is as it were a pregnant woman new with child, having *conceived* the seed, and it always presseth onward, till it openeth the head.

94. And then also the sweet quality presseth forth in *little* leaves, like a woman who is in travail and bringing forth, but the little leaves or *blossoms* have no more its colour and form, but the form of all the qualities; for now the sweet quality must bring forth the *children* of the other qualities.

95. And when this *sweet mother* hath brought forth the fair, green, blue, white, red and yellow flowers, blossoms or children, then she groweth *quite* weary, and cannot long nourish or nurse these children, neither can she have them long, seeing they are but her *step-children*, which are very tender.

96. And so when the *outward* heat presseth upon these tender children, all the qualities in the children come to be kindled, for the spirit of life qualifieth or floweth in them.

97. And seeing they are *too weak* for this strong spirit, and cannot elevate themselves, they yield or surrender their noble power, and that smells so *lovely* and with so pleasant a savour that it rejoiceth the very heart, and maketh it laugh; but they *must wither* and fall off, because they are too tender for this spirit.

98. For the spirit draweth from the *head* or *bud* into the blossoms, and the head or bud is formed according to the *kind* of all the qualities ; the astringent quality attracteth or collecteth the body of the bud or head, and the sweet quality softeneth it and spreadeth it abroad, and the bitter quality parteth or *distinguisheth* the matter into members, and the heat is the *living* spirit therein.

99. Now all the qualities labour or work therein, and bring forth their fruit or children, and *every* child is qualified or conditioned according to the kind and property of *all* the qualities.

100. This they drive and act so long, till all the *matter* is quite dried, till the sweet quality or sweet water is dried up, and then the *fruit falls off*, and the *stalk* drieth also and falleth down.

And this is the End of Nature in this World.

101. Concerning this, much higher things are to be written, which you will find concerning the creation of this world : This is *only* brought in for a *similitude*, and described in the briefest manner.

102. Now the *other* form of the qualities, or of the divine powers, or of the seven spirits of God, is especially to be observed or known by the *instance* or example of heat.

103. First there is the ground, or the corporeal

being, although in the Deity, or in the creatures, it [the heat] hath no peculiar or *several* body, for all the qualities are one in another as *one*, however the operation of every quality is perceived in particular and *severally*.

104. Now in the body or fountain is the heat, which *generateth* the *fire*, and which is a form or kind of thing that a man *can* search into; and out of the heat goeth the light *through* all the spirits and qualities; and the *light* is the *living* spirit, which a man *cannot* search into.

105. A man *can* search into its *will*, and know what it willeth, or *how* it is: For it proceedeth in the sweet quality, and the light riseth up in the *sweet* quality in the sweet water, but *not* in the other qualities.

106. For example: If the sweet quality hath the predominance thou canst kindle all things in this world, and so make them burn and give light, but where the other qualities are predominant thou canst kindle nothing; for though thou mayest bring heat into a thing yet thou canst not bring the spirit into it, to make it give light. Therefore all qualities are the children of the sweet quality, or of the sweet water, because the spirit riseth up only in the water.

107. Art thou a rational man, in whom is the spirit and *understanding*? then look all about in the world, for there thou wilt find it *thus*.

108. Thou *canst* kindle wood that it give *light*,

for the water is chief upper regent, or predominant therein; so likewise in *all* sorts of herbs on earth, wherein the *sweet* water is predominant.

109. Thou canst *not* kindle light in a *stone*, because the astringent or *harsh* quality is chief or predominant therein: neither canst thou kindle light in *earth*, unless the other qualities be first vanquished and *boiled out of it*, which is seen in *gunpowder*; yet this light is but a flash or a spirit of *terror*, wherein the devil in the anger of God representeth himself, which I will describe and *demonstrate* more largely in another place.

Objection.

110. But thou wilt say that a man *cannot* kindle the *water* to make it give *light*.

Answer.

111. Yes, dear man, here lieth or sticketh the Mystery. The wood which thou kindlest is not very *fire*, but a dark or opaque *stock*, still the fire and light take their original from thence.

112. But thou must understand this concerning the *sweet* quality of the *water*, and not concerning the stick or block; but it is to be understood ¹ Or oiliness. concerning the ¹*unctuosity* or fatness which is the spirit therein.

113. Now in the elementary water on earth the sweetness is *not* the chief or upper regent, but the astringent, bitter and sour quality; else

the water were not *mortal*, but were as *that* water is out of which heaven is created.

114. That I will demonstrate to thee *thus*, viz. that the astringent, sour and bitter quality is predominant in the *elementary* water on earth.

115. Take rye, wheat, barley, oats, or what you will, wherein the sweet quality is *predominant*, soak or steep it in the elementary water, afterwards *distil* it, then the sweet quality will *take away* the predominancy from the others; and afterwards kindle that water, and then you will *see* the spirit which is remaining in the water of the [1] unctuosness or fatness of the corn, which overcame the water. [1] Or oiliness.

116. This thou *seest* also in flesh: The flesh neither burneth nor shineth nor giveth light, but its [2] *fat* burneth and shineth or giveth light. [2] Or oil, or tallow.

Question.

117. Thou mayest perhaps ask, How comes that to pass, or in what manner is it so?

Answer.

118. Behold, in flesh the *astringent* or sour, and the bitter qualities are predominant; and in the fat the *sweetness* is chief and predominant; therefore fat creatures are always merrier and frolicker than the lean, because the *sweet spirit* floweth more abundantly in them than in the lean.

119. For the light of nature, which is the spirit of life, shineth more in them than in the lean: For in that light in the sweet quality standeth the *triumphing* or the joy, for the astringent or harsh and bitter qualities triumph therein, for they rejoice that they are refreshed, fed, given to drink and enlightened from the *sweet* and light quality.

120. For in the astringent or harsh quality there is *no* life, but an astringent, cold, hard death; and in the bitter quality there is no light, but a *dark*, bitter and raging pain, a house of trembling, horror, and fierce, wrathful, fearful *misery*.

121. Therefore when they are guests *feasting* at the sweet and light quality, then are they affected, and pleasant, very joyful and triumphing *in* the creature.

122. Therefore *no* lean creature is merry, unless it be that *heat* is predominant therein: That is, though it be lean, and hath *little* of the fat or oil in it, yet perhaps *sweetness* is very abundant there.

123. On the other side, many creatures have *much* fatness, and yet are very melancholy or sad, which is because their fatness is *inclined* to the condition of the elementary water, wherein the astringent or harsh, and bitter qualities are somewhat *strong*.

Of the Language of Nature.

124. Art thou a rational man? then observe this: The spirit which moveth on high,* aloft from the heat, taketh its *exit*, rising and shining in the sweet quality; therefore the *sweet* quality is its friendly or kind *will*, and reigneth in meekness; and meekness and humility are its proper house or *habitation*.

125. This is the pith or *kernel* of the deity, and therefore IT is called GOTT, GOD, because it is sweet, meek, friendly and bounteous or good, GUTIG; and therefore is IT called *Barm-hertz-ig* (warm-heart-ed or merciful), because its sweet quality *riseth up* in the astringent or sour and bitter qualities, and refresheth, moisteneth and *enlighteneth* them, that they might *not* remain a dark valley.

126. For understand but thy [1] *mother tongue aright*; thou hast as deep a ground *therein* as there is in the *Hebrew* or *Latin*: Though the learned elevate themselves in these, like a proud arrogant [2] bride; it is no great matter, *their* art is now on the [3] lees, or bowed down to the dust.

[1] The mother tongue expounded according to the Language of Nature.

[2] Braut.

[3] Turba.

127. *The spirit sheweth and declareth, that yet before the end, many a layman will know and understand more than now the wittiest or most cunning doctors know; for the gates of heaven set themselves open; those that do not blind them-*

* "moveth on high"—*empöret (gebäret)*. See Ch. 3., par. 67.

*selves shall and will see it very well; the Bride-groom crowneth his bride.   AMEN.**

BARM - HERTZ - IG.

¹ Barm-hertz-ig, warm-heart-ed, or merci-ful.

128. Observe, ¹the word BARM- is chiefly formed upon thy *lips*, and when thou pronouncest BARM- then thou shuttest thy mouth, and snarlest † in the hinder part of the mouth; and

* Between the 127th and the 128th pars. St M. inserts the following note :—

"One must presume that the following explanation has its origin in the 'mother-tongue,' which the author elsewhere calls 'language of nature.' It is possible that in the last analysis, words corresponding in meaning, but out of the most diverse languages, would shew relations, if not uniform, at least very close to a universal base, were our mind sufficiently open to grasp both the activity and the universality of the language of nature. Without this conjecture, the author's application of the latter to the German word '*barmhertzig*' would repel the more superficial minds, since it could not take place in the case of French or any other ordinary language." See par. 126.   J. B. does not *identify* the two expressions, "mother-tongue" and "language of nature," since he compares his mother-tongue to Hebrew or Latin. The point is, that he means to shew how perfectly the "language of nature" is applicable to his "mother-tongue." St M. has no doubt been misled by the fact that *Mutter-Sprache* (mother-tongue), when translated into the French *langue-mère*, signifies root-language, and not native language.

† "snarlest" (*knarren*) and "snarleth" (par. 129)—the 1730 ed. has "*karren*," which is obviously a misprint. The word denotes a rattling noise, and J. B. applies it to the rolling of the "r." In the second instance, however, "snarleth" is in the original "*murret*," which denotes a low growl or muttering sound. St M. gets over the difficulty by rendering the sentence, "*vous retirez le son en arrière*," "thou drawest back the sound," which elucidates the idea.

this is the astringent quality, which environeth or *encloseth* the word; that is, it figureth, *compacteth* or contracteth the word together, that it becometh hard, or soundeth, and the bitter quality separateth or cutteth or *distinguisheth* it.

129. That is, when thou pronouncest BAR, the last letter R snarleth * and murmureth like a *trembling* breath, and thus doth the bitter quality, which is a trembling.

130. Now the word BARM- is a dead word, void of understanding, so that no man understands what it meaneth; which signifieth that the *two* qualities, astringent, and bitter, are a hard, dark, cold and bitter being, which have *no* light in them: And therefore a man cannot understand their power *without* the light.

131. But when a man saith BARM-HERTZ, he fetcheth or presseth the second syllable out from the *deep* of the body, out from the heart, for the *right* spirit speaketh forth the word HERTZ, which riseth up aloft from the *heat* of the heart, in which the light goeth forth and floweth.

132. Now observe, when thou pronouncest BARM, then the two qualities, the astringent and the bitter, form, frame or *compact* together the word BARM, very leisurely or slowly; for it is a long, *impotent*, feeble syllable, because of the weakness of the qualities.

* See footnote † on opposite page.

133. But when thou pronouncest -HERTZ- then the spirit in the word -HERTZ- (heart) goeth forth *suddenly*, like a flash of lightning, and giveth the [1]distinction and understanding of the word.

134. But when thou pronouncest -IG, then thou *catchest* or captivatest the spirit in the midst of the other two qualities, so that it *must stay* there and form the word.

135. Thus is the divine power also; the astringent and bitter qualities are the *Salitter* of the divine omnipotence, the sweet quality is the pith or kernel of the *Barm-hertz-ig-keit*, warm-heart-ed-ness, or mer-ci-ful-ness, according to which the whole being, with *all* the powers, is called GOTT (GOD).

136. The *heat* is the kernel of the spirit, out of which the *light* goeth and kindleth itself in the *midst* or centre of the sweet quality, and becometh captivated by the astringent and bitter qualities, as in the midst or centre *wherein* the Son of God is generated, and that is the very *Hertz* (heart) of God.

137. The light's flame or flash, which in the twinkling of an eye, or in a moment, shineth into all the powers, even as the sun doth in the whole world, is the *Holy Ghost*, which goeth forth from the clarity or brightness of the Son of God, and is the flash of lightning and sharpness; for the *Son* is generated in the midst or centre of the

other qualities, and is caught by the other qualities.

Understand this high thing rightly.

138. When the Father speaketh or pronounceth the WORD, that is, generateth his *Son* (which is always done for ever and eternally), then that *Word first* taketh its original in the astringent quality; therein it fixeth, conceiveth or *compacteth* itself; and in the sweet quality it taketh its fountain, spring or source, and in the bitter quality it *sharpeneth* and moveth itself, and in the heat it riseth up and *kindleth* the middle sweet fountain or source.

139. Now it burneth *jointly* or equally alike in all the qualities of the kindled fire, and the fire burneth forth from the qualities; for *all* qualities burn, and that fire is one fire, and not many several fires.

140. That fire is the very *Son of God*, who is thus generated always from eternity to eternity: This I can *demonstrate* by the heaven and the earth, the stars and the elements, and by all the creatures, stones, leaves and grass, yea in the devil himself; and that, not with dead, slight, insignificant arguments, *void of understanding*, but with clear, quick, *living* and invincible firm arguments, even *above*, beyond and to the refutation of all men's reason, convincingly and undeniably; and lastly, in opposition against

all the devils and the gates of hell; and I would do it here, if it would not take up *too* much room.

141. Yet it shall be *treated of* all along in *this* whole book, in all the articles and *parts* thereof; but you shall find it more particularly in that part concerning the creation of the *creatures*, as also concerning the creation of *heaven* and *earth* and of all things, which will be fitter to be done *then*, and *more easily* apprehended by the Reader.

Now observe :

142. Out of that fire goeth forth the *flash* or the light, and moveth or boileth in all the powers, and hath or *containeth* in itself the fountain and sharpness of all the powers, because it is generated, through the *Son*, out of all the powers of the *Father* ; and so then it reciprocally maketh all the powers in the Father *living* and moving ; and through that *spirit* are all the *angels* formed and imaged out of the Father's *powers*.

143. That spirit formeth and preserveth and *supporteth all*, all vegetation, all colours and all creatures, both in heaven and in this world, and *above* the heaven of heavens. For the birth or *geniture* of the holy *Trinity* above all is thus and no otherwise, neither will it be otherwise in all eternity.

144. But when the fire is kindled in a creature, that is, when a creature elevateth itself *too high*

or too much (as *Lucifer* and his legions did),
then the light extinguisheth or goeth out, and the
fierce, wrathful and hot source, the source of the
hellish fire, riseth up, that is, the spirit of the
fire riseth up in the fierce quality.

145. Observe here the *circumstances* how this
is done, or how it can come to be done. Therefore consider : an angel is formed, figured, composed or compacted together out of *all* powers,
as I have described it at large.

146. Now when he elevateth himself, he
elevateth himself *first* in the astringent quality,
which he gripeth close together, as a woman who
is in travail, and *presseth* himself, whereby the
hard quality becometh so hard and *sharp* that
the sweet water can force or prevail with it *no
more*, and so can rise up no more meekly or
mildly in the creature, but is captivated and *dried
up* by the astringent quality, and changed into a
hard, sharp, fierce coldness.

147. For it becometh too empty and [1]dry by   [1] derb.
the astringent *contraction*, and loseth its bright
lustre, and its unctuosity, fatness or oiliness
(wherein the *light spirit* riseth up, which is the
spirit of the holy *angelical* and *divine* life)
becometh so hard compacted and pressed together
by the astringent quality, whereby it is dried up
like sweet dry *wood*.

148. So when the bitter quality riseth up in
the exsiccated or dried sweet quality, then the

sweetness *cannot* mollify it, and saturate it with its sweet light water, because it is dried up.

149. There the bitter quality raveth and *rageth*, and seeketh for rest and food, and finds it not, and moveth or boileth in the body as a lingering poison.

150. Now when the heat *kindleth* the sweet quality, and would mitigate its heat in the sweet water (whence it riseth up and *shineth* in the whole body), there it finds nothing but a hard, dry, sweet source or quality, there is no sap or *moisture*, the sap being quite exsiccated or dried up by the astringency.

151. Then the heat kindleth the sweet source or quality, with an intent to be *refreshed*, but there is no sap left, the sweet source or quality is now burning and *glowing* only, even as a *hard*, dried or burnt stone, and can *no more* kindle its light. And so the whole body remaineth now a dark valley, in which there is nothing but a fierce hard coldness in the astringent quality, and in the sweet quality a hard glowing fire only, wherein the fierce *wrathful* heat riseth up in all eternity, and in the bitter quality there is a raving, a raging, a stinging and a *burning*.

152. Thus you have here the true description of an *expulsed* angel or of a devil, as also the cause thereof, and that not written in a similitude *only*, but in the spirit, through *that power* out of which all things are come to be.

153. O man! behold thyself herein, look before thee and behind thee, nothing is in vain.

154. This great history or *action*, of how it came to pass and how it went, you will find it at large concerning the fall of the devil.

V. *Of the Fifth Circumstance or Species.*

155. The Fifth quality, or the fifth spirit of God among the seven spirits of God, in the divine power of the Father, is the *gracious, amiable,* blessed, friendly and joyful *love.*

156. Now observe what is the fountain of the *gracious, amiable,* blessed and friendly love of God; observe it exactly, for it is the very pith, marrow or *kernel.*

157. When the heat in the *sweet* quality riseth up, and kindleth the sweet source, fountain or spring, then that fire burneth in the sweet quality; now seeing the sweet quality is a thin or transparent lovely *pleasant* sweet fountain or spring-water, it allayeth the heat and *quencheth* the fire, and so there remaineth in the sweet fountain-spring of the sweet water only the *joyful* light.

158. The heat is only a gentle soft *warming,* even as it is in a man who is of a *sanguine* complexion, wherein also the heat is only a friendly, cheerly warming, if the party liveth temperately, and keepeth a *due measure.*

159. That friendly *courteous* love-light-fire goeth along in the sweet quality, and riseth up

into the bitter and astringent qualities, and so *kindleth* the bitter and astringent qualities, *feeding* them with its sweet *love-sap*, refreshing, quickening and enlightening them, and making them *living* or lively, cheerful and friendly.

160. And when the sweet, light, love-power cometh to them, so that they *taste* thereof and get its life, O, there is a friendly meeting, *saluting* and triumphing, a friendly welcoming and great love, a most friendly and *gracious*, amiable and blessed kissing, and well-relishing taste.

161. There the Bridegroom kisseth his bride : O gracious amiable *blessedness* and great love! how sweet art thou? How friendly and courteous art thou? How pleasant and *lovely* is thy relish and taste? How ravishingly sweet ·dost thou smell? O noble light and *bright* glory, who can apprehend thy *exceeding* beauty? How comely *adorned* is thy love? How *curious* and dainty are thy colours? And all this *eternally*! Who can express it?

162. Or why and what do I write, I, whose tongue doth but *stammer* like a child that is learning to speak? With *what* shall I compare it? or to what shall I liken it? Shall I compare it with the love of this world? *No*, that is but a mere dark valley to it.

163. O immense greatness! I *cannot* compare thee to anything, but *only* to the resurrection from the dead; there will the love-fire rise up *again* in

us, and embrace man courteously and friendly, and kindle again our astringent, bitter and cold, dark and *dead* quality, and embrace us most friendly.

164. O noble guest! O, *why* didst thou depart from us! O fierceness, wrath and astringency or severity, *thou* art the cause of it! O fierce wrathful devil! O, what hast *thou* done, who hast *sunk down* thyself and thy beautiful *bright angels into darkness? Woe, woe for ever!

165. O, was not the gracious, amiable, blessed and fair love in *thee* also? O thou high and lofty-minded devil! Why wouldst thou not be contented? Wert thou not a Cherubim? and was there anything *so* beautiful and bright in heaven as *thou*? For what didst thou seek? Wouldst thou be the whole or *total* God? Didst thou not know that thou wert a *creature*, and hadst *not* the fan and casting-shovel in thy own hand or power?

166. O, *why* do I pity thee, thou stinking goat? O thou cursed stinking devil! how hast *thou* spoiled us? How wilt thou excuse thyself? What wilt thou *object* to me?

Objection.

167. Thou sayest, if thy fall had not been, man would never have been thought of.*

* "never have been thought of" (*erdacht worden*), "thought out." St M. renders the idea very well: "*n'eût pas été conçu dans l'imagination divine*," "would not have been conceived in the divine imagination."

Answer.

O thou lying devil! Though that should be true, yet the *Salitter* out of which man is made (which is also from eternity, as well as *that* out of which thou art made), had stood in *eternal joy* and bright glory, and had likewise risen up in God, and had tasted of the *gracious*, amiable, blessed love in the seven spirits of God, and enjoyed the heavenly joy.

168. O thou lying devil, stay but a *little*, the spirit will discover thy shame to thee; tarry but a little while *longer*, and thy pomp, pride* and pageantry will be at an *end*. *Stay*, the bow is bent, the arrow will *hit* thee, and then *whither* wilt thou fall? The place is ready provided and prepared, it wanteth only to be kindled; wilt thou bring fuel † lustily to it, that thou be not frozen with cold? Thou wilt *sweat* very hard: Dost thou suppose thou shalt *obtain* the light again? *No*, but hell fire. Smell thy sweet love, *guess* at it, what is *that* called? *Gehenna*; yes, *that* will be in love with thee eternally.

169. Woe, woe, poor miserable *blinded* man, why sufferest thou the devil to make thy body and soul *so* dark and blind? O temporal good, and the pleasure and voluptuousness of *this life*!

---

* "thy pomp, pride," etc., lit., "thy show will be over."

† "wilt thou bring fuel." The German form is more emphatic, being in the imperative mood, "only bring fuel," etc.

thou blind *whore*, why dost thou go a wooing and a *whoring* to the devil?

170. O *security*! the devil watcheth for thee. O *high-mindedness*! thou art a hellish fire. O beauty, pomp or *bravery*! thou art a dark valley. O potency of dominion! thou art a raging and a tearing of the hellish fire. O self-vindication or vengeance! thou art the fierce wrath of God.

171. O *Man*! why will the world be too narrow for thee? Thou wilt needs have it *all* for thyself; and if thou hadst it, thou wouldst not have *room* enough. O, this is the devil's high-mindedness, who *fell* out of heaven into hell.

172. O man! alas, O man! why dost thou *dance* with the devil who is thine enemy? Art thou not afraid* that he will *thrust* thee into hell? Why dost thou go on so securely? Is it not a very narrow *stick* on which thou dancest? Under that small narrow bridge is *hell*! Dost thou not see how high thou art, and how dangerously and desperately thou goest? Thou dancest between heaven and hell.

173. O thou blind man! how doth the devil *mock* at thee? O, wherefore dost thou trouble heaven? Dost thou think thou wilt *not* have enough in this world? O blind man! is not heaven and earth thine? Nay, *God* himself too? What dost thou bring into this world, or what

* "art thou not afraid," or "dost thou not care," or "art thou not mindful."

dost thou take along with thee at thy going out of it? Thou bringest an *angelical* garment into this world, and with thy wicked life thou turnest it into a devil's mask or *vizor*.

174. O thou miserable man, return, the heavenly Father hath stretched forth both his arms and calleth thee; do but *come*, he will take thee *into* his love. Art thou not his child? He *doth* love thee. If he did hate thee, he must be at *odds* with himself. O no, it is not so: there is nothing in God but a *merciful*, amiable love and bright glory.

175. O ye *watchmen* of Israel! why do ye *sleep*? Awake from the sleep of whoredom, and dress or trim your *lamps*: The Bridegroom cometh, *sound* your trumpets.

176. O ye covetous, stiffnecked and drunken *roisterers*! how do you woo and go a whoring after the covetous devil? Thus saith the LORD, Will ye *not* feed my people which I have committed to your charge?

177. Behold I have set you upon *Moses'* chair, and entrusted you with my flock; but you mind nothing but the wool, and mind *not* my sheep, and therewith you build your great palaces. But I will set you on *the stool of pestilence*, and *my* own Shepherd shall feed my sheep *eternally*.

178. O thou fair world, how doth heaven complain of thee? How dost thou trouble the elements? O wickedness and malice! *when* wilt

thou leave, and give over? Awaken! awaken! and bring forth, thou sorrowful *woman*; behold thy *Bridegroom* cometh, and requireth *fruit* at thy hands: Why dost thou sleep? *Behold, he knocketh!*

179. O gracious, amiable, blessed love and clear bright light, *tarry* with us, I pray thee, for the evening *is* at hand. O truth! O justice and *righteous* judgment! what is become of thee? Doth not the spirit *wonder*, as if he had never seen the world before now? O, *why* do I write of the wickedness of this World? I *must* do it, and the world [1]curseth me for it. *Amen.*

[1] Or giveth me the devil's thanks for it.

THE NINTH CHAPTER

Of the Gracious, *amiable, blessed, friendly and* merciful *Love of God.*

The Great, *Heavenly and Divine* Mystery.

1. BECAUSE I write here of heavenly and divine things, which are *altogether strange* to the *corrupted*, perished nature of man, the Reader doubtless will wonder at the *simplicity* of the author, and be offended at it.

2. Because the condition and inclination of the corrupted nature is to gaze on *high* things alone, like a proud, wild, wanton and *whorish* woman, who always gazeth in her heat or burning lust after *handsome* men, to act wantonness with them.

3. Thus also is the proud, corrupted, perished nature of man, it stareth only upon *that* which is glittering and in *fashion* in this world, and supposeth that God hath forgotten the afflicted, and therefore plagueth them so, because he mindeth them not.

4. Corrupt nature imagineth that the Holy

Ghost regardeth only *high* things, the high arts and sciences of *this world*, the profound studies, and great learning.

5. But whether it be so or no, look but back, and then you will find the true *ground*. *What was* Abel? A shepherd. *What were* Enoch *and* Noah? Plain, simple men. *What were* Abraham, Isaac *and* Jacob? Herdsmen.

6. *What was* Moses, that dear man of God? A herdsman. *What was* David, when the mouth of the Lord called him? A shepherd.

7. *What were* the great and the small prophets? Vulgar, plain and mean people: *some of them* but country people and herdsmen, *counted the underlings or footstools of the world*: Men counted them but mere fools.

8. Though they did miracles and wonders, and shewed great signs, yet *the world* gazed on high things alone, and the Holy Ghost must be as the dust under their feet: For the proud devil *always endeavoured* to be king in this world.

9. *How came* our King JESUS CHRIST into this world? Poor, and in great trouble and misery, and [1] *had not where to lay his head.*

[1] Matt. viii. 20.

10. *What were* his Apostles? Poor, despised, illiterate fishermen. *And what were* they that believed their preaching? The poorer and meaner sort of the people. The High Priests and Scribes *were the* executioners of Christ,

[1] Luke xxiii. 21. [they] who [1]*cried out, Crucify him, crucify him.*

11. *What were they* that in all ages of the Church of Christ stood by it most stoutly and constantly? The poor, contemptible, despised people, who shed their blood for the sake of Christ.

12. *But who were they* that falsified and adulterated the right, pure Christian doctrine, and *always fought* against and opposed it? *Even* the learned doctors and scribes, popes, cardinals, bishops, and great dons or masters and teachers. *And why did the world* follow after them, and depend on them? But because they had * great respect, were in great *authority* and *power*, lived stately, and carried a port in the *world*. Even such a *proud whore* is the corrupt, perished human nature.

13. *Who was it* that purged *out of* the Churches in *Germany* the Pope's greediness of money, his idolatry, bribery, deceit and cheat-[1] Luther.ing? A poor despised [1]monk or friar. *By what* power and might? By the power of God the Father, and by the power and might of God the Holy Ghost.

Question.

14. *Then what is* yet concealed or remains hidden, the true doctrine of Christ?

* "But because they had," etc. "Only because they had a high standing and made a great show before the world."

Answer.

No; but the [1]philosophy, and the *deep ground* of God; the heavenly delightful habitation and pleasure; the revelation of the creation of *angels*; the revelation of the horrible *fall* of the devil; from whence *evil* proceedeth; the creation of this world; the deep ground and mystery of man, and of all creatures in this world; the Last Judgment and change of this world; the mystery of the resurrection of the dead; and of eternal life.

[1] That is, the real knowledge or the manner how the Mysteries spoken of in the doctrine of Christ, as they are in nature physically, or metaphysically in supernatural things, are to be understood convincingly, according to its true ground, and the capacity of the human heart.

15. *This* shall arise in the depth, in great plainness and *simplicity*. *But why not* in the height in art? [In order] that no man should dare to boast that he himself hath done it, and that *hereby* the devil's pride should be discovered and brought to nothing.

16. But why doth God so? *Of his great love* and [1]mercy towards all people and nations, and to shew hereby that now is *near at hand* the time of the restitution of all *whatsoever* is lost, wherein men shall behold and enjoy the *perfection*, and move in the *pure* light and deep knowledge of God.

[1] Barm-hertz ig-keit.

17. Therefore, *beforehand, will arise* the dawning of the day, or morning redness, whereby the *day may be known or taken notice of.*

18. *He that will now sleep, let him sleep still; and he that will awake and trim his lamp, let*

him awake still: Behold the Bridegroom cometh, and he that is awake and is ready accompanieth him into the eternal heavenly *wedding: But he that sleepeth at his coming, he sleepeth for ever,* eternally in the dark prison of fierceness or wrath.

19. Therefore I would have the Reader warned that he read *this book* with diligence, and not be *offended* at the meanness or simplicity of the author, for God looketh *not* to high things, for He *alone* is high: But *he careth for the lowly,* how to help them.

20. If you come *so far* as to apprehend the spirit and sense of the author, then you will need no *admonition,* but will rejoice and be glad in this light, and thy soul will laugh and *triumph* therein.

21. *Now observe,* The gracious, amiable, blessed love, which is the *fifth* fountain-spirit in the divine power, is the *hidden* source, fountain or quality which the corporeal being *cannot* comprehend or apprehend, *but* only when it riseth up in the body, and *then* the body triumpheth therein, and behaveth itself friendly, lovely and *courteously;* for that quality or spirit belongeth *not* to the imaging or *framing* of a body, but riseth up in the body, as a *flower* springeth up out of the earth.

22. Now this fountain-spirit taketh its original at *first* out of the sweet quality of the water.

Understand this, how it is, and observe it *exactly*.

23. *First* there is the astringent quality, *then* the sweet, and *next* the bitter: The sweet is in the *midst* between the astringent and the bitter. Now the astringent causeth things to be hard, cold and dark; and the bitter *teareth*, driveth, rageth and divideth or *distinguisheth*. These two qualities *rub* and drive each other so hard, and move so eagerly, *that* they generate the heat, which now in these two qualities is *dark*, even as heat in a *stone* is.

24. As when a man taketh a stone, or any hard thing, and *rubbeth* it against wood, these *two* things are heated: Now this heat is but a darkness, having *no* light therein: And so it is, in the divine power also.

25. Now the astringent and the bitter qualities, *without* the sweet water, rub and drive themselves *so hard* the one against the other, that they generate the dark heat, and so are *kindled* in themselves.

26. *And this* [process] *together* [with the agents therein] *is the wrath or anger of God, the source and original of the hellish fire.* As we see by *Lucifer*, who *elevated* and compressed himself so hard together with his *legions*, that the sweet fountain-water in him was *dried up*, wherein the light kindleth, and wherein the love riseth up.

27. *Therefore* now he is *eternally* an astringent,

hard, cold, bitter, hot and sour stinking fountain-source : For when the sweet quality in him was dried up, it *became* a sour stink, a valley of misery, and a house of perdition and woe.

Now further into the Depth.

28. When the astringent and the bitter qualities *rub* themselves so hard the one upon the other that they generate heat (the sweet quality, the sweet fountain-water, being therein in the midst or centre, *between* the astringent and bitter qualities), the *heat* becometh generated between the astringent and the bitter qualities in the sweet fountain-water, *through* [by means of] the astringent and the bitter qualities :

29. There the light kindleth in the heat in the sweet fountain-water, and *this is the beginning of life* : For the astringent and bitter qualities are the beginning and cause of the heat and of the light also, and *thus* the sweet fountain-water becometh a *shining* light, like the blue or *azure* light of heaven.

30. And that bright light fountain-water *kindleth* the astringent and the bitter qualities, and the heat (which is generated by the astringent and the bitter qualities in the sweet water), *riseth up* out of the sweet fountain-water through the astringent and bitter qualities, and in the astringent and bitter qualities the light *first then* becometh dry and shining, as also moveable and triumphing.

31. And when the light riseth up out of the sweet fountain-water *in the heat*, in the astringent and bitter qualities, then the bitter and astringent qualities *taste* the light and sweet water, and the bitter quality *catcheth* the taste of the sweet water, and in the sweet water is the *light*, but only of a sky-colour or *azure*, which is blue.

32. And then the bitter quality trembleth, and *dissolveth* the hardness in the astringent quality, and the light becometh dry in the astringent, and shineth clear, *much* brighter than the light of the sun.

33. In this rising up the astringent quality becometh meek, light, thin or *transparent* and pleasant or lovely, and obtaineth its life, whose *original* riseth up out of the heat in the sweet water, and this now is *the true fountain or well-spring of love.*

Observe this in the deep Sense.

34. How should love and joy *not* be there, where life is generated in the very centre or midst of death, and light in the midst of darkness?

Question.

Thou askest, *How* comes *that* to pass?

Answer.

35. If *my* spirit indeed did sit in *thy* heart, and spring up in thy heart, then *thy* body would find, feel and apprehend it.

36. But *otherwise* I cannot bring it into thy sense. Neither canst thou apprehend or understand it, *unless* the Holy Ghost kindle thy soul, so that *this* light itself shine in *thy* heart.

37. Then will this light itself be generated *in thee*, as in God, and rise up in *thy* astringent and bitter qualities, in *thy* sweet water, and triumph, as in God: Now when *this* is done, then will you *first understand my book*, and not before.

Observe:

38. When the light is generated in the bitter quality, that is, when the bitter and dry fountain-sources *catch* the sweet fountain-water of life, and *drink* it, then the bitter spirit becometh living in the astringent spirit, and the astringent spirit, which is as a spirit impregnated with child,* is impregnated with life, and must continually generate the life.

39. For the sweet water, and the light in the sweet water, rise up *continually* in the astringent quality, and the bitter quality triumpheth continually *therein*, and so there is nothing else but mere laughing and joy, and mere existing in love.

40. For the astringent quality *loveth* the sweet water.

41. First, because in the sweet water the spirit of light is generated, and saturateth or moisteneth

* "a spirit impregnated with child," lit., "a pregnant spirit."

the astringent, hard and cold qualities; also it enlighteneth them and warmeth them; for in water, light and heat the *life consisteth.*

42. Secondly, the astringent quality loveth the bitter, because the bitter quality in the sweet water, that is, in water, heat and light, triumpheth in the astringent quality, and maketh the astringent moveable or stirring, *wherein* the astringent also can triumph.

43. Thirdly, the astringent quality loveth the heat, because in the heat the light is generated, *whereby* the astringent quality is enlightened and warmed.

44. And the sweet quality also loveth the astringent.

45. First, because the astringent drieth it up,* *that* it becometh *not* thin or dim *like* the elementary water, and that its quality consisteth in power; and *because* in the astringent quality the *light,* which is [thus] generated therein, becometh *shining* and *dry.*

46. Besides, the astringent quality is a cause of the *heat* which is generated in the sweet water, wherein the light riseth up, and wherein the sweet water standeth in great *clarity, brightness* or glory.

47. Secondly, the sweet quality also loveth the bitter, because it is a cause of the *heat,* and also

* St M. translates: " *la qualité astringente la resserre,*" " the astringent quality contracts it."

because the bitter spirit triumpheth and *trembleth* in the sweet water, heat and light, and so maketh the sweet water moveable or stirring and *living*.

48. Thirdly, the sweet quality loveth heat *exceedingly*, so very much that I cannot compare it to anything; but you may take this for a *similitude*, though it comes very short of it: Suppose that in *two* young people of a noble *complexion*, these being kindled in the heat and fervour of burning love the one to the other, there is such a fire as this: that if each could creep into the body and *heart* of the other, or if they could transmute themselves into *one* body, they would do it.

49. But this *earthly* love is only cold water, and is not true fire: A man cannot find any *full* similitude of it in this *half-dead* world. In all *divine things* that receive the *true love-fire*, the resurrection of the dead at the last day alone is a perfect similitude.

50. But the sweet quality doth thus love the heat *because* it generateth therein the light-spirit, which is the spirit of life. For *life* existeth in the heat, for if the heat were not, all would be a dark valley: Now *so dear* as the life is, so dear also is the heat to the sweet spirit, and the light in the heat.

51. And the bitter quality also loveth *all* the other fountain-spirits. And first the sweet. For in the sweet water the bitter spirit is *refreshed*,

and therein it *quencheth* its great thirst; and its bitterness is therein mitigated; also it obtaineth its light-life *therein*: In the astringent it hath its body, wherein it triumpheth, cooleth and mitigateth itself; and in the heat it *hath* its power and strength, wherein its joy standeth.

52. And the hot quality also loveth *all* the other qualities; and the love is so *great* therein towards and in the others that it cannot be likened to anything, for it is generated from and out of the others.

53. The astringent and bitter qualities are the *father* of the heat, and the sweet fountain-water is its *mother*, which conceiveth, retaineth and generateth it: For the heat existeth through the astringent and bitter hard driving, which riseth up in the sweet quality, as in wood or fuel.

54. Wilt thou *not believe* this? Then open thy eyes, and go to a *tree*, look upon it, and bethink thyself; there you see first the *whole* tree, take a knife and cut a *gash* in it, and taste how it is; then you *first* taste the astringent, harsh, *choky* quality, which draweth thy tongue together, and that also *draweth* and holdeth together all the powers of the tree.

55. Then you taste the bitter quality, which maketh the tree moveable or stirring, so that it *springeth* and groweth green and flourisheth, and so getteth its branches, leaves and fruit.

56. *After that* you taste the sweet, which is very *gentle* and sharp; for it getteth the *sharpness* from the astringent and bitter qualities.

57. Now these *three* qualities would be dark and dead, if the *heat* were not therein: But as soon as the *spring* time cometh, that the sun with its *beams* reacheth and warmeth the earth, the spirit becometh living by the heat in the tree, and the spirits of the tree begin to grow green, *flourish* and blossom.

58. For the spirit riseth up in the heat, and *all* the spirits rejoice therein, and so there is a hearty love between them.

59. But the heat is generated through the power and *impulse* of the astringent and bitter qualities in the sweet water.

60. But they must use the heat of the sun to their kindling, because the qualities *in this world* are half dead, and are too weak; of which king Lucifer was the cause, which you will find, here following, concerning *his fall*, and concerning the creation of this world.

Of the friendly Love, gracious, amiable Blessedness and Unity *of the* Five *Qualifying or Fountain-Spirits of God.*

61. Though it be impossible for the hands of men to describe this sufficiently, yet the *enlightened* spirit of *man* seeth it; for it riseth up just in such a form and birth as the light [doth]

in the divine power, and also in [such a form and birth as] the qualities which are *in God* [rise up].

62. Only this is to be lamented concerning man, that his qualities are corrupted, perished, and *half* dead; and therefore it is that man's spirit [in its] or his qualities [in their] rising or kindling in this world, can come or attain to *no perfection*.

63. On the other hand, it is highly to be rejoiced at, that man's spirit, in his necessity, becometh *enlightened* and kindled by the Holy Ghost: [just] as the sun kindleth the cold heat in a tree or herb, whereby the cold *chilled* heat becometh living.

Now observe:

64. As the members of man's body love one another, so do the spirits also in the *divine* power; there is nothing else but a mere longing, desiring, and fulfilling, as also a *triumphing* and rejoicing the one in the other: For through these spirits come the *understanding* and distinction in God, in angels, in men, in beasts, in fowls and in *everything* that liveth.

65. For in *these five* qualities rise up the seeing, smelling, tasting and feeling; and so a *rational* spirit cometh to be.

66. When the light riseth up, then one spirit seeth another.

67. When the sweet spring or fountain-water

riseth up *in the light*, through all the spirits,
then the one tasteth the other; and then the
spirits become *living*, and the power of life
penetrateth through all.

68. In *that* power the one smelleth the other;
and through this qualifying *influence* and penetration the one feeleth the other.

69. So there is nothing else but a *hearty*, loving
and friendly aspect or seeing, a pleasant smell,
a good relishing or tasting, and a lovely feeling,
a gracious, amiable, *blessed* kissing, a feeding
upon and drinking of one another, and a lovely
walking and *conversing* together.

70. This is the gracious, amiable, blessed
BRIDE, which *rejoiceth in her* BRIDE-
GROOM; herein is love, joy and delight; here is
light and brightness or clarity; here is a pleasant
and lovely smell; here is a friendly and sweet taste.

71. And this for ever *without end*! How can a
creature sufficiently rejoice therein? O dear love
and gracious amiable blessedness! Surely thou
hast no end. No man can see any end *in thee*,
thy profound deep is unsearchable, thou art
everywhere all over thus; only in the fierce devils
art thou *not* thus, they have spoiled and perished
thee in *themselves*.

Question.

72. Now thou wilt say, *Where* then are these
gracious, amiable and blessed spirits to be met

with? Do they dwell only in themselves in *heaven*?

Answer.

73. This is the other open gate of the Deity, here thou must set thy eyes *wide* open, and rouse up or awaken the spirit in thy *half* dead heart: for this is not an obscure fiction, contrivance or phantasy.

Observe:

74. The seven spirits of God, in their circumference and *space*, contain or comprehend heaven and this world; also the *wide breadth and depth* without and beyond the heavens, even above and beneath the world, and in the world, yea *the whole Father*, who hath neither beginning nor end.

75. They contain also *all* the *creatures* both in heaven and in this world; and all the creatures in heaven and in this world are imaged, fashioned or framed out of these spirits, and live in them as in their own *propriety*.

76. Their life and their *reason* is generated in them in such a manner as the divine being is generated, and also in the *same* power.

77. Out of and from the same *body* of the seven spirits of God are *all things* made and produced, all angels, all devils, the heaven, the earth, the stars, the elements, men, beasts, fowls, fishes; all worms, wood, trees, also stones, herbs and grass, and *all* whatsoever is.

Question.

78. Now thou wilt ask, Seeing God is *every-where*, and is himself *All*, how cometh it then that there is in this world such cold and heat, such biting and striking among all creatures, and that there is almost nothing else but mere *fierce-ness* or wrath in this world?

Answer.

[79. " *The cause is, that, without* [apart from,
" outside of] *the light the first four forms of*
" *nature are one at enmity against the other;*
" *and yet they are the causes of life.*"]

80. Behold here the wickedness and malice which is the cause; viz. when king *Lucifer* did sit in his kingdom, like a *high-minded* proud bride, then his circuit, circle or orb contained or comprehended the place or *space* where *now* is the created heaven, which is made out of the water:

81. And also the place of the created world, even unto heaven, as also the *deep* where now the earth is, *all* that was a pure and holy *Salitter*, wherein the seven spirits of God were *complete* and pleasant, as now [they are] in heaven, although they are *still* complete and *full* in this world. But observe the circumstances rightly.

82. When king *Lucifer* elevated himself, then he elevated himself in the seven qualifying fountain-spirits, and *kindled them* with his eleva-

tion, so that all was wholly *burning*, and the astringent quality was so *hard* and compact, that it generated stones; and it was so *cold*, that it made the sweet spring or fountain-water turn *into ice*.

83. And the sweet spring water became very thick and stinking, and the bitter quality became very *raging*, tearing and raving, whence *poison* was generated, and the fire or heat was violently and zealously or fervently *burning* and *consuming*, and so there was a very great distemper and confused *mixture*.

84. *Upon this* king Lucifer was thrust out of his royal place or kingly *throne*, which he had in *that place* where now is the created heaven, and thereupon *instantly ensued* the creation of this world.

85. And the hard, spoiled or corrupt matter, which had *wrought forth itself* in the kindled seven qualifying or fountain-spirits, was *driven* together, from whence the earth and stones came to be, and, after that, all the creatures were created out of the *kindled Salitter* of the seven spirits of God.

86. Now the qualifying or fountain spirits became *so fierce* and wrathful in their kindling, that the one continually spoileth the other with its evil corrupt quality or source, and so also now do the creatures, which *were made out of* the qualifying or fountain spirits, and *live* in the same impulse, the one biting, beating, worrying and

annoying the other, all according to the kind or *disposition* of the qualities.

87. Upon this now the *total* or universal God hath decreed the *Last Judgment*, wherein he will separate the evil from the good, and set the good again in the meek, mild and pleasant delight, as it *was before* the horrible kindling of the devil, and will give that which |is fierce or *wrathful* to king *Lucifer* for an *everlasting* habitation.

88. And then there will be *two parts* or divisions of this kingdom, the one *men* will get, with their King JESUS CHRIST; the other the *devils* shall have with all ungodly men and wickedness.

89. This is a *short* introduction, that the Reader might the better understand the divine Mystery; when I write concerning *the fall of the devil*, and concerning the *creation* of *this* world, you will find all more at large, particularly described. Therefore I would have the Reader admonished, that he read *all in order*, and so he will come to the true ground.

90. It is true, that from the beginning of the world it was *not so fully* revealed to any man; but seeing God will have it so, I submit to his will, and will see what *God* will do with it.

91. For his way which is *before* him is for the *most part* hidden from me: But following *after* him the spirit seeth, even into the highest and profoundest depth.

THE TENTH CHAPTER

*Of the Sixth qualifying or fountain Spirit
in the Divine Power.*

1. THE Sixth qualifying or fountain spirit in
the divine power is the sound, tone,
tune or noise, wherein all soundeth and tuneth ;
whence ensued *speech*, language, and the *distinction* of everything, as also the ringing melody
and *singing* of the holy angels, and therein
consisteth the forming or framing of all *colours*,
beauty and ornament, as also the heavenly
joyfulness.

Question.

2. But thou wilt ask, What is the tone or
sound ? Or how taketh this spirit its source and
original ?

Answer.

3. *All* the *seven spirits* are generated one in
another, the one continually generateth the other,
not one of them is the first, nor is any one of
them the last ; for the last generateth as well

the first as the second, third, fourth, and so on to the last.

4. But why one is called the *first*, another the *second*, and so *on*, that is in respect to that which is the first in order to the imaging, framing and *forming* of a creature.

5. For all the seven are *equally* eternal, and none of them hath either beginning or end; and therefore, in that the seven qualities are continally *generating* one another, and that none is without the other, it followeth that there is ONE *Only Eternal Almighty* GOD.

6. For, if anything be generated out of or in the divine being, that thing is not formed or framed by or through *one* spirit alone, but by *all* the seven.

7. And if a creature, which is like or as the whole being of God, spoileth, elevateth and *kindleth* itself in a qualifying or fountain spirit, it kindleth not one spirit alone, but *all the seven* spirits.

8. And therefore that creature is a loathsome abomination before the *total* God, and before all his creatures, and must stand in eternal enmity and ignominy or shame *before* God, and before all the creatures.

9. The tone or *Mercurius* taketh its original in the *first*, that is, in the astringent and hard quality.

Observe in the Depth:

10. Hardness is the fountain or well-spring of the tone, but it *alone* cannot generate the same, yet it is the father thereof, and the whole *Salitter* is the mother; otherwise, if the hardness were both father and mother of the tone, then a hard stone also must have a ringing sound.   But a hard stone doth make only a noise, like a knocking, as a seed or *beginning* of a tone, and that it is, certainly.

11. But the tone of voice riseth up in the middle centre, in the flash or *lightning*, where the light is generated out of the *heat*, where the flash or lightning of life riseth up.

Observe how this is done:

12. When the astringent quality *rubbeth* itself with the bitter, so that the heat riseth up in the sweet spring or fountain-water, then the heat kindleth the *sweet* spring or fountain-water, like a flash of lightning, and that flash is the *light*; which in the heat goeth into the bitter quality, and there the flash is *distinguished* according to all the powers.

13. For all powers are discerned or distinguished in the bitter, and the bitter receiveth the flash of the light, as if it were *horribly* terrified, and goeth with its trembling and terror into the astringent and hard quality, and there it is *bodily* captivated.

14. And the bitter quality is now *impregnated* with the light, and trembleth in the astringent and hard quality, and stirreth therein, and is *captivated* in the astringent quality, as in a body.

15. And now when the spirits do move and would *speak*, the hard quality must open itself; for the bitter spirit with its flash breaketh it open, and then *there* the tone goeth forth, and is impregnated *with* all the seven spirits, which distinguish the word, as it was *decreed* in the centre, that is, in the middle of the circle, whilst it was yet in the *council* of the seven spirits.

16. And therefore the seven spirits of God have created a *mouth* for the creatures, that when they [the creatures] would utter their voice, which is their speaking, or [when they would] make a noise,* they need not first tear themselves open; and therefore it is that all the veins and powers or [1]qualifying or fountain spirits *go* into the tongue, that the tone or noise may come forth *gently.*

[1] conditioning.

[2] Mind or Meaning.

Here observe exactly the [2] *Sense and* Mystery.

17. When the flash riseth up in the heat, then first the sweet water *catcheth* or captivateth it, for therein it becometh shining. Now when the water catcheth the flash, that is, the *birth* of the light, then the sweet water is terrified, and being

* " make a noise " (*schallen*), " sound."

so thin and pliant or feeble, it yieldeth, very much trembling; for the heat riseth up in the light.

18. Now when the astringent quality, which is very cold, catcheth the heat and the flash, then it is *terrified*, as in a tempest of lightning; for when the heat cometh with the light into the hard cold, then it maketh a *fierce* flash, of a very fiery and light colour.

19. Then that flash *retireth* back, and the sweet water catcheth it, and riseth up in that *fierceness*, and in that rising and terrifying changeth itself into a green or azure or blue colour, and trembleth because of the fierce flash.

20. And the flash in itself *keepeth* its fierceness, from whence existeth the bitter quality, or the bitter spirit, which *now* riseth up in the astringent quality, and inflameth or *kindleth* the hardness with its fierce quality, and the light or flash *drieth* itself in the hardness, and shineth clear and bright, *far brighter* than the light of the sun.

21. But it is caught in the hard quality, so that it subsists in a bodily manner, and *must* shine *so* eternally, and the flash trembleth in the body, like a fierce rising up, whereby all the qualities are stirred, always and eternally.

22. And the flash of fire in the light trembleth and triumpheth thus continually, *and the sweet water softeneth* [or quencheth] *the fire also con-*

*tinually,** and the hardness is always the body, which retaineth, preserveth, and drieth it.

23. And this stirring in the hardness is the tone, so that [there is a] sound; and the light or flash maketh the ringing, and the sweet water maketh the ringing soft: so that a man can use the sound to the distinction of speech, or *articulation of syllables.*

Here observe *yet more plainly the Nativity* or Birth
of the bitter Quality.

24. The *original* of the bitter quality is when the flash of life in the heat riseth up in the astringent quality; and now when the flash of fire in the mixture of the water cometh *into* the astringent quality, then the spirit of the fiery flash *catcheth* the astringent and hard spirit, and both these together are an earnest *severe* fierce quality, which rageth and teareth vehemently, like a fiery violent fierceness.

25. I can liken it to nothing else but to a *thunder-clap*, when the fierce fire first falls down, so that it *dazzleth* the *sight*; that fierce fire is like the manner of the conjunction of these two.

Now observe:

26. When the fire-spirit and the astringent-spirit *struggle* and wrestle thus together, then

* The clause printed in italics is not in Sparrow's translation. It is here supplied from the German editions of 1682, 1715 and 1730. It is not in 1656, nor in Schiebler.

the astringent maketh a vehement hard *cold* astriction, and the fiery maketh a terrible fierce *heat*.

27. Now the rising up of the heat and of the astriction maketh a trembling, fierce, *terrible* spirit, which raveth and rageth, *as if* it would tear the Deity asunder.

But thou must understand this, exactly and properly.

28. This is *thus* in the original of the quality in itself; but in the *midst*, in the rising up of this *fierce* spirit, this [same] spirit is *caught* and mitigated in the sweet water, where its fierce source or fountain is *changed* into a trembling, bitter, and greenish colour, like a greenish duskiness, and it retaineth in itself the *condition* and property of all *three* qualities, *viz.* of the fiery, the astringent and the sweet; and so from these three existeth the *fourth* quality, *viz.* the bitter.

29. For from the fiery quality the spirit becometh *trembling* and *hot*, and from the astringent it becometh *severe*, astringent, hard and *corporeal*, so that it is a spirit which always subsisteth; and from the sweet it becometh meek or *mild*, and the fierceness changeth it into a gentle bitterness; which standeth now in the fountain or *well-spring* of the seven spirits of God, and helpeth continually to generate the other six spirits.

Understand this rightly.

30. It doth *as well* generate its father and mother, *as* its father and mother do generate it, for after that it is *corporeally* generated, it then, with the astringent quality, *always* generateth the fire *again*, and the fire generateth light, and the light *is* the *flash*, which always generateth the *life* again in all the qualifying or fountain spirits; whence the spirits have *life*, and always generate one another *again*.

31. But here thou must know that *one* spirit *alone* cannot generate another, neither can *two* of them do it, but the birth of a spirit standeth in the operation of *all* the *seven* spirits, *six* of them always generate the *seventh*, and so if *one* of them were not, then the *others* would not be either.

32. But that I sometimes take only two or three to the nativity or birth of a spirit, I do that because of my *own weakness*, for in [1] my corrupted brain I cannot bear them all seven at *once* in their perfection.

[1] The human nature being corrupted and perished in the fall of *Adam*.

33. I see them *all seven* very well, but when I speculate into them,* then the spirit riseth up in the *middlemost* fountain or well-spring, where the spirit of life generateth itself, which goeth now *upwards*, now *downwards*, it cannot apprehend

* "but when I speculate into them"; text, "*aber wenn ich speculire in sie.*" But when I look or gaze into them, to examine, inspect or observe them more closely or narrowly. (*Speculate*, 2. O.E.D.)

all the seven spirits in *one* thought, or at once, but only in *part.*

34. Every spirit hath its *own* quality or source, though indeed it is generated of the others ; and so it is with the *apprehension* of man ; he hath indeed the fountain of all seven spirits *in* him, but in what quality or fountain soever the spirit riseth up, the qualifying or fountain spirit *thereof,* wherein that same spirit is most *strongly* imaged, is that [one] which he comprehendeth most sharply in *that* rising up.

35. For even in the divine power one spirit, in its [1] rising up, doth *not go* through all the spirits equally *at once* ; for when it riseth up, then indeed it toucheth or *stirreth* them all at once, but it is caught in its rising up, so that it must lay down its stateliness and pomp, and not *triumph over all the seven.*

[36. " *It is the being or substance of the senses* " *and thoughts, otherwise, if a thought through the* " *centre of nature could penetrate all the forms,* " *then it were* free *from the band of nature.*"]

37. Thus also in man : When *one* qualifying or fountain spirit riseth up, then it toucheth *all* the others, and seeth all the others, for it riseth up in the middle or central fountain or well-spring of the heart, where, in the *heat,* the flash of light kindleth itself, wherein the spirit in its rising up, in the same flash, seeth through *all* the spirits.

[1] Or ascension.

38. But in our corrupted flesh it [the rising up] is only like a tempest of *lightning* : for if I *could* in my *flesh* comprehend the flash (which I very well see and know *how it is*), I could clarify or transfigure my body therewith, so that it would shine with a *bright* light and glory.

[" *For from the flash cometh the* light *of the* " *Majesty.*"]

And then it would no more resemble and be conformed to the bestial body, but to the angels of God.

39. But hearken, Friend, tarry yet a *little* while, and then give the bestial body for food to the worms : But when the total God shall *kindle* the seven spirits of God in the *corrupted* earth, then, if that same *Salitter* which thou sowest in the earth will not be capable of the fire, then thy qualifying or fountain spirits, which thou didst sow in thy life-time, and which are sown in thy *departure* from hence, will *rise* again in the same *Salitter* which thou hast sown, and will triumph therein, and become *a body* again.

[1] Or whose *Salitter.* See Ch. 10, verse 110, the *Salitter* which they have corrupted. And Ch. 11, verse 115, the corrupted *Salitter.*

40. But he [1] that will be *capable* of the kindled fire of the seven spirits of God, he shall *abide* therein, and his qualifying or fountain spirits shall rise in *hellish* pain, which I shall demonstrate clearly in its due place.

41. I cannot describe unto thee the whole Deity by the circumference or extent of a circle, for it is immeasurable ; but to *that spirit* which is in

God's love it is *not* incomprehensible : That spirit comprehends it well, yet but in part; therefore take one part after another, and then you will see the *whole.**

42. In this corruption we cannot get higher than with such a revelation,† neither doth this world enclose itself any higher, both as to the beginning and the end.

[43. "*I would very fain see* somewhat higher " *in this my anxious generating or birth, whereby* " *my sick Adam might be refreshed.*

44. "*But I look round about me in all the* " *world, and can find out* nothing ; *all is sick,* " *lame and wounded : moreover, blind, deaf and* " *dumb* "].‡

45. I *have read* the writings of very high masters, hoping to find therein the ground and true depth ; but I have found nothing, but a *half*

---

* See Cont. of this B., par. 39 *et seq.*, and Ch. 21, par. 66.

† "In this corruption we cannot get higher than with such a revelation." That is, man can get no higher knowledge of the whole Deity, or of this world as to its beginning and end, than is vouchsafed to him as a revelation by the spirit that is in God's love. "I cannot describe unto thee . . . the immeasurable, but that spirit which is in God's love . . . comprehends it well, but only piecemeal, part by part (*aber nur stückweise*); therefore take one part after another, and then you will see the whole" (par. 41).

‡ In Sparrow's translation, and also in the German ed. of 1656, these pars. are treated as part of J. B.'s original text, but Gichtel, in the 1682 ed., prints them as additions by J. B. in 1620.

dead spirit, which in anxiety travaileth * and laboureth for health, and yet, because of its great weakness, *cannot* attain perfect power.

46. Thus I stand yet as an anxious woman in travail, and seek *perfect* refreshing, but find only the scent or smell or savour in its rising up, wherein the spirit examineth what power *sticketh* in the true cordial, and in the meanwhile refresheth itself in its sickness with that *perfect smell* or savour, till the true *Samaritan* doth come, who will dress and bind up its wounds and heal it, and bring it to the eternal *inn* or lodging, then shall it enjoy the *perfect taste*.

47. This *herb*, which I mean here, from whose fragrancy my spirit taketh its refreshing, every country ploughman doth not know it, *nor* every doctor, the one is as ignorant of it as the other; it groweth indeed in *every* garden, but in many it is quite spoiled and bad: for the quality of the soil or ground is in *fault*. And therefore men do not know it, nay the *children of this Mystery* do hardly know it; although this knowledge hath been very rare, dear and precious, from the beginning of the world to this *time*.

48. Though in many men a source or fountain and quality hath risen up, but then suddenly pride pressed after it, and *spoiled* all; whereupon

---

* "in anxiety travaileth." Sparrow invariably uses the later spelling, "travelleth." The German reads, "*sich ängstet*," "anxiously labours," *i.e.* frets or worries itself.

it [pride] was loath to write it down in its mother-tongue; it supposed that was *too* childish a thing to do, it must shew it in a *deeper* language, that the world should see that it is manly; and for its *advantage* it kept it [the source or fountain and quality] in secret, and *daubed* it with deep strange names, that men might not know it; such a *beast* is the devil's disease of pride.

49. But hear, thou simple mother, who bringest all the children into this world, who afterwards in their rising up are *ashamed* of thee and despise thee, and yet are *thy* children whom thou hast brought forth.

50. *Thus saith the spirit, which riseth up in the seven spirits of* God, *which is thy Father: Despair not, behold, I am thy strength, and thy power, I will fill to thee a mild draught in thy age.*

51. *Seeing all thy children despise thee, whom thou didst bear, and hast given them suck in their childhood, and who will not give thee any attendance, or minister to thee in thy high or old age:*

52. *Therefore I will comfort thee, and will give unto thee a young SON in thy high or old age; he shall abide in thy house as long as thou livest, and attend thee or minister to thee, and comfort thee against all the raving and raging of thy proud children.*

Now here observe further concerning the Mercurius,
Tone or Sound.

[1] finite or
transitory ori-
ginal.

53. All qualities take their [1] beginning-original in their *middle* or centre: Therefore observe *where* the fire is generated; for *there* riseth up the flash of the life of all the qualities, and it is *caught* in the water, so that it remaineth *shining*; and it is dried in the astringency, so that it remaineth *corporeal*, and becometh shining, bright and clear.

Observe here :

54. For instance : Kindle some wood, and *then* you will see the mystery : The fire kindleth itself in the *hardness* of the wood; and this is now the astringent hard quality, the quality or source *Saturnus*, which *maketh* the wood hard and dry.

55. But now the *light*, that is, the flash, doth not consist in the hardness, otherwise a stone also would burn and give light, but the light subsisteth only in the *sap* of the wood, that is, in the

[2] Or oiliness. [2] water.

56. Whilst there is sap in the wood the fire *shineth* as a shining light; but when the sap is consumed in the wood the shining light *goeth out*, and the wood becometh a glowing coal.

57. Now behold: the fierceness which riseth up in the light consists *not* in the water of the wood, but when the heat riseth up in the hard-

ness, then is the flash *generated*, which the sap in the wood first catcheth, whereby the *water* becomes shining.

58. The fierceness or bitterness is generated in the midst or centre of the hardness, and the *heat* is generated in the flash, and therein also it subsisteth; and so far as the flash, that is, the *flame* of the fire reacheth, so far also reacheth the *fierceness* of the bitterness, which is the son of the hardness and heat.

59. But thou must know this mystery, that the bitterness is *already* in the wood, else the fierce bitterness would not so suddenly generate itself like *lightning* in the natural fire.

60. For as, when wood is kindled, the body of the fire generateth itself, in such a manner likewise is the *wood* generated in and above the earth.

61. But if the fierceness should be generated in the shining light, then surely it would reach *as far* also as the splendour or shining of the light, but it doth not so.

62. But thus it is; the flash is the *mother* of the light; for the flash generateth the light, and is the *father* of the fierceness, for the fierceness abideth in the flash as a *seed* in the father; and that flash generateth also the tone or sound.

63. When it goeth from the hardness and heat, then the hardness maketh a thumping, *knocking* sound in the flash, and the heat ringeth forth,

and the light in the flash maketh the ringing *clear*, and the water mitigateth or softeneth it, and then in the astringency and hardness it is caught and dried up, so that it is a *corporeal* spirit in all the qualities.

64. For *every* spirit in the seven spirits of God is impregnated with *all* the seven spirits, and they all are one in another as *one* spirit, not one of them is without the others.

65. Only the birth therein is *thus*, and so the one generateth the other, in and through itself, and the birth *lasteth* or continueth thus from eternity to eternity.

66. Here I will have the Reader warned that he rightly *consider* the divine birth. Thou must *not* think that one spirit standeth *by* another, as you see the stars of heaven stand one by another.

67. But all the seven are *one in another* as *one* spirit; as this may be conceived in man, who hath *several* thoughts, because of the operation of the seven spirits of God, which keep and reside in the *human body*.

68. But you may say to me, Thou art foolish in this; for *any member* of the whole body hath the *power* of the other.*

69. Yet in what quality soever thou excitest or *awakenest* the spirit, and makest it operative

---

* "But you must say [admit], unless you be foolish, that each one of the members of the whole body hath the power of the other."

or qualifying, according to that same quality the thoughts rise up, and *govern* the mind.

70. If thou stirrest or awakest the spirit in the fire, then there riseth up in thee the bitter and harsh *anger*; for as soon as the fire is kindled, which is done in the hardness and fierceness, *then* springeth up the bitter fierceness or wrath in the flash.

71.* For when thou, in thy body, liftest thyself against anything whatsoever, be it in love or wrath, thou kindlest the quality of that against which thou liftest thyself; and that [kindled quality] burneth in the corporeal whole of thy spirit; but in the flash this same fountain-spirit awakeneth.

72. For when thou lookest upon anything which doth *not please* thee, but is *against* or contrary to thee, then thou *raisest up* the fountain of thy heart, as when thou takest a stone, and therewith strikest fire on a steel, and so when the *spark* catcheth fire in the heart, *then* the fire kindleth.

73. At first it *gloweth*, but when thou stirrest the source or fountain of the heart more violently, then it is as when thou *blowest* the fire, so that the *flame* is kindled; and then it is high time to quench it, else the fire will be too great, and then

* A new translation of this par. has been substituted for Sparrow's rendering. "Quell-Geist" (fountain-spirit) has, in this particular par., been translated by St M. "spirit-source."

it *burneth* and consumeth, and doth hurt to *its neighbour.*

74. Thou askest, *How* can a man quench this kindled fire ?

75. Hearken, thou hast the *sweet* water in thee, pour that into the fire, and then the fire goeth out : If thou *lettest* it burn, then it consumeth in thee the sap that is in all the seven qualifying or fountain spirits, so that thou wilt become dry.

76. *When that is done, then thou art a hellish fire-brand, and a billet or faggot to lay upon the hellish fire, and then there is no remedy for thee eternally.*

77. But when thou lookest upon a thing which *pleaseth* thee, and awakenest the spirit in thine heart, then thou kindlest the fire in thine heart, which burneth first in the sweet water like a *glowing* coal.

78. Whilst it is but *glimmering* it is only a gentle, soft, longing delight or pleasing lust in thee, and doth *not* consume thee ; but if thou exhaltest thy heart still more, and thou kindlest the sweet quality or fountain, so that it becomes a *burning flame*, then thou kindlest all the qualifying or fountain spirits, and then the whole body burneth, and so mouth and hands fall on to work.

79. *This fire* is the most dangerous and hurtful, and hath spoiled most since the world began, and it is a *very hard* matter to quench it; for when it is kindled it burneth in the *sweet* water in the flash of life, and must be quenched through *bitterness,* which is scarce a water,* but much *rather* is a fire.

80. *Therefore* also there followeth a heavy, sad, sorrowful mind, when one is to forsake that which burneth in his love-fire in the sweet fountain water.

81. But thou must know, that thou, in the government of thy mind, art *thine own* lord and master, there will rise up *no* fire to thee in the circle or whole circumference of thy body and spirit, *unless* thou awakenest it *thyself.*

82. It is true that all thy spirits spring and move in thee, and rise up in thee, and indeed *always* one spirit hath *more* power in thee than [in] another [man].

83. For if the government of the spirits were the same in one man as in another, then we should *all* have *one* will and form; but all seven are in *the power* of thy compacted incorporated spirit, which spirit is the S O U L.

["84. *It hath in it the* first Principle; *the* " *spirit of the soul hath the* second; *and the astral*

* "scarce a water" (*gar ein elend Wasser*), "but poor [as] water." The word "*elend*" implies weakness and wretchedness.

" *or starry spirit in the elements hath the* third,
" *viz. this world.*"]

85. Now if a fire riseth up in one qualifying or fountain spirit, then that is *not concealed* or hidden from the soul, and it may instantly awaken the other qualifying or fountain spirits, which are *contrary* to the kindled fire, and *may* quench it.

86. But if the fire will be or becometh *too big*, then hath the soul a *prison*, wherein it may shut up the kindled spirit, *viz.* in the hard astringent quality, and the *other* spirits must be the gaolers, till their wrath is allayed, and the fire is *extinguished*.

Observe what that is.

87. When *one* qualifying or fountain spirit driveth thee too strongly, or presseth thee *too hard* to a thing which is against *the law of nature*, then thou must turn thine *eyes* away from it: If that will not help, then take *that spirit* and cast it into prison.

88. That is, turn thy heart *away* from temporal pleasure and voluptuousness, from fulness of eating and drinking, from the *riches* of this world, and think that to-day is the *last* day of the *end* of thy *body*; turn away from the *wantonness* of the world, and call *earnestly* to God, and yield or submit thyself to him.

89. When thou dost so, then the world *mocketh*

thee, and thou art a *fool* to them.   But bear *this* cross patiently, and let not the imprisoned spirit get out of prison again, but trust in God, and *he will set upon thee the crown of the divine joy.*

90. But if the spirit *breaketh out* of prison, then put it in again, *make good* thy part against it as long as thou livest, and if thou gettest so much advantage, that it doth not *wholly* kindle the source or fountain of thy heart, whereby thy soul *would* become a dry fire-brand of wood, each fountain or source having *yet* its sap, *when* thou departest from hence :

91. Then that kindled fire at the Last Judgment Day will not hurt thee ; nor will it cleave or *stick* in thy sappy spirits ; but after this anxious affliction and trouble thou wilt be, in the resurrection, *a triumphing angel of God.*

Question.

92. But now thou mayest say, Is there in God also a *contrary* will or opposition among or between the spirits of God ?

Answer.

93. No : Though I shew here their *earnest* birth, how earnestly and severely the spirits of God are generated, whereby every one may very well understand the great earnest *severity* of God :

94. Yet it doth *not therefore follow* that there

is a disunion or *discord* among them : for the very innermost, *deepest* birth * or geniture in the heart or kernel is only and altogether *so*, which no creature can apprehend in the body ; but in the *flash*, where the hidden spirit is generated, there it will be apprehended ; for that is also generated in *such* a manner, and in such a power as is here mentioned.

95. But unto me is opened the gate of my *mind*, so that I *can* see and discern it, else it would indeed remain concealed with me, and hidden to me, *till* the *day* of the resurrection from the dead ; yea, it hath been concealed from *all men* since the beginning of the world ; but I submit my will to God's will, let him do what he pleaseth.

96. In God *all* the spirits do triumph as *one* spirit, and one spirit always mitigateth or softeneth and loveth the others, so there is nothing but mere joy and delight : But their *severe* birth or geniture, which is effected or done in *secret*, must be so : † for life, under-standing, and [1] omniscience are *thus* generated ; *and this is an eternal birth or geniture, which is never otherwise.*

[1] Or all know-ingness.

* " for the very innermost, deepest birth," etc. "For it is in the heart or kernel alone, that the innermost, deepest birth thus takes place [as above described], and no creature can apprehend it [this birth] in the body, but [only] in the flash, where," etc.

† " must be so " = must be as it is, *i.e.* severe and secret.

97. Thou must not think that perhaps in heaven there is *some* manner of body which *only* is thus generated, *which* above all other things is called God.*

98. No; but the whole divine power which itself is heaven, and the heaven of *all* heavens, is *so* generated, and that is called G O D *the Father*; of whom all holy angels are generated, and live also in the same power; also the spirit of all angels in their body is always continually and eternally *thus generated*; in like manner also is [generated] the *spirit* of all men.

99. For this world belongeth as well to the body or [1] *corpus* of God the Father as the heaven doth; but in the locality or space of this world the *spirits* were kindled through king *Lucifer*, in his elevation, so that all things in this world are as it were languid and half dead: And *therefore* it is that we poor men are so very much blinded, and live in such great and *desperate* danger.

[1] substantiality or corporeity.

100. Yet thou must *not* therefore think that the heavenly light in this world, in the qualifying or fountain spirits of God, is *quite* extinct: No; there is only a darkness or dim *obscurity* upon it, so that we cannot apprehend it with our *corrupted* eyes.

* "Thou must not think that perhaps in heaven there may be some [particular] manner of body thus generated, and above all things called God."

101. But if God did [but] *once* put away that darkness, which moveth about the light,* and that thy eyes were opened, then in *that* very place where thou standest, sittest or liest thou wouldst see *the glorious countenance or face of God, and the whole heavenly gate.*

102. Thou needest not first to cast thine eyes up into heaven, for it is written: [1] *The Word is near thee, viz. on thy lips, and in thy heart.*

[1] Deut. xxx. 14. Rom. x. 8.

103. *Yea, God is so near thee, that the birth or geniture of the Holy Trinity is done or wrought even in thy heart, yea, all the three Persons are generated in thy heart, even God the Father, Son, and Holy Ghost.*

104. Now when I write here concerning the midst or *centre,* that the fountain of the divine birth or geniture is in the midst or centre, the meaning is *not* that in heaven there is a peculiar or *several* place, or a peculiar *several* body, wherein the fire of the divine life riseth up, out of which the seven spirits of God go forth into the *whole deep* of the Father.

105. No; but I speak in a corporeal or angelical or human way that the *Reader* may the better understand it, in such a manner as the angelical creatures were imaged or framed, and as it is in God everywhere *universally.*

* "moveth about the light" (*über dem Lichte schwebet*), "moveth [floateth] above the light," or "over the light."

106. For thou canst not nominate * any place, either in heaven or in this world, wherein the divine birth or geniture is *not thus*, be it in an angel, or in a holy man, or anywhere else.

107. Wheresoever one qualifying or fountain spirit in the divine power is *touched* or stirred, let the place be where it will or the thing what it will (*except* in the devils, and all wicked, damned men), there is the fountain of the divine birth or geniture directly at hand, and there *already* are all the seven qualifying or fountain spirits of God.

108. As when thou wouldst make a spacious, *creaturely*, circumscribed circle, and hadst the whole Deity peculiarly *apart* therein. Just as the Deity is generated in a creature, so it is also in the whole deep of the Father in all places and parts thereof, and in all *things*.

Note.

109. *And in such a manner is God an all-mighty, all-knowing, all-seeing, all-hearing, all-smelling, all-tasting, all-feeling God, who is everywhere, and proveth the hearts and reins of the creatures.*

110. And in such a manner heaven and earth are *his*; also in such a manner all the devils, together with all wicked men, must be *his* eternal

---

* "nominate," German *ernennen*, to nominate, to name; with a by-meaning of pick out, point out, indicate = (nominate, 1. b., to give a name or names to; to provide with a name. *Obs.*). [O.E.D.]

prisoners; and in the *Salitter*, which they have
corrupted and kindled in their place or space,
must *endure* eternal pain and torment, and moreover eternal shame and reproach.

111. For the total *glorious* face of God, together with all the holy angels, will shine bright
and gloriously above them and under them, and
round about *them* on every side.

112. And all holy angels, together with all
holy men, will eternally triumph above them,
below them and round about *them*, and for great
joy, delight and pleasantness will sing of God's
holiness, of their royal kingly government or
regimen, and of the gracious, amiable, blessed
fruit of the heavenly spring or *vegetation*; and
that will go forth according to the qualities of
the seven spirits of God, in many various *voices*.

113. On the contrary, the devils, with all
wicked men, will be *forced* into a hole, where
a hellish stink will well up and rise up, and the
hellish fire, and the hellish coldness and bitterness,
will *burn* after the manner of the kindled spirits
of God, eternally in their body, as also in their
courts, dominions, regions, space or circumference.

114. Nay, if they could be locked in or barred
up in a *hole*, that the angry face of God might
not touch them, then they might be quiet and
contented, and would not be necessitated to
endure eternal ignominy, shame and reproach.

115. But here is no help, their *torment* in-

creaseth and becometh but the greater; the more they bewail it, the *more* doth the hellish fierceness or wrath kindle itself, they must lie in hell, as dead bones, like singed scorched sheep in the fire, their *stink* and abomination *gnaweth* them.

116. They dare not lift up their eyes for shame, for they see in their circumference, courts or *regions*, nothing else but only a severe judge; and above them, and on all sides of them, they *see* the eternal joy.

[117. "*Not that they apprehend and behold it*, "*but they have a kind of knowledge thereof in* "*the* Centre."]

118. Here is lamentation and woe, *yelling* and crying, and no deliverance; it is with them as if it did *continually* thunder and lighten tempestuously.

119. For the kindled spirits of God generate themselves *thus:*

I. The hardness generateth a hard, raw, *rough*, cold and astringent quality.

II. The sweetness is grown *faint*, and gaspeth, like a glowing coal splits when there is no more sap in the wood, and there is *no* refreshment for it.

III. The bitterness *teareth* like a hot plague, and is as bitter as gall.

IV. The fire *burneth* as a fierce wrathful Sulphur.

V. Love is an *enmity* here.

VI. The sound is a mere beating, *rumbling* or

cracking,* like the noise of a fire breaking forth out of a hollow place, as if it were great *claps* of thunder.

VII. The circuit, region, court or *residence* of the body of the seven is a house of *mourning*.

120. Their food is *abomination*, and groweth from the fierceness of all qualities : Lamentation and woe, and that for ever without end ; there is no time there ; *another king* sitteth on their throne, which keepeth or holdeth a judgment for ever ; they are only his *footstool*.

121. O beauty, *pleasure* and voluptuousness of this world ! O riches and proud stateliness ! O might and *power* ! Thy unrighteous judgment and great *pomp*, with all thy pleasure and voluptuousness, lie all together on a heap, and are become a hellish fire !

122. Now eat and drink, now trim and dress thyself † therewith, and domineer therein, thou fair goddess, how art thou become a *whore*, and thy shame and reproach continue for ever !

---

* "a mere beating, rumbling or cracking." In this, and in several similar sentences where Sparrow has used such terms as the above, the original is "*Pochen*," a word difficult to render in English, but highly suggestive. It describes above all else a pulsation ; it might be the throbbing of an engine, or the beating of the human heart ; it might be the hammering of a pounding-machine, or the ticking of the "death-watch" insect ; but in every case it denotes a regular, continuous motion and alternating sound, and this both as a technical term and as a figurative.

† "trim and dress thyself" (*schmincke dich*), "paint thy face."

THE ELEVENTH CHAPTER

VII. *Of the Seventh Qualifying or Fountain Spirit in the Divine Power.*

1. THE Seventh spirit of God in the divine power is the *corpus* or body, which is generated out of the other *six* spirits, wherein *all* heavenly figures subsist, and wherein all things image and form themselves, and wherein all *beauty* and joy rise up.

2. This is the very spirit of nature, yea *nature itself*, wherein apprehensibility or comprehensibility consisteth, and wherein all creatures are formed in heaven and on earth. Yea *heaven* itself is therein formed; and all *naturality* in the whole God consisteth in *this* spirit.

3. If it were not for this spirit there would be neither angel nor man, and God would be an *unsearchable* being, subsisting *only* in an unsearchable power.

Question.

4. Now the question is: How is this form? Or in what manner is this so?

Answer.

If thou art a rational mercurial spirit, which *presseth* through all the seven spirits of God, and beholdeth, proveth and examineth them, how they are, then thou wilt, by the *explanation* of this seventh spirit, conceive and understand the *operation* and the *being* of the whole Deity, and apprehend it in thy sense or mind.

5. But if thou *understandest* nothing by this spirit, then let this book alone, and *judge* neither of the cold nor of the warmth therein : For *thou* art too hard bound and captivated in *Saturnus*, and art not a philosopher in this world.

6. Let thy *judging* alone, or else thou wilt receive thy *evil* wages for it ; therefore I will have thee faithfully warned of it. Tarry till thou comest into the other life, for then the heavenly gate *will* be opened to thee, and then thou also wilt understand this.

Now observe the Depth.

7. Here I must *lay hold* on the whole divine body in the midst or centre at the heart, and explain the whole body, how nature is or existeth, and there you will see *the highest ground*, how all the seven spirits of God *continually* generate one another, and *how* the Deity hath neither beginning nor end.

8. Therefore behold and see the longing, desired

pleasure of thy spirit, the eternal divine *joyfulness*, and the heavenly delight and corporeal joy, which in all eternity hath *no* end.

Now observe:

9. When the flash riseth up in the centre, then the divine birth standeth in its full operation: In God it is continually and *eternally* thus; but *not* so in us poor fleshly children.

10. In this life the triumphing divine birth lasteth in us men only *so long* as the flash lasteth, therefore our *knowledge is but in part*, whereas in God the flash standeth unchangeably, always eternally thus.

11. Behold, all the seven spirits of *God* are generated alike together at once; none of them is the first, and none of them is the last; but we must have an eye to the kernel, and consider how the divine birth or *geniture* riseth up, otherwise man understandeth it not.

12. For the creatures cannot comprehend *at once* all the seven spirits, one in another, but they look upon them; but when one spirit is touched or stirred, then that toucheth or stirreth all the others, and then the birth or geniture standeth in full power.

13. Therefore it hath a beginning *in man*, but none *in God*; and therefore I must also write in a *creaturely* manner, or else thou *canst not* understand it.

14. Behold, without the flash all the seven spirits were a dark valley, but when the *flash* riseth up between the astringent and bitter qualities, in the heat, then it becometh *shining* in the sweet water, and in the flames of the heat it becometh bitter, and triumphing and living, and in the astringent it becometh corporeal, dry and *bright*.

15. Now these four spirits move themselves in the flash, for all the four become living therein, and so now the power of these four riseth up in the flash, as if the *life* did rise up, and the *power* which is risen up in the flash is the love, which is the *fifth spirit*.

16. That power moveth so very pleasantly and amiably in the flash, as if a dead spirit did become living, and was suddenly in a moment set into great clarity or *brightness*.

17. Now in this moving one power toucheth or stirreth another : First the astringent beateth or striketh,* and the heat maketh in that beating or stroke a *clear* ringing sound, and the bitter power divideth the ringing, and the water maketh it mild and soft, and mitigateth it; and this is *the sixth spirit*.

18. Now the tone in all the *five* spirits riseth up like a melodious pleasant music, and remaineth so standing ; for the astringent quality exsiccateth it or drieth it up.

* "beateth or striketh" (*pochet*), "beating or stroke" (*Pochen*). See Ch. 10, par. 119.

19. So now, in the same sound *that is gone forth* (which now subsisteth, being dried) is the power of *all the six* qualifying or fountain spirits, and it is as it were the *seed* of the other six spirits, which they have there compacted or incorporated together, and made one spirit thereof, and which hath the quality of *all* the spirits : and that is *the seventh spirit of God* in the divine power.

20. Now this spirit subsisteth in its colour like azure or heaven-*blue*, for it is generated out of all the six spirits ; and when the flash, which standeth in the midst or centre in the heat, *shineth* into the other spirits, so that they rise up in the flash and generate the seventh spirit, then the *flash* riseth up also in the birth of the *six* spirits together in the *seventh*.

21. But because the seventh hath no *peculiar* quality in itself, therefore the flash in the seventh cannot be brighter, but it receiveth from the seventh the *corporeal* being of all the seven spirits, and the flash standeth in the midst or *centre* of these seven spirits, and is generated from all the seven.

22. The seven spirits are the *father* of the light, and the light is their son, which they always continually generate thus from eternity to eternity, and the light enlighteneth and always eternally maketh the seven spirits living and

joyful, for they all receive their rising and *life* in the power of light.

23. Again, they all generate the light, and all are together alike the father of the light, and the light generateth no one spirit, but maketh them *all* living and *joyful*, that they always continually stand in the birth.

24. Behold, I will shew it thee once more, that so by *any means* thou mayest apprehend it, that this high work *may not* take place in vain without profit to *thee*.

25. The astringent quality is the *first* spirit, and that attracteth or draweth together and maketh all dry : The sweet quality is the *second* spirit, and that softeneth or mitigateth the astringent : Now the *third* spirit is the bitter spirit, which existeth from the fourth and the first.

26. So when the third spirit in its rage *rubs* itself in the astringent, then it kindleth the *fire*, and then the *fierceness* in the fire riseth up in the astringent.   In that fierceness now the bitter spirit becometh *self-subsisting* ; and in the sweet it becometh meek or *mild* ; and in the hard it becometh *corporeal* ; and so now it subsisteth, and is also the *fourth* spirit.

27. Now the flash in the power of these *four* goeth forth in the heat, and riseth up in the sweet spring water or fountain ; the bitter maketh it *triumphing* ; the astringent maketh it *shining*,

dry and corporeal; and the sweet maketh it meek and *mild*; and so it receiveth its first shining and lustre in the sweet; and here now the flash, or the light, subsisteth in the midst or centre, as a *heart*.

28. Now when that light, which standeth in the midst or centre, shineth *into* the four spirits, then the power of the *four* spirits riseth up in the light, and they become living, and *love* the light; that is, they take it into them, and are impregnated with it, and that spirit which is so taken in is the love of the life, which is the fifth spirit.

29. Now when they have taken the love into them, then they qualify, act or *operate* for great joy; for the one seeth the other in the light, and so the one toucheth or stirreth the other.

30. Then the tone riseth up; and the hard spirit beateth, striketh or *thumpeth*;* but the sweet maketh that beating or striking *mild*; and the bitter *divideth* it according to the condition or kind of every quality; the fourth causeth the *ringing*; the fifth causeth *joyfulness*; and the compacted incorporated sounding is the *tone* or tune, or the *sixth* spirit.

31. In this tone riseth up the *power* of all the six spirits, and becometh a palpable body, to speak after an angelical manner, and subsisteth

---

* "beateth, striketh or thumpeth" (*pochet*), "beating," etc. (*Pochen*). See Ch. 10, par. 119.

in the power of the other six spirits, and in the light; and this is the *body* of nature, wherein all heavenly creatures, ideas, figures and sprouts or vegetations are imaged or fashioned.

The Holy Gates.

32. But the *light*, which subsisteth in the midst or centre in all the seven spirits, and wherein standeth the *life* of all the seven spirits, whereby all seven become triumphing and joyful, and wherein the heavenly *joyfulness* rises up:

33. This is *that* which all the seven spirits generate, and that is the *son* of all the seven spirits, and the seven spirits are its *father*, which generate the light; and the light generateth in them the *life*; and the *light* is the heart of the seven spirits.

34. *This light is the true Son of God, whom we Christians worship and honour, as the second Person in the Holy Trinity.*

35. *All the seven spirits of God together, are God the Father.*

36. For no one spirit of them is *alone* or without the others; they all seven generate one another; for if one were *wanting* the others could not be.

37. But the *light* is another *Person*, for it is *continually* generated out of or from the seven spirits, and the seven spirits rise up continually in the light; and the powers of these seven

spirits go forth continually in the glance or *splendour* of the light in the seventh [1] nature-spirit, and do form and image all in the *seventh* spirit; *and this out-going or exit in the light is the Holy Ghost.*

[1] Or spirit of nature.

38. The flash or stock or pith or the heart, which is generated in the powers, remaineth standing in the *midst* or centre, and that is the Son; and the splendour or *glance* in all the powers goeth forth from the Father and the Son, in all the powers of the Father, and formeth and imageth all in the seventh nature-spirit, according to the power and operation of the seven spirits, and according to their *distinction* and impulse. *This is the true Holy Ghost, whom we Christians honour and adore for the third Person in the Deity.*

39. Thus, O blind Jew, Turk, and Heathen, thou seest that there are *three Persons in the Deity*, thou canst not deny it, for thou livest and art or hast thy being *in the three Persons*, and thou hast thy life from them and in them, and in the power of these three Persons thou *art to rise* from the dead at the last day, and live eternally.

Note.

40. Now if thou hast lived well and *holily* in this world, according to the law of nature, and hast [1] *not* extinguished the clear flash, which is the Son of God, which *teacheth* thee the law of

[1] *Note.*

nature in thy seven qualifying or fountain spirits, and hast not put it out through a fierce elevation, which runneth on contrary to the [1] knowledge of nature, [2] then wilt thou with all Christians live in eternal joy.

Note.

[41. "*The* law of nature *is the* divine *ordinance* "*out of the centre of nature, he that can live* "*therein needs no other law, for he* fulfilleth *the* "*will of* God."]

42. For it lieth not in thy [3] unbelief to hinder it; thy unbelief doth *not take away* or make void the truth of God: but *faith* bloweth up the spirit of *hope*, and *testifieth* that we are God's children. The faith is generated in the flash, and wrestleth so long with God till it *overcometh* and gets the victory.

43. Thou *judgest* us, and thereby thou judgest thyself, in that thou blowest up the zealous or jealous spirit in anger and wrath, which extinguisheth *thy* light. [4] But if thou art grown on a *sweet* tree, and *suppressest* the evil influence or *suggestions*, and livest well and holily in the law of nature, that sheweth thee very well what is *right*, if thou art not indeed grown out from a *fierce* or wrathful twig or branch.

[44. "*Here is meant or* understood *out of or* "from *a quite Godless seed, whereout there often* "*groweth a* thistle; *though yet there were a* "remedy, *if the will were but once broken; but it*

Margin notes:
[1] Or conscience.
[2] *Note.*
[3] Or ignorance.
[4] *Note.*

" *is a rare and precious thing ; however, indeed on*
" a good tree *it is often so, that some branches*
" *do also wither.*"]

Note.

45. Moreover, thou art blind. For who shall
separate thee *from the love of God*, in which thou
art born or generated, and wherein thou livest,
if thou perseverest and continuest therein till
the end? Who shall separate thee from God, in
whom thou hast lived *here*?

46. That which thou hast *sown* in the ground,
that will spring up, be it rye, wheat, barley,
tares or thorns; that which is not combustible
or capable of the final or last fire, that will not
burn at all: But God will not *himself* corrupt
or spoil *his good* seed, but will husband, *till* and
manure it, that it may bear *fruit* in the eternal
life.*

47. Seeing then *all* live and have their being
in God, why do the *weeds* glory and boast against
the *wheat*? Dost thou think that God is a dissembler, and that he regardeth or respecteth *any*
man's person or *name*?

48. What man was the father of us all? Was
it not *Adam*? And when his son *Cain* lived
wickedly before God, why did not his father
Adam help him? But here it may be said: [1] *He* [1] Ezek. xviii.
that sinneth shall be punished. 4, 20.

* "husband, till," etc. (*bauen*), "build," *i.e.* develop,
cultivate.

49. If *Cain* had not *quenched* or extinguished his light, *who could have separated* him *from the love of God?*

50. So thou also, thou boastest thou art a Christian, and knowest the light, why dost thou *not* walk therein? Dost thou think the *name* will *make* thee *holy?* Tarry, Friend, till thou comest thither into the other world, then thou wilt know it by experience. Behold! *many* a Jew, Turk, and Heathen, who had indeed *their lamps well trimmed and furnished*, will *sooner* enter into the kingdom of heaven than thou who boastest.

Question.

What prerogative or advantage then have the Christians?

Answer.

51. Very much; for they *know the way of life*, and know *how* they should rise from the fall: But if any *will lie still*, then he must be thrown into the *ditch*, and there must perish with all the Godless Heathen.

52. Therefore take heed what thou dost, and consider what thou art; thou *judgest* others, and art *blind* thyself.

53. But the spirit saith thou hast no cause for it, *viz.* to judge him who is *better* than thou: Have we not all *one* flesh, and our

life subsisteth in God, be it in his love, or in
his anger? For *what thou sowest, that thou
shalt reap.*

Note.

54. God is not the cause thereof that thou art
lost: For the law to do right or *righteousness* is
written in *nature*, and thou hast *that very book*
in thy heart.

55. Thou knowest very well that thou *shouldst*
deal well and friendly with thy neighbour; also
thou knowest well that thou shouldst *not vilify*
thy own life, that is, thou shouldst not bemire
and *defile* thy own body and soul, and lay open
their shame.

56. Surely *herein* consisteth the pith and
kernel, and the love of God. God doth not regard
any man's *name* or *birth*, but he that moveth or
acteth in the love of God moveth in the *light*,
and the light is the heart of God. Now he that
sitteth in the heart of God, who can spew him out
from thence? No one; for he is begotten or
generated in God.

57. O thou blind, *half-dead* world, cease from
thy judging; O thou blind Jew, Turk, and
Heathen, desist from thy *calumniating*, and submit thyself in obedience to God, and walk in the
light, then thou wilt *see how* thou shouldst rise
from thy fall, and how thou shouldst arm thyself
in this world against the hellish *fierceness* and

wrath, and how thou mayst overcome, and live *with God* eternally.

58. Most certainly *there is but one God*; but when the veil is put away from thy eyes, so that thou seest and knowest *him*, then thou wilt also see and know *all* thy brethren, whether they be *Christians, Jews, Turks,* or *Heathen.*

59. Or dost thou think that God is the God of *Christians* only? Do not the *Heathen* also live in God, [1] *whosoever doth* right or *righteousness God* loveth and *accepteth him.*

¹ Acts x. 35.

60. Or what didst thou, who art a Christian, know [as to] *how God would* redeem and deliver thee from evil? What friendship and *familiarity* hadst thou with HIM? or what covenant hadst thou made with HIM, *when* God caused his Son to become man, or be incarnate, to redeem *mankind*? Is he only *thy* king? Is it not written, [2] *He is the comfort of all the Heathen.*

² Haggai ii. 7.

³ Rom. v. 18.

61. Hearken, [3] *By one man sin came into the world, and pressed through one upon all. And through one came the redemption into the world, and pressed through one upon all.* What therefore lieth in *any man's* knowledge? No! indeed, thou didst not know how God would deal with thee, when *thou wast dead* in sins.

62. Now as *sin* without distinction reigneth through one man over all, so *mercy* and redemption reign through one over all.

63. But unto those Heathen, Jews, and Turks,

blindness did befall, yet for all that they stand in an anxious birth, and *seek* for a rest; they *desire* grace, though they seek not for it at the right mark, or in the right place or limit: but *God* is *everywhere*, and looketh upon the ground of the *heart*.

64. But if in their anxious birth the light be generated *in them*, what art thou that judgest them?

65. Behold! thou blind man, I will demonstrate this to thee thus: Go into a meadow, there thou seest *several* sorts of herbs and flowers; thou seest some that are bitter, some tart, sweet, sour, white, yellow, red, blue, green, and many various sorts.

66. Do they not all grow out of the *earth*? Do they not stand one by another? Doth the one *grudge* the beauteous form of the other?

67. But if one among them lifteth up itself too high in its growth, and so *withereth*, because it hath not sap enough, how can the *earth* help it? Doth it not afford its sap to *that* as well as to the others?

68. But if *thorns* grow among them, and the mower cometh to reap his crop, he cutteth them down together, but he casteth out the thorns, and they are to be *burnt* in the fire; but the various flowers and good crop he gathereth, and causeth it to be brought into his barn.

69. Thus it is also with men, there are *diver-*

sities of gifts and accomplishments, endowments or aptitudes; one it may be is much *lighter* or brighter in God than another; but all the while they do not *wither in the spirit* they are not rejectable; but when the *spirit* withereth, then that is good and useful for nothing but for fuel, and is only as wood for the fire.

70. But if the Turks be of an *astringent* quality, and the Heathen of a *bitter*, what is that to thee? If the light becomes *shining* in the astringent and bitter qualities, then it gives light also.

71. But thou art generated in the heat, where the light riseth up in the *sweet* spring or fountain-water; have a care lest the heat *burn* thee; it is time, thou wouldst do well to *quench* that.

Question.

72. Thou sayest, Is it *right* then that the Heathen, Jews, and Turks, should persevere in their *blindness*?

Answer.

73. No; but this I say; How can he see, that hath *no eyes*? For what doth the poor lay or vulgar man know of the *tumults* which the priests have in their drunkenness? He goeth on in his simplicity, and generateth anxiously in his *spiritual* birth.

Question.

But then thou sayest, Hath *God* blinded the Turks, Jews, and Heathen?

Answer.

74. No; but when God kindled the light for them, then they lived after the pleasures, *voluptuousness* and lusts of their own hearts, and would not be led or directed *by the spirit*, and so the *outward* light extinguished.

75. But it is not therefore so *totally* extinguished that it *could not* be generated in man; for man is out of or from God, and liveth in God, be it either in love or in wrath.

76. Now if man be in a longing, should he not be *impregnated* in his longing? And so if he be impregnated once, then he can generate also. But as long as the *outward* light doth not shine to him, *therefore* he doth not know his [man's] Son, whom he hath generated.

77. But when the light *shall arise* on the last Judgment Day, then he will *see* HIM [Christ].

78. *Behold, I tell thee a mystery: The time is already that the Bridegroom crowneth his bride!*

79. Guess, Friend, where lieth the *crown*? Towards the *north*; for in the centre of the astringent quality the light will be clear and bright.

80. But from whence cometh the *Bridegroom*? From the midst or centre, where the heat generateth the light, and goeth towards the north into the astringent quality; there the light groweth *bright*.

81. What do these towards the *south*? They are in the heat fallen *asleep*, but a stormy tempest will awaken them; among these many will be terrified to *death*.

82. Then what do those in the *west*? Their bitter quality will rub itself with the others, but when they taste the sweet water, then will their spirit be *mild* and meek.

83. But what do these in the *east*? Thou art a lofty proud *bride* from the beginning; the crown was always offered to thee from the beginning, but thou thoughtest thyself *too fair* already; thou livest as the rest do.

Of the Operation and Property of the Divine and Heavenly Nature.

84. Now if thou wilt *know* what kind or manner of nature there is in *heaven*, and what kind of nature the holy *angels* have; also what kind of nature *Adam* had *before* his fall, and what, properly, the holy, heavenly or *divine* nature is; then observe the circumstances exactly concerning this *seventh* qualifying or fountain spirit of God, as followeth.

85. The seventh qualifying or fountain spirit of God is the qualifying or fountain spirit of *nature*: for the *other* six do generate the seventh; and the seventh, when it is generated, is then as it were the *mother* of the seven, which encompasseth the other six, and generateth them again:

for the *corporeal* and *natural* being consisteth in the seventh.

Observe here the Sense.

86. The *six* rise up in a full or a complete birth according to the power and *condition* of each of them, and when they are risen up, then is their power mingled one in another, and the hardness *drieth* it [the whole], and is as it were the whole being.

87. This corporeal exsiccation or drying, I call in this book the divine S A L I T T E R, for it is [1] therein *the seed of the whole Deity*, and [2] it is as it were a mother, which receiveth the seed, and always generateth fruit again, according to all the qualities of the *seed*.

[1] In the seventh fountain spirit of nature.

[2] the said seventh spirit.

88. Now in this rising up of the six spirits, there riseth up also the *Mercurius*, tone or sound of all the six spirits, and in the seventh nature-spirit it subsisteth [96][3] as in the *mother*; and then the seventh generateth all manner of fruits and colours, according to the *operation* of the six.

[3] [See Eds.' Note, p. ix.]

[89. "*By the word* [4]*SALITTER, in this* [4] "*book, is understood how, out of the* eternal centre "*of nature, the* second Principle *groweth and* "*springeth up out of the* first, *just as the* light "*springeth up out of the* fire, *wherein* two *spirits* "*are understood,* viz. first, *a* hot, second, *an* "*aërial one; whereas in the aërial life the true*

" *vegetation or growing consisteth, and in the*
" *fire-life is the* cause *of the quality.*

90. " *So when it is written, the* angels *are*
" *created out of* God, *then it is understood or*
" *meant out of* God's eternal nature, *wherein is*
" *understood or meant the* seven forms, *and yet*
" *the* divine *holy* nature *is not understood to be*
" *in the* fire, *but in the* light.

91. " *Yet the fire giveth or holdeth forth to us*
" *a* mystery *of the eternal nature, and of the*
" *Deity also, wherein a man is to understand*
" *two* Principles *of a twofold source, viz.* I.
" *a hot, fierce, astringent, bitter, anxious, con-*
" *suming one in the fire-source. And out of*
" *the fire cometh* II. *viz. the light, which*
" *dwelleth in the fire, but is not apprehended*
" *or laid hold on by the fire; also it hath another*
" *source than the fire hath, which is* meekness,
" *wherein there is a desire of* love, *where then,*
" *in the love-desire, another will is understood*
" *than that which the fire hath.*

92. " *For the fire will consume all, and causeth*
" *a high rising in the source, and the meekness*
" *of the light causeth entity or substantiality; viz.*
" *in the eternal light it causeth the water-spirit*
" *of eternal life; and in the third principle of*
" *this world it causeth water, together with the*
" *existency or original of the air.*

93. " *Thus the Reader is to understand this*
" *book as concerning three* Principles *or births;*

" viz. *one is the original of the eternal nature,*
" *in the eternal will or desire of God, which*
" *desire driveth itself on in great anguish till it*
" *cometh to the* fourth form, *viz. to the fire.*

94. " *Wherein the second, which is the light,*
" *existeth and replenisheth the eternal liberty*
" *besides or beyond nature, wherein we under-*
" *stand the holy* Ternary *in the light, without or*
" *beyond nature, in the power of the light, in the*
" *liberty, as another or second spring or source*
" *without being, and yet united with the fire's*
" *nature, viz. as fire and light together in one.*

95. " *The third Principle of this world is*
" *generated and created out of the first, that is,*
" *magically : As is clearly demonstrated in our*
" [1] second, *and* in our [2] third book, *unto which this*
" *book is only an introduction, and is the first*
" book, *which was not sufficiently apprehended by*
" *the author at the first time, though it appeared*
" *clearly enough, yet all of it could not be con-*
" *ceived ; also it was as when a torrent or stormy*
" *shower of rain passeth over a place, from*
" *whence vegetation and springing existeth ; for*
" *therein is the seed of the whole Deity.*"]

96. [See par. 88.][3]

97. But here thou must know that the *Deity*
doth not stand still, but worketh and riseth up
without *intermission*, as a pleasant wrestling,
moving or struggling.

98. Like *two* creatures which in *great love*

[1] Three Principles.

[2] Threefold Life.

[3] [See Eds.' Note, p. ix.]

play together, embracing, struggling and wrestling the one with the other; now one is above, by and by the other, and when *one* hath overcome it yieldeth or giveth over, and letteth the *other* rise up again.

99. Thou mayest also understand it thus, in a similitude, as when *seven persons* had begun a friendly sport and play, where one gets the upper hand above another, and a *third* comes to help *that one* which is overcome; and so there is a pleasant friendly sporting among them; whereas indeed they all have one and the *same* agreement or love-will together, and yet strive and fight or vie one against another in a way of *love*, in sporting and pastime.

100. Thus also is the *working* of the six spirits of God in the seventh; suddenly *one* of them hath a strong rising up, suddenly *another*; and thus they wrestle in love one with another.

101. When the light riseth up in this striving, then the Holy Ghost moveth in the power of the light, in the play of the other six spirits, and so in the seventh *spring up* all manner of fruits of life, and *all manner* of colours and vegetations, or ideas and forms.

102. Now as that quality is which is *strongest*, so the body of the fruit is imaged, and the colours also; in this striving or wrestling the *Deity* formeth itself into infinite and unsearchable variety of kinds and manners of images or ideas.

103. For the seven spirits are the *seven* head sources or springs, and when *Mercurius* riseth up therein, that stirreth all, and the bitter quality moveth it, and *distinguisheth* it, and the astringent *drieth* it up.

[104. " Nature *and the* Ternary *are not one and* " *the same ; they are distinct, though the Ternary* " *dwelleth in nature, but unapprehended, and yet* " *is an eternal band, as is plainly unfolded in our* " *second and third books.*"]

Now observe here, how the Imaging in Nature is in the seventh Spirit.

105. The sweet water is the *beginning* of nature, and the astringent quality draweth or attracteth it together, that it becomes natural and *creatural*, to speak in an angelical way.

106. Now being drawn together, it looketh like *azure* or sky-colour blue, but when the light or flash riseth up therein, then it looketh like the precious jaspis or *jasper stone*, or as I may call it in my language, a glassy sea, on which the sun shineth, and that very clear and bright.

107. But when the bitter quality riseth up therein, then it divideth and formeth itself, as if it were *alive* or lively, or as if the life did rise up there, in a *greenish* flourishing manner and form, like a green flash of lightning, to speak after the manner of men, so that it dazzleth a man's eyes, and *blindeth* him.

108. But when the heat riseth up therein, then the green form inclineth to a half red or *ruddy* form, as when a carbuncle stone shineth from the green flash or *beam* of light.

109. But when the light, which is the Son of God, shineth into this sea of nature, then it getteth its *yellowish* and whitish colour, which I cannot compare to anything ; you must be content to stay or tarry with this aspect or vision, till you *come into* the other life.

110. For this now is the true heaven of nature, which is out of or from God, wherein the *holy angels* dwell, and out of which they were created in the beginning.

111. Behold now, when the *Mercurius* or tone in this nature-heaven riseth up, there the divine and angelical joyfulness riseth up, for therein rise up forms, imagings, colours and angelical *fruits*, which blossom curiously, grow, spring, flourish and stand in *perfection*, as to all manner of bearing or fruit trees, plants and springing growths, of a gracious, comely, lovely, amiable, blessed prospect, vision or sight to be looked upon, with a most delicious, lovely, pleasant smell and taste.

112. *But here I speak with an angel's tongue, thou must not understand it earthly, like unto this world.*

113. It is with *Mercurius* in this manner or form also. Thou must *not* think that there is

any hard beating, striking, toning or sounding, or whistling and piping in the Deity, as when one taketh a huge trumpet, and bloweth in it, and maketh it to sound.

114. O *no*, dear man, thou half dead angel, that is not so, but all is done and consisteth in *power*; for the divine being standeth in power. But the holy angels sing, ring and trumpet forth with clear and *shrill sounding*; for to that end God hath made them out of himself, that they should increase and multiply the heavenly joy: [*And therefore were the angels made out of God.*]

115. Also such an image was *Adam*, as God created him, before his *Eve* was made out of him; but the corrupted *Salitter* did wrestle with the well-spring of life in *Adam*, till it overcame. And so *Adam* became weary, which made him fall into a *sleep*.   Here he was undone: And if the Barmhertzigkeit, or the *mercy* of God, had not come to help him, and made a *woman* out of him, he would have still continued asleep.

Of this we will speak in its proper Place.

116. This, as is mentioned above, is that fair, bright and holy heaven, which is thus in the *total* Deity, and which hath neither beginning nor end, whither no creature with its sense *can* reach.

117. Yet thou shouldst know this, that always in a place now *one* quality sheweth itself *more powerfully* than the others, now the second pre-

vaileth, now the third, then now the fourth, now again the fifth, now the sixth, then again now the seventh.

118. Thus there is an *eternal wrestling*, working and friendly amiable rising up of love ; where then in this rising up the Deity continually *sheweth* itself *more* and *more* wonderful, more incomprehensible and more unsearchable.

119. So that the holy angels cannot sufficiently *enough* rejoice themselves, nor sufficiently enough converse, walk and most lovingly sport therein, nor sufficiently enough sing that beautiful *Te Deum Laudamus*, We praise thee, O God, as to each quality of the great God, according to his wonderful revelation, and wisdom, and beauty, and fruit, and form.

120. For the qualities rise up *eternally*, and so there is not with them or among them either beginning, middle or end.

121. Although I have written here how all is come to be, and how all is framed, *formed* and imaged, and how the Deity riseth up, yet for all that thou must not think that it hath any rest, ceasing or extinction, and that afterwards it riseth up thus *again*.

122. O no : But I must write in *part* or by pieces, for the Reader's better understanding, that he might thereby apprehend *somewhat*, and so attain the sense and meaning thereof.

123. Nor must thou think that I have climbed

up aloft into heaven, and beheld it with my *carnal* or fleshly eyes. O no; hear me, thou *half-dead* angel, I am as thou art, and have no greater light in my *outward* being than thou hast.

124. Moreover, I am a *sinful* and mortal man, as well as thou, and I must every day and hour grapple, struggle and fight with the devil who afflicteth me in my corrupted lost nature, in the fierce or wrathful quality, which *is* in my flesh, as in all men continually.

125. Now I get the better of him, now he is too hard for me; yet for all that he hath *not* overcome or conquered me, though he often getteth the *advantage* over me : *For our life is as a perpetual warfare with the Devil.*

[126. " *This strife and battle is about that most* " *high, noble, victorious garland, till the cor-* " *rupted, perished Adamical man is killed and* " dead, *in which the devil hath an* access to man.

127. " *Of which the sophister will know* " *nothing ; for he is not generated of God, but is* " born of flesh and blood : *and though indeed the* " *birth standeth open for and towards him, yet* " *he will not enter ; for the devil withholds him :* " *God blindeth none.*"]

128. If he buffeteth me, then I must *retire* and draw back, but the divine power helpeth me *again*; then he also getteth a blow, and often loseth the day in the fight.

129. But when he is overcome, then the

heavenly gate openeth *in my spirit*, and then the
spirit seeth the divine and heavenly being; not
externally without the body, but in the fountain
or well-spring of the *heart* there riseth up the
flash in the *sensibility* or thoughts of the brain,
and therein the spirit doth contemplate or
meditate.

130. For *man* is made out of all the powers
of God, out of all the seven spirits of God, as
the *angels* also are. But now seeing man is
corrupted, therefore the divine birth doth not
always spring, qualify or operate in him; no,
nor in all men either: And though indeed it
springeth in him, yet the *high light* doth not
presently shine in all men; and though indeed
it doth shine, yet it is incomprehensible to the
corrupted nature.

131. For the Holy Ghost will not be caught,
held or *retained* in the *sinful* flesh, but riseth
up like a flash of lightning, as fire flashes and
sparkles out of a stone, when a man strikes fire
upon it.

132. But when the flash is caught in the
fountain of the heart, then the Holy Ghost riseth
up in the seven qualifying or fountain spirits,
into the brain, like the daybreak, dawning of the
day, or morning redness: Therein *sticketh* the
mark, aim or scope and knowledge.

133. For in *that light* the one seeth the others,
feeleth the others, smelleth the others, tasteth

the others, and heareth the others, and it is as if the whole Deity did rise up therein.

134. *Herein* the spirit seeth into the depth of the Deity; for in God, near and afar off is all one; and that same God, of whom I write in this book, is as well in his *Ternary* in the body of a holy soul, as in heaven.

135. From this God I take my knowledge, and from no other thing, neither will I know *any other thing* than that same God, and the same it is which maketh that assurance in my spirit, that I *steadfastly* believe and trust in him.

136. Though an angel from heaven should tell this [knowledge] to me, yet for all that I *could not* believe it; much less lay hold on it, for I should always doubt whether it were certainly so or no: But the *sun* itself ariseth in my spirit, and therefore I am most *sure* of it, and I myself do see the proceeding and birth of the holy angels, and of *all things* both in heaven and in this world.

137. For the holy soul is *one spirit with God*; though indeed it is a creature, yet it is *like* to the angels: Also the soul of man seeth much deeper than the angels; for the angels see only to* the heavenly pomp, but the soul seeth *both* the heavenly and the hellish, for it liveth *between* both.

* "see only to" (*sehen allein bis in*), "see only into," *i.e.* as far as into.

138. Therefore it must undergo * many hard bangs and pinches, and must every day and hour wrestle and struggle with the devil, that is, with the [1] *hellish qualities*, and so it liveth in great danger in this world; therefore this life is very well called the *valley of misery*, full of anguish, a *perpetual* hurliburly, pulling and haling, worrying, warring, fighting, struggling and striving.

[1] Or devilish conditions, inclinations and passions in us.

139. But the cold and *half*-dead body doth not *always* understand this fight of the soul: The body doth not know how it is with it, but is heavy and anxious; it goeth from one room or *business* to another; and from one place to another; it seeketh for ease and rest.

140. When it cometh thither, where it *would be*, yet it findeth no such thing; then doubtings and unbelief fall in between and come upon it; sometimes it seems to it as if God had *quite* cast it off; but it doth *not* understand the fight of the spirit, how the same is sometimes down, and sometimes gets aloft.

141. What vehement and furious war and fight there is between the *hellish* quality and the *heavenly*, which fire the devils *blow up*, and the holy angels *quench* it, I leave to every holy soul to consider of.

142. Thou must know that I write not here

---

* "it must undergo," etc. (*muss sich wol quetschen lassen*), "it must suffer itself to be crushed." See Ch. 19, par. 121.

as a story or history, as if it were *related* to me from another, but I must continually stand in that combat or battle, and I find it to be full of heavy strivings, wherein I am often struck down to the ground, as well as all other men.

143. But for the sake of the violent fight, and for the sake of the *earnestness* which we have together, this revelation hath been given me, and the vehement driving or impulse to bring it so to pass as to set all this down on *paper*.

144. But what the total sequel is, which may follow upon and after this, I do not *fully* know : Only sometimes, future Mysteries in the depth are shewn to me.

145. For when the flash riseth up in the centre, one seeth through and through, but cannot well apprehend or lay hold on it ; for it happeneth to such a one as when there is a tempest of *lightning*, where the flash of fire openeth itself, and suddenly vanisheth.

146. So it goes also in the soul, when it presseth or breaks quite through in its flight or *combat*, then it beholdeth the *Deity*, as a flash of lightning ; but the source, quality or fountain of sins covereth it suddenly again : For the *Old* Adam belongeth [1] to the earth, and doth not, with *this* flesh, belong [1] to the Deity. [1] Or into.

147. I do *not* write this for my own praise, but to that end that the Reader may know wherein my knowledge standeth, that he might not seek

that from me which I have not, or think me to
be *what I am not*.

148. But what I am, *that* are all men, who
wrestle in JESUS CHRIST our King for the
crown of the eternal joy, and live in the *hope* of
perfection; the *beginning* whereof is at the day
of the resurrection, which is now *shortly* near
at hand; which, in the circle of the rising or
horizon of the east in the flash, is very *well* to
be seen, in which nature sheweth itself as if it
would be daybreak.

149. Therefore take heed, that you be not
found asleep in your *sins*; truly the prudent
and the wise will take notice hereof, but the
wicked will *continue* in their sins.

150. They say, What ails the fool, when will
he have done with his dreaming? This is because
they are asleep in *fleshly* lusts. Well, well, you
shall see what kind of dream this will be.

151. I would willingly take ease and rest in
my *meekness*, if I were not put upon this work;
but *that* God who hath *made* the world is *too*
strong for me, I am the work of his hands, he
may set me and place me *where* he will.

152. Though I must be a *by-word* and spectacle
of scorn to the world and devils, yet my hope is
in God concerning the life to come; in him will I
venture to hazard myself, and not resist or *strive*
against the Spirit. *Amen.*

THE TWELFTH CHAPTER

Of the Nativity and [1] Proceeding forth or De-
scent of the Holy Angels, as also of their
Government, Order, and Heavenly joyous
Life.

[1] Rise, original, geniture, or springing forth.

[1. " VERBUM Domini, *The Word of the*
" Lord, by the Fiat *(that is, the say-*
" ing, Let there be angels), comprised the quali-
" fying or fountain spirits into a will; and that
" is the creation of the angels."]

Question.

2. Now the question is, What is properly an
angel ?

Answer.

Behold, when God [*Schuff*] created the angels,
then he created them out of the *seventh* qualifying or fountain spirit, which is nature, or the *holy*
heaven.

3. The word *Schuff* [created] thou must understand thus, as when a man says, [2] drawn together,
or [3] driven together; as the earth is *driven* or

[2] attracted.

[3] compacted.

compacted together : In like manner, when the whole God did move himself, then the astringent quality drew or drove together the *Salitter* of nature, and *dried* it, and so the angels came to be : Now *such* as the quality was in every place, in its moving, *such* also was the angel.

Observe the Depth.

4. There are seven spirits of God, all these *seven* have moved themselves, and the *light* therein hath moved itself also, and the *spirit*, which goeth forth out of the seven spirits of God, hath moved itself also.

5. Now the Creator intended, according to his *Ternary*, to create three [1] hosts, not one from another, but one *by* another,* as in a circle or sphere.

[1] armies, bands or companies.

6. Now observe : *As* the [2] spirits were therein in their moving, boiling or rising up, *so* also were the creatures : In the midst or centre of each host was the ·*heart* of each host incorporated or compacted together, out of which an angelical or great or chief prince proceeded or came to be.

[2] seven spirits of God.

7. And as the *Son* of God is generated in the midst or centre of the seven spirits of God, and is

* "not one from another, but one by another" (*nicht weit von einander, sondern eins am andern*), "not far [apart] from one another, but close [together] to one another." Instead of "far " and " close," St M., to bring out the idea more clearly, prints "*detachées*" (detached) and "*unies*" (united).

the life and Heart of the seven spirits of God, so
there was *one* angelical king created in the midst
or centre of his circumference, sphere, extent or
[1] region out of nature, also out of nature's heaven, [1] Or province.
out of the *power* of all the seven qualifying or
fountain spirits, and that now was the heart in
one host, and he had in him the quality, might,
power and strength of his *whole* host, and was
the fairest among them, or of them all.

8. Just as the Son of God is the heart and
life and strength of all the seven spirits of
God, so also is that *one* king of angels, in his
host.

9. And as there are seven principal qualities in
the *divine* power, out of which the Heart of God
is generated; so there are also some mighty
princely angels created in each host, according
to each head or chief quality, the number of
which I do not *exactly* know; and they are with
or near * the king, and are *leaders* of the other
angels.

10. Here thou must know that the angels are
not all of one quality, neither are they equal or
alike to one another in power and might: Indeed
every angel hath the power of all the seven
qualifying or fountain spirits, but in every one
there is somewhat of one quality more predominant and strong than another, and according
to that quality is he also glorified.

* " with or near " (*neben*), "by the side of, close to, near."

11. For such as the *Salitter* was in every place, at the time of creation, such also was the angel that came forth; and according to *that* quality which is strongest in an angel, he is also named and glorified.

12. As [in] the *flowers* in the meadows, every one receiveth its colour from its quality, and is named also according to its quality, so are the holy angels also: Some are strongest in the *astringent* quality, and those are of a [1]brownish light, and are nearest of quality to the cold.

[1] dusky or grey or dim white, like twilight.

13. So when the light of the Son of God shineth on them, then they are like a brownish or *purple* * flash of lightning, very bright and clear in their quality.

14. Some are of the quality of the *water*, and those are light, like the holy heaven; and when the light shineth on them, then they look like to a *crystalline* sea.

15. Some are strongest in the *bitter* quality, and they are like a [2]green precious stone, which sparkleth like a flash of lightning; and when the light shineth on them, then they shine and appear as a *greenish red*, as if a carbuncle did shine forth from it, or as if the life had its original there.

[2] Or *emerald*.

16. Some are of the quality of *heat*, and they

* "brownish or purple." Böhme uses only "*braun*," brown, and St M. renders it "*foncé*," darkish.

are the lightest and brightest of all, *yellowish* and reddish; and when the light shineth on them, they look like the flash or lightning of the Son of God.

17. Some are strongest in the quality of *love*, and those are a glance of the heavenly joyfulness, very light and *bright*; and when the light shineth on them, they look like [1] *light blue*, of a pleasant [1] Or *azure.* gloss, glance or lustre.

18. Some are strongest in the quality of the *tone* or sound, and those are light or bright also; and when the light shineth on them, they *look* like the *rising* of the flash of lightning, as if something would lift itself aloft there.

19. Some are of the quality of the *total* or whole nature, as a general mixture; and when the light shineth on them, they look like the holy *heaven*, which is formed out of all the spirits of God.

20. But the king is the heart of all the qualities, and hath his circumference, [2] *court*, [2] Or province. quarters or residence in the midst or centre, like a fountain: As the *sun* standeth in the midst among the planets, and is a king of the stars, and the heart of *nature* in this world, so great also is a *Cherubim* or king of angels.

21. As the six planets with the sun are leaders of hosts, and give up or submit their will to the sun, that it may reign and *work* in them, so all the angels give up or submit their will to the

king, and the *princely* angels are in *council* with the king.

22. But thou must know here that they all have a *love-will* one to another, none of them grudgeth the other* his form and *beauty*; for as it goeth among the spirits of God, so it goeth among these.

23. They all have *jointly* and equally the divine joy, and they equally enjoy the heavenly food, therein there is no difference.

24. Only in the colours and *strength* of power is there a difference, but *no* difference at all in the perfection; for every one hath in him the power of all the spirits of God; therefore when the light of the Son of God shineth on them, then each angel's quality sheweth itself by the *colour*.

25. I have reckoned up only some few of the forms and colours of them, but there are a *great many* more that might be written down, which I will omit for brevity's sake.

26. For as the Deity presenteth itself *infinitely* in its rising up, so there are unsearchable *varieties* of colour and form among the angels: I can shew thee no *right* similitude of it in this world, unless it be in a *blossoming* field of flowers in *May*, which yet is but a *dead* and earthly type.

---

* "none of them grudgeth the other," etc., "none grudgeth the other his form and beauty; for it is (or goeth) among them as among the spirits of God" (St Martin).

Of the Angelical Joy.

Question.

27. Now it may be asked, *What* then is it that the angels do in heaven? Or to what end and purpose hath God created them?

Answer.

28. You may observe this, you greedy, covetous, griping persons, you who in this world *seek* after pride, state, dignity, honour, fame, glory, power, money and goods, and *squeeze* out the sweat and blood of the poor, oppressed and distressed, and spend their labours upon your gallantry, bravery and stateliness, and *think* yourselves better than plain and simple lay, vulgar people, and suppose it is *what* God hath created you for.

Question.

Why hath God created angel-princes and not made them all *equal*, or alike?

Answer.

29. Behold, *God is the God of order*; and as it is, and as it goeth and moveth in his government in himself, that is, in his birth or geniture, and in his rising up, so also is the *order* of the angels.

30. Now as there are in him *chiefly* seven qualities, whereby the *whole* divine being is driven on, and sheweth itself infinitely in these

seven qualities, and yet these seven qualities are the chief or *prime* in the infiniteness, whereby the divine birth or geniture stands eternally in its order unchangeably:

31. And as in the *midst* or centre of the seven spirits of God the heart of life is generated, whence the divine joy riseth up; *thus* also is the order of angels.

32. The angel-princes were created according to the spirits of God, and the Cherubim according to the heart of God: And as the divine being worketh, so also do the angels.

33. That quality which riseth up in God's being, and chiefly sheweth itself in its *working*, as in the rising up of the tone or tune, or of the divine working, wrestling and fighting, that angelical prince who is most strongly *addicted* to that quality begins, in his rank or file and round, with his legions, with singing, ringing forth, dancing, rejoicing and jubilating.

34. This is *heavenly music*, for here every one singeth according to the voice of his quality, and the prince leadeth the choir or *chorus*, as a chanter or singing-master with his scholars; and the *king* rejoiceth and jubilateth with his angels, to the honour of the great God, and to the increasing and multiplying of the heavenly joys, and that is in the heart of God as a holy *sport* or scene; and to that end also are they created for the joy and honour of God.

35. Now when the heavenly music of the angel riseth up, then in the heavenly pomp, in the divine *Salitter*, there rise up all manner of vegetations, springings or sprouts, also all manner of figures, shapes or *ideas*, and all manner of colours; for the Deity presenteth, sheweth or discovereth itself in *endless* and unsearchable varieties of kinds, colours, ideas, forms and joys.

36. Now, that qualifying or fountain spirit in the *Deity* which doth shew itself then specially or more distinctly with its rising up and *love-wrestling*, as if it had become the prince or chief of them, that *very* angel-prince belonging to it beginneth instantly his heavenly music with his own legions, according to his quality, with singing, ringing forth piping melody, and in all the manners of heavenly *skill* and art, which riseth up in the spirits of God.

37. But when the centre in the midst riseth up, that is, when the birth or geniture of the Son of God sheweth itself specially or more distinctly, as a *triumph*, then there rise up the music, melodies or joys of all the *three* kingly governments or royal regiments of the whole creation of all the angels.

38. What manner of joy this *must* be, let every soul consider: I, in my corrupted nature, cannot apprehend it, much less can I write it.

39. By this song I invite or cite the Reader into the other life; there he himself will also be

of that choir or chorus, and then first will he give credit to this spirit. What he doth not understand here, that he will there behold [for himself].

40. Thou must know that this is not forged out of a stone; but when the flash riseth up in the centre, *then* the spirit seeth and knoweth it.

41. Therefore look to it, and be not too scornful in this place, else thou wilt be found a scorner and mocker before God, and then well mayest thou *fare* as king *Lucifer* did. Now it may be asked:

Question.

What then do the Angels when they sing not?

Answer.

42. Behold! what the Deity doth, that they do also, when the spirits of God *lovingly* generate one in another, and rise up one in another, as in a loving saluting, embracing, kissing and feeding one another; in which taste and smell the *life* riseth up, and the eternal refreshing; of which thou mayest read before at large.

43. Then the holy angels also walk and *converse* one with another friendly, graciously, amiably and blessedly in the heavenly circumference or region, and do behold the wonderful and pleasant form or *prospect* of heaven, and eat of the gracious, amiable, blessed and delicate fruits of *life*. Now thou wilt ask:

Question.

What do they talk of one with another?

Answer.

44. Behold! thou pompous, stately, *lofty* and proud man; the world is even *too narrow* for thee here, and thou thinkest there is *none* like thee, or equal to thee: Bethink thyself in this, whether thou hast *in thee* the manner, quality or condition of an angel, or of a devil.

To whom now shall I liken the Angels?

Answer.

45. I will liken them to *little* children who walk in the fields in *May*, among the *flowers*, and pluck them, and make dainty garlands and posies, carrying them in their hands *rejoicing*, and always talk together of the several forms or shapes of beautiful flowers, *leading* one another by the hand when they go to gather flowers.

46. And when they come home, they *shew* them to their parents; and the parents also rejoice in their children, and are merry and cheerly with them.

47. So do the holy angels likewise, they take one another by the *hand*, and walk together in the beautiful *May* of heaven, and parly or talk of the pleasant and fair spring or *fruits* in the heavenly pomp, and feed on the *delicate*, blessed

fruits of God, and make use of the beautiful heavenly flowers for their play or sport in their *scenes*, and make beautiful garlands, and rejoice in the delicious pleasant *May* of God.

48. Here is nothing but a cordial or hearty loving, a meek and gentle love, a friendly, courteous discourse, a gracious, amiable and *blessed* society, where the one always delighteth to see the others, and [where they delight] to honour one another.

49. They know of *no* malice, *cunning*, subtlety or deceit; but the divine fruits and pleasant loveliness are *common* among them; one may make use of these things *as well* as the others, there is no disfavour or hatred, no envy, no contrary or *opposite* will, but their hearts are knit together in love.

50. In this the *Deity* hath its highest delight, as parents have in their children, that its dear and beloved children in heaven behave themselves so well and so friendly; for the Deity in itself playeth *or sporteth* thus also, *one* qualifying or fountain spirit [springeth up] in another.

51. Therefore the angels can do no other than their Father doth, as also our angelical King JESUS CHRIST testified, when he was with us on earth, as it is written in the Gospel, where he saith: [1] *Verily the Son can do nothing of Himself; but what he seeth his Father do, the Son doth also:* Also, [2] *If you do not convert, and*

John v. 19.

[2] Matt. xviii. 3.

become like children, you cannot come into the kingdom of heaven.

52. Whereby he meaneth that *our hearts* should be knit together in love, as are the holy angels of God, and that we should deal friendly, courteously and kindly one with another, and love one another, and *prefer* one another in kindness and *respect*, as do the angels of God.

53. *Not* that we should *deceive* and belie one another, and tear the morsel out of others' mouths for very greediness and great covetousness, neither should one *outbrave* another in stateliness, fashions and *deportment*, and so despise another who cannot use his bad, devilish, cunning policy and *tricks*.

54. O no! the angels in heaven do *not* so; but they love one another, and rejoice in the beauty and loveliness of others, and none esteemeth or accounteth himself more excellent than the others; but *every* one hath his joy in the others, and rejoiceth in *another's* fair beauty, comely form and loveliness, whence then their love one towards another riseth up, so that they lead one another by the hand, and friendly kiss one another.

Observe the depth.

55. As when the flash of life riseth up in the centre of the *divine power*, wherein all the spirits of God attain their life, and highly rejoice, there is a loving and *holy* embracing, kissing, tasting,

touching or feeling, hearing, seeing and smelling, so also there is among the angels; when the one seeth, heareth, feeleth or toucheth another, then there riseth up in *his heart* the flash of life, and the one spirit embraceth the other, as it is in the Deity.

Observe here the Ground and highest Mystery of God's Angels.

56. If thou wilt now know from *whence* their love, humility and friendliness come, which rise up in their heart, then observe that which followeth:

57. Every angel is constituted as the *whole* Deity is, and is as a *little* god. For when God constituted the angels, he constituted or framed them *out of himself*.

58. Now God is the same in one place as he is in another; God is *everywhere* the Father, and Son, and Holy Ghost.

59. In these three names and *powers* stand heaven and this world, and all whatsoever thy heart can think upon, and though thou shouldst draw a little circle, which thou canst hardly look into, or which thou canst hardly discern, even less than the *smallest point* thou canst imagine, yet even *in that* is the *whole* divine power; and the Son of God is generated *therein*, and the Holy Ghost *therein* goeth forth from the Father and the Son; if not in love, then in wrath, as it is

written, [1] *With the holy thou art holy, and with* ¹ Psalm xviii. *the perverse thou art perverse.* 26.

60. They who *stir up* the wrath of God upon themselves, that wrath standeth also in *all* the spirits of God, in that place where it is awakened, stirred up or *provoked.* On the other side, where the love of God is awakened or stirred up, there it also standeth in the *full* birth or geniture of the *whole* Deity, of or in the place or thing wherein it is awakened.

61. Herein there is *no* difference, the angels are created, one as well as another, *all* out of the divine *Salitter* of the heavenly nature; only this is the difference between them, that when God constituted them, each quality in the great motion stood in the *highest* geniture or rising up.

62. Hence it is come to pass that the angels are of *various* and manifold qualities, and have several colours and beauties, and yet all out of or from God.

63. Yet *every* angel hath *all* the qualities of God in him, but one of them is strongest in him, after the same he is named, and in the same he is glorified.

64. Now, as the qualities in God *always* generate, rise up and heartily love the one the other, and the one always getteth its *life* from the other; and as the flash in the sweet water riseth up in the heat, from whence the life and the joy have their original; so it is also in an

angel, his *internal* birth or geniture is no otherwise than the external, which is without [apart from] him in God.

65. As the Son of God, without or distinct from the angels, is generated in the middle or central fountain *spring*, in the heat, in the sweet water, out of or from *all* the seven spirits of God, and re-enlighteneth back again all the seven spirits of God, *whence* they have their life and joy :

66. So also, in like manner, the Son of God in an angel is generated in the angel's middle or central fountain spring of the *heart* in the heat, in the sweet water, and re-enlighteneth back again all the seven qualifying spirits of *that* angel.

67. As the Holy Ghost goeth forth from the Father and the Son, and formeth, imageth, *figureth* or frameth and loveth *all* ; even so the Holy Ghost goeth forth in the angel, *into* his fellow brethren, and loveth them, and rejoiceth with them.

68. For there is no difference between the spirits of God and the angels, but *only this*, that the angels are *creatures*, and their *corporeal* being hath a beginning ; but their *power*, out of which they are created, is God himself, and is from eternity, and abideth in eternity.

69. Therefore their agility is as nimble and swift as the *thoughts* of a man, wherever they

would be, there also they are, instantly; moreover, they can be great or small, as they please.

70. *This is the true being of God in heaven,
yea heaven itself*: If thy eyes were opened, thou
wouldst see it plainly and clearly on earth, in *that*
place where thou art at present.

71. For since God can let the spirit of man see
it, which spirit is yet staying in the body, and
can reveal or manifest himself to him *in the flesh,*
surely he can well do it also when he is out of the
flesh, if he pleaseth.

72. O thou sinful house of *this* world, how art
thou encompassed with *hell* and *death*; awake,
the hour of thy regeneration is at hand; the daybreak, the day-spring, dawning or morning-redness
sheweth itself!

73. O thou foolish and dead world, *why* dost
thou require or demand *signs* and wonders? Is
thy whole body chilled and benumbed? Wilt
thou not awake from sleep?

74. Behold, a *great sign* is given thee, but thou
sleepest and seest it not: Therefore the Lord will
give thee a sign in his zeal or jealousy, which
thou hast awakened and *provoked* with thy sins.

*Of the whole Heavenly Delightfulness and
Habitation of all the Three Kingdoms of
Angels.*

75. Here the spirit sheweth that where every
angel is constituted, stated or settled, there *that*

place in the heavenly nature, wherein and out of which he is become a creature, is his *own* seat, which he possesseth by right of nature, as long as he abideth *in God's love.*

76. For it is the place which he hath had from *eternity*, before he was become a creature, and that *Salitter* stood in the same place out of which he existed, and *therefore* that seat remaineth to him, and is his by right of nature, as long as he moveth in God's love.

77. But thou must not think as if God were tied to it, and cannot or may not *expel* him from thence, if he should move or stir otherwise than God had created, settled or *stated* him at first.

78. For as long as he abideth in obedience and in love, the place is *his*, by right of nature; but when he exhalteth himself and kindleth that place in the wrathful fire, then he sets his Father's house on fire, and becomes a contrary will, or *opposite* to [against] the place out of which he is made, and maketh TWO out of that which was ONE before his exhaltation.

79. Now when he doth so, then he *keeps* his corporeal right of nature to himself, and that place also keepeth *its* own to itself: But seeing the *creature*, which hath a beginning, will oppose or set itself against the first being, which was before the creature was, and which had no beginning, and will needs spoil the place which is *none* of its making, wherein it was created a creature

in the love, and will *turn* that love into a wrath-fire, then it is only fair that the love should spew up the wrath-fire forth, together with the creature.

80. From hence also the [1]RIGHTS in this world exist, or have their original. For when a son resisteth his father, and striketh his father, then he loseth his paternal *inheritance*, and his father may thrust him out of his house; but so long as he continueth in obedience to his father, the father hath no right, authority or lawful power to disinherit him.

[1] Laws, customs, statutes, ordinances and polities.

81. This worldly [2]*Right* taketh its original from heaven; as also many other worldly rights, which are written in the books of *Moses*, take their beginning and original from the *divine nature* in heaven, which I shall demonstrate plainly in its due place, from the true ground in the Deity. Now one might object and say:

[2] *Jus.*

Objection.

Then an angel is fully bound and tied to that place in which he is created, and must not stir, nor can stir from thence.

Answer.

82. No: As little as the *spirits of God* are or will be tied in their rising up, that they should not move one among another, so little also are the *angels* quite [entirely] bound to their place.

83. For as the spirits of God rise up continually

one in another, and have a sport or game of love in their birth or geniture, and yet every spirit keepeth his natural *seat* or place in the birth or geniture of God; wherein it *never cometh to pass* that the heat is changed into the cold, or the cold into the heat, but each keepeth its natural place or *position*, and the one riseth up' in the other, from whence the life hath its original.

84. So the holy angels move, walk or *converse* in all the three kingdoms, one among another, whereby they conceive or receive their *conceptions*, one from the other; *that is*, from the other's beauty, comely form, friendliness, courtesy and virtue every one receives his highest joy, and yet *each* keepeth for his *own* propriety his natural seat or place in *which* he is become a creature.

85. Like one in this world, when he hath a dear and near kinsman, who *returns* home from *foreign* parts of the world, whom he had a very *hearty* desire and earnest longing to *see*, there is joy and friendly saluting, and bidding welcome, also a friendly loving discourse or conference between them, and so he treateth this loving and welcome *guest* in the best manner that he can; yet this is but cold water, in *respect* of the heavenly.

86. Thus the holy angels do one towards another; when the army or company of one kingdom cometh to the other, or when the army or com-

pany of one princely quality cometh to an army or company of another princely quality, there is nothing but mere loving * entertainment, saluting and *embracing* reception; a very gracious, amiable and blessed discourse and friendly respect; a very gracious, amiable, *blessed* and loving walking and playing together; a most *chaste* and humble exercise; a friendly kissing, and leading one another up and down: here beginneth the lovely choir and set *dancing*.

87. Like little children, when they go in *May* among the *flowers*, where many often meet together; there they have a friendly talk, and pluck or gather flowers many and diverse.

88. Now when this is done, they carry those flowers in their hands, and *begin* a merry round dance, and sing from the joy of their hearts, and rejoice. Thus also do the angels in heaven, when the *foreign* armies or companies meet together.

89. For the corrupted nature in this world *labours* in its utmost power and diligence, that it might bring forth heavenly forms, and many times little children might be their parents' school-masters and *teachers*, if parents could but understand, or would but take *notice* of them: But nowadays the corruption is unfortunately

---

* "nothing but mere loving," etc., lit., "nothing but pure love reception [or conception], gracious discourse and friendly deference; blessed intercourse, chaste and humble behaviour, friendly kissing and escorting [or leading], and here beginneth the lovely round dance."

with both young and old, and the proverb is
verified,

𝔚ie bie 𝔄lten fungen,
   So lerneten bie Jungen.

As the old ones sing,
   So th' young learn to ring.

90. By this high *humility* of the angels the
spirit admonisheth the children of this world,
that they should view and *examine* themselves,
whether they bear such a love one to another.
Whether there be such humility among them.
What kind of angels do they think they are.
And whether they are like to *these* or no : They
have [or possess] the *third* angelical kingdom
within themselves.

91. Behold, the spirit will here present a little
before thy eyes what *manner* of love, humility
and courteous friendliness there is in thee, thou
fair angelical *bride*; behold, I pray thee, thy fair
attire, What great joy may thy *bridegroom* take
in thee, thou beloved angel, that dancest daily
with the devil !

I.

92. First, If one be nowadays a *little* preferred
or advanced, and getteth but a little while into
an office, then others, that are in *no* preferment,
are no more *so* good as he, or fit for his company ;
he counteth the vulgar or layman his footstool,
he instantly endeavoureth by cunning and craft

to get the vulgar or layman's *goods* under his disposal; if he cannot compass it by tricks and *designs*, then he doth it by force, to satisfy his highmindedness.

93. If a simple man, that *cannot place* his words handsomely, cometh before him, then he taketh him up short, as if he were a *dog*; and if the man hath any business before him, then, in his eyes, only those of worldly esteem are in the right, and he lets them carry the cause, *right or wrong*: Take heed, Friend, what manner of princely angel indeed thou art; thou wilt find it well enough in the following chapter, concerning the fall of the devil; that will be *thy* looking-glass in which to see thyself.

II.

94. Secondly, If one nowadays hath learnt more in *worldly sciences*, or studied more than the vulgar or layman, in an instant no vulgar or layman is to be compared to him, because he [the layman] cannot *express* himself or speak according to art; nor [or, neither can he] follow the other's proud ways.

95. In brief, the *simple* plain man must be his *fool*, whereas he himself is indeed a proud angel, and is in his love but a *dead* man. This sort of *party* also will have its *looking-glass* in the following chapter.

III.

96. Thirdly, If one be *richer* nowadays than the other, then the *poorer* man is counted the fool; and if he can wear but better and more fashionable *clothes* or apparel than his neighbour, then the poorer man is *no more* worthy, or good enough to be in his company.

97. And so the old song is nowadays in full force and practice, which is this:

> Der Reich den Armen zwinget,
> Und ihm sein Schweiß abbringet,
> Daß nur sein Grosche Klinget.

> The rich man doth constrain the poor,
> And squeezeth out his sweat so sore,
> That's own great wealth abroad may roar.

These angels also are invited as guests to the next chapter for their looking-glass in which to see themselves.

IV.

98. Fourthly, There is for the generality such a *devilish* pride and stateliness, and such over-topping one another, such despising, belying, entrapping, circumventing, over-reaching, cheating, deceiving, betraying, extorting usury, coveting, envying, and hating one another, that the world *burneth* now as in the hellish fire: Woe, woe for ever!

99. O world, *where* is thy humility? *Where*

is thy angelical love? *Where* is thy courteous friendliness? At that very instant when the mouth saith, God save thee! the heart thinks, Yes, beware.

100. O thou excellent angelical kingdom, how comely dressed and adorned wert thou once? How hath the devil turned thee into a *murderous* den? Dost thou suppose thou standest now in the flower of thy beauty and glory? No! thou standest in the *midst* of hell: If thine eyes were but opened, thou wouldst see it.

101. Or dost thou think that the spirit is *drunken*, and doth not see thee? O, it seeth thee very well: Thy shame standeth quite naked before God, thou art an unchaste, wanton, lascivious woman, and goest a whoring day and night, and yet thou *sayest*, I am a chaste virgin.

102. O, how fair a looking-glass art thou, in the presence of the holy angels; do but smell thy sweet love and humility, doth it not smell or savour just like *hell*? All these parties are invited as guests to the following chapters.

Of the Kingly Primacy, or of the Power and Authority of the Three Angelical Kings.

103. As the Deity in its being is threefold, in that the efflux out of the seven spirits of God sheweth and generateth itself as *threefold*, viz. Father, Son, and Holy Ghost, *one* God; wherein the whole divine power consisteth, and all what-

soever is therein; and they are the *three Persons* in the Deity, and yet are not a divisible being or essence, but in one another as *one*:

104. So also, when God moved himself and created the *angels*, there came to be *three* special angels out of the best kernel of nature, out of the being of the *Ternary* in the *nature* of God, and in such power, authority and might, as hath the Ternary in the seven spirits of God; for the Ternary of God riseth up in the seven spirits of God, and is again the life and heart of all the seven spirits.

105. Thus also are the three angelical kings risen up, each in the nature of his host or place, and a natural lord of his place over the government of his angels; but the Ternary of the Deity retaineth to itself that place which is unalterable or unchangeable; and the king retaineth the dominion of the angels.

106. Now, as the Ternary of the Deity is one only being or substance in all *parts* in the whole Father, and is united together, as the members in man's *body*, and all places are as *one* place, though one place may have a different function from the others, as also the members of men have; yet it is the one body of God:

107. So also are the three angelical kingdoms *united* one in another, and not each *severed* asunder: No angelical king ought to say, This is my kingdom; or that there ought *no other*

king to come thereinto; though indeed it is his first *beginning*, original and natural inheritance, and remaineth also to be his: Yet *all* other kings and angels are his true natural brothers, generated out of or from one Father, and do inherit their Father's kingdom.

108. As the qualifying or fountain spirits of God have *each* of them the natural seat or possession of its birth or *geniture*, and retaineth its natural *place* to itself, and yet is, together with the other spirits, the one only God; so that if the other were not, *that* would not be either, and thus also they rise up one in the other:

109. So it is also with the chief or *principal* of the holy angels in his constitution; and is in no other *manner* than as it is in God; and therefore they live all friendly, peaceably and blessedly *one with another* in their Father's kingdom, as loving dear brethren; there are no bounds or bars how far any should go, and how far not.

Question.

Now the simple might ask, *Upon what do the angels walk?　Or upon what do they stay or set their feet?*

Answer.

110. I will here shew thee the right ground, and it is no otherwise in heaven than as thou here findest in the letter, for the spirit looketh

undisturbed into this depth, also it is very apprehensible.

111. The *whole* nature * of the heaven standeth in the seven qualifying or fountain spirits, and in the seventh consisteth *nature* or the apprehensibility of all the qualities: This now is very lightsome and solid † as a cloud, but very *transparent* and shining, like a chrystalline sea, so that a man can see through and through it all: Yet the whole depth upward and downward is wholly *thus.*

112. Now the angels also have such bodies, but more dry and close compacted or incorporated together, and their body also is the kernel of or out of nature, even the best or fairest splendour and *brightness* of or out of nature.

113. Now their foot doth stay upon the seventh spirit of God, which is solid ‡ like a cloud, and clear and *bright* as a chrystalline sea, wherein they walk upward and downward, which way soever they please. For their agility or nimbleness is as swift as the *divine power* itself, yet one angel

* "The whole nature," etc., lit., "The whole [universal] nature of the heavens consisteth in the virtue of the seven fountain-spirits, and in the seventh is (*bestehet*) nature or the apprehensibility (*Begreiflichkeit*) of all the qualities." The word "*Begreiflichkeit*" may be translated "intelligibility" and "palpability."

† "lightsome and solid" (*lichte und dicke*), "light [loose, open, like transparent material] and thick [in the sense of a certain degree of density, but not in the sense of solidity]."

‡ "solid" (*dicke*). See par. 111 above.

is more swift than another, and that according to the quality of each.

114. In that seventh spirit of nature rise up also the heavenly fruits and colours, and whatsoever is apprehensible or comprehensible, and is like to such a [1] *form* or manner as if the angels did dwell between heaven and earth in the deep, where they ascend and descend, and wherever they are, there their foot resteth, *as if* it stood upon the earth.

[1] Text **Forma.**

115. Antiquity hath represented the angels in pictures like men with wings, but they have *no need* of any wings, yet they have hands and feet as men have, but after a heavenly manner and kind.

116. At the day of the resurrection from the dead there will be no difference between the angels and men, they will be of one and the *same kind* of *form*; which I shall shew plainly in its due place; and our *King* JESUS CHRIST clearly testifieth the same, where he saith, [2] *In the resurrection they are like the angels of God.*

[2] Matt. xxii. 30.

Of the great Glory, Brightness and Beauty of the Three Angelical Kings.

117. This is the very cudgel or club which is flung at the *dog*, to make him run away; because of this song lord *Lucifer* could tear off his beard with regret [and vexation].

Observe here the Depth.

Concerning the King or great Prince MICHAEL.

118. MICHAEL signifieth the great *strength* or power of God, and beareth the name operatively, actually and in *deed*: For he is incorporated or consolidated together out of the seven qualifying or *fountain* spirits, as out of a kernel or seed of them, and standeth here now as in the stead of God the Father.

119. The meaning is *not* that he is God the Father, who consisteth in the seven spirits of the *whole* deep, and is not creaturely; but the meaning is, that in nature among the creatures there is also such a kind of creature, who is to reign among the *creatures*, who is *like* God the Father, as he is in the seven qualifying or fountain spirits.

119a. For when God made himself creaturely, then he made himself creaturely according to his *Ternary*: and as in God the *Ternary* is the greatest and chiefest, and yet his wonderful proportion, form and variety *cannot* be measured, in that he sheweth himself in his operation so *various* and manifold; so also hath he created three principal angel-princes, according to the *highest* primacy of his *Ternary*.

120. In accordance with that he created the princely-angels, according to the seven qualifying

or fountain spirits, answerable to their quality, viz. GABRIEL, an angel or prince of the tone or sound, or of swift or speedy messages; as also RAPHAEL; and others besides in the kingdom of MICHAEL.

121. Thou must not understand this, as if these royal angels were to rule in the *Deity*, that is, in the seven qualifying or fountain spirits of *God*, which are without or distinct from the creatures; no, but each over his creatures, or the creatures of his *own* dominion.

122. For as the *Ternary* of God reigneth over the infinite or *endless* being, and over the figures and several *various* forms or ideas in the Deity, and changeth, varieth and imageth or frameth the same:

123. So also are the three angelical kings lords over *their* angels, even to the heart and deepest ground, though they *cannot* corporeally or bodily vary or change themselves, as God himself *can* who hath created them; yet they rule them (viz. the angels) corporeally, and are bound or united to them, as body and soul are bound the one to the other.

124. For the king is their *head*, and they are the *members* of the king; and the [1] qualifying or fountain princely angels are the king's *counsellors*, or [2] *officers* in his affairs, like the five senses in man, or as the hands and feet, or the mouth, nostrils, eyes and ears, whereby the king *executeth* or accomplisheth his affairs.

[1] Or facultating, potentiating.

[2] instruments in employment.

125. Now as all angels are bound to the king, so is the king also bound to *God* his Creator, as body and soul; the body signifieth God; and the soul signifieth the angelical king, who is in the body of God, and is become a *creature* in the body of God, and abideth eternally in the body of God, as the soul doth in its nest. And therefore also hath God so highly glorified him, as his own *propriety*, or as the soul is glorified in the body.

126. Thus the king or great prince *Michael* looks like God the Father in his glorification, clarity or brightness, and is a king and prince of God upon the *mount* of God, and hath his office in the deep wherein he is created.

127. That circumference or space, region or province, wherein he and his angels are created, is *his* kingdom, and he is a *loving* son of God the Father in nature, a *creaturely* son, in whom the Father delighteth.

128. Thou must *not* compare him with the Heart or light of God, which is in the whole Father, which has neither beginning nor end, no more than hath God the Father himself.

129. For this prince *is* a creature, and *hath* a beginning, but he is *in* God the Father, and is bound and united with him *in his love*, as his dearly beloved son, whom he hath created out of himself.

130. Therefore he hath set upon him the *crown*

of honour, of might, power and authority, so that there is in heaven no higher nor more excellent nor mightier than he is, *except* God himself in his *Ternary.* And this is one king, rightly described, with a true ground in the knowledge of the spirit.

Of the second King LUCIFER, *now so called, because of his Fall.*

131. King LUCIFER, shut thy eyes here a little, and stop thy ears a little, that thou mayest neither hear nor see, or else thou wilt be horribly *ashamed* that another sitteth upon thy seat, and so thy shame shall be fully discovered yet before the end of the world, which thou hast kept so closely *concealed* in secret, and suppressed ever since the beginning of the world, wheresoever thou couldst : I will now describe thy kingly primacy, not for thee, but for the *benefit* of man.

132. This high and mighty, glorious and beautiful king, *lost* his right name in his fall : For he is now called LUCIFER, that is, one carried forth or expelled out of the light of God.

133. His name was *not so* at the beginning : for he was a creaturely prince or king of the heart of God in the bright light, even the brightest among the *three* kings of angels.

Of [1] *his Creation.*

[1] Lucifer's.

134. As *Michael* is created according to the quality, manner and property of God the Father,

so was *Lucifer* created according to the quality, condition and beauty of God the Son, and was bound to and united with him in love, as a dear son or heart, and his heart also stood in the *centre* of light, as if he had been God himself; and his beauty or brightness transcended all.

135. For his circumference, conception or chief mother, was the Son of God, and there he stood as a king or prince of God.

136. His court, province, place, region or quarters, wherein he dwelt with his whole army or company, and wherein he is become a *creature*, and which was his kingdom, is the created heaven and this world, *wherein* we dwell with our King JESUS CHRIST.

137. For our King sitteth in divine *omnipotence*, where king *Lucifer* sat, and on the kingly throne of *expulsed* Lucifer, and the kingdom of king Lucifer is now become HIS: O prince *Lucifer*, how dost thou relish that?

138. Now as God the Father is bound and united in great love with his Son, so was king Lucifer also bound with king *Michael* in great love, as one heart or one God, for the fountain or well-spring of the Son of God *hath* reached even into the heart of Lucifer.

139. Only, the light which he had in his body, he had for his *own* propriety, and while it shone with or agreeable to the light of the Son of God, which was externally without or distinct from

him, they both qualified, incorporated and united
together as one thing, though they were two,
yet they were bound or united together, as body
and soul.

140. And as the light of God reigneth in all
the *powers* of the Father, so he also reigned in
all *his* angels, as a mighty king of God, and wore
on his head the fairest crown of heaven.

141. Here at present I will leave him a little
scope, because I shall have so much to do concerning him in the next chapter. Let him make a
show a little yet here in the *crown*, it shall
suddenly be plucked away from him.

Of the third Angelical King, called URIEL.

142. This gracious, amiable, blessed prince and
king hath his *name* from the light, or from the
flash or going forth of the light, which signifieth
rightly *God the Holy Ghost*.

143. For as the Holy Ghost goeth forth from
the light, and formeth, figureth and *imageth* all,
and reigneth in all, such also is the power and
gracious, amiable blessedness of a Cherubim, who
is the king and heart of all his angels ; that is,
when his angels do but *behold* him they are all
then infected and *touched* with the will of their
king.

144. For as the will of the heart infects and
stirs all the members of the body, so that the
whole body doth as the *heart* hath *decreed* or

concluded; or as the Holy Ghost riseth up in the centre of the heart, and enlighteneth all the members in the *whole* body; so the Cherubim with his whole glance or lustre and will infects all his angels, so that they all are together as one body, and the *king* is the heart therein.

145. Now this glorious and beautiful prince is imaged and framed according to the kind and *quality* of the Holy Ghost, and is indeed a glorious and fair prince of God, and is united with the other princes in love, as *one* heart.

146. These are now the *three* princes of God in the heaven. And when the *flash* of *life*, that is, the Son of God, riseth up in the middle or central circle in the qualifying or fountain spirits of God, and sheweth itself triumphantly, then the Holy Ghost also riseth upwards triumphantly: In this rising up the Holy *Trinity* also riseth up in the heart of these three kings, and each of them triumpheth also according to his kind and quality.

147. In this rising up the armies or companies of *all* the angels of the *whole* heaven become triumphant and joyful, and that melodious *TE DEUM LAUDAMUS* (WE PRAISE THEE O GOD) riseth up.

148. In this rising up of the heart, the *Mercurius* in the heart is stirred up or awakened, as also in the whole *Salitter* of heaven there riseth up in the Deity the *miraculous*, wonderful

and fair beautiful imaging of heaven, in several manifold various colours and manners, and each spirit presenteth itself in its own peculiar form.

149.* I can compare this to nothing, except to the finest of [1] precious stones, such as the ruby, the emerald, the topaz, the onyx, the sapphire, the diamond, the jasper, the jacinth, the amethyst, the beryl, the sardonyx, the carbuncle and the like.

[1] Such as are mentioned in Exod. xxviii. 17; xxxix. 10, and Rev. xxi. 19.

150. In *such* manner and colours the [2] heaven of God's nature sheweth or presenteth itself in the rising up of the spirits of God: Now when the light of the Son of God *shineth* therein, then it is like a bright clear *sea* of the colours of the above-mentioned precious stones or jewels.

[2] Or God's nature's heaven.

Of the wonderful Proportion, Alteration or Variation, and Rising up of the Qualities in the heavenly Nature.

151. Seeing then the spirit bringeth into knowledge the *form* and manner of heaven, I cannot choose but write it thus down, and let his will be done, who will have it so.

152. Although the devil will raise scorners and mockers to *vilify* it, I do not much regard that; I am satisfied with this gracious, amiable and blessed *revelation* of God; they may mock so long till they find it by experience with eternal

* A new translation of this par. has been substituted for Sparrow's rendering.

shame, then the fountain of remorse or shame will surely *gnaw* them.

153. Also I have not gone up to heaven, and *beheld* it with my fleshly eyes, much less hath any told it me ; for though an angel should come *and tell it me*, yet I could not apprehend or *conceive* it without enlightenment from God, much *less* believe it.

154. For I should always stand in doubt, whether it were a good angel sent of God [1] or no, seeing the [1] devil can transform or clothe himself in the form of an angel of light, to seduce men.

155. But because it is *generated* in the centre or circle of life, as a bright shining light, like unto the heavenly birth or rising up of the Holy Ghost, with a fiery driving or impulse of the spirit, therefore I cannot resist or withstand it, though the *world* always make a mock of me for it.

156. The spirit testifieth that there is yet a very little time remaining, and then the flash in the whole circle of this world will rise up, to which end this spirit is a forerunner. *Messenger* and proclaimer of the day.

157. Then whatsoever man is not found in the *birth* of the Holy Ghost at that time, in him the birth will never rise at all, but he abideth in the quality or source of darkness, as a dead, hard flint-stone, in which the source or quality

of fierceness, wrath and corruption riseth up
eternally.

158. There he will be a mocker eternally in
the birth of the hellish abomination: for whatsoever quality the tree is of, such also is its fruit.

159. Thou livest between heaven and hell,
into whichsoever thou *sowest*, in that thou shalt
reap also, and that will be thy food in eternity:
If thou sowest scorn and contempt, thou wilt
also reap scorn and contempt, and that will be
thy food.

160. Therefore, O Child of man! have a care,
trust not too much upon *worldly* wisdom, it is
blind, and is born blind; but when the flash of
life is generated *therein*, then it is no more blind,
but seeth.

161. For Christ saith, [1] " *You must be born* ¹ John iii. 3,
anew, or else you cannot enter into the kingdom 7.
of heaven.

162. Truly it must be generated in such a
manner in the Holy Ghost: which riseth up in
the sweet spring or fountain-water of the heart,
in the flash.

163. *Therefore hath Christ ordained or insti-*
tuted the Baptism or New Birth or Regeneration
of the Holy Ghost, in the water, because the birth
of the light riseth up in the sweet water in the
heart.

164. Which is a very great Mystery, and hath
been also kept *secret* from all men since the

beginning of the world till *now* : which I will demonstrate and describe plainly in its due place.

Now observe the Form and Posture of Heaven.

165. When thou beholdest this world thou hast a *type* of heaven.

I. The *stars* signify or denote the angels : for as the stars must continue unaltered till the end of this time, so the *angels* also in the *eternal time* of heaven must remain unaltered for ever.

166. II. The *elements* signify or denote the wonderful proportion, variety, *change* and alteration of the form and posture of heaven : For as the deep * between the stars and earth always alter and change in their *form*, suddenly it is fair, bright and light, suddenly it is lowery and dark, now wind, then rain, now snow, suddenly the deep is blue or *azure*, suddenly greenish, by and by whitish, then suddenly again dusky.

167. Thus also is the change and alteration of *heaven* into many several colours and *forms*, but not in such a manner and kind as in this world, but all *according* to the rising up of the spirits of God, and the light of the Son of God shineth therein eternally : But the rising up in the birth differs in the *degrees* more at one time than at

---

* "For as the deep," etc. Or, "For as the deep between the stars and the earth always changeth in its form, being now fair and bright, now dull [or dark]; now [there is] wind, now rain, now snow; now is the deep azure, now greenish, now whitish, or again dark."

another.   *Therefore the wonderful wisdom of God is incomprehensible.*

168. III. The *earth* signifieth or denoteth the heavenly nature, or the seventh spirit of nature, in which the ideas or *images*, forms and colours rise up.

169. IV. The *birds* or *fowls, fishes* and *beasts*, signify and denote the several forms or shapes of figures in heaven.

170. Thou art to know this, for the spirit in the flash testifieth the same, that in heaven there arise *all manner* of figures or shapes like the beasts, fowls, birds and fishes of this world, but in a *heavenly* form or manner, clarity or brightness and kind, as also all manner of trees, plants and flowers.

171. But as they rise, so they go away again, for they are not incorporated or compacted together, as the angels are : for these figures are so formed in the birth of the rising qualities, in the spirit of nature or *nature-spirit.*

172. If a figure be imaged in a spirit, so that it *subsisteth* ; and if another spirit wrestleth with this, and gets the *better*, then it comes to be divided, and indeed changed or altered, all according to the *kind* of the qualities ; *and this is in God as a holy sport, play or scene.*

173. *Therefore* also the creatures, as beasts, fowls or birds, fishes and worms in this world, are not created to an eternal being, but to a

transitory one, as the figures in heaven also *pass away*.

174. This I set down here only for a manuduction or introduction : You will find it described more at large concerning the *creation* of this world.

THE THIRTEENTH CHAPTER

Of the terrible, doleful, and lamentable, miserable Fall of the Kingdom of Lucifer.

1. I WOULD have all proud, covetous, envious and wrathful men *invited* to look into this glass, and there they will see the original of their pride, covetousness, envy and wrath, also the *issue* and final requital or wages thereof.

2. The *learned* have produced many and various monsters concerning the beginning of sin, and original of the devil, and scuffled one with another about it; every one of them thought he had the axe by the handle, yet it continued hidden from them *all* till this very time.

3. But since it will henceforth be *fully* revealed, as in a clear looking-glass, therefore it may well be supposed or expected *that the great day of the revelation of God is now near at hand,* wherein the fierceness and the kindled fire will be *separated* from the light.

4. Therefore let none make himself stark blind,

for *the time of the restitution of whatsoever man hath lost is now near at hand: the day dawneth, or the morning-redness breaketh forth; it is high time to awake from sleep.*

Question.

Now it may be asked, *What is the source or fountain of the first sin of* Lucifer's *kingdom?*

Answer.

5. Here we must *again* take in hand the highest depth of the Deity, and see out of what king Lucifer became a creature, or what was the first source or fountain of evil or *malice* in him.

6. The devil and his *crew* continually excuse themselves, and so do all wicked men who are begotten in corruption, saying, God doth them *wrong* in thrusting them out or rejecting them.

7. Nay, this present world doth dare to say that God hath *decreed* or concluded it so in his *predestinate* purpose and council that some men should be *saved*, and some should be *damned*; and they say, to that end also God hath rejected prince *Lucifer*, that he should be a spectacle of God's *wrath*.

8. As if hell, or malice and evil, *had been* from eternity, and that it was in God's predestinate purpose that creatures should and *must* be therein; and so they pull and *hale* and bestir themselves to prove it by *Scripture*, though indeed

they have neither the knowledge of the *true* God, nor the *understanding* of the Scriptures, though also some erroneous things are *brewed* from the Scriptures.

9. Christ saith, [1] *The devil was a Murderer and liar from the beginning, and did not stand in the truth.* But seeing these justifiers and disputers assist the devil so steadfastly, and *pervert* God's truth, and change it into lies, in that they *make* of God a thirsty and fierce wrathful devil, and such a one as hath created and still willeth evil, so all of them, together with the devil, are *jointly* murderers and liars. [1] John viii. 44.

10. For as the devil is the *founder* and father of hell and damnation, and hath himself built and *prepared* for himself the hellish *quality* to be his royal seat, so also such writers and *scribblers* are the *master*-builders of lies and damnation, who help to confirm and establish the devil's lies, and to make of the merciful, loving and friendly God, a murderer and furious destroyer, and so pervert and turn the truth of God into lies.

11. For God saith in the Prophet, [2] *As true as I live, I have no delight or pleasure in the death of a sinner, but that he turn and live;* and in the *Psalms* it is thus, [3] *Thou art not a God that hast pleasure in wickedness.* [2] Ezek. xxxiii. 11. [3] Psalm v. 4.

12. Besides, God hath given laws to man, and hath *forbidden* the evil, and *commanded* the

good. Now if God would have the evil, and also the good, then he would be at odds with himself, and it would follow that there would be destruction or destructiveness in the *Deity*, one quality running counter against the other, and the one spoiling and corrupting the other.

13. Now how all this is come to pass, or how *wickedness* hath taken its first source, original and beginning, I will declare in the highest simplicity in the greatest depth.

14. To which end the spirit inviteth and citeth, summoneth or *warneth* all men that are seduced into errors by the devil, that they come and present themselves before the looking-glass of this *school*, wherein they shall see and inspect the murderous devil, even into his very heart.

15. Then he that will not take heed and *beware* of his lies, whilst he may very well do it, there is no *remedy* for him neither here nor hereafter : he that soweth and will *sow* with the devil, must *reap* with the devil also.

16. *In the centre of the flash it is shewn that the harvest is white already, wherein every one will reap what he hath sown.*

17. Here, my *entrusted* talent, which I have received, I will let out for interest, profit and increase, as I am commanded to do, and he that will deal with me * in. *this* way of gain or usury,

* "deal with me," etc., lit., "deal with me and make the best of it [*i.e.* of the talent]."

it shall be free for him, he may freely do it, *whether* he be a Christian, a Jew, a Turk or a Heathen; it is all the same to me; my warehouse shall stand open for every one, none shall be tricked or deceived, but shall be dealt with in all fairness.

18. Every one should here have a care to deal so well that he bring in some gain of *use-money* for his Master: for I am afraid that not every merchant will be *fitted* to deal with my wares; for to some they will be very strange and *uncouth*; neither will every one understand my language.

19. I would therefore have every one warned that he deal circumspectly and *warily*, and not be conceited that he is rich, and cannot grow poor; truly I have very admirable and *wonderful* wares to sell, every one will not have understanding and skill to know what to do with them.

20. Now if any one should in drunkenness or fulness * fall upon them, and plunge himself into perdition, let him bear his own blame; he hath need of a light *in his heart*, that his *understanding* and mind may be well governed.

21. Else let him forbear to come into my warehouse, or he will but deceive his own expectation; for the ware which I have to sell is very precious and dear, and requireth a very sharp and acute *understanding*: Therefore have a care, and do

---

* "in drunkenness or fulness" (*in seiner vollen Weise*), "as if in drunkenness [*i.e.* in the fulness of self-satisfaction]."

not climb aloft where you see no ladder is, else you will fall.

22. But to me is shewn the ladder of *Jacob,* upon which I am climbed up, even into heaven, and have received my ware, to offer for sale: Therefore if any one will climb up after me, let him take heed that he be not drunken, but he must be girt with the sword of the spirit.

23. For he must climb through a horrible deep, a *giddiness* will frequently come into his head; and besides, he must climb through the midst or centre of the kingdom of hell, and there he will feel by experience what a *deal* of scoffings and upbraidings he must endure.

24. In this combat I had many hard trials to my *heart's* grief: My sun was often eclipsed or *extinguished,* but did rise again; and the oftener it was eclipsed or put out, the *brighter* and clearer was its rising again.

25. I do not write this for my own *praise,* but that if it go so with you, you should not despair about it; for there belongeth and is requisite a mighty enduring hard labour and stoutness, for him that fighteth with the devil, *between* heaven and hell; for the devil is a potent prince.

26. Therefore have a care that thou put on the coat of mail or [1] *habergeon* of the spirit, else do not venture to come *near* my warehouse, or thou wilt deal wrongfully [evilly] with my wares.

[1] corslet or breast-plate.

27. Thou must *renounce* the devil and the world, if thou wilt enter into this fight, else thou wilt not overcome : But if thou *overcomest not*, then let my book alone, and meddle not with it, but *stick* to thy old matters, *else* thou wilt receive but evil wages for thy pains : [1] *Be not deceived,* [1] Gal. vi. 7. *God will not be mocked.*

28. Truly it is a narrow and strait passage or *entrance*, through the gates of hell, for them that will press *in* to God; they must endure many *pangs*, crushings and squeezings from the devil.

29. For the *human* flesh is very young and tender, and the *devil* is rough and hard, also dark, hot, bitter, astringent and cold, and so these *two* are very ill *matched.*

30. Therefore I seriously exhort the Reader, and would have him faithfully warned, as it were with a *Preface* to this great Mystery, that if he do *not* understand it, and yet longeth and would fain have the meaning or understanding thereof, that he would pray to God for his Holy Spirit, and that he would *enlighten* him with the same.

31. For without the illumination thereof you will *not understand* this Mystery; for there is a strong lock and bar before it *in the spirit of man,* that must be first unlocked or opened; and that, *no man* can do, for the Holy Ghost is the *only* key to do it withal.

32. Therefore if thou wilt have an open gate into the Deity, then thou must move, stir and walk *in God's love*; this I have set down here for thy consideration.

Now observe:

[1] Or faculty.

[2] NATURA.

33. Every angel is created in the *seventh* [1] quali-fying or fountain spirit, which is [2] N A T U R E, out of which his body is compacted or incorporated together, and his body is given him for a pro-priety, and the same is *free* to itself, as the whole Deity is free.

34. He hath no impulse or driving, without or distinct from himself; his impulse and mobility standeth *in his body*, [3] which is of such a kind and manner as the *whole* God is; and his light and knowledge, as also his life, is generated in that manner as the whole divine being is generated.

[3] Viz. the body.

35. For the body is the incorporated or com-pacted spirit of nature, and encompasseth or encloseth the other six spirits; these generate themselves *in the body*, just as it is in the *Deity*.

36. Now *Lucifer* had the fairest, most beautiful and most powerful body in heaven, of or among *all* the princes of God, and his light, which he hath, and which is continually generated in his body, that [light] hath incorporated itself *with* the Heart or Son of God, as if they were *one* thing.

37. But when he saw that he was so fair and beautiful, and found or felt his inward birth and

great power or authority, then his spirit, which he had generated in his body, and which is his ANIMAL (or animated) or *life*-spirit, or son or heart, exalted itself, intending to triumph over the divine birth, and to lift up or extol itself *above* the Heart of God.

[*Note, The author calls the soulish birth the* ANIMAL *birth, from* anima, *which signifieth the* soul; *but seeing the Scripture otherwise understandeth by the word* animal *the perished or corrupted* soul, *or* animalem hominem, *the* animal *man, or the corrupted natural man,* that is, the Adamical bestial man, *and so he being advertised of it, he altered that expression, and used it no more any further.*]*

Here observe the Depth.

38. In the middle or central fountain or well-spring, which is the heart, where the birth riseth up, the astringent or harsh quality rubs itself with the bitter and the hot; and there the *light* kindleth, which is the *son*, and of the son the light is always impregnated in its body, and that enlighteneth and maketh it *living*.

---

* The *Note* is printed by Gichtel in the 1682 edition, and is reproduced as a footnote by Schiebler. In the editions of 1715 and 1730 it is absent; but whenever the expression "animal spirit" occurs in the text, in this particular sense, it is invariably printed "animalischer (seelischer) Geist." See Ch. 15, pars. 42-49. In par. 42 Böhme himself has added a note on the meaning of this term.

39. Now that light in *Lucifer* was so fair, bright and beautiful, that he *excelled* the bright form of heaven, and in that light was perfect *understanding*; for all the seven qualifying or fountain spirits generate that same light.

40. But now the seven qualifying or fountain spirits are the father of the light, and may *permit* or suffer the birth of as much light as they please; and the light *cannot* exalt or raise itself higher than the qualifying or fountain spirits will permit or give it leave.

41. But when the light is generated, then it *enlighteneth* all the seven qualifying or fountain spirits, so that all seven are [become] understanding, and all seven do give their will to the *birth* of the light.

42. But now, every one hath power and might to *alter* its will in the birth of the light, according as there is *need*: Now if that be so, then the spirit cannot triumph thus, but must lay down its splendour.

43. Therefore it is that all seven spirits are in full power, every one of them hath the reins in its hand, that it may hold in and *check* the *generated* spirit from triumphing any higher than is *fit* for it.

44. But the seven spirits, which are in an angel, and which generate the light and understanding, are bound and united with the *whole* God, that they should not qualify any other way,

either higher or more vehemently, than God himself; but that there should be one and the same
manner and way between *them both*.

45. Seeing they are but a part or piece of
the whole, and not the whole itself, for God hath
therefore created them out of *himself*, that they
should qualify, operate or act in such a manner,
form and way as God himself doth.

46. But now the qualifying or fountain spirits
in *Lucifer* did not so; but they, seeing that they
sat in the highest primacy or *rank*, moved themselves so hard and strongly that the spirit which
they generated was very fiery, and climbed up in
the fountain of the heart, like a proud *damsel* or
virgin.

47. If the qualifying or fountain spirits had
moved, qualified or acted gently and lovely, as
they *did* before they became creaturely (as they
were *universally* in God, before the creation),
then had they generated also a gentle, lovely,
mild and meek son in themselves, which would
have been *like* to the Son of God; and then the
light in *Lucifer* and the light of the Son of God
had been *one* thing, one qualifying, operating,
acting and affecting, one and the same lovely
kissing, embracing and struggling.

48. For the great light, which is the Heart
of God, would have *played* meekly, mildly and
lovingly with the *small* light in *Lucifer*, as with
a young son, for the *little* son in *Lucifer* should

have been the dear *little* brother of the Heart of God.

49. To this end God the Father hath created the angels, that as he is manifold and *various* in his qualities, and in his *alteration* or variegation *** is incomprehensible in his love-play, so the *little* spirits also, or the little lights of the angels, which are as the Son of God, should play or sport very *gently* or lovely in the great light before the Heart of God, that the joy in the Heart of God might here be *increased*, and that so there might be a holy sport, scene or play in God.

50. The seven spirits of nature in an angel should play and rise up *gently* in God their Father, as they had done before their creaturely being, and rejoice in their new-born son, which they have generated out of *themselves*, which is the light and understanding of their body.

51. That light should rise very gently or mildly in the Heart of God, and *rejoice* in the light of God, as a child with its mother; and so there should be a hearty loving and friendly kissing, a very meek and pleasant taste or relish.

52. In this the tone should rise up and sound, with *singing* and ringing forth, in praising and jubilating : also all the qualities should rejoice therein, and every spirit should *exercise* or prac-

---

* "alteration or variegation" (*Veränderung*), "transformation," *i.e.* power of transformation.

tise its divine work or labour, as God the Father *himself* doth.

53. For the seven spirits had this in perfect knowledge, for they were united and *actuated* with God the Father, so that they *could all* see, feel, taste, smell and hear what God their Father *did*, or wrought and made.

54. But when they elevated themselves in a sharp or strong kindling, then they did *against* nature's right otherwise than God their Father did, and this was a stirring quality or rising up *against* or contrary to the whole Deity.

55. For they kindled the *Salitter* of the body, and generated a high triumphing son, which in the astringent quality was hard, rugged or rough, dark and cold, and in the sweet was *burning*, bitter and fiery ; the tone was a hard *fiery noise*; the love was a lofty *enmity* against God.

56. Here now stood the kindled bride in the seventh nature-spirit, like a *proud beast*; now she supposed she was beyond or above God, nothing was like her now : Love grew *cold*, the Heart of God could not touch it, .for there was a *contrary* will or opposition between them. The Heart of God moved very meekly and lovingly, and the heart of the angel moved very darkly, *hard*, cold and fiery.

57. The Heart of God should now *unite* and qualify with the heart of the angel, but that could *not* be ; for there was now hard against

soft, and sour against sweet, and dark against light, and fire against a pleasant gentle warmth, and a hard knocking * or rumbling against a loving melodious song.

Question.

Hearken, Lucifer, *Where lieth the fault now, that thou art become a devil? Is God in fault, as thou lyingly sayest?*

Answer.

58. O no, *thou* thyself art faulty, the qualifying or fountain spirits in thy body, which thou thyself art, have generated thee *such* a little son: Thou canst not say that God hath kindled the *Salitter* out of which he made thee, but thy qualifying or fountain spirits have done it; whereas thou wert clearly before a prince and a king of God.

59. Therefore, when thou sayest God created thee thus, or that he hath *without sufficient* cause spewed thee up out of thy place, then art thou a liar and murderer; for the *whole* heavenly host or army beareth witness against thee, that thou hast *thyself* erected and prepared this fierce quality for thyself.

60. If it be not so, then go before the face of God, and *justify* thyself. But thou seest it plain enough without that; and besides, thou darest not look on that matter: Wouldst not thou *fain*

* "hard knocking" (*Pochen*). See Ch. 10, par. 119.

have a friendly kiss of the Son of God, that thou mightest once be eased or refreshed? If thou art in the right, then do but once look upon HIM: Perhaps thou mayest be made sound or whole again.

61. But stay a little, *another* sitteth on thy throne, he is kissed, and he is an obedient son to his Father, and doth as the Father doth.

62. Stay yet a little while, and the *hellish* fire will kiss thee; in the meanwhile make much of this Latin, till more groweth out of it; thou wilt *suddenly* lose thy crown. Now one might ask,

What then, in Lucifer, *is properly that Enmity against God, for which he was thrust and driven out of his Place?*

63. Here I will shew you exactly the pith, kernel and *heart* of Lucifer, and then you will see what a devil is, or *how* he is become a *devil*. Therefore take heed, and do not invite or entertain him as a guest, for he is the arch-sworn enemy of God, and of all angels and men, and that in his eternity.

64. Now if thou understandest and apprehendest *this* aright, then thou wilt not make of God a devil, as some do, who say, *God hath created the evil*, and that his will is that some men should be lost; which men, that say so, help to increase the devil's *lies*, and bring upon themselves the severe judgment, by their

perverting God's *truths*, and so turning them into lies.

Now observe:

65. The whole Deity hath in its innermost or beginning birth, in the pith or kernel, a very tart, terrible *sharpness*, in which the astringent quality is a very horrible, tart, hard, dark and cold attraction or drawing together, like *winter*, when there is a fierce, bitter, cold frost, when water is frozen into ice, and besides it is very intolerable.

66. Then think or suppose, if in such a hard winter, when it is so cold, the *sun* should be taken away, what kind of hard frost, and how very rough, *fierce* and hard darkness would it be, wherein no life *could* subsist.

67. After such a manner and kind is the astringent quality in the innermost kernel or pith *in itself*, and to itself alone, without the other qualities *in God*; for the austereness or severity maketh the attraction or drawing together, and fixation or glutinousness of the body, and the hardness drieth it up, so that it subsisteth [1] as a creature.

¹ creaturely.

68. And the bitter quality is a *tearing*, penetrating and cutting bitter quality or source: for it *divideth* and driveth forth from the hard and astringent quality, and maketh the mobility.

69. Between these two qualities is heat generated from its hard and fierce bitter rubbing,

tearing and raging, which riseth up in the bitter and hard quality, as a *fierce* wrathful kindling, and presseth quite through, as a *hard* fiery *noise*.

70. From whence existeth the hard tone, and in that rising up or climbing, it is environed and *fixed* in the astringent quality, so that it becometh a body which subsisteth.

71. Now if there were *no* other quality in this body, which could quench the *fierceness* of these four qualities, then there [1] would be a perpetual enmity therein.   For the bitter [1] would be against the astringent, in that it stormeth or teareth so vehemently therein, and *breaketh open* the astringent.

72. Then the astringent also would be against the bitter, in that it attracteth, draweth together and holdeth fast the bitter *captive*, that it could not have its own course.

73. The heat would be against both, in that with its fierce, wrathful kindling and rising up it maketh all hot, *burning* and raging, and is fully or totally against the cold.

74. So the tone would be a great enmity in all the others, in that it penetrateth forcibly through all, like a *tyrant*.

75. *Thus, this is the very deepest and innermost hidden birth of God*, according to which he calleth himself *an angry* zealous or *jealous God*, as may be seen by the [2] Ten Commandments on mount *Sinai*.

[1] Or were.

[2] Exod. xx. 5. Deut. v. 9.

76. In this quality standeth *hell* and eternal perdition, as also the eternal enmity and murderous den, and such a creature the *devil* is come to be.

77. But now, seeing he is a sworn arch-enemy of God, and though indeed the disputants and helpers of the devil will needs force it so in *arguments* (that God willeth the good and also the evil, and that he hath created *some* men to damnation), therefore and thereupon the spirit of God *citeth* them, upon pain of eternal enmity, to come before this looking-glass, wherein their *heart* shall be laid open ; and they shall see *what* God is, and *who* the devil is, or *how* he is become a devil.

78. If thy heart be not bolted and barred up in death, through thy *stubborn* wilfulness and blasphemy, and *drowned* in horrible sins, purposing not to desist from them, or leave them, then *awake*, and behold ; I take heaven and earth, also the stars and elements, and all the creatures, and man himself also in his whole substance, to witness, and so I will prove it also *plainly* and clearly in its due place, with all these forementioned things, especially when we come to treat of the *creation* of all the creatures.

79. If these things will *not* give thee satisfaction, then pray to God that he would *open* thy heart, and then thou wilt know and *see* heaven and hell, as also the *whole* Deity with all its qualities ; and then no doubt thou wilt forbear,

and justify the devil no more : *I am not able to open thy heart for thee.*

Now observe the true ¹ birth or geniture of God.   ¹ Or the divine birth.

80. Behold, as I have mentioned above, the birth or geniture of God in its innermost being, in *these* four qualities, is thus sharp or tart.

Thou must understand it exactly.

81. The astringent quality is thus sharp in its own proper quality in *itself*, but it is not alone, or without the others ; neither is it generated of or in itself, as being wholly free, but the other six spirits generate it, and they also hold it by the reins, and may let their reins and *authority* go as far only as they please.

82. For the sweet spring or fountain-water is suddenly a whip, scourge or lash upon the astringent quality, and mitigateth, softeneth or suppleth it, so that it groweth very thin, gentle, mild and soft, as also very *bright*.

83. But that it is thus sharp in itself, is to the end that a *body* may be imaged or framed through its attracting or drawing together, otherwise the Deity *would not* subsist, much *less* a creature.

84. In this sharpness God is an all-comprehensible, and all-fixing or all-fastening sharp God : for the birth, geniture and sharpness of God is *thus* everywhere.

85. But if I should describe the Deity in its birth or *geniture* in a small round circle, in the highest depth, then it is *thus*:

In a Similitude.

86. Suppose a WHEEL standing before thee, with seven *wheels* one so made in the other that it could go on *all* sides, forward, backward and cross ways, without need of any turning back or stopping.*

87. In its going, that always-one wheel, in its turning about, *generateth* the others, and yet none of them vanish out of sight, but that all seven be visible or in sight.

88. The seven wheels always generating the *naves* in the midst or centre according to their turning about, so that the nave stand always free without alteration or removing, whether the wheels go forward or backward or cross ways or upward or downward.

89. The nave always generating the *spokes*, so that in their turning about they stand right and direct from the *nave* to the *fellies* of the wheel: and yet none of the *spokes* to be out of sight, but still turning about thus one with another, going whithersoever the *wind* driveth it, and that without need of any turning back or *stopping*.

* See Ch. 19, par. 81 *et seq.*

Now observe what I shall inform you in the
application of this.

90. The *seven wheels* are the seven spirits of
God, the one always generating the others, and
are like the turning about of a wheel, which hath
seven wheels *one in another*, and the one always
wheeleth itself otherwise than the others in its
station or position, and the seven wheels are
hooped round with *fellies*, like a round *globe*.

91. And yet that a man may see all the seven
wheels turning round about severally apart, as
also the whole *fitness* or compass of the frame,
with all its fellies and spokes and naves.

92. The *seven naves* in the midst or centre
being as it were *one nave*, which doth fit everywhere in the turning about, and the wheels continually generating these naves, and the naves
generating the spokes continually in all the
seven wheels, and yet none of the wheels, as
also none of the naves, nor any of the fellies
or spokes, *to be out of sight*, and as if this
wheel had *seven* wheels, and yet were all but
one wheel, and went always *forward*, whithersoever the wind drove it.

Now behold, and consider:

93. The seven wheels one in another, the one
always generating the others, and going on every
side, and yet none out of sight, or turning back;

these are the *seven* qualifying or fountain *spirits* of God the Father.

94. They generate in the seven wheels in each wheel a nave, and yet there are not seven naves, but *one* only, which fitteth in all the seven wheels : This is the heart or *innermost* body of the wheels, wherein the wheels run about, and that signifieth the *Son* of God.

95. For all the seven spirits of God the Father generate continually in their circle, and that is the Son of all the seven spirits, and all those qualify or *act* in his light, and [the Son] is in the midst or centre of the birth, and *holds together* all the seven spirits of God, and they in their birth turn about therewith thus.

96. That is, they climb either upward or downward, backward or forward, or crossways, and so the Heart of God is *always* in the midst or centre, and fitteth itself to every qualifying or fountain spirit.

97. Thus there is *one* Heart of God, and *not* seven, which is always generated from all the seven, and is the heart and *life* of all the seven.

98. Now the *spokes*, which are always generated from the naves and wheels, and which fit themselves to all the wheels in their turning, and are their root, stay and fastening in which they stand, and out of which they are generated, signify God the *Holy Ghost*, which goeth forth from the Father and the Son, even as the spokes go out

from the nave and wheel, and yet *abide* also *in* the wheel.

99. Now as the spokes are many, and go always about with and in the wheel, so the Holy Ghost is the *workmaster* in the wheel of God, and formeth, imageth and frameth all in the whole or total God.

100. Now this wheel hath seven wheels one in another, and one nave, which fitteth itself to all the seven wheels, and all the seven wheels *turn on that one nave*: Thus God is one God, with seven qualifying or fountain spirits one in another, where always one generateth the others, and yet is but one God, just as these seven wheels are but *one* wheel.

Now observe :

101. The wheel in its incorporated structure and frame signifieth the *astringent* quality, which attracteth or draweth together the whole corporeal being of the Deity, and holdeth it, and drieth it, so that it *subsisteth.*

102. The *sweet* spring or fountain-water is generated by the driving about or *rising up* of the spirits, for when the light is generated in the heat, then the astringent quality is amazed or terrified for great joy, and this is a submitting or lying down or growing thin, and the *hard* corporeal being sinketh down like a meekness or mildness.

103. Now the terror * or the *glance* of the light riseth up in the astringent quality very *gently* and shivering, and trembleth, which now in the *water* is bitter, and the light drieth it, and maketh it friendly and sweet.

104. Therein standeth *life* and *joy*; for the terror or flash riseth up in all the qualities, like the wheel before mentioned which turneth about, and then there all the seven spirits rise up one in another, and generate themselves, as in a *circle*, and the light is shining in the midst or centre of the seven spirits, and re-shineth back again in all the spirits, and all the spirits *triumph* therein, and rejoice in the light.

105. As the seven wheels turn about upon one nave, as upon their heart, which *holds* them, and they hold the nave, so the seven spirits generate the heart, and the *heart* holds the seven spirits, and so there arise *voices*, and *divine* joyfulness of ¹ hearty loving and kissing.

¹ Or glorious.

106. For when the spirits with their light move or boil, turn about and rise one in another, then the life is *always* generated; for one spirit always affordeth to the others its taste or relish, that is, it is *affected* by the others.

107. Thus one tasteth and feeleth another, and

* " the terror " (*der Schrack*). This word, peculiar to Böhme, is very aptly rendered by St M., "*explosion*" or "bursting forth." In the next par. it is made identical with "flash," "*Schrack oder Blitz.*"

in the sound one heareth another, and the tone presseth forth from all the seven spirits *towards* the heart, and riseth up in the heart in the flash of the light, and then rise up the voices and *joyfulness* of the Son of God; and all the seven spirits triumph and rejoice in the Heart of God, each according to its quality.

108. For in the light in the *sweet* water all astringency and hardness and bitterness and heat are mitigated and made pleasant, and so there is in the seven spirits nothing else but a *pleasant* striving, struggling and wonderful generating, like a divine holy sport or scene of God.

109. But their sharp or tart birth, of which I have written above, abideth *hidden* as a kernel, for it becometh mitigated by the light and the sweet water.

110. Just as a sour bitter green apple is *forced* by the sun, that it becometh very pleasant or lovely to be eaten, and yet all its qualities are tasted; so the Deity keepeth its qualities also, but striveth or struggleth gently, like a pleasant lovely sport or scene.

111. But if the qualifying or fountain spirits should *extol* or lift up themselves, and penetrate suddenly one into another, driving hard, rubbing and thronging, crowding or squeezing, then the sweet water would be *squeezed* out, and the fierce heat would be kindled, and then would rise up the *fire* of the seven spirits, as it did in *Lucifer*.

112. *This is now the true birth or geniture of the Deity, which hath been so from eternity in all corners and places whatsoever, and abideth so in all eternity.*

113. But in the kingdom of *Lucifer*, ¹the *destroyer*, it is otherwise, as I have written above concerning the *fierceness*; and in this world, which is now half kindled also, it is likewise after another manner, and will be so till the day of the restitution; of which I shall write when I treat concerning the *creation* of this world.

114. Now in this glorious, lovely and heavenly *Salitter* or divine qualities, the kingdom of *Lucifer* also was created without any greater motion than in the others.

115. For when *Lucifer* was created, he was altogether *perfect*, and was the fairest prince in heaven, adorned and endued with the fairest *clarity* or brightness of the Son of God.

116. But if *Lucifer* had been spoiled or destroyed in the moving of the creation, as *he pretendeth*, then he had *never had* his perfection, beauty and clarity, but would have been *presently* a fierce dark devil, and not a Cherubim.

Of the glorious Birth and Beauty of King Lucifer.

117. Behold, thou murderous and lying spirit! here I will describe thy *royal* birth, how thou wert in thy creation, how God created *thee*, and

how thou becamest so beautiful, and to what *end* God created thee.

118. If thou sayest any other thing than this, which heaven and earth and all the creatures testify, then thou liest; nay, the whole *Deity* testifieth against thee, that God created thee for his *praise* out of himself, to be a prince and king of God, as he did prince *Michael*, and prince *Uriel*.

Now observe :

119. When the Deity moved itself to creation, and would form, image or frame creatures in *its body*, it kindled not the qualifying spirits, else they would have *burnt* eternally, but it stirred them **very** gently or softly in the astringent quality.

120. That drew or attracted the divine *Salitter* together, and dried it, so that it became a *body*, and so the whole divine power of all the seven qualifying or fountain spirits of that place or room, as far as that of the angels *reached*, was captivated in the body, and became the propriety of the body, which neither can nor will be destroyed again in *eternity*, but will remain the body's propriety or proper own in eternity.

121. Now the captivated or incorporated power of all the seven qualifying or fountain spirits had its *propriety* in the body, and is risen in the body, and hath generated itself in the same

manner as the whole *Deity* generateth itself from all the seven qualifying or fountain spirits.

122. One quality hath always generated the others alike, and none of them have vanished or gone out of sight, just as it is in the *whole* God; and then the whole body, as it is also in the Ternary, generated itself just as the Deity generateth itself, without or distinct from the body in the *Ternary*.

123. But this I must mention here, viz. that *Lucifer*, the king, was incorporated together out of his whole kingdom, as the heart of the whole place or room thereof, so *far* as his whole angelical host or army reached when it was created, and so far as that circumference or circle, region or quarter reached, wherein he with his angels became a creature, and which God before the time of creation had enclosed or concluded as a room or space for a kingdom, whose circuit or extent comprehendeth *heaven and this world*, as also the *deep of the earth*, and of the whole circle, sphere or circumference of this *whole world* of the heavens and stars.

124. According to the qualities were his [Lucifer's] qualifying or fountain princes created, which are his kingly counsellors, and so also were all his angels created.

125. Yet you are to know that *every* angel hath *all* the seven spirits in him, but one of the seven is chief or principal.

Now behold!

126. When the king was thus incorporated or *compacted* together, as one comprehending his whole kingdom, then instantly, the same hour, and in the same *moment*, when he was incorporated or compacted together, the birth of the Holy *Trinity* of God, which he had for a propriety in his body, rose up and generated itself without, distinct from the creature, in God.

["*Understand, for a propriety in the* liberty, "*not essentially, but as the fire shineth forth or* "*gloweth through the iron that is flaming hot,* "*and the iron remaineth iron still; or as the* "*light replenisheth or filleth the darkness, the* "*dark source or quality being changed into light,* "*and so becometh joyful, and yet in the centre* "*remaineth a darkness, which is understood to* "*be nature; for a spirit is replenished only with* "*the Majesty.*"]

127. For in the driving together of the body, presently likewise rose up the birth also in great triumph, as in a new-born king, *in God*; and all the seven qualifying or fountain spirits shewed themselves very joyful and *triumphing*.

128. And instantly, in the same *moment*, the light was generated and rose up out of the seven spirits in the centre of the heart, as a new-born son of the king, which also instantly, in a moment, transfigured the *body* of all the seven qualifying

or fountain spirits from the centre of the heart; and externally from without the light of the Son of God transfigured it.

129. For the birth of the new son in the heart of *Lucifer* also penetrated through the whole body, and was glorified from the Son of God, which was without, distinct from the body, and was in a friendly manner welcomed with the *greatest* beauty of heaven, according to the beauty of God the Son, and it was to him as a loving heart or propriety, with which the whole Deity qualified or *operated*.

130. Then instantly the spirit of the new-born son in the heart also went forth from the light of *Lucifer* through his *mouth*, and united, qualified or co-operated with the holy Spirit of God, and was with highest joy received and embraced, as a dear *little* brother.

131. Now here standeth the beauteous bride: what shall I write of her now? was she not a *Prince* of God, as also the most beautiful, moreover, in God's love also, and as a *dear* son of the creatures?

Of the horrible, proud, and henceforth doleful lamentable Beginning of Sin. The highest Depth.

Observe here:

132. When king *Lucifer* was thus fairly, gloriously, beauteously, highly and holily framed

or built, he should *surely* have now begun to praise, honour and magnify his *Creator*; and should do that which God his Creator doth.

133. *Viz.* God his Creator qualifieth or operateth very *meekly*, lovingly and joyfully, and one qualifying or fountain spirit of God always loveth the other, and infecteth itself with the other, and always helpeth the other to image, form and frame all in the *heavenly pomp*.

134. Whereby in the heavenly pomp such **fair** beauteous forms, ideas, *figures* and vegetations always spring up, as also *various* colours and fruits; and this the qualifying or fountain spirits of God do *in God*, as a holy play, sport or scene.

Now behold!

135. Seeing then God had incorporated or compacted together out of himself *eternal creatures*, they should not qualify or operate in the heavenly pomp in such a way and manner as to be *like God* himself.

136. No, by no means; for they were not thus imaged or framed for *that end*: For the Creator had for this cause incorporated or *compacted* the body of an angel together, to be more dry * than he [the Creator] is in his body, that he might be and *remain to be* God; so that the qualities

---

* "to be more dry," etc., lit., "to be more dry than He, in His Divinity was and remained."

should be harder and tougher, that the tone or sound might be audible.

137. So that when the seven qualities in an angel, in the centre of the heart, do *generate* the light and the spirit or *understanding*, that then that same spirit, which in the light of the heart goeth forth at the mouth of the angel, in the *divine* power, should, as an audible sound in the power of all the qualities *in God*, sing and ring forth as a melodious *music*, and in the forming, imaging, framing or qualifying of God, rise up as a pleasant, hearty, loving voice, in *God's forming*.

138. And when the Holy Ghost formeth the heavenly fruit, then should the tone, which should rise up in the praising of God from the angels, be also together in the *forming* or imaging of the fruit; and so on the other side again, the fruit should be the *food* of the angels.

139. Therefore also we pray in *Our Father*, [1] saying, ℭℑℬ uns unſer taglich Brodt (GIVE *us our daily bread*) so that the *tone* or word, ℭℑℬ (GIVE), which we thrust forth from our *centre* of the light, through the animated, animal or [2] soulish spirit, out at the *mouth* forth from us, into the divine power, should, in the divine power, as a [3] fellow-forming or [4] fellow-generating, *help* to image or frame unſer taglich Brodt (*our daily bread*), which afterwards Der Vater gibet Uns (*the Father giveth to us*) for food.

140. Then, when *our* tone is thus incorporated

[1] Matt. vi. 11.

[2] psychical.

[3] co-forming.

[4] co-generating.

in *God's* tone, so that the fruit is formed, imaged or framed, it must needs be *wholesome* or healthful for us, and so we are in God's love, and have that food to make use of, as by the right of nature, being our spirit in God's love did *help* to image and form the same.

141. *Herein standeth the innermost and greatest depth of God.* O man, consider thyself! I will more *largely* declare it in its due place.

142. Now for such an end hath God created the angels, and they do so too :* for their *spirit,* which in the centre or heart goeth forth from their light in the power of all the seven qualifying or fountain spirits, *that* goeth forth at their mouth, as God the Holy Ghost goeth forth from the Father and Son, and helpeth to form, image or frame all in God (that is to say, in the divine nature) through the *Mercurius,* song and speaking and sport or scene of joy.

143. For as God worketh in nature to the producing of *all* manner of forms, ideas, images, vegetations, springings, fruits and colours, so do the angels also, in very great simplicity or sincerity ; and though they should *scarce* touch the least twig,† or scarce rejoice in the beauteous

---

* "and they do so too." The translation is literal; the sense is, of course, "and they work it out," that is, they work out the end for which they have been created.

† "touch the least twig," lit., "ride upon a stick "=ride upon a hobby-horse. St M. translates simply, "play as children."

flowers in the heavenly *May*, and discourse and confer never so little, weakly, meanly or simply thereof; yet nevertheless that very tone or speech riseth up together in the divine *Salitter*, and helpeth to co-image and frame or form all.

144. Thou hast many *examples* thereof in this world, that if some creature or man look upon a thing, it perisheth because of the poison or venom in the creature : * On the other side again, some men, as also beasts and other creatures, can with their tone or words change or *alter* the malignity or evil of a thing, and bring it into a *right* form.

145. That now is the *divine* power, which all the creatures are subjected to ; for all whatsoever it is that liveth and moveth is in God, and *God himself is all*, and all whatsoever is formed or framed, is formed *out of* HIM, be it either out of love or out of wrath.

The Head-Spring or Fountain-Vein of Sin.

146. Now *Lucifer* being so royally imaged or framed, that his spirit in his forming and imaging rose up in him, and was received or embraced of God very excellently and lovingly, and was set or put into *glorification*, then instantly he should

---

* "that if some creature or man look upon a thing, it perisheth because of the poison or venom in the creature," or, "for many a creature or man cannot look upon a thing without corrupting (*verdirbet*) the same, because of the poison in that creature or man."

have begun his angelical *obedience* and course, and should have moved (as *God himself* did) as a loving son in the house of his Father; and that he did not.

147. But when his light was generated in him in his heart, and that his qualifying spirits were instantly affected or *environed* with the high light, they then became so highly rejoicing that they elevated themselves in their body against the right of nature, and presently began as it were a higher, *statelier*, more pompous or active qualifying or operation than God himself *exercised*.

148. But these spirits elevating themselves thus, and triumphing so eagerly and vehemently one in another, and rising up against the right of nature, by that means they kindled the qualifying or fountain spirits an exceeding deal too much; *viz.* the astringent quality attracted or compacted the *body* too hard together, so that the sweet water was *dried* up.

149. And the powerful and great bright flash, which was risen up in the sweet water in the *heat*, from whence the bitter quality existeth in the sweet water, that rubbed itself so horribly hard with the astringent quality, as if it would break in pieces for great *joy*.

150. For the flash was so bright, that it was as it were intolerable to the qualifying or fountain spirits, and therefore the bitter quality or source trembled and rubbed itself so hard in the astrin-

gent, that the heat was kindled *contrary* to the right of nature, and the astringent also dried up the sweet water by its hard attracting together.

151. But now the quality of heat was *so severe*, furious and eager, that it bereaved the astringent quality or source of its power; for the heat existeth in the fountain or source of the *sweet* water.

152. But the sweet water being dried up through the astringent attracting together, therefore could not the heat any more rise to a flame or to any light (for the light existeth in the unctuosity or *oiliness* of the water), but *glowed* like a red-hot iron, or like iron not quite glowing, but very *dimly* and darkly; or as if you should put a very hard *stone* into the fire, and should let it lie there in great heat as long as you please, yet it would not be *glowing* light, because it hath too little water or *oiliness* in it.

153. Thus now the heat kindled the dried water, and the light could *no more* elevate and kindle itself, for the water was dried up, and was quite consumed by the fire or great heat.

154. The meaning is not here, as if the spirit of the water were *swallowed* up or devoured, which dwelleth in all the seven qualities, but its quality or upper place or *predominancy* was changed into a dusky hot and sour quality.

155. For here in this place the sour quality hath taken its *first original* and beginning, which

now also is *inherited* in this world, which is not in heaven in God after *such* a manner at all, nor in any angel; for it is and signifieth the house of *affliction*, trouble and misery, and is a forgetfulness of all good.

156. Now when this was done, the qualifying or fountain spirits *rubbed* themselves one upon another in that manner and way as I have mentioned *above*, concerning the *figure* of the sevenfold wheel, for they ever do, and rise up one in another, to taste one another, or to *affect* one another, from whence life and love exist.

157. Now in all the spirits there was nothing else but a mere *hot*, fiery, *cold* and hard corruption, and so one evil quality tasted the others, whereby the whole body grew so very fierce and wrathful; for the heat was against the cold, and the cold against the *heat*.

158. So the sweet water being dried up, the bitter quality (which existed and was generated by the *first flash*, when the light kindled itself) rose up in the body through all the spirits, as if it would *destroy* the body, and so raved and raged like the rankest or worst poison.

159. From thence existed the *first* poison, wherein we poor men now in this world have enough to *chew* upon, and thereby the bitter *poisonous death* is come into the flesh.

160. Now in this raging and tearing the life of *Lucifer* was generated, that is, his *dear* little son

in the circle or centre of his heart; and what manner of life and dear little son came to be, I offer to any *rational* soul to consider of.

161. For *such* as the father was, *such* was the son also, *viz.* a dark, astringent, cold, hard, bitter, hot, sour, stinking fountain or source, and the love stood in the bitter quality, in its *penetrating* taste and relish, and became an enmity against all the qualifying or fountain spirits in the body of the high-minded *arrogant* king.

162. Thus the tone rose up through the penetrating of the bitter quality through the *heat* and *dried* water, and through the astringent hard quality, into the *heart*, into the little, new, dear son.

163. Here the spirit *went forth*, and as he was generated in the *heart*, so he went forth now at the *mouth*; but how welcome a guest he was before God, and in God, also before the holy angels of the other kingdoms, I leave to *thee* to consider of.

164. He should now have united with the Son of God, as one heart and one God: Alas for ever! Who can write or express this sufficiently?

THE FOURTEENTH CHAPTER

How Lucifer, *who was the most beautiful Angel in Heaven, is become the most horrible Devil.*

The House of the murderous Den.

1. HERE, *king Lucifer*, pull thy hat down over thy eyes, lest thou shouldst see how man will take off thy crown away from thee, thou canst *no more* rule in heaven; stand still a little while, we must first *view* thee, and observe what a beauteous fair bride thou art, and whether the filth of thy whoredom may *not* be cleansed and washed away from thee, that thou mayest be fair again; we will a little describe thy *chastity* and virtue.

2. *Come on* ye philosophers, and ye lawyers and advocates, that justify and defend king *Lucifer*! Come near and bring him to the *bar*, whilst he hath yet the *crown upon him*, for here we will hold a *court* of judgment against male-factors for him; if you can *maintain* his cause to be right, then he shall be your king; if not, then

347

he shall be turned out and cast down into hell; and another shall get his royal crown, who will *govern* better than he.

Now observe:

3. When *Lucifer* had thus horribly spoiled and destroyed himself, all his qualifying or fountain spirits were at enmity against God, for they all qualified or acted much *otherwise* than God, and so there *came to be* an eternal enmity between God and *Lucifer*.   But now it might be asked:

Question.

How long did Lucifer *stand in the Light of God?*

The Depth.

Answer.

4. When the royal body of *Lucifer* was incorporated or compacted together, in that very *hour* the light kindled itself also in *Lucifer*.

5. For as soon as his qualifying or fountain spirits in the building of the body *began* to qualify or operate, and to generate themselves according to the right of nature, *then* rose up the flash of life in the heart in the sweet spring or fountain-water, and so the royal body was *ready furnished or complete*, and the spirit went forth in the heart from the light through the mouth *into* the heart of God.

6. And so he was a most exceeding beautiful prince and king, and very *dear* and acceptable to the divine being, and was received and *embraced* with great joy.

7. In like manner also the spirit *went forth* from the heart into all the qualifying or fountain veins of the body, and kindled all the seven spirits, and so the royal body was glorified instantaneously, and there he stood as a king of God, in an unsearchable clarity or brightness, transcendently *excelling* the whole heavenly host or army.

8. Now in this clear and light flash the seven qualifying or fountain spirits were *instantly* kindled, as a man kindleth a fire, for they were affrighted at the terrible clarity or brightness of their spirit, and so instantly at the *first* flash *suddenly* became highly triumphing, proudly lifted up and joyful to excess, and so moved themselves towards a *higher birth*.

9. But if they had *continued* in their seats, and had qualified or operated, as [1] they had done from eternity, then that high light had *not hurt* them.

10. For they were *not* new spirits made of any *new* thing, but they were the *old* spirits, which had no beginning, which had been in God from eternity, and they *knew very well* the right of the Deity and the right of nature, and *how* they [the spirits] should move and stir.

11. Also when God figured or framed the body together, he did *not* beforehand destroy the quali-

[1] Viz. the seven spirits of nature, of which they were constituted.

fying or fountain spirits, but figured or framed the body of king *Lucifer* together out of the kernel of that which was the *best*, wherein was the best knowledge of all.

12. Else if the qualities had been dead beforehand, there had been a necessity for a new life, and it would have been in *doubt* whether the angels *could* have subsisted eternally.

Conceive it aright.

13. God created angels out of himself, for this reason, that they might be harder and drier incorporated or compacted together than the ideas, figures, shapes or forms, which, through the qualifying or operating of the spirits of God in nature rise up, and which also through the moving of the spirits *vanish* or pass away again ; that the light of the angels, in their hardness, should shine the clearer and *brighter*, and that the tone of the body should sound the clearer and shriller,* whereby the joyfulness should increase the more in God. *This was the cause that God created angels.*

14. But it is said, the angel generated *a new light*, or *a new spirit*. That is to be understood as followeth :

---

* "shriller," lit., "more sonorous." Sparrow has in most cases printed "shrill," where the German is "*hell*," "clear, distinct, sonorous." He probably intended thereby to emphasize the idea of pitch, over and above the idea of sonority.

15. When the qualifying or fountain spirits were incorporated or compacted together, then the light shone much brighter and clearer in the body, and from or out of the body, *than* it did *before*, in the *Salitter*; for there then rose up a much clearer and brighter flash in the body than before, whilst the *Salitter* was thin and dim.

16. Therefore the qualifying or fountain spirits became stately and proud, and supposed they had a *much fairer* little son or light than the Son of God was; and therefore they would also the more earnestly and eagerly qualify or operate, and elevate themselves, and so despised the qualifying or acting which is in God their Father; and they despised the birth of the Son of God, as also the *exit* or going forth of God the Holy Ghost, and supposed *they could do it*; because they were so gloriously incorporated or compacted together, therefore they would now *exalt* themselves gloriously and stately, and shew forth themselves, as if they were the most fair and beauteous *bride* of heaven.

17. *They knew very well* that they were not the whole or total God, but were only a *piece* or *part* thereof; they also knew very well how *far* their omnipotence reached or extended; and yet they would no more have their *old* condition, but would be higher than the whole or *total God*, and supposed thereby that they would have their place, region, quarters or court above

the whole or total Deity, above *all* kingdoms *whatsoever*.

18. Therefore they elevated or extolled themselves, intending to kindle or *inflame* the whole God, and to govern or rule the whole God by their power and might. All forms and *ideas* should rise up in the qualifying and acting of his [Lucifer's] spirit. He would be *lord of the Deity*, and would not endure any co-rival.*

19. *Now this is the root of covetousness, envy, pride and* [1] *wrath*; for in the *fierce* qualifying or acting and boiling rose up the wrath, and burnt like fire of heat and cold, and was also *bitter* as gall.

[1] Or anger.

20. For the qualifying or fountain spirits had in themselves no impulse from without, but the impulse to pride elevated itself *within* the body, in the council of the seven qualifying or fountain spirits; these *agreed* and united in a compact, that they alone would be God.

21. But because they could not begin it in their old seat, and so bring it to effect, therefore they *dissembled* or played the hypocrite together, and flattered one with another, and so combined, intending to extol themselves against the birth of God, and would needs qualify or work in the *highest depth*, and then nothing could be like them, seeing they were together the *most mighty* prince in God.

* "would not endure any co-rival," lit., "no other was to be lord beside him " (*neben*), alongside, by the side of.

22. The astringent quality was the *first* murderer, flatterer and hypocrite, for when it saw that it generated so fair and bright a light, then it compressed itself together *yet harder* than God had created it to be, intending to be *much more* terrible, and to draw together all in its whole region, circuit or circumference, and keep it *fast*, as a *stern* severe lord.

23. So then, in a degree, it effected somewhat, from whence earth and stones have their *original*; which I will write of when I treat concerning the *creation* of the world.

24. The bitter quality was the *second* murderer, which, when it rose up in the flash, did *tear* with breaking and great power in the astringent quality, as if it would break the *body* in pieces.

25. The astringent quality permitted this tearing, or else it was very well able to have *staid* and captivated the bitter spirit, and to bathe or *steep* it in the sweet water, till its high mind had been *allayed* and gone: But the astringent quality would needs have *such a little brother*, because such little brother was so serviceable to its turn; else, seeing the bitter spirit *taketh* its original from the astringent quality, as it were from its father, the astringent quality could well have *stopped* or hindered that.

26. The heat is the *third* murderous spirit, which *killed* its mother, the *sweet* water; but the astringent spirit is the cause thereof, for by its

stern, severe *attracting* together and hardening,
it hath thus vehemently awakened and kindled
the fire by the bitter quality; for the fire is the
sword of the astringent and bitter quality.

27. But since the fire riseth up in the sweet
water, therefore itself hath the *whip* or scourge
in its own power, and might have *staid* or kept
back the astringent quality in the water, but the
heat also became a *flatterer* or hypocrite, and
dissembled with the *great* quality, *viz.* the
astringent, and did *help* to destroy the sweet
water.

28. The tone is the *fourth* murderer; for it
taketh its *ringing* sound in the fire, in the sweet
water, and riseth up very gently and lovely in
the *whole* body.

29. Yet it did not so here, but after it was
risen up in the water, in the astringent quality,
it also dissembled [or played] with the astringent
quality and broke out or burst forth *furiously*,
like a thunder-clap, whereby it would prove and
shew forth *its new Deity*: and so the fire rose
up, as when there is a *tempest* of lightning,
intending thereby to be *so great* as to be above
all things in God.

30. And this they * practised so long till they
had *murdered* their mother, the sweet water;
and therein the whole *body* became a dark valley,

---

* "they," *i.e.* the tone, and the heat, and the bitter and
the astringent qualities.

and there was no more remedy or council in God that could help here: For love was turned into enmity, and the whole body became a black dark Teufel (*devil*).

31. Of the word (Teufel) Teu= hath its original from hard beating, drumming or thumping;* and the word or syllable =fel hath its original from the Falle, and so lord Lucifer is called Teufel (*devil*), and is no more called a *Cherubim* or *Seraphim*. Here it may be asked:

Question.

Could not God have hindered and prevented the pride of *Lucifer*, that he might have abstained from his high-mindedness?

Answer.

32. This is a high question, on which all those lay hold that *justify* and plead the cause of the devil; but they are all *cited* to appear at the court of justice held for trial of criminal *malefactors*: let them have a care *how* they plead for their master, else the sentence of judgment will be *pronounced* against him, and he will lose his *crown*.

The wonderful Revelation.

33. Behold, king *Lucifer* was the head in his whole region, circuit or circumference, also he

* "beating, drumming or thumping" (*Pochen*). See Ch. 10, par. 119.

was a *mighty* king, and was created out of the *kernel* or marrow of his whole region and circumference, also he would fain have kindled that whole circumference by his elevating, that so all might have burned and qualified, or operated *as he* did in his own body.

34. Though indeed the Deity, without or distinct from his body, would have meekly and gently qualified or *acted* towards him, and would have *enlightened* and exhorted him to *repentance*, yet now there was no other will in *Lucifer*, but that he would *needs* rule over the Son of God, and kindle that whole region or circumference, and in such a way he *himself* would be the *whole* God, above and over all the angelical hosts or armies.

35. Now when the Heart of God with his *meekness* and *love* made haste towards *Lucifer*, he despised it, and thought *himself* far better than it, and then stormed back again with fire and coldness in *hard* claps of thunder *against* the Son of God, supposing the Son of God must be in subjection under him, and that he himself was *lord*; for he *despised* the light of the Son of God.

Question.

Then thou askest: How? Had he such power?

Answer.

36. Yes, he had; for he was a *great part* of the Deity, and besides, was from or out of the kernel thereof, for he made an *attempt* also upon that king and great prince *Michael*, to spoil and destroy him, who at last *fought* with Lucifer, and overcame him, since [or because] the power of God in *Lucifer's* kingdom also fought vehemently against *its* king, till at last he was thrust down from his kingly seat, as one that was [1] *vanquished.*

[1] Rev. xii. 7–9.

Objection.

Now thou wilt say, God should have enlightened his *heart*, that he *might* have repented.

Answer.

37. No! Lucifer would receive no light other than his own, for he *scorned* the light of the Son of God, which did shine without, distinct from his body, seeing he had such a *glittering* light in himself, and so he elevated himself more and more, till his water was quite dried up and burnt, and his light was quite put out; and then *all was done* with him.

[" *This water here, is* the water of eternal life, " *generated in the light of the Majesty, but in* " *the centre it is like the sulphur or brimstone*

" *spirit, or* like unto aquafortis, *or the water of*
" *separation.*"]

Concerning the fall of all his angels, one might
ask :

Question.

How comes it, that at this time all his angels
did also fall ?

Answer.

38. As *this* lord commanded, so *his* subjects
obeyed; when he elevated himself, and would
be God, his angels, seeing it, *followed* their lord,
doing as he did, all made a proffer to *assault*
and storm the Deity.

39. For they were all in subjection under
Lucifer, and he ruled *in all* his angels, for he
was created out of the pith or kernel of that
Salitter, out of which *all* his angels were created,
and he was the heart and lord of all his angels.

40. *Therefore* they all did as he did, and all
would sit in the primacy of the Deity, and would
rule powerfully in the whole region, circuit or
circumference, over and above the *whole divine*
power : They were all of one *will,* and would
not suffer *the same* to be taken from them. Now
thou wilt ask :

Question.

Did *not* the whole, total or universal God *know*
this, before the time of the creation of angels,
that it would so come to pass ?

Answer.

41. *No* : For if God had known it before the time of the creation of angels, it had then been an eternal *predestinate* purposed will in God to have it so, and it had been *no enmity* against God, but God had indeed at the beginning created and made *him* a devil.

42. But God created and made him *a king of light*, and when he became disobedient, and would be above the whole or total God, then God *spewed him out* of his seat, and in the midst or *centre* of *our time* created another king out of the *same* Deity out of which lord *Lucifer* was created ; (understand it aright, out of the *Salitter*, which was without, *distinct* from the body of king *Lucifer*), and set him on the royal throne of *Lucifer*, and gave him might, authority and power, as *Lucifer* had before his fall.

43. *The same King is called* JESUS CHRIST, *who is the Son of God and of man.*

44. This I will demonstrate clearly and at large in its proper place.

[45. " Note, *This is explained in the second* " *and third books:* God *knew this very well* " *according to his* wrath, *but* not *according to* " *his love, according to which* God *is called* " God, *into which no fierceness nor imagination* " *entereth, neither is there any searching in the* " *love concerning the* hellish *creature.*

46. "*This foregoing* question *is understood or meant thus : as when I say*, God knoweth not the evil ; *also*, God willeth not the evil, *according to the tenure of the Scripture ; then I understand or mean that in his love (which alone is the one only* [1] Good, *and is alone called* God) *there is* no *glimpse of evil revealed or manifested ; otherwise, if any evil were revealed or manifested therein, then the love were not* meekness *and* humility *alone*.

¹ Or Goodness.

47. "*But in the outspeaking of his Word, wherein the nature of the spiritual world existeth, wherein perceptibility or sensibility is understood to consist, and wherein* God calleth himself an angry, *zealous or* jealous God, and a consuming fire, *therein, indeed*, God hath known the evil * *from eternity, and that in case he should once move himself* [2] *therein, that the source or quality thereof would become creaturely also, but therein is he* not called God, *but a consuming fire*.

² in that, according to which he is called a consuming fire.

48. "*I understand the abovesaid question magically, taking notice how* God's love *and* wrath *differ, and are distinguished, and how the knowledge of evil, viz. of the devil and of* the fall, *is discerned to differ from his well-*

* "therein, indeed, God hath known the evil," etc., lit., "therein, indeed, God hath known from eternity that, should he once move himself in that source or quality, the same would become creaturely also ; but therein [in that source] he is not called God," etc.

" *spring or source, from whence the* fall *also took*
" *its* original.

49. " *So also in God's* love *there is only the*
" *fountain and knowledge of* joyfulness, *for every*
" *science or root causeth or produceth its like.*

50. " *For if I should say,* God's love *had*
" *willed the* evil, *or that there was a false*
" [1] *science or root in God's love and meekness,* [1] Text,
" *then I should speak contrary to the Scripture :*   *Scientz.*
" *For what* God's love *knoweth* sensibly or
" *feelingly in itself, that it also willeth, and*
" *nothing else. And what God's wrath knoweth*
" *sensibly in itself, that he also knoweth, and*
" *nothing else.**

51. " *From hence, in the creation,* good *and*
" *evil are existed : I exhort the Reader to con-*
" *ceive our very deep sense aright, and not*
" *mistake or go astray here, but to read our* other
" *writings, where these things are sufficiently*
" *explained.*"]

Of the great Sin, and contrary or opposite Will ;
  and of the eternal Enmity *against* God *of*
  King Lucifer, *together with his whole Host*
  or Army.

52. This is the right looking-glass of man ;
before this court of justice for malefactors the

* The last clause of this par. does not appear in Sparrow's
translation, neither is it in the German edition of 1656, nor
in Schiebler's edition. It is in the German editions of 1682,
1715 and 1730.

spirit inviteth and citeth all men to stand as before a looking-glass, wherein they may see themselves, and what the *hidden, secret sin* is.

53. This hath remained hidden ever since the world began, and was never so fully and totally revealed in any *heart* of man : I myself also do wonder much more than the Reader can wonder at this high revelation or manifestation.

54. I do *not* write this for my own glory ; for my glory standeth in my hope of that which is to come : I am a poor sinner as well as other men, and I also ought to come before *this glass*.

55. But I marvel that God should reveal himself thus fully to such a simple man, and that God thus *impelleth* him also to set it down in writing ; whereas there are many *learned* writers who could set it forth and express it better, in a more *flourishing* style, and demonstrate it more exactly and fully than I, who am a *scorn* and a *fool* to the world.

56. But I neither can nor will oppose him ; for I often stood in great striving *against him*, that if it were not his impulse or will, that he would be pleased to take it *from me* ; but I find, that with my striving against him I have but merely gathered *stones* for this building.

57. Now I am climbed up and mounted so very high that I dare not look back, for fear a giddiness should overtake me, and I have now but a short *length* of ladder to the mark, to which it is

the whole desire, longing and delight of my heart to reach fully. When I go *upward* I have no giddiness at all ; but when I look back and would return, *then* am I giddy, and afraid to fall.

58. Therefore have I put my confidence in the strong God, and will *venture*, and see what will come of it. I have no more than one body, which nevertheless is mortal and corruptible, I willingly venture *that* ; if the light and knowledge of *my* God do but remain with me, then I have sufficiently enough for *this life and the life to come.*

59. Thus I will not be angry with my God, though for his *name's sake* I should endure shame, ignominy and reproach, which springeth, buddeth and blossometh for me *every day*, so that I am almost inured to it : I will sing with the prophet *David*, [1] *Though my body and soul should faint and fail, yet thou, O God, art my trust and confidence ; also my salvation, and the comfort of my heart.*

[1] Psalm lxxiii 26.

60. *Sin* hath *seven* kinds, forms, species or sorts ; among which there are *four* special wellsprings or sources : And the *eighth* kind or sort is the *house of death.*

Now observe :

61. The *seven forms* are the seven qualifying or fountain spirits of the body ; when these

are kindled each spirit generateth a special or particular enmity against God.

62. Out of these seven are generated *other four* new sons, and they together are the *new god*, which is wholly against the *old God*, as two professed armies of enemies, which have sworn eternal enmity one against the other.

The first Son is PRIDE. *The second Son is* COVET-OUSNESS. *The third Son is* ENVY. *The fourth Son is* WRATH.

63. Now let us view these in the ground from whence *all* hath its original, and see how it is an enmity against God : and therein you will see what is the beginning and *root of sin*, and wherefore *in God* it *cannot* be suffered or endured.

64. Therefore come on, ye *philosophers* and *lawyers*, you that will maintain, and undertake to prove it, that God created the *evil* also, and that he willeth the same ; also that it is his *predestinate* purpose that the *devil fell*, and that many *men* are *damned* ; otherwise God could have altered all, and turned it some other way.

The Citation, or Summons.

65. Here the spirit of our kingdom for the third time *citeth* you, together with your prince *Lucifer*, whom you defend and justify, before the final Court of Justice for criminal malefactors ; give in your answer there.

66. For as to these *seven* kinds or forms, and *four* new sons, the right shall be prosecuted in the heavenly Father's *house.*

67. If you can prove and maintain that the *seven spirits* of *Lucifer* have of right and equity generated *these four* new sons, so that they of *right and equity* should govern heaven and the whole Deity, then king *Lucifer* shall be re-enthroned, and set upon his seat, and his kingdom shall be restored to him again.

68. If *not*, then a *hell* or hole, burrow or dungeon shall be given to him for an everlasting prison, and *there* shall *he* together with his sons be imprisoned for *ever* : and you should take heed lest a Court of Justice be held, and pass upon you also.

69. Now seeing then you will plead the right of the *devil's* cause, wherewith shall he requite you, or with what *fee* shall he reward you? He hath nothing in his power but the hellish abomination ; what will then be your recompense? Guess, Sir, even the best of all that he hath, the best fruits and apples in his orchard, and the best perfumes and incense of his *garden.*

Of the First *Kind or* Form.

70. The *first* spirit is the *astringent* or harsh quality, which in God is a gentle attracting or drawing together, a drying and cooling or refreshing, and is made use of in and for the imaging or

forming of things ; and though in its depth it be somewhat sharp or *tart*, yet it tempereth itself with the *sweet water*, so that it is meek, soft, pleasant and full of joy.

71. When the light of the sweet water cometh *into it*, then it willingly, friendly and freely *yieldeth* up its birth thereunto, and maketh it [the sweet water] dry and shining *bright*.

72. When the tone or *tune* riseth up in the light, then it [the astringent quality] also giveth up its tone, tune and ringing sound very *gently* and brotherly thereunto.

73. Also it receiveth the *love* from all the spirits.

74. Also the *heat* favoureth it, giving way friendly, that it [the heat] may be cooled, and so the astringent quality is a friendly will in and with *all* the qualities ; it readily helpeth also to image or frame the spirit of *nature*, and to form therein all manner of shapes, figures, fruits and growths or vegetations, according to the *will* of all the six spirits.

75. It is a very *humble* father to its children, and loveth them *heartily*, and playeth with them friendly, for it is the right *father* of the *other six* spirits, which are generated in it, and it helps to generate them all.

76. Now when God constituted *Lucifer* with his host or army, he created them out of *this* friendly Deity, out of himself, out of the place

of heaven and of this world, there was no other matter to make them of, this living *Salitter* was very gently and softly attracted or drawn together without any *killing* or slaying it, or without any *great* stirring or motion.

77. These spirits, thus incorporated or compacted together, had the knowledge, the skill and the eternal, infinite and unbeginning *law* of God, and knew full well, I. How the Deity had generated them.

78. II. They knew also well, that the Heart of God had the *primacy* in the whole Deity.

78a. III. They knew well also, that they had no more for their proper own, to deal with and to *dispose of*, than their own compacted, incorporated *body*; for they saw very well that the Deity generated itself without, severally, distinct, apart from their body, as it had done *from eternity*.

79. IV. They knew likewise very well that they were not the *whole* room or place, but were therein to increase the joy and wonderful proportion, variety and *harmony* of that same place, and were to *accord*, qualify and act friendly with that room or place of the Deity, and in a friendly manner affect the qualities that are without, distinct from their bodies.

80. V. They had also *all power* to dispose of all the ideas, figures and growths or vegetations, as they would; all was a hearty love-play, sport or *scene* in God; they had not at all moved God

their *Creator* to any contrary will, though they had *broken* all the heavenly ideas, figures or vegetations and growths, and had made of them all *mere horses to ride on*; * God had still always caused enough of *others* to come up instead of them, for it had all *been* but a play or scene in God.

81. For to that very *end* also they were created, that they should play and sport with the ideas, figures and growths or vegetations, and *dispose* of them for their *own* use as they pleased.

82. For the ideas or figures have in a manner [1]framed themselves thus from eternity, and [2]have *passed away* and altered *again* through the qualifying or fountain spirits: *For this was the eternal play, sport or scene of God, before the times of the creation of the angels.*

[1] That is, have come and gone perpetually.

83. Thou hast a very good *example* and instance of this, if thou wilt but see, and wilt not be stark blind here; *viz.* in the beasts, fowls and all vegetations or growths in this world: *All these* were created before man was created, who is and signifieth the second host or army, which God created *instead* of expelled *Lucifer*, out of the place of *Lucifer*.

Question.

But now, what did the astringent or harsh quality do in *Lucifer*?

* "mere horses to ride on," that is, playthings.

Answer.

84. When God had thus *gently* incorporated it, or compacted it together, then it found and felt itself to be mighty and powerful, and saw that it had or possessed a *body* more beautiful than the figures were, that were without, distinct from it; *thereupon* it became high minded, and elevated itself in its body, and would be more severe and eager than the *Salitter* was, which was without, distinct from its body.

85. But seeing [1] it could not do anything *alone*, it *flattered* and played the hypocrite with the other spirits, so that they followed it as their *father*, and did all that they saw it do, each in its own quality.

[1] The astringent or harsh spirit.

86. Now being thus agreed, they generated also *such* a spirit, which came forth at the mouth, at the eyes, at the ears, and at the nostrils, and affected or *mixed* itself with the *Salitter* that was without, distinct from the body.

87. For the intent and purpose of the astringent or harsh quality, seeing it was so glorious, when the kernel was incorporated or compacted together out of the whole kingdom, its intent was, that it also through *its* spirit, which it did generate by or with the other spirits, would rule powerfully with the sharpness externally, without its own body, in the whole *Salitter* of God, and

that all should stand and be in or under its *own* power and authority.

88. It would image, frame and form all through its own spirit which it *generated*, as the whole Deity did; it would have the *primacy* in the whole Deity: This was its purpose.

89. But seeing it could not effect this in its true *natural* seat, it thereupon elevated itself, and kindled itself.

90. So by this kindling it kindled its *spirit* also, which now went forth at the mouth, the ears, the eyes and the nostrils, as a very fierce, *furious* spirit, and strove against the *Salitter* in its [the Salitter's] place, as a furious, storming, raging lord, and kindled the *Salitter*, and attracted or drew all forcibly together.

Thou must understand it aright.

91. The astringent or harsh quality in the spirit that *went forth* kindled the astringent or harsh quality which was in the place of its *region*, or in nature, *viz.* in the seventh qualifying or fountain spirit, and ruled powerfully in the astringent quality in the *Salitter*; and that, the astringent quality in the *Salitter* would not have, but strove with the sweet water against this spirit; but all would *not* help, the storm grew hotter and hotter, the longer the greater, till at length the astringent or harsh quality of the *Salitter* was kindled.

92. And so when this was done, then the storm grew *so hot* that the astringent quality drew the *Salitter* together, so that *hard stones* proceeded from it; whence the stones in *this* world have their original: and the water in the *Salitter* was also attracted or drawn together, so that it became very thick,* as it is now at present in this world.

93. But when the astringent quality was kindled in *Lucifer*, then it became very cold; for the *coldness* is its own proper spirit, and thereupon now it kindleth with its cold fire also all in the *Salitter*.

94. Hence the water of this world became so cold, dark and thick; and hence it is that all is become so hard and palpable, which was *not* so before the times of the angels.

95. This now was a great contrary will in the *divine Salitter*, a great battle and strife, and an eternal *enmity*.   But now thou wilt say,

Objection.

God should have withstood him, that it might not have come so far.

Answer.

96. O dear blind man! it was not a man nor a beast that stood here before God.   But it was

---

* "thick." The idea is that of density. The quality in the Salitter, that later became physical water, was "densified," and thus made more grossly manifest. Whence became water, as we have it.

God against *God*; one strong one against another: Besides, how should God withstand him? With the friendly *love*? That could not avail, for *Lucifer* did but *scorn* and despise *that*, and would himself be God.

97. Should God withstand him then with anger or wrath, (which indeed must be done at *length*), then God must have kindled himself in his qualities in the *Salitter*, wherein king *Lucifer* dwelt, and must in the strong zeal or jealousy strive and fight against him, which he did; and so this striving made this kingdom so dark, *waste* and evil, that another creation must *needs* afterwards follow upon it.

98. Ye philosophers and *jurists* or lawyers of prince *Lucifer*, here you must first defend the astringent or harsh quality in *Lucifer*, and *answer* whether it hath dealt righteously or *no*, and prove it in nature. I do not *accept* of your extorted, wrested, bowed, stretched, and far-fetched texts of Scripture, *brought in* by head and shoulders for a *proof*, but I will have living testimonies.

99. And I will also set before you *living* testimonies, *viz.* the created and comprehensible heaven, the stars, the elements, the creatures, the earth, stones, men, and lastly your dark, cold, hot, hard, rough, smoky, wicked prince *Lucifer* himself; *all these* are come into this present condition through his *elevation*.

100. Here bring in your *defence*, and answer for your spirit; if not, it will be condemned. For this is God's *jus*, right or law, which law hath no beginning, and is, that the child which is generated of the mother should be *humble* before the mother, and be obedient to her; for it hath its life and body from the *mother* who hath generated it.

101. Also the *house* of the mother, as long as the mother liveth, is not the child's proper own; but the mother keeps the child with her in love, she nourisheth it, and putteth on it the best and finest *attire* which she hath, and giveth the same to it for its *own*, that her joy may be increased by the child, and that she may have *joy* in it.

102. But when the child *rebelleth* and resisteth against the mother, and takes away all from the mother, and *domineers* over her, and moreover striketh at her, and forceth her to change into a *low* condition, contrary to right and equity, then it is but *just* that the child should be expelled out of the house, and left to sit behind the *hedge* * and quite lose its child's portion and inheritance.

103. Thus it was between God and his child *Lucifer*. The Father put on him the fairest attire, *hoping* to have joy in him: But when the child got the *robe* and ornament, he despised the Father, and would *domineer* over the Father,

---

* "left to sit "—a literal translation of a form which means, "to be put away," "to be kept out."

and would ruin his Father's house; and besides, struck at the Father, and would not be *advised* or taught to do otherwise.

Of the Second *Species, Form, Sort or Spirit of* Sin's *Beginning in* Lucifer.

104. The *second* spirit is the *water*: As the astringent or harsh quality is the *father* of the other six spirits, which attracteth or draweth them together, and so *holds* them, so the sweet water is the *mother* in which all spirits are conceived, kept and generated, that softeneth and saturateth them, wherein and whereby they get their life, and then the *light* and joyfulness riseth up therein.

105. Thus king *Lucifer* in the same manner did get the sweet water for his corporeal government, and indeed the very kernel and *best* thereof. For God put on to his little son the best ornament, robe and attire of all, hoping to have great joy in him.

Question.

Now what did this *astringent* or harsh quality with its *mother*, the sweet water?

Answer.

106. It flattered with the *bitter* quality, and with the *heat*, and persuaded them that they should elevate themselves and be *kindled*, and so together they would destroy their mother, and

turn her into a *sour* form or property, whereby they would domineer with their spirit very sharply over the *whole* Deity: All must bow down and incline to them; and they would form, frame, figure and image all with their *sharpness*.

107. According to this false or wicked conclusion and result they *agreed* to do one and the same thing, and so *dried up* the sweet water in *Lucifer's* body; the heat kindled it, and the astringent dried it, and then it became very sour and sharp.

108. When in this qualifying or acting they had generated the *spirit* of *Lucifer*, then the *life* of the spirit, which riseth up in the water, as also the *light*, became very sour and sharp.

109. Now this sour spirit also *stormed* with all its powers against the sweet water, which was without, distinct from the body, in God's *Salitter*, and thought *itself* must needs be the prime and chief, and should in its *own* power form, frame and image everything.

110. This was the *second enmity* against God, from whence is existed the *sour* quality in this world, for it was not so from eternity; as you have an *example* thereof in this, *viz.* if you set any *sweet* thing in the *warmth*, and let it stand therein, it groweth *sour* of itself; as also water, beer or wine in a vessel will do; but none of the other qualities alter, but only into a *stink*, which is caused by the quality of water. Now thou wilt ask,

Question.

Why did God suffer Lucifer's *evil spirit*, which proceeded out of the body of *Lucifer*, to come *into Himself*? Could God *not* hinder it?

Answer.

111. Thou must know, that between God and Lucifer there was no other difference, than there is between *parents* and *their children*; nay, there was yet a *nearer* relation between them: For as parents generate a child out of their body according to their image, and keep it in their house, as a natural *heir* of their bodies, and cherish it, thus near also is the *body* of Lucifer to the Deity.

112. For God had generated him out of his body, and therefore also made him the *heir* of his goods, and gave him for a possession the whole region or extent of the place in which he created him.

The highest Depth.

113. But here you must know what it was with which *Lucifer* fought against God, and so *moved God to anger.* For he could *not* do it with his body; for his body reached no farther than the place where he then stood; he could effect *little* with that, but it was *something else.*

Be attentive here.

114. The spirit, which is generated from or out of all the seven qualifying spirits in the *centre* of

the heart, the same doth (whilst it is yet in the body, when it is generated) qualify, mix or *act* in and with God, as one substance or thing, nor is there any difference.

115. And when that *same spirit*, which is generated in the body, seeth anything through the eyes, or heareth through the ears, or smelleth through the nostrils, then it is already in *that thing*, and worketh, laboureth or acteth therein, as in its own propriety.

116. And if the same be *pleasing* to it, it eateth thereof, and infecteth itself with the thing, and wrestleth therewith, and maketh a mixture or *temper* together; let the thing be as far off as it will, even so far as the *originality* of its kingdom in God reacheth, so far can the spirit govern or rule in a *moment*, and is withheld or hindered by nothing.

117. For it is and comprehendeth the *power*, as God the Holy Ghost doth; and in this there is no difference at all between God the Holy Ghost and the spirit of the body, but *only* this, that the Holy Spirit of God is the *whole fulness*, and the spirit of the body is but a *piece* or *part*, which presseth through the whole fulness, and wherever it cometh, there it is mixed or *affected* with the place, and presently ruleth *with* God in the same place.

118. For it is of God and in God, and cannot be withheld or hindered, but only by the *seven*

nature-spirits of the body, which generate the animated or soulish spirit; they have the *reins* in their hand, and generate it as they please.

["*God's Spirit hath all the well-springs, but* "*distinguisheth itself in three Principles, where* "*three sources or qualities arise, the first in the* "fire *according to the first Principle, and the* "second in the light *in the second Principle, and* "*the third in the* spirit *of this world in the* aërial "*and astral source.*"]

119. When the astringent or harsh quality, as the *father*, formeth the word or *son*, or spirit, then it stands captive in the centre of the heart, and is examined or *tried* by the other spirits, whether it be good or no. Now if it pleaseth the fire, then the fire letteth the *flash* (in which the bitter spirit standeth) go through the *sweet* water, wherein it conceiveth the *love*, and goeth therewith into the astringent quality.

120. Now when the flash returns with the love into the astringent quality again, together with the *new*-generated spirit or *will*, then the astringent quality *rejoiceth* in the new young son, and elevateth itself.

121. Then the *tone* lays hold thereon, and goeth forth therewith at the mouth, eyes, ears and nostrils, and executeth that which is decreed in the council of the seven spirits: for as the *decree* of the council is, so also is the spirit; and the *council* can alter the same as it will.

122. Therefore the original lust sticketh in the circle of the heart, in the *council* of the seven spirits; and as they generate the spirit, so also it is.

123. So in this manner lord Lucifer brought the *Deity* into anger and wrath; ["*that is, kindled the* eternal nature *according to the first Principle*;"] seeing he, together with all his angels, as a *malicious devil*, fought or strove against the Deity, intending to bring and subdue the *whole* circumference, circuit or region under his *innate* spirits, that they should form, frame, figure and image all, and the whole circumference, region or extent should *bow, yield* and suffer itself to be ruled and formed by the kindled *sharpness* of the innate spirits.

124. [1] As this hath a being or substance, *form* or condition in angels, so it hath also a being, substance, *form* or condition in man. Therefore bethink and consider yourselves, *you* that are proud, covetous, thievish, extorting usurers, calumniating, blasphemous, envious, and whorish or lascivious, what manner of little son or *spirit* you send into God.

["*The soul was originally comprehended in* " *the eternal nature with the Word* Fiat, *which is* " *God's nature according to the* first *Principle* " *and eternal original of nature; and if it* " *kindleth itself in the* original, *then it kindleth* " *God's* wrath *in the eternal nature.*"]

[1] Or as this condition is in angels, so there is such a condition in man also.

Objection.

Thou wilt say, We do not send this *into God*, but only into our *neighbour*, or into his work which we like and have a [1]mind to.

Answer.

125. Now shew thou me any *place*, to which thou sendeth thy covetous or lustful spirit, where God is *not*; be it to man, beasts, garments, fields, money or *anything* whatsoever. From him is all, and he is in all, [2]he himself is *all*, and he upholdeth and supporteth all.

Objection.

Then thou wilt say, But he is with his *wrath* in many things which are so hard and evil that they are not suitable to or capable of the Deity.

Answer.

126. Yes, dear man, all this is true: The wrath of God is certainly *everywhere* all over, in silver, gold, stones, fields, garments, beasts and men, and all whatsoever is comprehensible and palpable; otherwise they would not be so hard and harsh to be felt, as they are.

127. But thou must know that the *kernel* of love also sticketh in all in the hidden centre, unless it be altogether too evil; and *so* evil a thing man hath *no* liking for at all.

["*God possesseth* all, *only as to* nature, *he is*
"*not the* essence, *he possesseth* himself."]

Or dost thou think thou dost well, if thou
bathest or soakest thyself in God's wrath? Take
heed, that it doth *not kindle* thy body and soul,
and so thou wilt *burn* therein eternally, as befell
Lucifer.

128. But when God shall bring forth the hidden
things, at the end of this time, then you will
discern in what God's love or wrath hath *been*.
[1] Therefore have a care, and take heed, and *turn* [1] *Note.*
thy eyes from evil, or else thou undoest thyself,
and so bringest thyself into *perdition*.

129. *I take heaven and earth to witness, that I
have performed here as God hath revealed to me,
that it is his will*.

130. Thus hath king *Lucifer* in his body turned
the sweet water into a sour sharpness, intending
therewith, in his haughty-mindedness, to *rule* in
the *whole* Deity.

131. He hath brought it so far to pass that, in
this world, with that sharpness, he reacheth *into*
the *heart* of all living creatures, as also into
vegetables, leaves and grass, and into all other
things, as a king and prince of this world.

132. And if the divine love were *not yet* in the
whole nature of this world, and if we poor men
and creatures had not in and about us *the*
Champion *in the fight*, we should all perish in
a moment, in the hellish horrible abominations.

133. Therefore we sing very rightly thus;

Mitten wir im Leben seynd.   Mit dem Todt umfangen;
Wo sollen wir dann fliehen hin, das wir Gnad erlangen?
       Zu dir Herr Chrift alleine.
Da ift nun Der Held im Streit, Zu dem wir fliehen muffen,
       Welcher ift unfer König,
       JESUS CHRISTUS.

*In the midst of this our life, death doth us round
       embrace,*
*Whither shall we flee away, that we may obtain
       grace?*
       To thee Lord Christ alone.
*This is the Champion in the fight, to Him 'tis we
       must flee,*
       Who is our King,
       JESUS CHRIST.

134. He hath the Father's love in him, and
fighteth in *divine power* and might against the
kindled hellish abomination. To him we must
flee; and he it is that preserveth and *retaineth*
the love of God in all things in this world; else
all would be lost and perish.

     Nur hoffe, wart, und beit,
     Es ift Noch eine Kleine Zeit,
     Bis Teufels Reich darnieder leit.

     Now hope, pray, and wait
     But a small time, and then strait
     *Th' devil's kingdom will be quite down laid.**

* "Now hope, pray," etc., lit., "Only hope, wait and pray,
there is but a little time, until the kingdom of the devil is put
down."

135. Ye philosophers and jurists or lawyers, that make God to be as a devil, in saying that he willeth evil, bring in your plea, and answer once more here, and try whether you can *maintain* your cause to be just ; if not, then the sour, *sharp*, tart *spirit* in Lucifer shall be also condemned, as a destroyer and as the enemy of God, and of all his *heavenly* hosts and armies.

THE FIFTEENTH CHAPTER

Of the Third *Species, Kind or Form and
Manner of* Sin's *Beginning in* Lucifer.

1. THE third spirit in God is the *bitter* spirit,
which existeth in the flash of life : for the
flash of life riseth up in the sweet water through
the rubbing or *fretting* of the astringent and hot
quality ; but the body of the flash abideth in the
sweet water, subsisting very meekly as a *light*
or heart, and the flash is very trembling, and by
the terror, and fire, and water, and astringent
spirit, it becometh bitter through the *original* of
the water, in which it riseth up.

2. And that flash, or raging terror, or bitter
spirit, is caught or laid hold on by the astringent
quality, and in the clear bright light in the
astringent spirit is *glorified*, and exceeding highly
joyful ; which now is the mobility, or the root
of life, which in the astringent quality imageth,
frameth and formeth the word, or maketh it
distinct or separable, so that in the body a
thought or will doth exist.

3. Now this highly triumphing and joyous spirit is very fitly and excellently, in the divine *Salitter*, used to the imaging or framing; because it chiefly moveth in the tone or tune, and in the love, and is *nearest* to the heart of God in the birth, and bound or united therewith in joy, which indeed is itself also the spring and source of joy, or the *rising up* in the heart of God.

4. And there is no difference here, but only such as is between the body and soul in man; and so the *body* signifieth or resembleth the seven qualifying spirits of the Father; and the *soul* signifieth or resembleth the only begotten Son of God the Father.

[" *The* spirit *of the soul signifieth* or repre-" senteth *the* heart *of God; and the* soul *the eye* " *of God in the first Principle; as is declared in* " *our third book, Concerning the Threefold Life* " *of Man.*"]

5. Now as the body generateth the soul,* so the seven spirits of God generate the Son; and as the soul is a peculiar *distinct* thing when it is generated, and yet is *united* with the body, and cannot subsist without the body, so also is the *Son* of God, when he is generated, a peculiar,

---

* "as the body generateth the soul." Note, by St M.: "In order to avoid misunderstanding of these expressions, let the reader refer to the Preface, and to other passages, which will clearly shew how far the author was from materialistic doctrines."

several, distinct *thing* also, and yet cannot subsist without the *Father*.

Now observe,

6. Just in such a kind and manner also was the bitter quality in *Lucifer*, and [it] had no cause to elevate itself, neither had it *any* impulse to it from anything, but followed the proud loftiness of the astringent quality, as its father, and supposed also that it would reign in *its* kind and manner over the whole Deity, and so kindled itself in its elevation.

7. Now when it had *half*-generated the animated or soulish spirit in the body, that spirit became in this kind and manner a fierce, stinging, raging, kindled and tearing spirit, bitter as *gall*; and is rightly the quality of hell. fire, a very fierce and enemicitious hostile being.

8. Now when this spirit in the animated or soulish spirit, out of or from the heart of *Lucifer* and his legions, roved (*or speculated*) into the Deity; ["*that is, brought its will thereinto, as* "*into the* genitrix;"] then it was no other than a tearing, breaking, stinging, murdering and poisonous *burning*: Concerning which Christ said, [1] *The devil is a liar and murderer from the beginning; and hath not continued in the truth.*

[1] John viii. 44.

9. But *Lucifer* intended by that means to be above God; none could domineer and rule so terribly as he himself, all must stoop to him; he would with his spirit in the whole Deity rule

as a powerful king over all; seeing he was the
fairest and *most beautiful* he would needs *also*
be the most *potent*.

10. But he saw and knew very well the divine
meekness, and *humble* being in God his Father;
moreover he knew also very well, that it stood
in such meekness from eternity, and that he also
should generate in such meekness, as a loving
and *obedient* son.

11. But now seeing he was so beauteously and
gloriously imaged or formed as a king in nature,
his beauteous form and feature tickled* him,
and so he thought with himself, *I am now God,*
and formed or framed out of God, who can
vanquish me? Or who can alter or change me?
I *myself* will be lord, and with my sharpness
rule in all things, and my *body* shall be the
image which shall be worshipped; I will prepare
and erect for myself a *new* kingdom: for the
whole circumference, extent or region is mine,
I alone am God, and none else.

12. And in his pride he struck and smote
himself with darkness and blindness, and made
himself a *devil*, and that he must be, and abide
so *eternally*.

[" *In God he knew only the* Majesty, *and not*
" *the* Word *in the centre, which hath the fan or*
" *casting shovel: He blinded himself with the*
" astringent *darkness; for he would needs in-*

* "tickled" (*stach*), lit., "stung."

" *flame himself, and rule in the fire over the*
" *light, and over the meekness.*"]

13. Now when these evil, devilish spirits (understand the centre of the genitrix) moved or boiled
in God's *Salitter*, and made havock, or spoiled
all therein, then there was nothing but stinging,
burning, murdering, robbing, and a mere opposite
or contrary will.

14. For the heart of God delighted in love
and *meekness*; and *Lucifer* would needs turn the
same by force into a raging tyranny: So there
was nothing but enmity, and a contrary or
opposite will; for by force he kindled the *Salitter*
of God, which had *rested* from eternity, and stood
in its meekness.

15. Concerning this kindling in this circumference or extent, it is that God calls himself
[1] *an angry, zealous or jealous God against*
those that hate him; that is, against those who
kindle his wrath and *fierceness still more* with
their *diabolical* spirits, with swearing, cursing,
blaspheming, and all manner of furious fierceness
and wrath, which *stick* in the heart, with pride,
covetousness, envy and anger. All that whatsoever is in thee, thou castest into God; [" *that is,*
" *into the* genitrix *of nature, and therefore that*
" *must be proved and tried through the fire, and*
" *the soul's spirit also, and the* wickedness *or*
" *malice must abide and remain in the fire.*"]
Now thou askest, How can that be?

[1] Exod. xx. 5.
Deut. v. 9.

Answer.

16. When thou openest thy eyes, and seest the [1] being of God, then thou *prickest* as it were with thorns into the being of God, and movest or stirrest up the wrath and anger of God.

[1] Which is everywhere in this world, in every creature.

17. When a tone or noise soundeth in thy *ears*, so that thou receivest or catchest it up from the being of God, then thou infectest it, as if thou didst dart thunderclaps into it.

18. Consider what thou dost with thy *nostrils*, and with thy *mouth*, whence thy dear new-born little son rusheth forth with thy speech, as a little son of all the seven spirits; and observe whether it doth not *storm* and assault in God's *Salitter*, as *Lucifer* did.   O, there is no difference at all in this!

19. But again, on the other side, God saith, [2] *I am a merciful God to those that love me; those I will do good to, and bless them, to a thousand generations.*

[2] Exod. xx. 6. Deut. v. 10.

Here observe:

20. Such are those who, contrary to the kindled wrath-fire, do, with their *love*, meekness and industrious earnest yearnings and *kindlings* of love with their prayers, *quench* the wrath-fire, and press on against the kindled fierceness.

21. Here indeed is many a hard blow or crushing; for the kindled wrath-fire of God falls many times so heavy upon them, and they know not

where to bestow themselves; heavy mountains lie upon them, the *love-cross* presseth sore, and is heavy.

22. But this is their comfort and *strong helmet* against the fierceness and the kindled fire; according as the kingly prophet *David* saith, [1]*To the honest* or *the upright the light riseth up in the darkness.*

[1] Psalm cxii. 4.

23. In this strife and fight against the wrath of God, and the kindled fierceness of the *devils,* and of all *wicked* men, the light riseth up in the heart of the honest and upright; and the friendly love of God *embraceth* him, that he may not despair in his cross, but strive further still against the wrath and fierceness.

24. If there were not at all times some honest upright men on earth, who *quench* the wrath of God with their opposing, the hellish fire had kindled itself long ago; and then it would have been well seen *where* hell is, which men do *not* now believe.

25. But thus saith the spirit; as soon as the fierceness overcometh the opposition of love in this world, then the *fire* kindleth itself, and then there is *no* more *time* in this world.

26. But that the fierceness doth terribly burn now at present, it needs no proof here, for, by *woeful experience,* it is known as clear as the day. *Behold, there riseth up yet a little fire, in the opposition against the wrath, out of a singular especial love-restraint of God: When this also*

groweth weak, then is the end of this time. See *Sig. Rerum*, Ch. 10, par. 11.

27. But whether *Lucifer* hath done rightly, in that he hath awakened and stirred up the fierceness in the *Salitter* of God, whence this world is become stinging, venomous, thorny, rocky, envious and evil, false or wicked, let the *attorneys*, proctors, advocates and defenders of *Lucifer* answer, and plead and justify it if they can; if *not*, then this third *bitter*, stinging, venomous spirit shall be *condemned* also.

Of the Fourth *Kind, Species, Form or Manner of Sin's Beginning in* Lucifer.

28. The fourth spirit of God is *heat*, which is generated between the bitter and the astringent qualities, and is conceived or bred in the sweet water, and is *shining* and giving light, and is the true fountain of life.

29. For in the sweet water it is very meek, from whence love existeth, and is only a loving *warmth*, but no *fire*.

30. Though indeed it be in the hidden kernel of the fire's quality or original, yet *that* fire is not kindled or burning, for it is generated in the *sweet* water.

31. Now where the water is there is no burning fire, but a pleasing warmth, and a gentle qualifying or *vivifying*; but if the water should be dried up, then there would be burning fire *there*.

32. Thus lord *Lucifer* thought also, that if *he did* but kindle his fire, then he might domineer forcibly in the divine power; for he thought it would have burnt *eternally*, and also have given light; his purpose was not to put out the light, but he would have it burn continually in the fire; he thought he would dry up the water, and then the light would move, stir or *shine*, in the burning fire.

33. But he *knew not*, that if he kindled the dried water, that the kernel, that is, the unctuosity, oil or heart of the water would be *consumed*, and that the light would turn into darkness, and the water turn into a sour *stink*.

34. For the oil or unctuosity in the water is generated through meekness or well-doing, and that is the unctuosity, oil, unction, marrow or fatness wherein the light becomes *shining*. But if the unctuosity be burnt up, then the water is turned into a sour stink, and moreover becometh very dark.

35. Thus it befell the pride of *Lucifer*: he triumphed a little while with his kindled light; but when his light was *spent* and burnt up, then he became a black devil.

36. But he supposed he would eternally reign thus in his burning light in the whole divine power, as a very terrible god, and so with his fire-spirit he *wrestled* with the *Salitter* of God, intending to kindle the whole circumference or extent of his kingdom.

37. And indeed he hath done somewhat, in that he hath set the *divine* power into a burning, which appeareth even in the sun and stars; also the fire in the *Salitter* in the elements is often kindled, so that it seemeth as if the *deep* were of a burning fire; of which I shall speak in another place.

["*He stept back out of the* meekness *into the* "*anxious* fire-will, *and fell into* darkness. *The* "*Reader is advertised that he must not under-* "*stand in any place, as if the devil had kindled* "*or fired the light of* God; *no, but the forms of* "*nature only, out of which the* light *shineth.* "*For he hath not comprehended the* light, *as* "*little as the fire doth, which cannot lay hold on* "*the light: But he entered into the fire, and is* "*expelled into the darkness, and hath neither* fire "*nor light,* besides, *without or distinct from*[1] *his* "*creature.*"]

[1] Or his own creatureliness.

38. Now in this quality king *Lucifer* hath prepared for himself the right hellish bath or lake. He *dares not* say that God hath framed or erected the hellish quality for him, but he himself hath done it: Moreover, he hath *offended* the Deity, and turned the powers of God into a hellish bath or lake, for his own *eternal habitation.*

39. For when he and all his angels had kindled in their bodies the qualifying or fountain spirit of the fire, then the unctuosness, marrow or fatness *burnt* in the sweet water, and the flash or terror, which riseth up fiercely in the birth of the light,

became raging and tearing, burning and stinging, and a being or substance of a mere *opposite* or contrary will.

40. Here, in this quality, the *life* was turned into *a sting of death*; for through heat the bitter quality grew so fierce, stinging, raging and burning, as if the whole body were mere fiery stings; these did tear and rage in the astringent quality, as if one did thrust red-hot bodkins through the body.

41. On the other side, the *cold fire* of the astringent quality was in a mad furious rage against the heat, and against the bitter venom or poison, like a great uproar or hurliburly; and now, furthermore, in the body of *Lucifer* there was nothing else but a murdering, rubbing, fretting, burning and stinging, a most horrible hellish fire.

42. This *fire-spirit*, and right devil's spirit, elevated itself now also in the centre of the heart, and would *rule* through the animated or soulish spirit, [" *Hereby is understood the* spirit " of the will, *out of the centre, which is generated* " *out of the* genitrix, *viz. out of the seven qualify-* " *ing or fountain spirits*, which is the image of " God,"] in the *whole* divine power, and kindle the whole *Salitter* of God as a new and potent God; and so the formings and heavenly imagings should rise up in a horrible fiery quality, and suffer themselves to be imaged and framed according to this *fierceness*.

43. Now when I write of the animated *soulish spirit*, then you must exactly know *what it is*, or *how it is*, else thou wilt read this birth or [1] geniture in vain, and it will happen to thee as [1] Or nativity. it did to the wise Heathen, who climbed up to the very face or countenance of God, but could not *see* it.

44. The [2] *spirit of the soul* is very much more [2] Or soulish spirit. subtle, and more incomprehensible than the body, or the seven qualifying or fountain spirits, which hold, retain and form the body ; for it goeth forth from the seven spirits, as God the Holy Ghost goeth forth from the Father and the Son.

45. The seven qualifying or fountain spirits have their compacted or incorporated body out of nature, that is, out of the seventh nature-spirit in the *divine* power ; which in this book I call *the Salitter of God*, or the *Comprehensibility*, wherein the heavenly figures or shapes arise.

46. And that is *a spirit*, as all the rest of the seven spirits are, only the other six are an incomprehensible being therein ; for the divine power generateth itself in the comprehensibility of the seventh nature-spirit, as it were hidden or concealed, and incomprehensible to the creatures.

47. But the animated or *soulish* spirit generateth itself in the heart, out of or from the seven qualifying or fountain spirits, in that manner as

the Son of God is generated, and keepeth its seat in the heart, and goeth forth from that *seat* in the divine power, as the Holy Ghost from the Father and the Son ; for it hath the same subtleness as the Holy Spirit of God, and it uniteth, qualifieth or operateth with God the Holy Ghost.

48. When the animated or soulish spirit goeth forth out of the body, then it is *one* thing with the hidden Deity, and is together the midst or centre in the imaging or framing of a thing in nature, as God the Holy Ghost himself is.

49. An example whereof you have in this : as when a *carpenter* will build a curious house or artificial piece of architecture, or when any other *artist* goeth about the making of some artificial work, the *hands*, which signify *nature*, cannot be the first that begin the work : but the seven spirits are the first workmasters about it, and the animated or soulish spirit sheweth to the seven spirits the form, figure or shape of it.

50. Then the seven spirits image or frame it, and make it comprehensible, and then the hands *first* begin to fall to work, to make the structure according to the image or frame contrived : For a work must be first brought to the sense, before you can make it.

51. For the soul comprehendeth the *highest* sense, it beholdeth what God its Father acteth or maketh, also it co-operateth in the heavenly imaging or framing : and therefore it maketh a

description,* draught, platform or model for the nature-spirits, shewing how a thing should be imaged or framed.

52. According to this delineation or prefiguration of the soul, all things in this world are made ; for the corrupted soul worketh or endeavoureth continually to bring forth or frame heavenly forms, but cannot bring that to effect, for the *materials* for its work are only the earthly corrupted *Salitter*, even a *half-dead* nature, wherein it cannot image or frame heavenly ideas, shapes or figures.

53. By this you may understand what great *power* the spirits of the expelled angels have had in the heavenly nature ; and of what manner of substance this perdition or *corruption* is ; how in their place they have corrupted and spoiled nature in heaven with their horrible kindling, from whence the horrible fierceness which is predominant in *this* world exists.

54. For the kindled nature burneth still continually until the Last Judgment Day, and this kindled fire, source or quality, is an eternal *enmity* against God.

55. But yet whether this kindled fire-spirit hath *right* therein, and whether God himself hath kindled it, from whence the wrath-fire existed, let the Electionists or Predestinarians, or those that dispute so about Election, justify it, and

* " it maketh a description," etc., lit., " it draweth [round] a model," etc.

prove it in *nature*, if they can; if not, then this fire-spirit is to be condemned also.

Of the Fifth *Kind, Species, Form or Manner of* Sin's *Beginning, in* Lucifer *and his Angels.*

56. The fifth qualifying or fountain spirit in the divine power, is the gracious, amiable and blessed *love*, which is the very glance or aspect of *meekness* and humility, which is also generated in the flash of life.

57. For the flash, as a crack, penetrateth suddenly, whereby joy existeth, and then the stock of the kindled light in the sweet water abideth standing, and *presseth* gently through the fire after the flash, even into the astringent quality, and mitigateth the fire, and maketh the astringent quality beautifully mild and soft or subtle, which is also a birth or geniture of the water.

58. But when the fire tasteth the *mild*, sweet and pliant taste, then is it mitigated and formeth itself into a meek warmth, very lovingly, and there riseth up a very *friendly* life in the fire, and penetrateth the astringent quality with this pleasing, lovely, gentle warmth, and allayeth or stilleth the *cold fire*, and mollifieth or suppleth the hardness, attenuateth the thick, and maketh the dark to be light.

59. But when the bitter flash, together with the astringent quality and the fire-spirit, tasteth this meekness, there is nothing else then but a

mere longing, desiring and replenishing, a very
gentle, pleasant tasting, wrestling, kissing and
love-birth : For the *severe* births of all the
qualifying or fountain spirits become, in this
[inter]penetration very gentle, pleasant, humble
and friendly, and the very *Deity* rightly subsisteth
therein.

60. For in the first four qualifying or fountain
spirits standeth the divine birth or geniture;
therefore they must be very earnest and strong
also, though they, too, have among them their
meek mother, the sweet water ; and in the fifth
standeth the gracious, amiable and blessed love ;
and in the sixth the *joy*, and in the seventh the
framing, imaging or *comprehensibility*.

61. Now, *Lucifer*! come on; with thy love;
how hast *thou* behaved thyself? Is *thy* love also
such a well-spring or fountain as this? We will
now view that also, and examine what manner of
loving angel thou art turned into.

Observe :

62. If *Lucifer* had not elevated and kindled
himself, then his fountain of love would be no
other than that in God, for there was no other
Salitter in him than there is in God.

63. But when he elevated himself, *intending*
to rule the whole Deity with his animated or
soulish spirit, then the stock and heart of light,
which is the kernel, marrow or pith of *love* in

the sweet water, became a fierce and hotly pursuing fire, source or quality, from whence in the whole body existed a very trembling, burning government and birth or geniture.

64. Now when the animated or soulish spirit was *generated* in this severe and astringent fire's birth, then it pressed very furiously forth from the body into nature, or the *Salitter* of God, and *destroyed* the gracious, amiable and blessed love in the *Salitter*; for it pressed very fiercely, furiously and in a fiery manner through all, as a raging tyrant, and supposed that itself *alone* was God; *itself* alone would govern with its sharpness.

65. From *hence* now existeth the great contrary opposite will and eternal enmity between God and *Lucifer*; for the power of God moveth very *softly*, meekly, pleasantly and friendly, so that its birth cannot be conceived of or *apprehended*, and the spirits of *Lucifer* move and tear very *harshly*, astringently, in a fiery manner, swiftly and furiously.

66. An example whereof you have in the kindled *Salitter* of the stars, which because of this kindled fierceness must *roll* with the vanity, even to the Last Judgment Day: *then* the *fierceness* will be separated from them, and be given to king *Lucifer* for an eternal house.

67. But that this is a great opposite, contrary will in God, needs no proof. But a man may

think, in case such a fierce fire, source or quality should rise in his body, what an *untowardness* and contrary will he would have in him, and how often the whole body would be in a rage and fury.

68. Which indeed befalls those who lodge the devil within them; but so long as he is but a guest, he lieth *still* like a tame whelp; but when he becometh the *host* himself, the master of the house, then he stormeth and maketh *havock* in the house, as he did to the body of God.

69. Therefore it is that the wrath-fire of God is yet in the body of God which is in this world, till the end, and many a creature is swallowed up and *devoured* in the wrath-fire, of which much is to be written, but it is referred to its proper place.

70. But now, whether God himself hath created and kindled this enmity and fierce fire-source in *Lucifer*, they are to plead for and justify who dispute for Predestination, Foreseeing, and the Election of Grace, and they are to prove it in nature, if they can; if not, then this *corrupted* fire-source, which stands in the place or stead of love, shall be condemned also.

Of the Sixth *Species, Kind, Form or Manner of* Sin's *Beginning in* Lucifer *and his Angels.*

71. The sixth qualifying or fountain spirit in the divine power is the *Mercurius*, or *tone* or tune, wherein the distinction and heavenly joy rise up.

72. This spirit taketh its original in the fire-flash, that is, in the bitter quality, and riseth up in the flash through the *sweet* water, wherein it mitigateth itself, so that it becometh clear and bright, and is caught or held in the astringent quality, and there it *toucheth* or stirreth all the spirits; and from this touching or stirring riseth up the tone; its rising source or quality standeth in the flash, and its body or root standeth in the sweet water in the *love*.

73. Now this tone or tune is the *divine joyfulness*, the triumphing, wherein the divine and meek love-play, sport or scene in God riseth up, as also the formings, imagings and all manner of *ideas*, shapes and figures.

74. But here thou must know that this quality penetrateth very gently and pleasantly with its touching or stirring, through all the spirits, in such a way and manner as when a *pleasant* and meek fire of joy riseth up in the heart of a man, in which fire of joy the animated or soulish spirit triumpheth, as if it were in *heaven*.

75. Now this spirit doth *not* belong to or concern the imaging or framing of the body, but it belongeth to the distinction, *diversifying* and mobility, especially to the joy, and to the distinction or difference in the imaging or *shaping*.

76. When the animated or soulish spirit in the centre of the heart, in the midst or centre of the

seven qualifying or fountain spirits, is generated, so that the *will* of the seven spirits is incorporated or compacted together, then the tone bringeth it forth from the body, and is its *chariot*, on which the spirit rideth, and executeth that which is decreed in the *council* of the seven spirits.

77. For the tone goeth through the animated or soulish spirit into the nature of God, and into the *Salitter* of the seventh qualifying or fountain spirit in the *divine* power, which is its inceptive or beginning mother, and uniteth, qualifieth or co-operateth with the same in the forming or framing, and also in the distinguishing or diversifying of the imaging or *shaping*.

78. Therefore when king Lucifer, in the tone, changed or *transmuted* his high-spirited horse into a fiery restiveness or motion* in all the seven spirits, that was a terrible contrary or *opposite* will in the *Salitter* of God.

79. For when his animated or soulish spirit was generated in his body, then he *stung forth* from his body into the *Salitter* of God, as a fiery serpent out of a hole.

80. But when the mouth *opened to speak*, that is, when the seven spirits had incorporated or compacted the word together in their will, and sent it through the tone into the *Salitter* of God, then it was no otherwise than if there

* "fiery restiveness or motion." St M. has, "*une réaction ignée*," "a fiery reaction."

went a fiery thunderbolt into God's nature; or as a fierce serpent, which tyrannizeth, raveth and rageth as if it would *tear* and rend nature all to pieces.

81. Hence taketh its original that the devil is called [1] *the old serpent*; and also, that there are adders and *serpents* in this corrupted world, moreover, all manner of vermin or venomous broods of worms, toads, flies, lice and fleas, and all such like things whatsoever; and from hence also *tempestuous* weather of lightning, thundering, flashing, and hailstones take their original in this world.

[1] Rev. xii. 9.

Observe:

82. When the tone riseth up in the divine nature, then it riseth up gently from all the seven qualifying or fountain spirits *jointly* together, and generateth the word or ideas, figures and shapes very gently.

83. That is, when one qualifying or fountain spirit createth a will to the birth or geniture, then it presseth very *gently* through the other qualifying or fountain spirits, even into the *centre* of the heart, and there that will is formed and approved by all the spirits.

84. And then the other six spirits speak it forth in the tone, out from *God's* animated or soulish spirit; understand, out from the Heart of God, out from the Son of God, which abideth

standing in the centre as a compacted *incorporated* Word.

85. And the flash out of that same Word, or the stirring of the Word, which is the tone, goeth forth very *finely* and gently from the Word, and executeth, affecteth or performeth the will of the Word.

86. And that same forthgoing from the Word is the Holy Ghost, which formeth, frameth and imageth all whatsoever was decreed in the centre of the heart, in the *council* of the seven spirits of God the Father.

87. In such a gentle way and manner should king *Lucifer* also have generated, qualified or operated; and according to the *right* of the Deity, with his animated or soulish spirit in the *Salitter*, or in the nature of God, he should have *helped* to image or frame things, as a *dear* son in nature.

88. Just as a son in the house helps his father to drive or *manage* his work, according to his father's way and profession, kind and art; so, in the *great house* of God the Father, according to the manner and way of God, should Lucifer also, with his angels, have *helped* with his animated or soulish spirit to image all the forms, ideas and vegetations in the *Salitter* of God.

89. For the whole *Salitter* should be a house of pleasure and *delight* for angelical bodies, and all should rise up according to the delight of their

spirit, and they should so image themselves that they would never at all have *any* displeasure in any figure, shape or creature, but their animated or soulish spirit should be co-operative in every imaging; and then the *Salitter* would have been the creature's proper own.

[" *The* imaging *out of the heavenly* essences *is* " *performed* magically, *all according to the will* " *and ability or potentiality of nature and the* " *creatures.*"]

90. If they had but continued. in their meek birth or geniture, according to the *divine right*, then all had been their own, and their will would have been always *fulfilled* eternally, and nothing had been among them and in them but merely the joy of love; to speak after an earthly manner, as it were an *eternal laughing*, and a perpetual rejoicing in an eternal hearty delight. For God and the creatures had been one heart and one will.

[" *The image out of or proceeding from the* " *soul's fire, and the love or the divine centre,* " *are in one essence.*"]

91. But when *Lucifer* exalted himself, and kindled his qualifying or fountain spirits, then the animated or soulish spirit went forth in the *tone* out of or from all the bodies of *Lucifer's* angels into the *Salitter* of God, as a fiery serpent or *dragon*, and imaged and framed all manner of fiery and poisonous forms and images, like to wild, cruel and evil beasts.

92. And from hence the wild, fierce and evil beasts in this world have their *original*. For the host or army of *Lucifer* had kindled the *Salitter* of the stars and of the earth, and *half* killed, spoiled and destroyed it.

93. But when God, after the fall of *Lucifer*, made or prepared the creation of this world, then all was created out of the same *Salitter* wherein *Lucifer* had his seat: So afterwards the creatures also in this world must needs be created out of that same *Salitter*, which then formed themselves according to the condition or kind of the kindled qualities, evil and good.

94. That beast, which had most of the fire or the bitter or the astringent quality in the *Mercurius*, became also a bitter, hot and fierce beast, all according as the quality was predominant or *chief* in the beast.

95. This I set down here only for a manuduction; you will find it demonstrated more at large concerning the *creation* of this world.

96. Now, whether this fiery tone or *dragon-spirit* in *Lucifer* and in his angels be right, and whether God hath thus created him, let the advocates of *Lucifer*, who make God to be as a devil, justify it here by their answer, and prove it in *nature*, if they can, whether God be such a God as willeth the evil, and hath created the evil.

97. *If not*, then shall this spirit also be condemned to the eternal prison; and they should

give over their lying and blaspheming of God; or else they are *worse* than the wild Heathen or Pagans, who know nothing of God, *who* notwithstanding live in God, and shall *sooner* possess the kingdom of heaven than many of these blasphemers of God shall, which I shall also demonstrate in its proper place.

THE SIXTEENTH CHAPTER

Of the Seventh *Species, Kind, Form, or Manner of* Sin's Beginning *in* Lucifer *and his Angels.*

1. HERE thou shouldst open thy eyes *wide,* for thou wilt see the hidden secret things which have been kept hidden from all men since the world began. For thou wilt see the murderous den of the *devil*, and the horrible sin, enmity and perdition.

2. The devil hath taught man *sorcery* or *witchcraft*, thereby to strengthen and fortify his kingdom. But if he had revealed to man the right, true, fundamental ground, which lurked behind or *under* sorcery, many would have let it alone altogether, and not have meddled with it at all.

3. *Come on ye jugglers and sorcerers or witches,* you that go a wooing and a whoring after the devil : Come to my school : I will shew you how, with your *necromancy* or art, you are carried into hell.

4. You rejoice [maliciously] with this ; that the devil is in subjection to you, and ye suppose that

ye are gods : Here I will describe the original and *ground* of *necromancy*, for I am become also a [1]searcher into nature, but not after your way and manner, but to *discover your shame* by a divine revelation, for an advertisement to this last world, and for a sentence of condemnation upon *their* skill and knowledge ; for the judgment followeth upon knowledge.

[1] Natur-kündiger. Naturalist, physicus or natural philosopher.

5. Seeing the bow of *fierceness* is already bent, let every one look to himself, lest he be found within the limit of the mark. *For the time is at hand to awake from sleep.*

6. Now the seventh form, or the seventh spirit in the divine power, is *nature*, or the issue or *exit* from the other six. For the astringent quality attracteth the *Salitter* together, or the fabric or product of all the six spirits, even as a magnet or loadstone attracteth to itself the *Salitter* of the iron ; and when it is attracted together, then it is a *comprehensibility*, in which the six spirits of God qualify, act or operate in an *incomprehensible* way or manner.

7. This seventh spirit hath a colour and condition or kind of its own, as all the other spirits have ; for it is the *body* of all the spirits, wherein they generate themselves as in a body : Also out of this spirit all *figures*, shapes and forms are imaged or fashioned ; moreover, the angels also are created out of it, and *all* [2]*naturality standeth therein.*

[2] natureliness or the universal nature.

8. And *this spirit* is always generated from the six, and subsisteth always *continually*, and is never missing or wanting, nor doth ever pass away, and it again continually generateth the six; for the other six are in this seventh as in a mother, enclosed or encompassed; and they receive their nourishment, power and strength *always* in their mother's body or womb.

9. For the seventh spirit is the *body*, and the other six are the *life*, and in the middle centre is the heart of *light*, which the seven spirits continually generate as a light of life; and that light is their son; and the welling out or penetration through all the spirits expandeth itself aloft * in the heart, in the exit or rising up of the light.

10. And this is the spirit of all the seven spirits, that goeth forth out of the heart of God, which there, in the seventh spirit, formeth and frameth all, and wherein the qualifying or fountain spirits, with their love-wrestling, shew themselves endlessly.

11. For the Deity is like a wheel, which with its *fellies* and *spokes*, and with all the *naves*, turneth about, and is fellied together, as seven wheels, so that it can go any way, forward, backward, downward, upward and crossways, without turning back.

12. Whereas yet always the form of all the

* "expandeth itself aloft"—*empöret (gebäret) sich.* See Ch. 3, par. 67.

seven *wheels*, and the one only *nave* in the centre of all the wheels, is fully in sight, and so it is not understood how the wheel is made; but the wheel always appears more and more *wonderful* and marvellous, with its rising up, and yet abideth also in its own place.

13. In such a manner the Deity is continually generated, and never passeth away, or ceaseth or vanisheth out of sight; and in this manner also is the *life* in angels and mén continually generated.

14. According to the moving of the seven spirits of God the figures and creatures of the *transitoriness* are *formed*, but not thus generated; though indeed the birth or geniture of all the seven spirits sheweth itself therein, yet their quality standeth only in the séventh nature-spirit, which the other six spirits do form, figure, frame, *alter* and *change*, according to their *wrestling* and rising up.

15. Therefore also the figures, and *transitory* forms and creatures, are changed according to the condition of the *seventh* nature-spirit, in which they rise up.

16. The angels are not alone imaged or framed out of the seventh nature-spirit, as the transitory creatures are, but when the Deity moved itself to the creating of angels, then in *every* circle, wherein each angel was incorporated or compacted together, there the Deity, with its *whole*

substance and being, was *incorporated* or compacted together, [" *Understand, the* two *eternal*
" *Principles*, viz. *the* fire *and the* light, *and yet*
" *not the quality or source of the fire, but the*
" *essence of it*,"] and became a body, and yet the
Deity continued in its *seat*, as before.

Understand this well:

17. The angel's body, or the *comprehensibility*,
is from or out of the *seventh* spirit, and the birth
or geniture in that body is the *six* qualifying
or fountain spirits; and the spirit or the heart,
which the six spirits generate in the centre of
the body, in which the light riseth up, and the
animated or soulish spirit out of the light, which
also qualifieth, uniteth or operateth with the
Deity, without, distinct from the body, that
signifieth the heart of God, out of which the
Holy Ghost goeth forth.

18. And it was * also from or out of the heart
of God, co-united or mixed in the body of the
angel in their first compacting or *incorporating*
together; therefore the angel's government in
the *mind* generateth itself as the Deity doth.

19. And as in the seventh nature-spirit of
God, which existeth out of the other six, there
doth *not* stand the whole perfect knowledge of

---

* "And it was" = "And the soulish spirit was"; meaning,
that there was, through the soulish spirit, an admixture of the
heart of God incorporated in the body of the angels in the first
compaction.

the other six spirits, for it *cannot* search or dive into their deep birth or geniture, in that they are its *father*, and generate it out of themselves.

20. So also the whole, full and *perfect knowledge* of God doth not stand in the *angelical* body, but in the *spirit*, which is generated in the heart, which goeth forth from the light, which qualifieth or operateth also with the heart and spirit of God, wherein the whole, full and *perfect knowledge* of God standeth.   But the body cannot apprehend that animated or soulish spirit; as also the seventh nature-spirit comprehendeth not the *deepest birth* or geniture of God.

21. For when the seventh nature-spirit is generated, then it is dried by the astringent quality, and is as it were staid and kept by its father, and cannot *go back* again into the deep, that is, into the centre of the heart, where the son is generated, and from whence the Holy Ghost goeth forth; but must hold still as a *generated* body, and must give way to the qualifying or fountain veins, that is, to the *spirits*, to qualify, work and labour therein as they please.

22. For it is the proper house and habitation of the six spirits, which they continually build according to their pleasure, or as a garden of delight into which the master of it *soweth* all manner of seeds, according to his pleasure, and then enjoyeth the fruit thereof.

23. Thus the other six spirits continually erect this garden of delight and pleasure, and *sow* their fruits thereinto, and feed upon it to strengthen their might and joy; and this is the garden in which the angels dwell, and walk up and down in, and *wherein* the heavenly fruit groweth.

24. But the wonderful proportion or variety of harmony, which appeareth in the growths or vegetations and figures and forms in this garden, ariseth from the *qualification* or operation, and from the loving, wrestling or struggling of the other spirits.

25. For that which is predominant or chief in the striving, imageth or formeth the growth and vegetation according to its kind, and the others always *help* to promote it; now the one, now the other, now the third, and so on.

26. Therefore also there arise so many diverse growths, vegetations and figures as are altogether unsearchable and incomprehensible to the *bodily reason* of the angels; but to the animated or *soulish reason* of the angels they are wholly, fully and perfectly comprehensible.

27. This is also wholly hidden as to my body, but not as to my animated or soulish spirit, for so long as my animated or soulish spirit qualifieth or worketh with and in God it comprehendeth the same; but when it falls into *sin*, then the door is shut against it, which the devil bolteth

up fast, and which must, with great labour and industry of the *spirit*, be set open again.

28. I know very well that the wrath of the devil will mock and scoff in the hearts of many wicked men, at *this revelation*. For he is mightily ashamed because of this revelation; he hath also given my soul many a pang and crush for it; but I leave it to the direction of God, who will have it so; I cannot resist him, though my earthly body should go to wrack for it, yet my God will *glorify me* in my knowledge.

29. The glorification of *this* my knowledge I desire, and no other; for I know that when this my spirit in my new body, which I shall get at the day of my *resurrection*, out of this my now *corrupted* body, shall arise, that it will appear like the Deity, as also like the holy angels.

30. For the triumphing joyous light in my spirit sheweth it me sufficiently, in which I have also *searched* into the depth of the Deity, and described it rightly, according to my gifts and the impulse of the spirit, though in great *feebleness* and weakness, in that my *original* and *actual sins* have often bolted the door against me, and the devil hath danced before it, as a whorish woman, and rejoiced at my captivity and anguish; yet that will bring *very little* profit to his kingdom.

31. Therefore I must now look for no other than his fierce wrath, *but my stay, trust and*

refuge is the Champion in the Fight, who hath often delivered me from his bands, in this Champion I will *fight* against him, till my departure out of this life.

Of the terrible, lamentable and miserable Perdition of Lucifer *in the* Seventh Nature-Spirit. *The sad Mourning House of Death.*

32. If all trees were writers or clerks, and all branches were pens, and all hills were books, and all waters were ink, yet they could not *sufficiently describe* the lamentable misery which *Lucifer*, together with his angels, hath brought into his place or whole space of that world wherein he was created.

33. For he hath made the house of *light* to be a house of *darkness*, and the house of *joy* to be a house of mourning, lamentation and *sadness*; that which was the house of pleasure, delight, vivifying and *refreshing*, he hath made to be a house of thirst and *hunger*; the house of *love* to be a house of eternal *enmity*; and the house of *meekness* to be a house of knocking, rumbling,* *thundering* and lightning; the house of *peace* to be a house of lamenting and eternal *howling*; the house of *laughing* to be a house of eternal trembling and *horror*:

34. The birth or geniture of light, munificence and *well-doing* to be an eternal hellish pain and

* "knocking, rumbling" (*Pochen*). See Ch. 10, par. 119.

torment; the *food* of *pleasing relish* to be an eternal abomination and stink, a *loathing* of all fruits; and the house of *Lebanon* and cedars to be a stony and *rocky* house of fire; the *sweet* scent or relish to be a *stink*, and a house of ruin and desolation, an end of all good; the *divine body* to be a black, cold, hot, eating, *corroding*, and yet not consuming devil, who is an *enmity* against God and his angels: And so he hath all the heavenly hosts or armies against him.

Now observe:

35. The *learned* have had many disputations, questions, conceits and opinions concerning the fierce malignity and evil that is in all the creatures in this world, and even in the very sun and stars; moreover, there are some so very poisonous and venomous beasts, worms and vegetables in this world, that thereupon rational men have justly *wondered*, and some have concluded peremptorily, *That God must needs have willed the evil also*, seeing he hath created so much that is evil; and some have laid the blame and fault thereof upon the fall of *Adam*, and some have imputed it to the work and doings of the devil.

36. But seeing all the creatures and vegetables were created *before* the time of man, therefore the fault ought not to be laid upon man; for man gat not the *bestial body* in his creation, but it first came to be so in his fall.

37. Neither hath man brought the malignity,. poison and venom into the beasts, birds, worms, and stones, for he *had* not their body ; otherwise if he had brought malignity and fierceness or wrath into all creatures, then he, like the devils, could never obtain God's mercy.

38. Poor man did not fall out of a resolved, purposed will,* but through the poisonous, venomous infection of the devil, else there had been no remedy for him.

39. Now this true information thou wilt find described here following, not from a zeal to vilify anybody thereby, but *in love*, and as a humble information and instruction from the abyss of my spirit, and for an assured comfort to the poor, sick old *Adam*, who now lieth at the point of his *last departure* from hence out of this world.

40. For *in Christ* we are all one body, therefore also this spirit would heartily fain have it so, that its fellow-members might be *refreshed* with a draught of the precious wine of God *before* their departure from hence, whereby they might encounter and stand in the great fight with the devil, and obtain the *victory*, that the victory of the devil in this modern drunken world might be disappointed and destroyed, and the great name of the LORD might be sanctified.

* "out of a resolved, purposed will," or, "on account of" or "in consequence of, an intentional will."

Now behold !

41. When king *Lucifer*, together with his angels, was so gloriously, beautifully and divinely created, as a Cherubim and king in God, then he suffered his bright, beauteous form to *befool* him, in that he saw how noble, glorious and fair a spirit *rose up* in him.

42. Then *his* seven qualifying or fountain spirits thought they would elevate and kindle themselves, and so they also would be as fair, glorious and mighty as the animated or *soulish spirit*, and thereby would domineer, by their own power and authority, in the *whole* court, circumference, dominion or extent as a new god.

43. They saw very well that the animated or *soulish spirit* qualified, mixed or operated with the heart of God; and thereupon they were resolved they would elevate and *kindle* themselves, hoping to be as bright, illustrious, deep and almighty as the *deepest ground* in the centre of the heart of God.

44. For they thought to elevate the natural body, (which was compacted together or incorporated out of the nature-spirit of God), up into the *hidden birth* or geniture of God, that their seven qualifying or fountain spirits might thus be as high, and as *all-comprehensible* as the animated or soulish spirit.

45. And the animated or soulish spirit would

triumph over the centre of the heart of God, and the heart of God should be subjected under it ; and so the seven spirits of God would image, frame and form all, by *their* animated or soulish spirit.

46. And this high mind and self-will was directly and *wholly* against the birth or geniture of God ; for the body of the angels should abide and remain in its seat, and *be* nature, and, as a humble mother, hold still and be quiet, and should not have the omniscience, and own self rational comprehensibility of the heart, or of the deepest birth or geniture of the *Holy Trinity* ; but the seven spirits should generate themselves in their natural body, as is done in God.

47. And their comprehensibility should not be in the *hidden kernel*, or in the innermost birth or geniture of God, but the animated or soulish spirit, which they generate in the centre of their heart, should *qualify*, mix or operate with the innermost birth or geniture of God, and help to form all figures, shapes and images, according to the pleasure, delight and will of the seven spirits, whereby, in the divine pomp, all might be but *one* heart and one will.

48. For the birth or geniture of God also is thus ; the seventh nature-spirit doth not *reach back* into its father, which generateth it, but holdeth still and is quiet as a body, and letteth the father's will, which is the other six spirits, to form and image in it how they please.

49. Neither doth any one spirit particularly and severally reach, with its corporeal being, after the heart of God, but includeth, closeth or *joineth* its will with the others, in the centre, to the birth or geniture of the heart, so that the heart and the seven spirits of God are *one* will.

50. For this is the law of the *comprehensibility*, that it doth not elevate itself up into the *incomprehensibility*; for the power which, in the centre or midst, is compacted together or incorporated out of all the seven spirits is incomprehensible and unsearchable, but not invisible; for it is not the power of one spirit alone, but of all seven.

51. Therefore one spirit in its own body, besides and distinct from its [1]instanding or innate instant birth or geniture, *cannot* reach into the whole heart of God, and examine, try and search all; for, besides and distinct from its instanding birth or geniture, it comprehends only its *own* birth or geniture in the heart of God; but *all* the seven spirits, *jointly* together, comprehend the whole heart of God.

["*So also in man. But understand it as to* "*the image of God*, viz. *in the soul's spirit; not* "*in the fiery essence of the soul; but in the* "*essence of the* light, *wherein the* image *of God* "*standeth.*"]

52. But in the instanding or innate birth or geniture of the spirits, where the one still generateth the other, there *every* spirit generateth

[1] Inste-
henden
Gebuhrt.

all the seven spirits, but yet only in the rising flash of the life.

53. But the heart, when it is generated, is singular or distinct, viz. *a peculiar person*, and yet not separated from the spirits; but the spirits cannot transmute or *change themselves*, in their first birth or geniture, one into another.

54. Also the second cannot change itself into the third, which is the *exit* of the spirit; but every birth or geniture abideth in its seat; and yet all the births or genitures together are but the *one* only *God*.

55. But seeing the body of *Lucifer* was created out of nature, [which is] the most *outward* birth or geniture, therefore it was unjustly done that he should elevate himself into the *innermost* and deepest, which he could not do [1] in the divine right, but must only so elevate and kindle himself that thereby the qualifying or fountain spirits might be set or put into the sharpest penetrating and *infecting*.

[1] Or *Jure divino.*

56. I verily suppose, indeed, that thou, fair Necromancer, hath changed thyself to purpose; and mayest well also teach men *thy black art*, that they perhaps might also become such potent gods as *thou* art.

57. Ye blind and proud necromancers, jugglers and sorcerers, your art consisteth in your changing the *elements* of your body by your conjurations and instruments of the qualities or qualifying

properties, which you make use of to that purpose, and ye think ye have *right* so to do; but is it not against the birth or geniture of God? If you think not, make that appear.

58. How can you well suppose that you can change yourselves into *another form*? Indeed you suffer the devil thus to play the ape with you, and *cheat* you; and all this while you are but *blind* in your own skill. Though you have learned your art never so well, yet you do not know the purpose it driveth at; for the pith and heart therein is the changing or altering of the qualifying or fountain spirits, as *Lucifer* did, when he would needs be God.

Now thou askest, How can that be?

Answer.

59. Behold, when the corporeal, qualifying or fountain spirits set their will into sorcery or witchcraft, then the animated or soulish spirit, which they generate, and which in the *astral elementary* quality ruleth in the hidden and deepest centre, is clearly already a sorcerer or witch, and hath changed, transformed or metamorphosed itself into sorcery or *witchcraft.*

60. But the bestial body cannot follow so suddenly and nimbly, but must be charmed to it by *characters* and *conjurations*, and by some instruments for that purpose, whereby the animated or soulish spirit maketh the bestial

body invisible, and changeth it into such a
form as the will of the qualifying or fountain
spirits was in, at the beginning of its purpose
to a *metamorphosis* or transmutation.

61. The bestial flesh cannot well *change* itself,
or put itself into another birth or geniture, but
is brought into a slender and inferior base form,
as of a beast, of wood, or such like thing which
hath its body qualifying or boiling in the
elements, as in their fountain.

62. But the astral spirits can well clothe
themselves in another form or shape, but that
continueth *so long only* as the birth or geniture
of nature above their pole or zenith permitteth
them.

63. For when it changeth itself with its *wheel-
ing* and penetrating, so that another qualifying
or fountain spirit becomes chief or predominant,
then their art lieth down upon the ground, and
their Deity in the first qualifying or fountain
spirit, in which they had begun their art, hath
an *end*.

64. Now if it be to last *any longer*, then it
must be made again *afresh* according to the
qualifying or fountain spirit then ruling at that
present, or the *devil* with his animated or soulish
spirit must be in the astral spirits of the body,
which instantly and suddenly changeth it, or
else *his art* is here also at an end.

65. For nature will *not* suffer itself to be

juggled with at all times and hours, as the spirits would *have* it, but all must be done according to that spirit which then at that present time is lord and chief or *predominant*.

66. It is *not* that spirit of God which is lord and chief in nature, which *causeth* or maketh the juggling, but it is made in the *fierceness* of the *Salitter*, which lord *Lucifer* hath kindled with his elevation, and which is his eternal kingdom.

67. But when the power or might of that spirit is allayed, then the kindled fire can be *no more* useful to the juggler.

68. For the wrath-fire in nature is not, during this time of the world, the devil's *own* house of his power; for the love standeth *hidden* in the centre of the wrath-fire, and *Lucifer*, together with his angels, lieth imprisoned in the *outward* wrath-fire, even until the Judgment of God: Then he will have the wrath-fire separated from the love, for an eternal bath or lake, and he will wash his juggler's head and face withal, doubtless.

69. This I set thee down here for a *warning*, that thou mayest know what manner of *ground* sorcery or witchcraft hath, not in such a way as if I would write any heathenish sorcery or witchcraft, neither have I learned any; but the animated or soulish spirit beholdeth their juggling, which in the *body* I do not understand.

70. But seeing it runneth counter, quite contrary to the love and meekness of the birth or

geniture of God, and is a contrary or *opposite* will in the love of God, so that he is loath to hurt man, unless pressing necessity driveth him to it, therefore will the spirit have the *wrath-bath* or lake of nature set apart to be an eternal parching or drying place for jugglers, perverters or changers of God's ordinance or order : And therein they may practise and shew forth their new deity.

Of the kindling of the Wrath-Fire.

71. Now when king *Lucifer*, together with all his angels, kindled himself, then the wrath-fire rose up *instantly* in the body, and the gracious amiable and blessed *light* was extinguished in the animated or soulish spirit, and became a fierce, furious, devilish spirit, all according to the *kindling* and will of the qualifying or fountain spirits.

72. Now this animated or soulish spirit was bound or united with the Deity, in nature, and could qualify, mix or operate in and with the same, as if it were one and the same thing ; and that now *darted forth* out of the bodies of the devils into the nature of God, like a thief and a *murderer* that desired to rob, murder and spoil all, and bring all under its power, and so kindled all the seven spirits in nature. And then there was nothing else but an astringent, bitter, fiery and cracking *burning*, tearing and raging.

73. Thou must *not think* that the devil hath thus powerfully and mightily overcome the Deity. No; but he hath kindled the wrath of God, which, indeed, had otherwise *rested eternally* in secret, and so he hath made the *Salitter* of God to be a murderous *den*; for if fire be cast into a heap of straw, and the straw kindled, it will *burn*. God hath not, on that account become a devil.*

74. Moreover, the wrath-fire of God doth *not reach* in nature into the innermost kernel of the heart, which is the Son of God, much less into the secret glory or holiness of the spirit, but into the birth or geniture of the six qualifying or fountain spirits, in the *place* where the seventh is generated.

75. For in that place, or in this birth or geniture, is lord *Lucifer become a creature*, and his dominion did reach no farther or deeper than so; but if he had continued in the *love*, then his animated or soulish spirit had reached even to the *centre* of the heart of God, for love presseth or penetrateth *through* the whole Deity.

76. But when his love was extinguished, then the animated or soulish spirit could *no more* reach into the heart of God, and so his attempt was in vain; but he raved and raged in nature,

---

* The last clause of this par. is absent from Sparrow's translation, and it does not appear in the German ed. of 1656, nor in Schiebler's ed. It is in the German eds. of 1682, 1715 and 1730.

that is, in the seventh qualifying or fountain spirit of God.

77. But seeing the power of all the seven spirits stood *in this one*, therefore also all the seven were kindled in the wrath, but yet only in the *outward* and *comprehensible* qualification or constitution.

78. For the devil could not touch the heart, neither could he touch the *innermost* birth or geniture of the qualifying or fountain spirits ; for his *glory* of the seven spirits was already mortified in the first flash of kindling, and was presently held captive and imprisoned in the first *exit* of the animated or soulish spirit.

79. In *this hour* king *Lucifer* prepared for himself the hell and eternal perdition, which now standeth in the *outermost* qualifying or fountain spirit of the nature of God, or in the outermost birth or geniture of this world.

80. But when *nature* kindled itself thus horribly, then the house of joy came to be a house of trouble, affliction and misery. For the astringent quality became kindled in *its own house*, which is a very hard, cold and dark essence, like a cold, hard frosty winter, which only attracted the *Salitter* together, and dried it up, so that it became rugged, cold and sharp like stones, wherein the heat was captivated, imprisoned, and also attracted together, and so formed or framed into a hard, cold, dark essence.

81. When this was done the light in nature was extinguished in the outermost birth or geniture also, and all became very dark, perished and *spoiled*; the water became very cold and thick, and stayed here and there in the *clefts*. This is the original of the elementary water on earth.

82. For before the times of the world the water was very thin or rarified, like air, and then the life was generated therein also, which water is now so *mortal*, corrupted, perished and spoiled, and so rolleth and runneth to and fro.

83. The gracious, amiable and blessed love which rose up in the flash of the life, became a fierce and bitter venom or poison, a very murderous den, *a sting of death*: The tone or tune became like the hard knocking or loud *rumbling* of stones, and a house of lamentation.

84. Briefly, all was a mere dark and miserable being in the whole circumference, extent or dominion, in the outermost birth or geniture of the kingdom of *Lucifer*.

85. But thou must not think that nature was thus *corrupted* and kindled even to the innermost ground, but only the outermost birth or geniture; but the innermost, in which the seven qualifying or fountain spirits generate themselves, retained its own right to itself, seeing the *kindled* devil could not reach into it.

86. But now the inner birth or geniture hath

the fan or casting-shovel in its hand, and will one day *purge* its floor, and give the chaff or husks to the kingdom of *Lucifer* for eternal food.

87. For if the devil *could* have reached into the innermost birth or geniture, then instantly the whole circumference, court or extent of his kingdom would have been the kindled *burning hell*.

88. But now he must lie *captivated* and imprisoned in the outermost birth or geniture, even till the Last Judgment Day, which is at hand, and very near *to be expected*.

89. But *Lucifer* hath kindled *his qualifying or fountain spirits* even in the innermost birth or geniture, and now *his* qualifying or fountain spirits generate an animated or soulish *devil's* spirit, which is an eternal enemy of God.

90. For when God was angry in *his* outermost birth or geniture in nature, then it was not his purposed *determinate* will to be kindled, neither hath he effected that kindling; but he hath drawn the *Salitter* together, and thereby hath prepared an eternal *lodging* for the devil.

91. For the devil cannot be expelled *quite out*, away, beyond God, into another kingdom of angels; but a place must be *reserved* to him for a habitation.

92. Neither would God *presently* give him the kindled *Salitter* for an eternal habitation, for the *internal* birth or geniture of the spirits stood yet *hidden* therein.

93. For God intended to do somewhat *else* with it, and so king *Lucifer* would be kept a *prisoner* till another angelical host or army, out of the same *Salitter*, should come in *his* stead, which are *men*.

94. Now come on, ye advocates [or justifiers] of *Lucifer*, maintain the cause of your king now, and shew whether he hath done right in kindling of the *wrath-fire* in nature; if not, then he must *burn* therein eternally, and your *lies* against the truth must burn with him.

95. These are the seven kinds, species, forms or manners of sin's beginning, and eternal *enmity* against God.

Now followeth briefly concerning the four new little sons *of* Lucifer, *which he hath generated in himself in his corporeal regimen, for which he was expelled from his place, and is become* the most horrible devil.

Of the First *Son,* Pride.

Now it may be asked, What *moved* Lucifer *to this,* that he *would* needs be above God?

Answer.

96. Here thou must know, that without, distinct from himself, he had no impulse at all to his pride, but his beauty and brightness *deceived* him. When he saw that he was the fairest and most beautiful prince in heaven, then he *despised*

the friendly qualifying, mixing, operating and generating of the Deity, and thought with himself that he would *rule* with his princely power in the whole Deity; all must stoop and bow to *him*.

97. But when he found that he could not effect it, then he kindled himself, intending to do it some other way; and so then the Son of Light became a Son of Darkness; for he *himself* consumed the power of his sweet water, and made it to be a sour stink.

Of the Second Son, [1] Covetousness.   [1] Avarice

98. The second will was *covetousness*, which grew out of pride, for *Lucifer* thought with himself that he would *reign* over all kingdoms, as a sole god; all should bow to him, he would form and frame *all* with his own power; and besides, also his *beauty* so deceived him that he thought he would have all in his sole possession.

99. This modern world would do well to speculate on this pride and covetousness, and to consider *how* it is an enmity against God; and that thereby they go *headlong* to the devil, and there must have their jaws and throats open eternally to rob and devour, and yet find nothing but *hellish* abomination.

Of the Third Son, [2] Envy.   [2] Or Spite.

100. This son is the very [3] *gout* of this world; [3] Podagra. for it taketh its original in the flash of pride and

covetousness, and standeth on the root of life as pricking and bitter gall.

101. This spirit also came at first from pride, for pride thought and said to itself, Surely thou art *beautiful*, and mighty *potent*; and covetousness thought and said to itself, All must be *thine*; and envy thought and said to itself, All which is not obedient unto thee thou must *kill* with thy stinging; and thus it stung at the other gates of angels. But all was in vain, for its power and might reached *no farther* than the extent of the *place* out of which it was created.

Of the Fourth Son, ¹ Wrath.

102. This son is the very *burning* hellish fire, and taketh its original also from pride. For when *Lucifer* with his antagonistic envy could *not* fill his pride and covetousness, then he kindled the *wrath-fire* in himself, and roared therewith into God's nature, as a fierce lion, and from whence then arose the wrath of God and *all evil*.

103. Of which much were to be written, but [in the present book] you will find it more apprehensibly at the place concerning the creation: For there are to be found *living* testimonies enough, so that none need doubt whether the things be so or no.

104. Thus king *Lucifer* is the beginning of *sin* and the *sting of death*, and the kindling of

God's wrath, and the beginning of all evil, a corruption, perdition and destruction of this world; and whatever evil is done, there *he* is the first author and *causer* thereof.

105. Also he is a murderer and father of lies, and a founder of hell, a spoiler and corrupter, and destroyer of all that is *good*, and an eternal enemy of God, and of all good angels and men; against whom I, and all men that think to be saved, must daily and hourly *struggle* and fight, as against the worst and arch enemy.

The final *Condemnation.*

106. But seeing God hath *accursed* him as an eternal enemy, and *condemned* him unto eternal imprisonment, where God now seeth his hour-glass more and *more* plainly before his eyes; and seeing his hellish kingdom is *revealed to me* by the spirit of God; so I, together with and among all holy souls of men, curse him also, and renounce and *defy* him as an eternal *enemy*, who hath often spoiled and torn up my vineyard.

107. Moreover, I defy also all his [1] lawyers and helpers, and will, with the divine grace, from henceforth *fully* reveal his kingdom, and demonstratively prove, that [2] *God is a God of love and meekness, who willeth not the evil,* and [3] *who hath no pleasure in the perdition of any, but willeth that all men should be* helped or *saved.* Then I will shew and prove also that *all evil*

[1] Jurists.

[2] Psalm v. 4.

[3] Ezek. xviii. 23 ; xxxiii. 11. 1 Tim. ii. 4.

cometh from the devil, and taketh its original from him.

Of the final *Fight and* Expulsion *of King* Lucifer, *together with* all his Angels.

108. Now when this horrible *Lucifer*, as a *tyrant* and raging spoiler of all that is good, shewed himself thus terribly, as if he would kindle and destroy *all*, and bring all under his jurisdiction, then all the heavenly hosts and armies were against him, and he also against *them all*; there now the fight began, for all stood most terribly, one *party against another*.

[1] Rev. xii. 109. And the great prince [1] *Michael* with his legions fought against him; and the devil with his legions had *not* the *victory*, but was driven from his place, as one vanquished.

Now it may be asked, What manner of fight was this? How could they fight one with another *without* weapons?

Answer.

110. The spirit alone understandeth this *hidden* secret, which spirit must fight daily and hourly with the *devil*, the outward flesh *cannot* comprehend it; also the astral spirits in man cannot understand it, neither is it comprehended by man at all, unless the animated or soulish spirit unite, qualify and operate with the *innermost* birth or geniture in nature, in the centre, where

the light of God is set opposite against the devil's kingdom, that is, in the third birth or geniture, in the *nature* of this world.

111. When it uniteth,* qualifieth or operateth with God in *this seat*, then the animated or soulish spirit carrieth it † into the *astral*; for the astral must in this place fight hourly with the devil.

112. For the devil *hath* power in the outermost birth or geniture of man, for his seat is there. [This seat is] the murderous den of perdition, and the house of misery and *woe*, wherein the devil *whetteth* the sting of death, and through his animated or *soulish* spirit he reacheth in into the heart of man, in man's outermost birth or geniture.

113. But when the astral spirits are *enlightened* from the animated or soulish spirit, which in the light uniteth with God, then they grow *fervent*, and very longing and desirous of the light. On the other hand, the animated or soulish spirit of the devil, which ruleth in the outermost birth or geniture of man, is very terrible and angry, and of a very contrary or *opposite* will.

* "When it uniteth," etc. The word which Sparrow has translated "it" is in the original "er," and may refer either to "man," or to "the animated or soulish spirit" St M. has chosen the former, and prints: "Lorsque dans ce siége, *l'homme inqualifie* avec Dieu, alors l'esprit *animique*," etc. "When in this seat, man uniteth . . . then the animated or soulish spirit," etc.

† "carrieth it." Here "it" refers to "the light."

114. And then there riseth up the striving or *fighting fire* in man, just as it rose up in heaven with *Michael* and *Lucifer*, and so the poor soul comes to be miserably crushed, *stretched*, tormented and put upon the rack.

115. But if it getteth the victory, then it bringeth with its piercing penetration its light and knowledge into the outermost birth or geniture of man; for it presseth back with force through the seven spirits of nature, which here I call the astral spirits, and governeth in the council [or counsel] of reason.

116. Then man first knoweth what the devil is, how much an enemy he is to him, and how *great* his power is; also how he must fight with him very *secretly* every day, hour and moment.

117. Which thing *reason*, or the outward birth or *geniture* of man, without the experience of this fight or battle, *cannot* comprehend. For the third or outermost birth or geniture in man, which is the *carnal* or fleshly birth, and which man through the first fall in his lust hath raised and prepared for himself, is the devil's castle or *fort* of prey or robbery and dwelling-house, wherein the devil, as in a *bulwark*, fighteth with the soul, and giveth it many a hard knock on the head.*

118. Now this birth of the *flesh* is *not* the

* "knock on the head" (*Kopfstoss*)—an obsolete word which denotes a blow given from above on the top of some object.

mansion-house of the soul, but in its strife the soul goeth in with its light into the *divine* power, and fighteth against the murder of the devil.*

119. On the other hand, the devil with his poison shooteth and *darteth* at the seven qualifying or fountain spirits which generate the soul, intending to destroy and to *kindle* them, that thereby he may get the whole body for his own propriety.

120. Now if the soul would willingly bring its light and knowledge into the *human* mind, then it must fight and strive hard and stoutly, and yet hath a very *narrow* passage to enter in at; it will often be knocked down by the devil, but it must stand to it here, like a *champion* in the battle. And if it now gets the *victory*, then it hath conquered the devil; but if the devil prevails and gets the better, then the soul is *captivated*.

121. But seeing the fleshly birth or geniture is not the soul's *own* proper house, and that it cannot possess it as an *inheritance*, as the devil doth, therefore the fight and the battle lasteth as long as the house of flesh lasteth.

122. But if the house of flesh be once destroyed, and that the soul is not *yet* conquered or vanquished in its house, but is free and unimprisoned, then the fight is *ended*, and the devil must be gone from this spirit *eternally*.

---

* "fighteth against the murder of the devil" = "fighteth against the murder that is being committed by the devil."

123. Therefore this is a very difficult *article* to be understood; nay, it cannot be understood at all, except by experience in *this* fight. Though I should write *many* books thereof, yet thou wouldst understand *nothing* of it, unless thy spirit stand in *such* a birth or geniture, and that the knowledge be generated in thyself; otherwise thou canst neither comprehend *nor believe* it.

124. But if thou comprehendest this, then also thou understandest the strife or the fight which the *angels* held with the devils. For *the angels have not flesh nor bones*, no more have the devils.

125. For their bodily or *corporeal* birth standeth only in the seven qualifying or fountain spirits, but the animated or *soulish* birth in the angels uniteth, mixeth or operateth with God; but it is *not* so in the devils.

126. Therefore thou must here know, that the angels with their animated or *soulish* birth, in which they qualify and unite with God, have striven and fought in *God's power* and spirit against the kindled devils, and turned them out from the light of God, and driven them together into a *hole*, that is, into a narrow court, quarter or compass, like a prison, which is the place or space in, upon and above the earth, up to the moon, which is a goddess of the earthly birth or geniture.

127. So far reacheth their extent now, till the last day, and then they will get a house in that

place where the *earth* now is and standeth, and this will be called *the burning hell*.

[" *That is, in the outermost birth in the dark-* " *ness, wherein they reach not the second Prin-* " *ciple and source or fountain of the* light."]

128. Lord *Lucifer*, wait for it, and in the meanwhile take this for an assured prophecy concerning it; for thou wilt get the kindled *Salitter* in the outermost birth or geniture, (which thou thyself hast so prepared and fitted), to be thy *eternal house* to dwell in.

129. But not in such a form as [that in which] it now standeth, but all will be *separated* in the kindled wrath-fire; and the dark, hot, cold, rugged, hard, bitter, stinking refuse, will be *left thee* for an eternal inn and lodging.

130. Thou wilt be such an eternal, almighty god therein, as a *prisoner* in a deep prison or dungeon, where thou wilt neither attain nor see the eternal light of God. But the kindled bitter wrath of God will be thy boundaries, out of which thou canst never get.

THE SEVENTEENTH CHAPTER

Of the lamentable and miserable *State and Condition of the* corrupt perished Nature, *and Original of the four Elements,* instead of *the holy Government of God.*

1. ALTHOUGH God be an eternal, almighty regent or governor, whom none can resist, yet *nature* in its kindling hath now gotten a very monstrous strange government, such as was *not* before the times of the wrath.

2. For the six qualifying or fountain spirits did generate the seventh nature - spirit before the times of the wrath, in the place of this world, very meekly and *pleasantly,* as is now done in heaven, and not so much as the least spark of wrath or anger rose up therein.

3. Moreover, all was very bright and light therein, neither was there need of any *other* light; but the fountain or well-spring of the Heart of God enlightened *all,* and was a light in all, which did shine everywhere all over incessantly without any obstacle. For nature was very

rarified and thin or transparent, and all stood merely in power, and was in a very pleasant *lovely* temper.

4. But as soon as *in nature* the fight began with the proud devil, then in the seventh nature-spirit, in the court, region or extent of *Lucifer*, which is the place of this world, all gat *another* form and operation.

5. For nature gat a twofold source, and the outermost birth or geniture in nature was kindled in the wrath-fire, which [1] fire now is called the *wrath of God*, or *the burning hell*.

[1] nature-fire, God's anger, hell.

Note.

6. Here is required most inward sense or perception to understand this; for the place where the light is generated in the heart alone comprehendeth it, the *outward* man doth not comprehend it at all.

7. But behold! when *Lucifer* with his host or army stirred or *awakened* the wrath-fire in the nature of God, so that God was moved to anger in nature in the place of *Lucifer*, then the outermost birth or geniture in nature gat *another* quality, which was very fierce, astringent, cold, hot, bitter and sour.

8. The moving or boiling spirit, which *before* qualified or operated very meekly in nature, became, in its outermost birth or geniture, very exhalted and *terrible*, which now, in the outer-

most birth, is called the *wind*, or the element of *air*, in regard of its elevation or expansion.

9. For when the seven spirits kindled themselves in their outermost birth or geniture, then they generated such a *violent* moving spirit; and so the sweet water, which before the times of the wrath was very rarified and thin and incomprehensible, grew very thick and elevated and swelled, and the astringent quality grew very sharp and cold-fiery or fierce-cold, for it got a strong attracting together, like *salt*.

¹ Or saltpetre.   10. For the saltwater or ¹ salt, which still to this day is found in the earth, hath its original and descent from the *first kindling* of the astringent quality; and so the stones also have their beginning and descent from thence, as also the earth.

11. For the astringent quality now attracted the *Salitter* very strongly together, and dried it, whence the *bitter* earth is proceeded; but the stones are from the *Salitter* which at that time stood in the power of the tone or tune.

12. For as nature, with the working, wrestling and rising up of its birth or geniture, stood in the time of the kindling, just *such* a *matter* attracted itself together.

Now it may be asked, How then is a comprehensible or palpable son come to be out of an incomprehensible mother?

Answer.

13. Thou hast a *similitude* of this, in that the earth and stones are proceeded out of the incomprehensibility.

14. For behold, the deep between heaven and earth is also incomprehensible, and yet the elementary qualities *sometimes* generate living comprehensible flesh therein, as grasshoppers, flies, and worms or creeping things.

15. Which is caused by the *strong* attracting together of the qualities, in which attracted *Salitter* the life is suddenly generated. For when the heat kindleth the astringent quality, then the life riseth up, for the bitter quality stirreth itself, which is the original of life.

16. So in like manner the *earth* and *stones* have their descent; for when the *Salitter* kindled itself in nature, then all became very rugged, thick and dark, like a thick dark mist or cloud, which the astringent quality dried up hard with its coldness.

17. But seeing the light in the outermost birth was extinguished, the heat also was captivated in the comprehensibility or palpability, and could *no more* generate its life. From thence *death* came into nature, so that nature or the corrupt earth could no more help it, and thereupon *another* creation of light must needs follow, or else the earth would have been an *eternal* indissolvable

death; but now the earth generateth or bringeth forth fruit in the power and kindling of the *created* light.

Now one might ask, What is the condition then of this *twofold* birth or geniture? Is God then extinguished in the kindling of the wrath-fire, in the place of this world, so that nothing else is there but a *mere* wrath-fire? Or is the *one* only God become a *twofold God*?

Answer.

18. Thou canst not better comprehend, apprehend or understand this, than in and by thy *own body*, which, through the first fall of *Adam* with all its [the body's] birth or geniture, fitness, faculties and will, is become just such a house as the place of this world is come to be.

19. First, thou hast the *bestial* flesh, which is come to be so through the lustful longing bite of the apple, for it is the house of *corruption*. For when *Adam* was made out of the corrupted *Salitter* of the earth, that is, out of the seed, or [1] mass, or lump which the Creator extracted out of the corrupted earth, he was not then at first such flesh, else his body had been created *mortal*, but he had *an angelical power-body*, in which he should have subsisted eternally, and should have eaten angelical fruit, which did grow for him in Paradise before his fall, *before* the LORD cursed the earth.

[1] Text, *Massa.*

20. But seeing the seed, or mass, or lump, out of which *Adam* was made, was somewhat infected with the corrupt disease or malady of the devil, *Adam therefore* longed after his mother, that is, to eat of the fruit of the corrupted earth, which then in its outward comprehensibility was become so evil, and in the wrath-fire was become so hard, palpable and comprehensible.

21. But seeing *Adam's spirit* longed after that fruit which was of the quality of the corrupted earth, *therefore* also nature formed or framed such a tree for him as was *like* the corrupted earth.

22. For *Adam* was the heart in nature, and therefore his animated or soulish spirit did *help* to image, fashion or form *this tree*, of which he would fain eat.

23. But when the devil saw that the *lust* was in *Adam*, then he stung confidently at the *Salitter* in *Adam*, and infected *yet* more and more the *Salitter* out of which *Adam* was made.

24. Then *it was time* that the Creator should frame a *wife* for him, who afterwards set the *sin on work*, and did eat of the false, evil or corrupt fruit. Else if *Adam* had eaten of the tree *before the woman* had been made out of him, then it would have been far *worse* than it is.

25. But seeing this requireth a high and deep description, as also requireth much room, therefore seek for it concerning the *fall* of *Adam*, where you will find it largely described.

So now I return to the forementioned Similitude.

26. Now when *Adam* did eat of the fruit, which was good and evil, then he suddenly gat such a body also. The fruit was corrupt or perished, and palpable, as to this day all fruits now on earth are; and so such a fleshly and palpable or comprehensible body *Adam* and *Eve* gat instantly.

27. But now the flesh is *not* the whole man; for this flesh cannot comprehend or apprehend the Deity, else the flesh were not mortal and corruptible, or fading and transitory; for Christ saith, [1] *It is* [2] *the spirit that quickeneth, the flesh profiteth nothing.*

[1] John vi. 63.
[2] Or the spirit is the life.

28. For *this flesh* cannot inherit the kingdom of heaven, but is only a *seed* which is sown into the earth, out of which will grow an impalpable or incomprehensible body, such as the *first* was before the fall. But the spirit is eternal life, which uniteth, qualifieth or mixeth with God, and comprehendeth the *internal* Deity in nature.

29. Now as man in his *outward* being is *corrupted*, and as to his fleshly birth or geniture is in the wrath of God, and is moreover also an *enemy* of God, and yet is but one man, and not two; and on the other hand, in his spiritual birth or geniture he is a child and *heir of God*, who ruleth and liveth with God, and qualifieth, mixeth or uniteth with the innermost birth or geniture

of God; thus also is the place of this world come to be.

30. The outward comprehensibility or palpability in the whole nature of this world, and of all things which are therein, standeth all in the *wrath-fire* of God, for it is become thus through the kindling of nature; and lord *Lucifer* with his angels hath his dwelling now in the same outward birth or geniture which standeth in the wrath-fire.

31. But now the Deity is *not so separated* from the outward birth or geniture, as if they were *two* things in this world; if so, man could have *no hope*, and then this world did not stand in the power and love of God.

32. But the Deity *is* in the outward birth, hidden, and hath the fan or casting shovel in its hand, and will one day cast the chaff and the kindled *Salitter* upon a heap, and will draw away from it its inward birth or geniture, and give them to lord *Lucifer* and his *crew* of followers for an eternal house.

33. In the *meanwhile* lord *Lucifer* must lie *captive* and imprisoned in the outermost birth in the nature of this world, in the *kindled* wrath-fire; and therein he hath great power, and can reach into the *heart* of all creatures with his animated or soulish spirit in the outermost birth or geniture, which standeth in the wrath-fire.

34. Therefore the soul of man must fight and

strive continually with the devil, for *he still presents before it the crab-apples of Paradise*—

    [" *That is, the fierce source of malignity,* " *wherewith the soul is infected.*"]

—and invites it also to bite thereof, that he thereby may also bring it into his prison.

35. If that will not succeed to his purpose, then he strikes many a hard blow at the head,* and that man must continually *lie under the cross,* affliction and misery in this world.

36. For he hideth the noble grain of mustard-seed, so that *man doth not know himself.* And then the world supposeth that the man is thus plagued and smitten of God, whereby the devil's kingdom remaineth always *hidden* and undis-covered.

37. But stay a little; thou hast given me also many a blow, I have experimental knowledge of thee, and here I will open thy door to thee a little, that *another also* may see what thou art.

    * " many a hard blow at the head " (*Kopfstoss*).   See Ch. 16, par. 117.

THE EIGHTEENTH CHAPTER

Of the Creation *of Heaven and Earth; and
of the* first Day.

1. MOSES writeth in his [1] first book *as if* [1] Genesis. he had been *present*, and had beheld all with his eyes; but without doubt he received it in writing from his forefathers: It may be *he*, in the spirit, might well have discerned somewhat *more* herein than his forefathers did.

2. But because at that time, when God created heaven and earth, there was *yet no man* who saw it, therefore it may be concluded that *Adam* before his fall, while he was yet in the deep knowledge of God, knew it in the spirit.

3. But yet when he fell, and was set into the *outward* birth or geniture, he knew it no more, but kept it in remembrance, only as a dark and veiled story; and this he left to his posterity.

4. For it is manifest, that the first world before the deluge or flood knew *as little* of the qualities and birth or geniture of God as this last world wherein we now live knoweth: For the external

fleshly birth or geniture could *never* apprehend or *understand* the Deity, otherwise somewhat more would have been written of it.

5. But seeing through the *divine grace* in this high article this great mystery hath been somewhat revealed to *me*, in *my spirit*, according to the inward man, (which qualifieth, mixeth and uniteth with the Deity), therefore I *cannot* forbear to describe it according to my *gifts*. And I would have the Reader faithfully admonished not to be offended at the *simplicity* of the author.

6. For I do it not out of a desire of *boasting* and vainglory, but in a humble information to the Reader, (that thereby the works of God might be *somewhat* better known, and the devil's kingdom revealed and laid open, seeing this present modern world moveth and liveth in all malice, wickedness and *devilish* vicious blasphemies) and that the world might once see in what kind of power, impulse or driving it liveth, and in what kind of *inn* it taketh up its lodging.

7. I do it to try whether I may, with the *entrusted* talent, happily get gain of usury, and not return it to my God and Creator again singly and empty, without improvement, like the *lazy* servant who had stood idle in the vineyard of the Lord, and would require his wages without having laboured at all.

8. But if the devil should raise mockers and despisers, who would say it doth not become me

to climb so *high* into the Deity, and to dive so *deeply* thereinto :

9. To all of them I give this for an answer : That I am not climbed up into the Deity, neither is it possible for such a mean man as I am to do it ; but the Deity is climbed up into me, and from *its love* are these things revealed to me, which otherwise I, in my half-dead fleshly birth or geniture, must needs have let alone altogether.

10. But seeing I have such an impulse upon me, I let *him* act and move in me, he who knoweth and understandeth what it is, and whose pleasure it is that I should do it ; I, poor man of earth, dust and ashes, could *not* do it. But the spirit inviteth * and citeth all such mockers and despisers [to come] before the *innermost* birth or geniture of God in this world, [and] to desist from their wickedness and malice : If not, then they shall be spewed out as *hellish chaff* into the *outermost* birth or geniture in the wrath of God.

Now observe :

11. When God was now moved to anger in the *third* birth or geniture, in the court, quarters or region of *Lucifer*, which was all the space and

---

* "But the spirit inviteth," etc. St M. renders this clause : "But the spirit inviteth all these mockers and these scorners of the innermost birth," etc. This gives an entirely different meaning, which, though it *may* be the real sense intended by J. B., hardly seems warranted by the original, " *vor* die innerste Geburt."

room or extent of this world, then the light was *extinguished* in the third birth or geniture, and all became a darkness, and the *Salitter* in the third birth or geniture was rough, wild, hard, bitter, sour, and in some parts stinking, stagnant and morass-like, all according to the birth or geniture of the qualifying or fountain spirits then at that time working.

12. For in that place wherein the *astringent* quality was predominant, there the *Salitter* was attracted together and dried, so that hard dry *stones came to be*; but in those places where the astringent spirit and the bitter were equally alike predominant, there sharp small gravel and *sand* came to be, for the raging bitter spirit brake the *Salitter* all to pieces.

13. But in those places where the *tone*, together with the astringent spirit, was predominant in the water, there copper, iron, and such like rocky ores of minerals came to be: but where the *water* was predominant, together with all the spirits jointly and equally, there the wild earth came to be, and the water was here and there like a cloud or vapour held *captive* in the clefts and veins or spaces of the rocks; for the astringent spirit, as the father of corrupted nature, held it captive with its sharp *attracting* together.

14. But the *bitter* spirit is the chief cause of the black earth, for through its fierce bitterness the *Salitter* became killed in its outermost birth

or geniture, from whence existed the wild or *barren* earth.

15. But the *heat* in the astringent spirit chiefly helped to make the hardness; but where that [hardness] came to be, there it [the heat] generated the noblest and most precious *Salitter* in the earth, as gold, silver, and precious stones.

16. For when the *shining light*, by reason of the hard, dry and rough matter, became extinguished, then it was together dried up and incorporated in the heat, which is the father of the light.

Yet you must understand it thus:

17. Where the hot spirit in the *sweet water* was predominant in love, there the astringent spirit attracted the matter together, and so thereby the noblest ores of minerals and precious stones were generated.

18. But concerning precious stones, as carbuncles, rubies, diamonds, smaragdines or emeralds, onyxes and the like, which are of the *best* sort, they have their original where the *flash* of the light rose up in the love. For that flash becometh generated in the meekness, and is the heart in the centre of the qualifying or fountain spirits; therefore those stones are also meek, full of virtue, delightful, pleasant and lovely.

Now it might be asked, Why in this world is man so in love with gold, silver and precious stones, above all other things, and useth them for a ¹defence or protection, and for the maintenance of his body?

¹ Eccles. vii. 12. With money and treasures men defend themselves, as with a shield.

Answer.

19. Herein lieth the *pith* or kernel; for gold, silver, and precious stones, and all bright ores of minerals, have their original from the *light*, which shone before the times of wrath in the outermost birth or geniture of nature, that is, in the *seventh* nature-spirit: So now, seeing every man is as the whole house of this world, therefore all his qualifying or fountain spirits love the *kernel*, or the best thing that is in the corrupted nature, and that they use for the defence, protection and ²maintenance of themselves.

² Or livelihood.

20. But the innermost kernel, which is the Deity, that they can nowhere comprehend, for the *wrath* of the fire lieth before it, as a strong ³wall, *and this wall must be broken down with a very strong storm or assault, if the astral spirits will see into it.* But the door standeth open to the animated or soulish spirit, for it [the animated or soulish spirit] is withheld by nothing, but is as God himself is, in his innermost birth or geniture.

³ Or bulwark.

Now then it might be asked, How then shall I understand myself in or according to the threefold birth or geniture in nature?

The depth!

21. Behold, the *first*, innermost and deepest birth or geniture standeth in the centre, and is the *heart* of the Deity, which is generated by the qualifying or fountain spirits of God; and this birth or geniture is the *light*, which yet, though it be generated out of the qualifying or fountain spirits, no qualifying or fountain spirit of itself alone can comprehend, but every qualifying or fountain spirit comprehendeth only its own instanding, innate place or seat in the light; but all the seven spirits jointly together comprehend the whole light, for they are the father of the light.

22. Thus also the qualifying or fountain spirits of *man* do not *wholly* comprehend the innermost birth or geniture of the Deity, which standeth in the light; but every qualifying or fountain spirit reacheth, with *its* animated or *soulish* birth or geniture, into the heart of God, and uniteth, qualifieth or mixeth *therewith* in that place.

23. And that is the hidden birth or geniture in nature, which no man by his own reason, wit or *capacity* can comprehend; but the *soul* of that man alone who standeth in the light of God comprehends it, and no other.

The Second *Birth or Geniture in Nature,*
are the seven Spirits of Nature.

24. This birth or geniture is more *intelligible* and comprehensible, but yet also only to *the*

children of this Mystery. The ploughman doth not understand it; though he seeth, smelleth, tasteth, heareth and feeleth it, yet he but looks on it, and knoweth not *how* the being thereof is.

[" *By this is meant or understood the corrupt* " *reason in its own wit, ingenuity or capacity,* " *without the spirit of God. The* doctor, *as well* " *as the* ploughman, *is here meant, the one is as* " *blind as the other concerning the* Deity; *and* " *sometimes the peasant or ploughman exceeds* " *the doctor in knowledge, if the peasant cleaves* " *close to God.*"]

25. Now these are the spirits wherein all things stand, both in heaven and in this world, and from these the *third* and outermost spirit is generated, wherein corruptibility standeth.

26. But [1] this spirit, or this birth hath *seven* kinds or species, *viz.* the astringent, the sweet, the bitter, the hot: these four generate the *comprehensibility* in the third birth or geniture.

[1] Or third spirit.

27. The fifth spirit is the love, which existeth from the light of the life, which generateth *sensibility* and *reason.*

28. The sixth spirit is the tone, which generateth the *sound* and joy, and is the spring or source rising up through all the spirits.

29. In these six spirits now standeth the spirit of life, and the will or reason and *thoughts* of all the creatures; and all arts, inventions, formings

and imagings of all that which standeth in the *spirit* in the *incomprehensibility.*

30. The seventh spirit is nature, in which standeth the corporeal being of all six spirits, for the six spirits generate the seventh.   In this spirit standeth the corporeal being of angels, devils, and men, and it is the *mother* of all the six spirits, in which they generate themselves, and in which they also generate the light, which is the heart of God.

Of the Third *Birth or Geniture.*

31. Now the third birth or geniture is the comprehensibility or palpability of nature, which (*before* the time of God's wrath) was rarified and transparent, lovely, pleasant and bright, so that the qualifying or fountain spirits could see *through* and *through* all.

32. There was neither stone nor earth therein, neither had it [the third birth or geniture] need of any such created or contracted light as now; but the light generated itself *everywhere* in the centre, and all stood in the light.

33. But when king *Lucifer* was created, then he excited or awakened the wrath of God in this *third* birth or geniture; for the bodies of the angels came to be *creatures* in this third birth.

34. Now then, seeing the devils kindled their own bodies, intending thereby to domineer over the whole Deity, *therefore* the creator also, in his

wrath, kindled this *third* spirit, or this third birth or geniture in nature, and imprisoned the devil therein, and made an eternal lodging therein for him, that he might not be *higher* than the *whole* God.

[" *Understand, in the outward sources or* " *qualities; for the outermost of all, is also the* " *innermost of all.*"]

35. But seeing the devils kindled themselves out of pride, *wantonness* and wickedness; *therefore* they were quite thrust out from the birth or geniture of the light; and they can neither lay hold of nor comprehend it *eternally.*

36. For the light of their heart, which qualified, mixed or united with the heart of God, they themselves have extinguished, and instead *thereof* have generated a fierce, hot, astringent, bitter, hard and stinking devilish spirit.

37. But now thou must *not think* that thereupon the whole nature or place of this world is become a mere bitter wrath of God. No; here lieth the point: the *wrath* doth not comprehend the innermost birth or geniture in nature, for the *love* of God is yet hidden in the centre, in the whole place of this world; and so the house which lord *Lucifer* is to be in is *not fully* separated, but there is still in all things of this world both love and wrath *one in the other*, and they always wrestle and strive one with the other.

38. But the devils cannot lay hold on the wrestling of the light, but only on the wrestling of the wrath, wherein they are *executioners* or hangmen, to execute the justice or law, which was pronounced in God's wrath against *all* wicked men.

39. Neither *ought* any man to say that he is generated in the wrath-fire of the total corruption or perdition, *out of God's predestinate purpose.* No; the corrupted earth doth not stand in the total wrath-fire of God, but only in its *outward* comprehensibility or palpability, wherein it is so hard, dry and bitter.

40. Whereby every one may perceive that this poison and *fierceness* doth not belong to the love of God, in which there is nothing but *meekness.*

41. Yet I do not say this, as if every man were *holy* as he cometh from his mother's womb, but as the tree is, so is its fruit. Yet if a mother beareth or bringeth forth a child of the devil, the fault is not God's, but the parents' wickedness.

42. Yet if a wild twig be planted in a sweet soil, and be *engrafted* with some other of a better and sweeter kind, then there groweth a mild tree, though the twig were *wild*. For here all is possible; the evil is as soon changed into good, as the good into evil.

43. For every man is *free*, and is as *a god* to himself; in this life man may *change* and alter himself either into wrath or into light. Such

clothes or garments as a man puts on, transfigure him. And what manner of body soever man *soweth* into the earth, such a body also groweth up from it, though in another form, clarity and brightness, yet all according to the quality of the *seed*.

44. For if the earth were *quite* forsaken of God, then it could never bring forth *any* good fruit, but mere bad and evil fruit. But seeing the earth standeth yet in God's love, therefore his wrath will not burn therein eternally, but the love *which hath overcome* will spew out the wrath-fire.

45. Then will the burning hell begin, when the love and the wrath shall be *separated*. In this world the love and the wrath are the one in the other in *all* creatures, and that which overcometh in the wrestling inheriteth the house by right, whether it be the kingdom of hell, or the kingdom of heaven.

46. I do not speak so, as if the beasts in their birth or geniture were to inherit the kingdom of heaven : *No* ; for they are like the corrupted earth, evil and good ; but if they be sown again into their mother the earth, then they are earth.

47. But the *Salitter* in a good beast will not therefore be left to the devil for a propriety, but will in the separated part, in the nature of God, eternally blossom—

["*That is, their* figure *will stand as a*

" *shadow upon the* holy *ground, in the*
" wonders, *viz., in the eternal* Magia :"]
—and bring forth other *heavenly* figures. But
the *Salitter* of the beast [1] of God's wrath will, in ¹·from, or
the wrath of God, bear eternal *hellish* fruits.   belonging to.

48. For if the earth be once kindled, then in
the wrath burneth the fire, and in the love the
light ; and then *all* will be separated, for the one
cannot comprehend the other *any more.*

49. But in this present time everything hath
a twofold source and quality ; whatsoever thou
buildest and sowest here in the *spirit*, be it with
words, works or thoughts, *that* will be thy eternal
house.

50. Thus thou seest and *understandest* out of
what the earth and stones are come to be.   But
if that kindled *Salitter* should have continued to
be thus in the whole deep of this world, then
the whole place thereof would have been a *dark
valley* ; for the light was imprisoned, together
with and in the *third* birth or geniture.

51. Not that the light of the heart of God in
its *innermost birth* is imprisoned : No ; but the
lustre and the shining thereof, in the *third* birth
or geniture, was incorporated with, and in, the
outermost comprehensibility ; and therefore it is
that men are in love with all those things which
stand in *that Salitter.*

52. But seeing the whole deep, in the third
birth or geniture, was very dark in regard of the

corrupted Salitter of the earth and stones, *therefore the* Deity could not endure it so to be, but created and compacted together the earth and stones, as in *one lump*, or as on a heap. *Concerning which*, Moses [1] *writeth thus:*

¹ Gen. i. 1.

Am   Anfang   schuff GOTT Himmel und Erden.
In the beginning created GOD heaven and earth.

53. These words must be considered exactly, [2] what they are. For the word (Am) conceiveth itself in the *heart*, and goeth forth to the *lips*, but there is captivated and goeth back again sounding, till it cometh to the place from whence it went forth.

² Or how these *German* words are framed in the articulation by the instruments of speech ; that what they signify according to the language of nature may be understood.

54. This signifieth now, that the [3] sound went forth from the heart of *God*, and encompassed the whole place or extent of this world ; but when [4] it was found to be *evil*, then the sound returned again into its own place.

³ voice of God.

⁴ the place of this world.

55. The word or syllable (An) thrusteth itself out from the heart, and *presseth forth* at the mouth, and hath [5] an after-pressure ; * but when it is spoken forth, then it *closeth* itself up in the midst or centre of its seat with the [6] upper gums, and is *half* without and *half* within.

⁵ Or murmuring sound.

⁶ Or palate.

56. This signifieth that the heart of God had a loathing against the *corruption*, and so thrust away the corrupted being from himself, but *laid hold* on it again in the midst or centre at the heart.

* "after-pressure," that is, a lingering emphasis. St M. aptly renders this, "*une longue trace*," "a long track or trail."

57. As the tongue breaketh off or divideth the word or syllable, and keeps it half without and half within, so the heart of God would *not wholly* reject the kindled *Salitter*, but the malignity, malice and impulse of the devil; and the other part should be re-edified or built again *after* this time.

58. The word or syllable (⸗fang) goeth *swiftly* from the heart out at the mouth, and is *stayed* also by the hinder part of the tongue and the gums; and when it is let loose, it maketh another swift pressure from the heart, out at the mouth.

59. This signifieth the sudden *rejection* at the riddance and thrusting out of the devils, together with the corrupted *Salitter*; for the strong and swift spirit thrusteth the breath *strongly* away from it, and *retaineth* the true tone of the word or expression with it at the hindermost gum, and that is the true spirit of the word or syllable.

60. This signifieth that the corrupted *fierceness* is thrust out eternally from the light of God, but the inward spirit, which is *loaded* therewith against its will, shall be set again in its first house.

61. The last after‑pressure (⸗ang) signifieth that the innermost spirits in the corruption are not *altogether* pure, and therefore they need a sweeping away, *purging* or consuming of the wrath in the fire, which will be done at the end of this time.

62. The word (Schuff) conceiveth itself *above* and *under* the tongue, and shutteth the teeth in the upper and lower gums, and so presseth itself *close* together, and being held together, and spoken forth again, then it openeth the mouth again swiftly, like *a flash*.

63. This signifieth the astringent spirit's *strong* driving together of the corrupted *Salitter*, as a lump on a heap.

64. For the teeth *retain* the word, letting the spirit go forth *leisurely* between the teeth. This signifieth that the astringent quality holdeth the earth and stones *firmly* and fast together; and yet, for all that, *letteth* the spirits of the earth spring up, grow and bear blossoms out of the astringent spirit; which signifieth the *regeneration or restitution of the spirits of the earth*.

65. But that the mouth is swiftly opened again *after* the word is ended, it signifieth, concerning the deep above the earth, that God the Lord will nevertheless dwell there, and *reserve* his regimen for himself, and hold the devil as a prisoner in the wrath-fire.

66. The word (Sott) conceiveth itself in the *midst* or centre, upon the tongue, and is thrust thither out of the heart, and leaveth the mouth *open*, and stayeth sitting on its royal seat, and soundeth without and within; but when it is spoken forth, then it maketh *another* pressure between the upper teeth and the tongue.

67. This signifieth that when God created heaven and earth, and all the creatures, he *nevertheless* remained in his divine, eternal, almighty seat, and *never* went away from it at all, and that HE alone is ALL. The last pressure signifieth the sharpness of his spirit, whereby in a moment he *effecteth* all in his whole body.

68. The word (Himmel) conceiveth itself in the heart, and is thrust forth to the lips, there it is *shut* up, and the syllable (*mel*) setteth the lips open again, and is held on the middle of the tongue, and so the spirit goeth forth on *both sides* of the tongue out of the mouth.

69. This signifieth that the *innermost* birth is become shut up from the outermost by the horrible sins, and is incomprehensible to the outward corrupted birth or geniture.

70. But seeing it is a word with a *twofold* syllable, and that the second syllable (*mel*) openeth the mouth again, it signifieth that the *gates* of the Deity have been opened again.

71. But that by the word or syllable (*mel*) it is conceived again upon the tongue, and held fast with the upper gums, and that in the meanwhile the spirit goeth out on both sides of the tongue.

72. This signifieth that God would again give to this corrupted kingdom or place in God, a *King* or *great* Prince, who would open again the innermost birth or geniture of the clear and

bright *Deity*, and thereby the Holy Ghost would go forth on both sides, that is, out of the innermost depth of the Father and of the Son, and would go forth *again* into this world, and would new regenerate this world again through the *New King*.

73. The word (unb) conceiveth itself in the heart, and is stayed and compacted, or *incorporated* by the tongue on the upper gums; but when it is *let loose*, it maketh another pressure from the heart, out at the mouth.

74. Now this signifieth the difference or *distinction* between the holy birth or geniture and the earthly. This syllable cometh indeed from the heart, but is stayed by the tongue on the upper gums, so that one cannot *yet* perceive what kind of word it is; and this signifieth that the earthly and corrupt birth or geniture cannot lay hold on, or apprehend the innermost birth or geniture, but is [1] foolish and silly.

[1] a foolish or silly virgin.

75. The last pressure from the heart signifieth that [2] it will indeed qualify, mix or *unite* with the *innermost* birth or geniture in its sensibility, perception or thoughts, but *cannot* apprehend it in its reason; therefore this syllable or word alone by itself is dumb, and hath no signification or understanding in itself alone, but is used only for distinction's sake, with some *other* word.

[2] the earthly birth.

76. The word (Erben) is thrust forth from the heart, and is conceived on the *hinder* part upon

the tongue, at the *hinder* gums, and *trembleth*; the tongue is used about the first syllable (𝔊𝔯𝔷), yet not steadily, but the tongue [1] recoils inwards [1] Or staggers. at the nether gums, and *croucheth* as it were before an enemy, trembling.

77. The other syllable (𝔷𝔟𝔢𝔫) is conceived by the tongue and *upper* gums, and leaveth the mouth open, and the spirit of formation goeth forth at the *nostrils*, and will not go forth together in this word out at the *mouth*; and though it carrieth forth somewhat indeed along with it, yet the true tone or noise of the true spirit goeth forth only through or at the nostrils, or organ of smelling.

This is a great Mystery.

78. The word or syllable (𝔊𝔯𝔷) signifieth the *kindled* astringent and bitter quality, the earnest *severe* wrath of God, which trembleth at the hinder part of the gums, before which the tongue is as it were afraid, and croucheth at the nether gums, and flieth as it were from an enemy.

79. The word or syllable (𝔷𝔟𝔢𝔫) conceiveth itself *on* the tongue again, and the spirit attracteth the power and virtue out of the word, and therewith goeth forth *another way* at the nostrils, and so goeth therewith up into or *towards* the brain before the royal seat. This signifieth that the outermost *Salitter* of the earth is *eternally* rejected from God's light and *holiness*.

80. But that the spirit layeth hold on the *power* and virtue of the word, and goeth another way through the nostrils into the brain before the throne of the senses or *thoughts*, signifieth that God will *extract* the heart of the earth from the wrath of wickedness; and *use* it to his eternal royal praise.

Observe:

81. He will extract from the earth the *kernel*, and the best or the good spirit, and will *regenerate* it anew, to his honour and glory.

82. *Here, O man, consider thyself well*, and mind what manner of seed thou sowest into the earth, the very same will spring up, and bear blossoms and fruit *for ever*, either in the love or in the wrath.

83. But when the good shall be separated from the evil, then thou wilt live in *that part* which thou hast laboured for here, be it either in heaven, or in hell-fire.

84. *In* [1] *whatsoever thou endeavourest, labourest and actest here, into that thy soul goeth when thou diest.*

[1] Whether heavenly or hellish, good or evil matter or thing.

85. Or dost thou think that this which I have set down here my spirit hath sucked out of the corrupted earth, or out of an old felt hat?

86. Truly no, for the spirit at this time of my description and setting it down did *unite* and qualify or mix with the deepest birth or geniture

of God. In that I have received my knowledge, and from thence it is sucked ; not in great earthly joy, but in the anxious birth or geniture, *perplexity* and trouble.

87. For what I did hereupon undergo, suffer and endure from the devil and the hellish quality, which as well doth rule in my *outward* man as in all men whatsoever, this thou canst not apprehend, unless thou also *dancest* in this round.

88. Had not our philosophers and doctors always played upon the fiddle of pride, but had played on the *musical instrument* of the prophets and apostles, there would have been far another knowledge and *philosophy* in the world.

89. Concerning which, in regard of my imbecility, want of literature or learning and study, as also the slowness and dulness of my *tongue*, I am very *insufficient*, but not so simple in the knowledge. Only I cannot deliver it in profound language, and in the *ornament* of eloquence, but I rest contented with my gift I have received, and am a *philosopher among the simple*.

Concerning the Creation of the Light in this World.

90. Here shut the eyes of thy *flesh* a little, for here they will profit thee nothing, seeing they are *blind* and dead, and open the eyes of thy spirit, and then I will rightly *shew thee* the *creation* of God.

Observe:

91. When God had driven the corrupted *Salitter* of earth and stones, (which had generated itself in the outermost birth by the *kindling*), together on a heap as in a lump, then, for that cause, the third birth or geniture in nature in the *deep*, above the earth, was not pure and bright, because the wrath of God did *yet burn* therein.

92. And though the innermost birth or geniture was light and bright, yet the outermost, which stood in the wrath-fire, could not *comprehend* it, but was altogether dark.

[1] Gen. i. 93. For *Moses* [1] writeth,

Und es war Finster auf der Tieffe.

And it was dark on the deep.

The word (auf) *on*, signifieth the *outermost* birth or geniture, and the word (in) signifieth the *innermost* birth or geniture.

94. But if the innermost birth had been dark, then the wrath of God had *rested* in this world eternally, and it would never have been light; but the wrath hath *not* thus touched or reached the heart of God.

95. Therefore he is a sweet, friendly, bounteous, good, meek, pure and *merciful* God, according to his heart in the *innermost* birth or geniture in the place of this world, and still continues so to be; and his meek love presseth forth from his

heart into the *outermost* birth or geniture of the wrath, and quencheth the same, and therefore Sprach Er, *He said*, Es werde Licht, *Let there be light*.

Here observe the sense in the highest depth.

96. The word (Sprach) or *said*, is spoken after the manner of men : Ye philosophers, open your eyes. I will, in my simplicity, teach you the Sprach Gottes, the speech, speaking or language of God, as indeed it must be.*

97. The word (Sprach) conceiveth itself *between* the teeth, for they bite or join *close* together, and the spirit hisseth forth through the teeth, and the tongue boweth or *bendeth* in the middle, and setteth its forepoint, as if it did listen after the hissing, and was *afraid*.

98. But when the spirit conceiveth the word, that *shuts* the mouth, and conceiveth it at the hinder gums upon the tongue in the hole or *hollowness*, in the bitter and astringent quality.

99. There the tongue is *terrified*, trembleth and croucheth to the nether gums, and then the spirit *cometh* forth from the heart, and closeth the word, which conceiveth itself at the hinder gums, in the astringent and bitter quality, in the wrath, and goeth forth mightily and strongly through the fierceness, as a king and a prince,

* "as indeed it must be." St M. has, "as indeed it ought to be."

and also *openeth* the mouth, and ruleth with a strong spirit from the heart through the *whole* mouth within, and also without the mouth, and maketh a mighty and *long syllable*, as a spirit which hath broken the wrath.

100. Against which the wrath, with its *snarling* in the astringent and bitter quality, at the hinder gums in the hollow on the tongue, *struggleth*, and keeps its right to itself, and keepeth its seat in its place, and lets the *meek* spirit come forth from the heart, through itself [the wrath], and thundereth with its [the wrath's] snarling after the meek spirit, and so *helps* to form or frame the word, yet with its *thundering* cannot get away from its seat, but abideth in its hollow hole, as a captive prisoner, and appears terrible.

This is a great Mystery.

101. Here observe the sense and meaning; if thou apprehendest it, then thou *understandest* the Deity aright, if not, then thou art yet blind in the *spirit*.

102. *Judge not*, else here thou runnest counter against a strong gate, and wilt be imprisoned; if the wrath-fire catcheth thee, then thou wilt remain *eternally* therein.

103. Thou child of man, behold now, how great a *gate* of heaven, of hell, and of the earth, as also of the whole Deity, the spirit openeth to thee.

104. Thou shouldst *not* think that God at that time did speak in that way as men do, and that it is but a *weak*, impotent word, like *man's* word.

105. Indeed man's word conceiveth itself just in such a *form*, manner, proportion, quality and correspondency; only the *half-dead* man doth not understand it: This understanding is very noble, dear and precious, for it is generated only in the knowledge of the *Holy Ghost*.

106. But God's word, which he spake then in power, hath encompassed heaven and earth, and the heaven of heavens; yea, and the *whole* Deity also.

107. But it frameth and conceiveth itself first between the teeth closed or *clapped* together, and *hisseth*, which signifieth that the Holy Ghost at the beginning of the creation went through the firmly closed *wall* of the third and outermost birth or geniture, which standeth in the *wrath-fire* in this world.

108. For it is written, *And it was dark on the deep, and the spirit of God moved on the water.* The *deep* signifieth the *innermost* birth or geniture; and the *darkness* signifieth the *outermost* corrupt birth or geniture, in which the wrath burned. The *water* signifieth the allaying or *mitigation* of the spirit.

109. But that the spirit doth *hiss* through the teeth signifieth that the spirit *is gone forth* from the heart of God through the wrath; but that

the teeth remain *closed* together, whilst the
spirit hisseth, and do not open themselves,
signifieth that the wrath *hath not* comprehended
or reached the Holy Ghost.

110. But that the tongue doth *crouch* towards
the nether gums, and is sharp at the point, and
will not be used about the hissing, signifieth
that the *outward birth* or geniture, together with
[1] The natural
man cannot
perceive the
things of God.
all the creatures which are therein, [1] *cannot*
comprehend or reach to apprehend the *Holy
Spirit*, which goeth forth out of the innermost
birth or geniture out from the heart of God,
neither can they hinder him by their power.

111. For he goeth and penetrateth through
all shut or closed doors, closets and births, and
needs no opening of them; as the teeth cannot
stay or hinder the spirit or *breath* from going or
passing through them.

112. But that the lips stand open, when it is
come hissing through the teeth, signifieth that
[2] The Holy
Ghost.
[2] he with his going forth out of the heart of God,
in the creation of this world, hath *opened* again
the *gates* of heaven, and is gone through the
gates of God's wrath, and hath left the *wrath* of
God strongly shut and bolted up, and hath left
the devil his eternal kindled wrath-house *close*
locked up, out of which he cannot come eternally.

113. It further signifieth that the Holy Ghost
in like manner hath an *open gate* in the wrath-
house of this world, where he may drive and

perform his work, *incomprehensibly* as to the gates of hell, and where he gathereth or congregateth a *holy seed* to his eternal praise, against or without the will of the strong, fast, hellish gates, and altogether incomprehensibly as to *them*.

114. But in the same way as the spirit effecteth his going forth, and his conceived or intended will, through the teeth, and yet the *teeth* do not stir, *nor can* they comprehend the will of the spirit, so the Holy Ghost also, without the apprehension or comprehension, either of the *devil* or of the *wrath* of God, buildeth or erecteth continually a holy seed or temple in the house of *this* world.

115. But that the whole word (Sprach) *said*, formeth or conceiveth itself at the *hinder* gums on the tongue in the *hollow* hole in the centre of the astringent and bitter quality, and *snarleth*, signifieth that God hath conceived or framed the place of this world at the heart in the midst or centre of it, and hath built to himself again a house to his praise, against all the grumbling, murmuring and *snarling* of the devil, in *which* he ruleth with his Holy Ghost.

116. And in the same way as the spirit goeth forth from the heart through the grumbling, murmuring and snarling of the bitter and astringent quality, very *strongly* and powerfully, and with its going forth ruleth in the astringent and bitter quality, incomprehensibly as to the astrin-

gent and bitter quality, as a potent king, so also the spirit of God ruleth in the *outermost* birth or geniture of this world (in the wrath-house) *mightily*, and generateth to himself a temple therein, incomprehensibly to the wrath-house.

117. But that the astringent and bitter spirit doth so *grumble* and murmur, when the spirit from the heart goeth through its house, and ruleth powerfully, signifieth that the wrath of God, together with the devils, are, in the house of this world, *set* in opposition to the love, so that *both* these, all the time of this world, must fight and *strive* one against the other, as two armies in the field; *from whence also wars and fightings among men, and among beasts, and all creatures, have their original.*

118. But that the astringent and the bitter qualities conceive themselves *together* with the word, and unite and agree one with the other, and yet the spirit of *the heart alone* speaketh forth the word at the mouth, signifieth that *all* creatures, which were produced and put forth by the word alone, *viz.* the beasts, fowls, fishes, worms, trees, leaves, herbs and grass, were formed from the *whole* body, being good and evil.

119. And that in all these there *would stand* both the angry and corrupt quality, and also the love of God; and yet all would be *driven on* by the spirit of love, though those two would disturb, rub, plague, squeeze and *vex* each other.

Note.

120. Whereby then, in many a creature the wrath-fire would be so very *hard kindled* that the body, together with the spirit, will afford and produce an eternal wrath-*Salitter* in hell.

121. For the spirit, which is generated in the heart, must in its body walk through the midst or centre of the *hellish* gates, and may very *easily* be kindled; they are as wood and fire, which will burn, if thou pourest no water in among them.

122. *O man, thou wast not, by the Word, created together with and as the beasts, from good and evil; and if thou hadst not eaten of good and evil, then the wrath-fire would not have been in thee; but by that means thou hast also gotten a bestial body: It is done: The love of God take pity, and have mercy in that behalf.*

123. But, that *after* the conceiving and compacting of the word together in the astringent quality at the hinder gums upon the tongue, the mouth *openeth* itself *wide*, and the compacted and united spirit goeth forth together at the mouth, which spirit is generated out of the heart and also out of the astringent and bitter quality, signifieth that the creatures would live in great anguish and *adversity*, and would not be able to generate through one body, but through *two*.

124. For the astringent and bitter quality receives the power from the spirit out of the heart, and infecteth or affecteth itself therewith: Therefore is nature now become *too weak* in the spirit of the heart, and is not able to deliver [itself from] its own innermost birth of the heart; and *for that cause* nature hath brought forth a male and a female.

125. Thus it denoteth also the evil and the good will in the whole or *universal* nature, and in all the creatures; that there would be a continual wrestling, fighting and destroying; from whence this world is *rightly called* a valley of misery, full of crosses, persecutions, toils and labours. For when the spirit of creation entered into the midst, and *interposed* its power, it was fain to make and form the creation in the *midst* or centre of the kingdom of hell.

126. Now seeing the outermost birth or geniture in nature is *twofold*, that is, both evil and good, *therefore* it is that there is a *perpetual* tormenting, squeezing, lamenting and howling; and the creatures in this life are subject to torments and afflictions, so that *this evil world is justly called a murderous den of the devil.*

127. But that the astringent and bitter spirit *sitteth still* in its seat at the hinder gums on the tongue, and *thrusteth* forth * the word at the

* "thrusteth forth" (*bellet*), "soundeth forth," or "crieth forth." The literal meaning is, "barketh forth."

mouth, and yet cannot get away from thence, signifieth that the devil and the wrath of God *would* indeed be domineering in all the creatures, yet would not have *full power* in them, but must *stay* in prison ; and that there they would belch forth or blow into all the creatures, and plague them, but would *not* overcome them, unless the creatures themselves are minded to tarry there in that place.

128. Just as the *meek* spirit of the heart goeth through the astringent and bitter quality, and overcometh it ; and though it be indeed infected with the astringent and bitter spirit, yet it *teareth* and breaketh thorough, as a conqueror : But if it should *wilfully* sit still in the hollow hole * in the astringent and bitter spirit, and suffer itself to be taken captive, and *would not* fight, then the fault were its own.

129. Thus it is also with those creatures that will continually *sow* and *reap* in the hellish fire, especially *that man* who liveth in a *continual desire* of pride, covetousness, envy and wrath, and will at *no time* fight and strive against them with the spirit and fire of *love* ; such a one himself attracteth the wrath of God, and the burning hellish fire, upon his body and soul.

130. But that the tongue doth *crouch* so

---

* "in the hollow hole." This rendering is correct according to the 1682 ed., but the 1715 and 1730 eds. have, "*in der Hölle*," "in hell."

much towards the nether gums when the word goeth forth, signifieth and denoteth the animated or *soulish* spirit of the creatures, especially of *man*.

131. The word which conceiveth itself at the upper gums, and which qualifieth or uniteth with the astringent and bitter spirit, signifieth the *seven spirits of nature*, or the astral birth or geniture, in which the devil ruleth, and the Holy Ghost *opposeth* him therein, and overcometh the devil.

132. But the tongue signifieth the *soul*, which is generated from the seven spirits of nature, and is the *son* ; and so now when the seven spirits will, *then* the tongue must stir, and must perform their *demands*.

133. If the astral spirits would not prove false, and would not woo the devil, to commit adultery with him, then they would *hide* the animated or *soulish* spirit, and hold it fast in their *bands* as a treasure, when *they fight* with the devil : Just as they hide and cover the tongue as their best jewel, when they wrestle with the astringent and bitter quality.

134. Thus you have a short and *real* introduction concerning the word which God hath spoken, rightly described in the knowledge of the *spirit*, faithfully imparted according to my gifts, and the *talent* I am entrusted with.

Now it may be asked, What then is it that

God *spake*, when he said, *Let there be light*, and there was light?

The Depth.

135. The *light* went forth from the innermost birth or geniture, and kindled itself in the outermost. [1] It *gave* again to the outermost a *natural* [1] Note. peculiar light of its own.

136. Thou must *not think* that the light of the sun and of nature is the heart of God, which shineth in secret. No; thou oughtest not to *worship the* light of nature, it is not the heart of God, but it is a *kindled light* in nature, whose power and heart stand in the unctuosity or *fatness* of the sweet water, and of all the other spirits in the *third* birth or geniture, and is *not* called God.

137. Though it be generated *in* God and *from* God, yet it is but the *instrument* of his handiwork, which cannot apprehend and *reach back* again to the clear Deity in the deepest birth or geniture, as the flesh cannot apprehend or reach the soul.

138. But it must *not* so be understood as if the Deity were *separated* from nature; no, but they are as body and soul : *Nature* is the body, and the *heart of God* is the soul.

Now a man might ask, What kind of light then was it that was kindled? Was it the sun and stars?

Answer.

139. No, the sun and stars were *first* created but on the fourth day, out of *that* very light : *
There was a light arisen in the seven spirits of nature which had no peculiar distinct *seat* or place, but did shine everywhere all over, but was *not bright* like the sun, but like an azure blue and light, according to the kind and manner of the qualifying or fountain spirits ; till afterwards the right creation and kindling of the *fire* in the water, in the astringent spirit, followed, *viz.* the sun.

* "light" = luminous, transparent, full of light. See Ch. 3, par. 50.

THE NINETEENTH CHAPTER

Concerning the Created Heaven, *and the Form of the* Earth, *and of the* Water, *as also concerning* Light *and* Darkness.

Concerning *Heaven.*

1. THE true *heaven*, which is our own proper human heaven, into which the soul goeth when it parteth from the body, and into which *Christ our King* is entered, and from whence it was that he came from his Father, and was born, and became *man* in the body or womb of *the Virgin Mary*, hath hitherto been *close hidden* from the children of men, and they have had many opinions about it.

2. Also the learned have scuffled about it with many strange scurrilous writings, falling one upon another in calumnious and disgraceful *terms*, whereby the holy name of God hath been reproached, his members wounded, his temple destroyed, and the holy heaven *profaned* with their calumniating and malicious enmity.

3. *Men have always* been of the opinion that

heaven is many hundred, nay, many thousand miles distant from the face of the earth, and that God dwelleth only in that heaven.

4. Some [1] *naturalists* or artists have undertaken to measure that height and distance, and have produced many *strange* and *monstrous* devices. Indeed, *before* this my knowledge and *revelation* of God, I held *that* only to be the true heaven, which in a round circumference and sphere, very azure of a light blue colour, extends itself *above* the stars, supposing that God had therein his *peculiar being*, and did *rule* only in the *power* of his holy spirit in this world.

[1] Physici. Studiers of natural philosophy, called physics; or the mathematicians.

5. But when this had given me many a hard blow and *repulse*, doubtless from [2] the spirit, which had a great longing yearning towards me, at last I fell into a very *deep melancholy* and heavy sadness, when I beheld and contemplated the great deep of this world, also the sun and stars, the clouds, rain and snow, and considered in my spirit the *whole* creation of this world.

[2] the Holy Spirit.

6. Wherein then I found to be in all things, *evil and good*, love and anger, in the inanimate creatures, *viz.* in wood, stones, earth and the elements, as also in men and beasts.

7. Moreover, I considered the little spark of light, *man*, what he should be esteemed for with God, in *comparison* with this great work and fabric of heaven and earth.

8. But finding that in all things there was evil

and good, as well in the *elements* as in the creatures, and that it went as *well* in this world with the wicked as with the virtuous, honest, and Godly; also that the *barbarous* people had the best countries in their possession, and that they had *more prosperity* in their ways than the virtuous, honest and Godly had.

9. I was *thereupon* very melancholy, *perplexed* and exceedingly troubled, no Scripture could *comfort* or satisfy me, though I was very well acquainted with it, and *versed* therein; at which time the devil would by no means stand idle, but was *often* beating into me many heathenish thoughts, which I will here be silent in.

10. But when in this *affliction* and trouble I elevated my spirit (for I then understood very little or not at all what it was), I *earnestly* raised it up into God, as with a great storm or onset, wrapping up my whole heart and mind, as also all my *thoughts* and whole will and resolution, *incessantly* to wrestle with the love and mercy of God, and not to give over, until he blessed me, that is, until he *enlightened me with his holy spirit*, whereby I might *understand* his will, and be rid of my sadness. *And then the spirit did break through.*

11. But when, in my resolved zeal, I gave so hard an assault, storm and onset upon God, and upon all the gates of hell, as if I had more reserves of virtue and power ready, with a *resolution to*

hazard my life upon it, (which assuredly were not in my ability *without* the assistance of the spirit of God), *suddenly*, after some violent storms made, my spirit *did break through* the gates of hell, even into the innermost birth or geniture of the Deity, and there I was *embraced* with love, as a bridegroom embraceth his dearly beloved bride.

12. But the greatness of the triumphing that was in the spirit I *cannot express*, either in speaking or writing; neither can it be compared to anything, but to *that* wherein the life is generated in the midst of death, and it is *like* the resurrection from the dead.

13. In this light my spirit suddenly saw through all, and *in* and *by* all the creatures, even in herbs and grass it knew God, who he is, and how he is, and what his will is: And suddenly in that light my will was set on by a mighty *impulse*, to describe *the being of God*.

14. But because I could not at once apprehend the *deepest* births of God in their *being*, and comprehend them in my *reason*, there passed almost *twelve* years, before the exact understanding thereof was given me.

15. It was with me as with a young tree that is planted in the ground, and at first is young and *tender*, and flourishing to the eye, especially if it comes on lustily in its growing: But [it] doth not bear fruit at once; and though it blossoms, the blossoms fall off; also many a cold wind,

frost and snow pass over it, *before* it comes to any growth and bearing of fruit.

16. So also it went with this spirit: The first fire was but a *seed*, and not a constant lasting light: *Since that time* many a cold wind blew upon it; but the will never extinguished.

16*a*. This tree was also often tempted to try whether it would bear fruit, and shew itself with blossoms; but the *blossoms* were struck off till this very time, wherein it standeth in its first fruit, in the growth or vegetation.

17. *From this light now it is that I have my knowledge*, as also my *will, impulse and driving*, and therefore I will set down this· knowledge in writing according to my gift, and let God work his will; and though I should *irritate* or enrage the whole world, the devil, and all the gates of hell, I will look on and wait what the LORD intendeth with it.

18. For I am much too *weak* to know his purpose; and though the spirit affordeth in the *light* to be known some things which are *to come*, yet according to the outward man I am too weak to comprehend the same.

19. But the animated or *soulish* spirit, which qualifieth or uniteth with God, that comprehends it well; but the *bestial body* attains only a glimpse thereof, just as if it lightened: For thus presenteth itself the innermost birth or geniture of the soul, when it teareth through the *outermost*

birth or geniture in the elevation of the Holy Ghost, and so breaketh through the gates of hell; but the outermost birth presently *shuts* again; for the *wrath* of God bolteth up the firmament, and holds it captive in its power.

20. Then the knowledge of the outward man is *gone*, and he walketh up and down in an *afflicted* and anxious birth or geniture, as a woman with child, who is in her travail, and would *always* fain bring forth her child, but *cannot*, and is full of throes.

21. Thus it goeth also with the bestial body, when it hath *once tasted* of the sweetness of God, then it continually hungereth and thirsteth after this sweetness: But the *devil* in the power of God's wrath opposeth exceedingly, and so a man in such a course must *continually* stand in an anxious birth or geniture; and so there is nothing but fighting and warring in his births or genitures.

22. I write this not for mine own glory, but for a *comfort* to the Reader, so that if perhaps he be minded to walk with me upon my *narrow* bridge, he should not suddenly be discouraged, dismayed and distrustful, when the gates of hell and God's wrath meet him, and *present* themselves before him.

23. When we shall come together *over* this narrow bridge of the fleshly birth or geniture, to be in yonder green meadow, to which the wrath of God doth *not* reach or come, then we shall

greatly rejoice at all our damages and hurts which we have sustained; though indeed at present the world doth account us for *fools*, and we must suffer the devil in the power of God's wrath to domineer, and to rush and roar over us: It should not trouble us, for it will be a more excellent *reputation* to us in the other life, than if in this life we had worn a royal crown; and there is so very *short a time* to get thither, that it is not worth the being called a *time*.

Now observe:

24. If thou fixest thy thoughts concerning heaven, and wouldst fain *conceive* in the mind what it is, and where it is, and how it is, thou *needest* not to swing or cast thy thoughts many thousand miles off, for that place, or that heaven, is *not thy* heaven.

25. And though indeed that is united with thy heaven as *one* body, and so together is *but the one* body of God, yet thou art not in that very place which is become a creature, aloft, many hundred thousand miles off; but thou art in the *heaven* of this world, which containeth also in it a deep, such as is not of any human number (or is not circumscriptive).

26. For the *true heaven* is everywhere, even in that very place where thou standest and goest, and so when thy spirit apprehendeth the innermost birth or geniture of God, and presseth in

through the astral and fleshly geniture, then it is *clearly* in heaven.

27. But that there is assuredly a *pure* glorious heaven in all the three births or genitures aloft above the deep of this world, in which God's being, together with that of the holy angels, riseth or *springeth up* very purely, brightly, beauteously and joyfully, is *undeniable*, and he is *not* born of God that denieth it.

But thou must know,

28. That the place of this world with its innermost birth and geniture uniteth or qualifieth with the heaven aloft *above us*, and so there is one heart, one being, one will, *one God, all in all.*

29. But that the place of this world is not called heaven, and that there is a firmament or fast enclosure between the *upper* heaven above us, hath this understanding or meaning, as followeth.

30. The upper heaven compriseth the two kingdoms, that of *Michael*, and that of *Uriel*, with all the holy angels that are *not fallen* with *Lucifer*, and that heaven *continueth* as it was from eternity, before the angels were created.

31. The other heaven is this world, in which *Lucifer* was a king, who kindled the outermost birth or geniture in nature; and that now is the *wrath* of God, and cannot be called God or heaven, but *perdition*.

32. Therefore the upper heaven closeth itself

so far in its outermost birth or geniture, and reacheth so far as the *wrath* of God reacheth, and so far as the government or dominion of *Lucifer* hath reached, for the corrupted or perished birth or geniture cannot comprehend the *pure*.

33. That is, the outermost birth or geniture of this world cannot comprehend the outermost birth or geniture of heaven *aloft* above this world, for they are one to the other as the life and the death, or as a *man* and a *stone* are one to the other.

34. Therefore there is a strong firmament or enclosure between the *outermost* birth or geniture of the upper heaven, and that of this world; for the firmament between them is *death*, which ruleth and reigneth everywhere in the outermost birth in *this* world, and this world is so bolted up therewith that the *outermost* birth of the *upper* heaven cannot come into the outermost birth of this world; there is a great cleft* or gulf between them. Therefore in our outermost birth or geniture we cannot *see* the angels, neither can the angels dwell with us in the *outermost* birth of this world; but in the *innermost* they dwell with us.

[35].[1]

36. And if or as we fight with the devil, they keep off his blows in the innermost birth, and are the defence and protection of the *holy* soul.

[1] [The numbers follow Sparrow's text. "35" is absent. —Eds.]

37. Therefore we can neither see nor compre-

* "cleft"—a literal translation of *Kluft*, gulf or chasm.

hend the holy angels; for the outermost birth of *their body* is incomprehensible to the outermost birth or geniture of this world.

38. The second birth of this world standeth in the life, for it is the *astral* birth, out of which is generated the *third* and holy birth or geniture, and therein love and wrath *strive* the one with the other.

39. For the second birth standeth in the seven qualifying or fountain spirits of this world, and is in all places and in all the creatures, as also in man: But the Holy Ghost also ruleth and reigneth in the *second birth*, and helpeth to generate the *third* holy birth or geniture.

40. But this third birth or geniture is the clear and *holy heaven*, which qualifieth or uniteth with the heart of God without, distinct and above all heavens, as one heart; also they are the one heart, which, as *an almighty, incomprehensible* God, holdeth and *beareth up* or sustaineth the place of this world, and holdeth the devil captive in the outermost birth in the anger-fire.

41. *And out of this heart* JESUS CHRIST, *the Son of God, in the womb or body of the Virgin* Mary, *went into all the three births or genitures, and assumed them really, that he might, through and with his innermost birth or geniture, take the devil, death and hell captive in the outermost birth, and overcome the wrath of God, as a king and victorious prince; and, in*

*the power of his geniture or birth in the flesh,
press through all men.*

42. And so by this entering of the innermost
birth of the heart of the heaven of this world
into the *astral* and outermost, is JESUS
CHRIST, the Son of God and of *Mary*, become
the *Lord* and *King* of this our heaven and earth,
who ruleth and *reigneth* in all the three births
or genitures over sin, the devil, death and hell,
and so *we with him* press through the sinful,
corrupted and outermost dead birth or geniture
of the flesh, *through death* and *the wrath of God*
into our heaven.

43. *In this heaven* now *sitteth our King*
JESUS CHRIST, *at the right hand of God*,
and encompasseth or surroundeth all the three
births, as *an almighty Son of the Father*, who is
present in and throughout all the three births
in this world, in all corners and places, and comprehendeth, holdeth and beareth up or sustaineth
all, as a new-born Son of the Father, in the
power, and upon the seat or *throne*, of the *once*
great, mighty, potent, and *now expelled*, accursed
and damned king *Lucifer*, the devil.

44. Therefore, thou child of man, be not discouraged, be not so timorous and despondent; for
if thou sowest in thy zeal and earnest sincerity
the *seed of thy tears*, thou dost not sow it in
earth, but in *heaven*; for in thy astral birth thou
sowest, and in thy animated or soulish birth

thou reapest, and in the kingdom of heaven thou possessest and enjoyest it.

45. While thou livest in this struggling or *striving* birth or geniture thou must buckle to, and suffer the devil to ride upon thee; but so hard as he striketh thee, so hard thou must strike him again, if thou wilt defend thyself. For when thou fightest against him, thou *stirrest up* his wrath-fire, and destroyest his nest, and this is then as a great *combustion*, and as a great strong battle maintained against him.

46. And though thy body may suffer pain, yet it is much worse with him when he is vanquished, for then he roareth like a lion that is *robbed* of her young whelps, for the fierceness and wrath of God *tormenteth* him; but if thou lettest him lodge *within* thee, then he groweth fat and *wanton*, and will *vanquish thee* in time.

47. Thus thou hast a real description of *heaven*: And though perhaps *thou* canst not in thy reason conceive it, yet *I can* very well conceive it; therefore consider rationally and seriously what God is.*

48. Thou seest in this world nothing but the *deep*, and therein the stars, and the birth or geniture of the elements: Now wilt thou say, God is

* "therefore consider rationally and seriously," etc. Sparrow has added "seriously," presumably because the German *vernünftig* expresses not so much the idea of thinking according to the rational faculty, as thinking "in reasonableness," *i e.* in a patient, open and temperate attitude of mind.

not there? Pray then, what was there in that place *before* the time of the world? Wilt thou say, There was nothing? Then thou speakest *without* reason, for thou must *needs* say that God was there, or else nothing would have come to be there.

49. Now if God was *there* then, who hath thrust him *out* from thence or vanquished him, that he should be there *no* more? But if God is there, then he is indeed in his *heaven*, and, moreover, in his *Trinity*.

50. But the devil hath kindled the bath or lake of wrath, whence the earth and the stones, also the elements, are become so fluctuating, as also cold, bitter, and hot. And so he hath [1] *destroyed* the outermost birth or geniture.

[1] killed or murdered.

51. Whereupon now this treatise, and my whole purpose therein, is to describe how the outermost birth is come to be living and *revived* again, and how it regenerateth itself again. From [2] thence also in the creatures the *bestial flesh* is come to be; but *sin* in the flesh is the *wrath* of God.

[2] the wrath bath.

Another question, which is chiefly treated of in this book, is this, viz. Where then shall the wrath of God come to be?

Answer.

52. Here the spirit answereth, that at the *end* of the time of *this* corrupted birth or geniture, *after* the resurrection from the dead, this place

or space where the earth now is will be left to the *devil* for a propriety or possession and *house of wrath*, yet *not* through and in all the three births or genitures, but only in the *outermost*, in which he *now* standeth: But the innermost will hold him captive in its might and strength, and use him for a *footstool*, or as the dust under its foot, which innermost birth he will never be able either to comprehend or to *touch*.

53. For it hath *not* this understanding or meaning, that the wrath-fire should be *extinguished*, and be no more; for then the devils also must become *holy* angels again, and live in the holy heaven; but that not being so, a hole, burrow or dungeon in this world must remain to be *their* habitation.

54. If man's eyes were but *opened*, he would see God everywhere in his heaven; for heaven standeth in the innermost birth or geniture everywhere.

55. Moreover, *when Stephen saw the heaven opened, and the Lord JESUS at the right hand of God*, there his spirit did not first swing itself up aloft into the upper heaven, but it penetrated or pressed into the *innermost* birth or geniture, wherein heaven is everywhere.

56. Neither must thou think that the *Deity* is such a kind of being as is *only* in the upper heaven, nor that the soul, when it departeth from the body, goeth up aloft into the upper heaven many hundred thousand miles off.

57. It *needeth* not do that, but it is set or put into the innermost birth, and there it is with God, and in God, and with all the holy angels, and can now be above, and now beneath; it is not *hindered* by anything.

58. For in the innermost birth the upper and nether Deity is *one body*, and is an open gate: The holy angels converse and walk up and down in the innermost birth of this world *by* and *with* our King JESUS CHRIST, as well as in the uppermost world aloft in their quarters, courts or region.

59. And where then would or should the soul of man *rather* be, than with its King and Redeemer JESUS CHRIST? For near and afar off in God is one thing, *one comprehensibility*, Father, Son and Holy Ghost, everywhere all over.

60. The gate of the Deity in the upper heaven is *no other*, also no brighter, than it is in this world: And where can there be greater joy than in that place, where every hour and *moment* there cometh to Christ beautiful, loving, dear, new-born children and angels, who are pressed or penetrated through death into life?

61. Doubtless they will have to tell of many fights: and where can there be greater *joy*, than where, in the midst or centre of death, life is generated continually?

62. Doth not every soul bring along with it a

new triumph? and so there is nothing else but an exceeding friendly welcoming and *salutation* there.

63. Consider, when the souls of children come to their parents, who in the body did generate them, whether heaven *can choose* but be there? Or dost thou think my writing is too earthly?

64. If thou wert come to this window, thou wouldst not then say that it is earthly : And though I must indeed use the *earthly* tongue, yet there is a true heavenly *understanding* couched under it, which in my outermost birth I am not able to express, either in writing or in speaking.

65. I know very well that the word concerning the three births cannot be comprehended or apprehended *in every man's heart*, especially where the heart is too much *steeped*, soaked or drowned in [1] the flesh, and bolted or barred up with the outermost birth.

[1] Or fleshly matters.

66. But I cannot render it otherwise than as it is, for it is just so ; and though I should write *mere* spirit, as indeed and truth it is no other, yet the heart understandeth *only* flesh.

Concerning the Constitution and Form of the Earth.

67. Many authors have written that heaven and earth were created out of NOTHING. But I wonder that, among *so many* excellent men, there hath *not one* been found that could yet

describe the true ground; seeing the same God which now is, *hath been* from eternity.

68. Now, where nothing is, there nothing can come to be: All things must have a *root*, else can nothing grow: If the *seven spirits of nature* had not been from eternity, then there would have come to be no angel, no heaven, also no earth.

69. But the earth is come from the corrupted *Salitter* of the outermost birth or geniture, which thou canst not deny, when thou lookest on earth and stones, for then thou must needs say that *death* is therein: On the other hand also thou must needs say that there is a *life* therein, otherwise neither gold nor silver, nor any plant, herb, grass or vegetable, could grow therein.

Now one might ask, Are there also all the three births or genitures therein?

Answer.

70. Yes: the life presseth through death; the *outermost* birth is the death; the *second* is the life, which standeth in the wrath-fire and in the love; and the *third* is the holy life.

An Instruction or Information.

71. The outward earth is a bitter stink, and is dead; and that every man understandeth to be so. But the *Salitter* is destroyed or killed through the wrath; for thou canst not deny but that *God's wrath* is in the earth, otherwise the

earth would not be so astringent, bitter, sour,
venomous and poisonous, neither would it en-
gender such poisonous, venomous, evil worms and
creeping things. But if thou shouldst *say* that *God*
hath created them *thus out of his purpose*, that
is as much as if thou shouldst *say* that God himself is evil, malice, malignity or wickedness.

72. Pray tell me, Why was the devil expelled
or thrust out? Surely thou wilt say, Because of
his pride, in that he would needs be above God.
But guess, Sir, with *what* the devil would be so:
What power had he to do it? Here tell me, if
thou knowest anything of it; if thou knowest
nothing, be *silent* and attentive.

73. Before the times of the creation he sat in
the *Salitter* of the earth, when the *Salitter* was
yet thin or transparent, and stood in a heavenly,
holy birth or geniture, and he was in the *whole*
kingdom of this world, therein was neither earth
nor stones, but a heavenly *seed*, which was
generated out of the seven qualifying or fountain
spirits of nature; for in the kingdom of this
world sprang up heavenly fruits, forms and ideas,
which were a pleasant, *delightful food* of angels.

74. But when the *wrath* did *burn* in the seed,
then the seed was killed and destroyed in death:
Yet not so to be understood as if it were therefore
altogether *quite* dead; for *how* can anything in
God die *totally*, that hath had its life from
eternity?

75. But I. The *outermost* birth or geniture was burnt up, frozen, drowned, stupefied, chilled and stark benumbed.

76. But II. The *second birth* or geniture generateth the life again in the outermost.

77. And III. The [1]*third* is generated between [1] birth. the first and the second, that is, between heaven and hell, in the *midst* or centre of the wrath-fire, and the spirit presseth through the wrath-fire, and generateth the *holy* life, which standeth in the power of the love.

78. And in this same birth or geniture will *those* dead arise who have sown a *holy* seed, and *those* who have sown in the *wrath* will arise in the wrath-fire: For the earth will *revive* and be living again, seeing the Deity in *Christ* hath regenerated *it* anew again through his *flesh*, and exalted *it* to the right hand of God: But the wrath-fire *abideth* in its own birth or geniture.

79. But if thou sayest that there is *no* life in the earth, thou speakest as one that is *blind*; for thou mayest see plainly that herbs and grass grow out of it.

80. But if thou sayest it hath but *one* kind of birth or geniture, thou speakest again also like one that is *blind*; for the herbs and wood which grow out of it are *not* earth, neither is the *fruit*, which groweth upon a tree, wood; so also the power and *virtue* of the fruit is *not* God either;

but ¹ God is in the centre, in the innermost birth in all the three natural births or genitures, *hiddenly*, but is not known, except ¹ *in the spirit of man* alone; also the outermost birth in the fruit doth not comprehend, conceive or contain *him*, but he containeth the outermost birth of the fruit, and formeth it.

Another Question is:

Why then is the earth so mountainous, hilly, rocky, stony and uneven?

Answer.

81. The hills came so to be in the driving together or *compaction*: For the *corrupted Salitter* was more abounding in one place than in another, according as the wheel of God was, as to its innate standing, or instant qualifying or fountain spirits.*

* "according as the wheel of God was, as to its innate standing, or instant qualifying or fountain-spirits," (*als nach das Rad Gottes mit seinen* instehenden *Quellgeistern ist gewesen*), "according as the wheel of God was, with its innate [*i.e.* involved, impelled and impelling] and instant qualifying fountain-spirits." Sparrow has used "innate standing" and "instant qualifying" to render one word alone in the German, "instehenden" (which here refers unmistakably to fountain-spirits, not to the wheel). *Instehend* means, literally, "in-standing" and "instant-ing," *i.e.* own, innate, involved, impelled and impelling. The phrase "instehenden Quellgeistern" means, not only that the fountain-spirits stand within the wheel (involved in it, and as it were constituting it and impelling it), but also that *they* are impelled to act, or qualify, instantly and invariably: where the wheel is, there they must operate. See also Ch. 13, par. 86 *et seq.*

82. For in *those* places where the sweet water in the standing wheel of God was chief or *predominant*, there much earthly, comprehensible or *palpable* water came to be.

83. But where the astringent quality in the bitterness in *Mercurius* was chief or predominant, there much *earth* and *stones* came to be.

84. But where the heat in the light was chief or predominant, there much *silver* and *gold*, as also some fair, *clear stones*, in the flash of the *light*, came to be; but especially where the love in the light was chief or predominant, there the most *precious stones* or jewels, as also the best, purest and *finest gold* came to be.

85. But when the lump of the earth was pressed and compacted together, then thereby the water came to be *squeezed* and pressed forth : But where the water was *enclosed* and pressed in with the astringent quality by hard rocks, there it is yet in the earth still, and hath since that time worn and made some great holes or veins for its passage.

86. In those places where there are great lakes and *seas*, there the *water* was chief or predominant over that place in that zenith or *elevation* of the pole; and there not being much *Salitter* in that place, there came to be as it were a dale or valley, wherein the water remained standing.

87. For the thin water seeketh for the valley,

and is a *humility* of the life, which did not exalt itself, as the astringent and the bitter qualities, and the fire's quality, have done in those creatures the *devils*.

88. Therefore it always seeketh the *lowest* places of the earth; which rightly signifieth or resembleth the spirit of *meekness*, in which the life is generated; as you may read concerning the creation of man, as also before, concerning the species or condition of water, meekness, and suchlike qualities.

Of Day and Night.

89. The *whole* Deity with all its powers and operations, together with its innate or instant *being*, as also its rising up, penetration, changing and alteration, that is to say the whole machine, fabric and work, or the whole generating or production, is *all* understood in the *spirit* of the [1] word.

[1] Of every word or syllable in every language or dialect.

90. For in what proportion or *harmony* soever, or in what innate or instant generating or production of qualities soever, the spirit comprehendeth, conceiveth and formeth the word, and goeth forth therewith, just *such* an innate or instant birth, penetrating, rising, wrestling and overcoming it hath also in *nature*.

91. For when man fell into sin, he was *removed* out of the innermost birth or geniture, and was set or put into the other *two* genitures, which

presently embraced him, and mixed, qualified **or** united *with* him and *in* him, as in their own propriety; and so man instantly received the spirit, and all generatings or productions of the *astral* birth, and also of the outermost birth or geniture.

92. Therefore now it expresseth * or speaketh forth *all words*, according to the innate, instant generating or production of nature; for the spirit of man, which standeth in the astral birth, and qualifieth or uniteth with the total universal nature, and is as it were the whole nature itself, that formeth the word, according to the innate, instant birth or geniture.

93. When the spirit of man seeth anything, then it giveth a name to that thing, according to the qualification or condition of the thing; but if it is to do this, then it must form or frame or put itself also into such a form, and generate itself also, with its tone, sound or articulation, just so as the thing to which it will give a name doth generate or compose itself. *Herein lieth the kernel of the whole understanding of the Deity.*

94. I do *not* write this, and bring it to light, that others after me should presently fall a writing, and publish the conceits of their own spirit herein, and cry them up for *sanctity*, or for a holy thing.

---

* "Therefore now it expresseth," etc. In the German "it" may refer either to "the spirit of the astral birth," or to "man." St M. takes "man" to be the antecedent.

95. Hearken, Friend, there belongeth more than so to this; thy animated or *soulish* spirit must first qualify, operate or *unite* with the innermost birth or geniture in God, and stand in the *light*, that it may *rightly* know and understand the astral birth or geniture, and that it may have a free and *open gate* into all the births or genitures; otherwise thou wilt *not* be able to write a holy and true philosophy, but a philosophy full of [1] lice and fleas, as it were, and so thou wilt be found a mocker against God.

[1] Or many evil beasts and creeping vermin.

96. I conceive already that the devil will get *many* a one to ride upon *his* proud prancing nag; and many will make themselves *ready* for the journey before they be well [2]*girt*; but I will not bear the blame for that.

[2] With the girdle of truth.

97. For what I here *reveal* or manifest I must do; for the time of breaking through is at *hand:* He that will *now sleep*, the stormy tempest of the fierceness will rouse him.

98. But now, that every one might have a care of his affairs and *doings*, I would have men faithfully warned, according to the impulse, driving and will of the spirit.

Observe:

[3] Gen. i.

99. The writer, *Moses*, saith, [3] *God separated the light from the darkness, and called the light day, and the darkness night, so out of evening and morning the first day came to be.*

100. But seeing these words, *evening* and *morning*, are contrary to the current of philosophy and reason, therefore it may be conceived *that Moses* was not the sole original author thereof, but that it was derived down to him from his forefathers, who reckoned *all* the *six* days of the creation in one *continued course*, and preserved and kept the memory of the creation from *Adam*, in an *obscure* word, and *so left* it to posterity.

101. For evening and morning were *not* before the time of the *sun* and *stars*, which most certainly and really were first created but on the *fourth day*, which I shall demonstrate from an assured, certain ground, concerning the creation of the sun and stars.

102. But there was *day* and *night*, which I will here declare according to my knowledge : Thou must here *once* more open wide the eyes of thy spirit, if thou intendest to understand it ; if *not*, then thou wilt remain *blind*.

103. *Though* this great work in man hath remained *hidden* till this very day, yet God be praised, it will now *once be day*, for the dayspring or morning-redness *breaketh forth*. The breaker-through, or opener of the innermost birth, sheweth and presenteth itself with its *red*, *green* and *white* flag, in the outermost birth upon the *rainbow*.

Observe :

Now thou objectest, How then could there be day and night, and not also morning and evening ?

Answer.

104. *Morning* and *evening* are and reach up from the earth to the moon only, and take their *original* from the light of the sun, and this maketh evening and morning, as also the *outward day*, and the *outward* dark *night*, as every one knoweth.

105. But there was not a *twofold* creation of evening and morning at that time ; but when evening and morning did once begin, they kept their *constant* course all along from that time to this.

Of the Day. (Tag.)

106. The word (Tag) conceiveth itself at the heart, and goeth forth at the mouth through the *way* or passage of the astringent and the bitter qualities, and doth *not* awaken or rouse up the astringent and the bitter qualities, but goeth forth *directly* through their place, which is at the hinder gums upon the tongue, very softly or *gently*, and incomprehensibly as to the astringent and the bitter qualities.

107. But when it cometh forth upon the tongue, then the tongue and the upper gums *close* the mouth ; but when the spirit thrusteth at the teeth, and will go forth, then the tongue *openeth*

the mouth at the teeth, and will go forth before the word, and at the mouth doth as it were leap forth for joy.

108. But when the word breaketh through, then the mouth *within* openeth wide, and the word conceiveth itself *once more* with its sound behind the astringent and the bitter qualities, and rouseth them up, as if they were *lazy* sleepers in the darkness, and goeth forth *suddenly* out at the mouth.

109. Then the astringent quality [1]drayleth after it, as a drowsy man who is awakened from sleep; but the bitter spirit which goeth forth from the fire flash lieth *still*, and heareth or regardeth *not, neither* doth it move. *These are very great things, and not so slight matters as the countryman supposeth.*

[1] [Drail, drayle, to trail, draggle, move laggingly. *Ox. Eng. Dic.*]

110. Now, that the spirit first conceiveth itself at the heart, and breaketh through all *watches* and guards till it come upon the tongue, unperceived or unobserved, signifieth that the light brake forth out of the heart of God, through the *corrupted*, outermost, fierce, *dead*, bitter and astringent birth or geniture in the *nature* of this world, incomprehensibly both as to death and the devil, together with the wrath of God; as it is written in the Gospel of St *John*, [2] *The light shineth in darkness, and the darkness comprehended it not.*

[2] John i. 5.

111. But that the tongue and the upper gums

close the mouth, when the spirit cometh upon the tongue, signifieth that the seven qualifying or fountain spirits of nature in *this* world, at the time of the creation, were *not mortified* and dead through the wrath of God, but were *lively*, active and *vigorous*. For the tongue signifieth or denoteth the life of nature, in which standeth the animated, *soulish* and holy birth or geniture : For it is a [1] type of the soul.

[1] prefiguration or resemblance.

112. But that the spirit suddenly *affecteth* the tongue, when the spirit cometh upon it, whereupon it leapeth for joy, and will go *before* the spirit forth at the mouth, signifieth that the seven qualifying or fountain spirits of nature, (which are called the *astral birth*), when the light of God, (which is called the *day*), rose up in them, suddenly gat the *divine* life and will, and so highly rejoiced ; as the tongue in the mouth here doth.

113. But that the *fore* gums widen *inward*, and give room for the spirit to do as it pleaseth, signifieth that the *whole* astral birth yielded itself very friendly and courteously to the *will* of the light, and did not awaken the fierceness in it.

114. But that the spirit, when it goeth forth at the mouth, conceiveth itself yet *once more* behind the astringent quality upon the tongue at the hindermost gums, and awakeneth or rouseth up the astringent quality, being as it were *asleep*, and then goeth suddenly forth at the mouth :

115. It signifieth, I. That the *astringent* spirit
indeed must hold, preserve and image or frame
all in the whole nature, but this is [only] *after*
the spirit of the light hath *first* formed it, and
that then the light first awakeneth the *astringent*
spirit, and giveth all into the hands *thereof* to
hold or preserve it.

116. And that must be, because of the outermost comprehensibility or *palpability*, which
must be held and sustained by the *astringent*
fierceness, else nothing would subsist in its *body*,
neither could the compressed, compacted earth
and stones subsist, but would be again a broken,
thick, muddy and *dark Salitter*, such as at first
moved in the whole deep.

117. It signifieth also, II. That this *Salitter*,
at last, when the spirit hath done with its
creation and *work* in this world, shall be roused
up and *revived* at the Last Judgment Day.

118. But that the spirit conceiveth itself
behind the astringent quality, and not *in* the
astringent quality, and so awakeneth or rouseth
it up, signifieth that the astringent nature will
not comprehend the light of God in its own
proper way, but shall *rejoice* in the light of the
grace, and be awakened or raised up thereby,
and *perform* the *will* of the light; as the bestial
body of man effecteth and performeth the will of
the spirit, and yet these are *not two* severed
things.

119. But that the bitter spirit *lieth still*, and neither heareth nor comprehendeth nor apprehendeth the work of the spirit, signifieth that the bitter wrath-fire, which ariseth in the flash of fire at the time of the birth or geniture of the *light*, is not awakened by the light, neither comprehendeth it, but lieth *captive*, imprisoned in the outermost birth or geniture, and must give leave to the spirit of light to do its work in nature, how it *pleaseth*, and yet can neither see nor hear nor comprehend the *work* of the light.

120. Therefore *no man* ought to think that the devil is *able* to tear the works of the light out of his [man's] heart, for he can neither see nor comprehend them : and though he rageth and raveth in the outermost birth in the *flesh*, as in his castle of robbery or fort of prey, do not despair; only take heed that *thou thyself* bring not the works of wrath into the *light* of thy heart. Then thy soul will be *safe enough* from the *deaf* and *dumb devil*, who is *blind* in the light.

121. Thou shouldst not suppose that which I write here to be as a *doubtful* opinion, questionable as to whether it be so or no : For the gates of heaven and of hell stand open to the spirit, and in the light it presseth through them *both*, and beholdeth them; also proveth or examineth them; for the astral birth or geniture liveth

between them both, and must endure to be squeezed.*

122. And though the devil *cannot* take the light from me, yet he often *hideth* or *eclipseth* it with the outward and fleshly birth or geniture, so that the astral birth or geniture is in *anxiety*, and in a strait, as if it were captivated or imprisoned.

123. These are only his *blows* and *strokes*, whereby the mustard - seed is overwhelmed, covered and obscured : Concerning which also the holy Apostle *Paul* saith, [1] *that a great thorn was given him in his flesh, and he besought the Lord earnestly to take it from him, whereupon the Lord answered, Let my grace be sufficient for thee.* [1] 2 Cor. xii. 7-9.

124. For he also was *come* to *this* place, and would fain have had the light without obstruction or hindrance, as *his own in the astral birth* or geniture. But *it could not be* ; for the *wrath* resteth in the *fleshly* birth, and must bear or endure the corruption or putrefaction in the flesh : But if the fierceness should be *wholly* taken away from the astral birth or geniture, then, in that [birth], man would be like God, and know all things, as God himself doth.

125. Which now [2] at present only *that soul* [3] in this life. which qualifieth, operateth or *uniteth* with the

* "and must endure to be squeezed"—*und muss sich wol quetschen lassen* = and must itself be willing to suffer the pain of being squeezed between the doors of heaven and of hell, as between a door and its jamb.

light of God knoweth, though it cannot *perfectly* bring it back again into the *astral* birth or geniture; for it is another person.

126. Just as an apple on a tree *cannot* bring its smell and taste back again into the tree, or into the earth, though it be indeed the son of the tree : So it is in *nature* also.

127. The *holy man* Moses *was* so high and deep in this light, that the *light* transfigured the astral birth also, whereby the outermost birth of the *flesh* in his *face* was transfigured; and he also desired to see the light of God *perfectly*, in the astral birth or geniture.

128. But that could *not* be; for the bar or bolt of the *wrath* lieth before it : For even the whole or universal nature of the astral birth in this world *cannot* comprehend the light of God, and therefore the heart of God is *hidden* and concealed, which, however, *dwelleth* in all places, and comprehendeth all.

129. Thus thou seest that the *day* was created before the time of the sun and stars; for when God said, [1] *Let there be light* : there the light brake through the darkness, but *the darkness did not comprehend it*, but remained sitting in its seat.*

130. Thou seest also how the wrath of God lieth hid and resteth in the *outermost birth* of nature, and *cannot* be awakened, unless men *themselves* rouse or awaken it, who with their

[1] Gen. i. 3.

* "remained sitting in its seat." See Ch. 25, par. 82.

fleshly birth or geniture qualify, operate or unite with the wrath in the *outermost* birth of nature.

131. Therefore if any one should be *damned* into hell, he ought *not* to say that God hath done it, or that God *willeth* it to be so; but *man* awakeneth or stirreth up the wrath-fire in *himself*, which, if it groweth *burning*, afterwards qualifieth, mixeth or uniteth with God's wrath and the hellish fire, as one thing.

132. For when thy light is extinguished, then thou standest in the darkness, and in the darkness the *wrath* of God is *hidden*, and so if thou awakenest it, then it *burneth* in thee.

133. There is fire even in a stone, and if you do not strike upon the stone, the fire remaineth *hidden*, but if you strike it, then the fire *springs* forth; and then, if any combustible matter be near it, that matter will take fire and burn, and so it cometh to be a huge fire; and thus it is with *man* also, when he kindleth the resting wrath-fire, which otherwise is at *rest*.

Of the Night. (Nacht).

134. The word (Nacht) conceiveth itself first at the heart, and the spirit *grunteth* with or in the astringent quality, yet not wholly comprehensible to the astringent quality; afterwards it conceiveth itself upon the tongue: But *all the while* it grunteth at the heart the tongue *shuts* the mouth, till the spirit cometh and conceiveth

itself upon the tongue, and then it openeth the mouth quickly, and lets the spirit *go forth.*

135. Now that the word conceiveth itself first at the heart, and *grunteth* with or in the astringent quality, signifieth that the Holy Ghost conceived itself *in the darkness* upon the heart of God in the astral birth or geniture of the seven qualifying or fountain spirits : But that it *grunteth* within or at the astringent quality, signifieth that the darkness was a contrary or *opposite will* against the Holy Ghost, at or against which the spirit was *displeased.*

136. But that it goeth likewise through the *dark* way or passage, signifieth that the spirit goeth forth also through the darkness, which is *yet* in a quiet rest, and generateth it to be light, if it holdeth still, and doth *not* kindle the fire.

137. Here is the cause for the judging world, which condemneth man in his mother's body or womb, to see and consider (for it doth not know) whether the wrath-fire of the parents be fully kindled in the fruit or not, since also the spirit of God moveth in the darkness which standeth in quiet rest, and can easily generate the darkness to be light. Towards this, moreover, the hour of man's nativity is very helpful to him ; and to many [it is] very harmful.

138. But that the mouth shutteth, when the spirit conceiveth itself upon the heart, and that the astringent quality grunteth against and *with*

or *in* it, signifieth that the whole court, extent
or place of this world was *very dark* in the astral,
and also in the outermost birth or geniture, and by
the *strong* going forth of the spirit became light.

139. But that the bitter spirit is not *awakened*,
whilst the spirit goeth through its place, signifieth that the *dark night* in the outermost birth
or geniture of this world hath never comprehended the light; also never will comprehend it
in all eternity.

140. Hence it is that the creatures see the
astral light with their eyes alone, else, if the
darkness were not yet in the outermost birth
or geniture, then the astral spirit could see
through wood and stones, as also *through the
whole earth*, and could not be hindered by anything, just as it is in heaven.

141. At the present time the darkness is
separated from the light, and *abideth* in the
outermost birth or geniture, wherein the wrath
of God resteth till the Last Judgment Day; but
then the wrath will be kindled, and the darkness
will be the house or habitation of eternal *perdition*, wherein lord *Lucifer*, together with all
wicked men who have sown into the darkness
in the soil of the wrath, will have his eternal
dwelling and *residence*.

142. But the astral birth, in which the natural
light now standeth, and wherein the *holy* birth
is generated, will be *also* kindled at the end of

this time, and the wrath and the *holy* birth will be *separated* asunder, for the wrath will not comprehend the holy birth or geniture.

143. But the wrath in the astral birth will be given to the house of darkness for a life, and *the wrath will be called the hellish fire: And the house of darkness*, which is the outermost birth, *will be called death:* And *king Lucifer* will be the *god therein*, and his angels and all damned men will be his ministers, officers and servants.

144. In this devouring abyss will rise up all manner of *hellish fruits* and *forms*, all according to the hellish quality and kind; as in heaven there spring up *heavenly fruits* and *forms*, according to the heavenly quality and kind.

145. Thus you may understand what the creation of heaven and earth signifieth and is, also what God made on the *first day*. Though indeed the first three days were not *distinguished* or severed asunder by evening and morning, but a time is to be reckoned and accounted as of twenty-four hours, as there is on high above the *moon* such a time and day.

146. Secondly, it is also therefore counted for a human day, because, doubtless, the *earth* instantly *began* its revolution and did turn round about once in such a period of time, while God was separating, and so till he had separated, the

¹ the earth.   light from the darkness; and thus ¹ it performed and finished its course the first time.

THE TWENTIETH CHAPTER

Of the Second Day

1. CONCERNING the second day, it is written thus: [1] *And God said, Let* [1] Gen. i. 6-8. *there be a firmament in the midst of the waters, and let it be a distinction or division between the waters: So there God made the firmament, and divided the waters under the firmament, from the waters above the firmament, and it was so done. And God called the firmament, heaven; and so out of the evening and the morning the second day came to be.*

2. This description sheweth once more that the dear man *Moses* was not the original author thereof; for it is written very obscurely and baldly, though indeed it hath a very *excellent* understanding and meaning.

3. Without doubt the *Holy Ghost* would not have it revealed, lest the devil should know all the mysteries in the creation. For the devil doth not know the creation of the *light*, viz. how heaven is made out of the midst or centre of the water.

521

4. For he can neither see nor comprehend nor apprehend the light and holy generation or production, which standeth in the water of the heaven, but he can see the generation or production only which standeth in the astringent, bitter, sour and hot quality, from whence existed the *outermost* birth or geniture, which is his royal fort or castle.

5. The meaning is *not* that he hath *no* power in the elementary water, to possess it; for the outermost corrupted birth or geniture in the elementary water *belongeth also* to the wrath of God, and *death* is also therein, as well as in the earth.

6. But the spirit in *Moses* meaneth here quite another *sort* of water, which the devil can neither understand nor comprehend: But if it should have been *declared* so long a time ago, then the devil would have *learned* it from man, and had without doubt strowed his hellish chaff *also* into it.

7. *Therefore* the Holy Ghost hath kept it hidden *almost* till the last hour before the *evening*, wherein his *thousand years are accomplished, and then he must be let loose again for a little season*, as is to be read in the [1] Revelation.

[" *After that* summer *cometh the last winter; but* " the sun *will shine warm yet, before that time.*"]

8. But seeing he is *now loose* from the chains of darkness, God causeth lights to be set up everywhere in this world, whereby men might

[1] Rev. xx. 3.

learn to know him, and *his feats* and wiles, and beware of him.

9. Whether he be *loose* or *no* I offer it to every one to consider; but view the world in the clear light, and thou wilt find, that at present the *four* new sons which the devil generated when he was thrust out of heaven, *do govern* the world, *viz.* 1. Pride, 2. Covetousness, 3. Envy, 4. Wrath; these rule the world at present, and are the *devil's* heart, his animated or *soulish* spirit.

10. Therefore view the world very well, and then thou wilt find that it *fully* qualifieth, uniteth and co-worketh with these *four new sons* of the devil. Therefore men have cause to look circumspectly to themselves. For *this is the time* of which all the prophets have prophesied; and Christ in the Gospel, saying, [1] *Thinkest thou that the Son of Man will find any faith, when he shall come again to judge the world?*

[1] Luke xviii. 8.

11. The world supposeth that it flourisheth now, and standeth in its *flower*, because the clear light hath moved over it. But the spirit sheweth to me that it standeth in the *midst* or centre of *hell*.

12. For it forsaketh the love, and hangeth on covetousness, extortion and bribery; there is *no mercy at all* therein: Every one crieth out, If I had but *money*! Those that are in authority and power *suck* the very marrow from the bones of men of low degree and rank, and feed upon the

sweat of their brows. Briefly, there is nothing else but lying, deception, robbing and murdering, and so [this world] may very justly be called the devil's *nest* and dwelling-house.

13. The *holy light* is nowadays accounted a mere history and bare knowledge, and that the spirit *will not work* therein; and yet they *suppose* that is faith which they profess with their *mouths*.

14. O thou blind and foolish world! full of the devil. It is *not* faith, to know that Christ died for thee, and hath shed his blood for thee, that thou mightest be *saved*: This *in thee* is but a mere history and knowledge, the devil also knoweth as much, but it profiteth him *nothing*; so thou also, thou foolish world, goest *no further*, but contentest thyself with the *bare* knowledge, and therefore this thy knowledge will *judge* thee.

15. But if thou wouldst know what the *true faith is*, then observe: *Thy heart must not qualify or co-operate with the four sons of the devil, in pride, covetousness, envy, wrath, extortion, oppression, lying, deceiving, murder, and tearing the bread out of thy neighbour's throat, studying day and night to do mischief, in bringing subtle devices and designs to effect, that thou mayest court and give satisfaction to the fourfold devil of pride, covetousness, envy and wrath, and exercise thyself in worldly pleasures and voluptuousness.*

16. For thus saith the spirit in its zeal, or in

the jealousy of God's wrath in this world: While thy *spirit* and *will* qualifieth or co-operateth with and in the four vices or sins of the devil, thou art not one spirit with God; and though thou didst every hour offer [the worship or prayer of] thy lips, and bow the knee before me, yet I will accept none of thy labour: Is not my breath, however, continually before me? What shall thy incense be to me in my fierce wrath? Dost thou think I will receive the devil into myself, *or exalt hell into heaven?*

17. Convert! Convert! and *strive against the malice and wickedness of the devil*, and incline thine heart towards the LORD thy GOD, and *walk in his will*. If thy heart will incline to me, saith the spirit, then will I also incline to thee: Or dost thou think that I am false and wicked, as thou art?

18. *Therefore* I say now, if thy heart doth not qualify, mix or co-operate with *God* in thy knowledge, out of a true purpose of *love*, then thou art a dissembler, liar and murderer in the sight of God. For God doth not *hear* any man's *prayer*, unless his heart be fully directed and bent in *obedience* to God.

19. Wouldst thou fight against the wrath of God? Then thou must put on the helmet of *obedience* and of *love*, otherwise thou wilt not break through; and if thou dost not break through, then thou fightest in *vain*, and re-

mainest to be a servant or minister of the devil, in one way as well as in another.

20. What good will thy knowledge do thee, if thou wilt not strive and *fight* therein? It is just as if one knew of a great treasure, and would not go for it; but, though he knoweth he might have it, would rather *starve* for hunger in the *bare* knowing of it.

21. Thus saith the spirit, *Many Heathen*, who have not thy knowledge, and yet strive or fight against the wrath, *will enter into the kingdom of heaven before thee.*

22. For who shall judge them, if their heart do qualify, unite or operate with God? For though they do *not* know him, and yet work and labour in his spirit, in righteousness, and in the *purity* of their heart, in *true love* one to another, ¹ *they testify assuredly that the law of God is in their heart.*

¹ Rom. ii. 15.

23. But seeing thou knowest it, and dost it *not*, and the others know it not, but yet *do* it, they, with their doing, judge thy knowledge; and thou art found to be a hypocrite, a dissembler, and an unprofitable servant, who wert put into the vineyard of the Lord, and *wilt not work* therein.

24. What dost thou suppose the Master of the house will say to thee, when he shall require and demand his *talent* with which he entrusted thee, *thou having buried it in the earth?* Will he not

say, *Thou perverse wicked servant, why didst thou
not put my talent out upon use, and then I could
have demanded the principal and the interest* or
profit?

25. And so the *sufferings of Christ* will be quite
taken from thee, and will be given to the Heathen,
who had but *one talent*, and yet yielded to
the Master of the house five; and thou wilt
have to *howl with the dogs.*

Now observe:

26. If we rightly consider how God separated
the *water under* the firmament, from the water
above the firmament, then great things will be
found therein.

27. For the water which *resteth on the earth*
is as corrupt and perished and mortal or dead a
being or thing as the earth is, and belongeth also
to the *outermost* birth, which with its comprehensibility, or as to its palpability, standeth in
death, even as the earth and stones do.

28. The meaning is *not* that the water is *quite*
reprobated, rejected or thrust out from God; for
the *heart* therein belongeth yet to the astral
birth or geniture, out of which the *holy* birth
becometh generated.

29. But death standeth in the outermost birth,
and *therefore* is the palpable water *separated*
from the impalpable.

Now thou wilt ask, How is that?

Answer.

30. Behold the water in the deep *above* the earth, which qualifieth, mixeth or uniteth with the *elementary* air and fire, that is the water of the *astral* birth or geniture, wherein standeth the *astral life*, and wherein *especially* the Holy Ghost moveth, and through which the *third* and innermost birth doth generate *incomprehensibly* as to the wrath of God therein : That water to our eyes seemeth like the air.

31. But that, in the deep above the earth, water, air and fire are *one in another*, every intelligent man may see and understand.

32. For thou seest that often the whole deep is very *clear* and pure, and then, in *a quarter of an hour*, is covered with watery clouds ; that is, when the stars from *above*, and the water upon the earth from *beneath*, kindle themselves, and so water is suddenly there also generated ; which would *not be*, if the wrath did not also stand in the astral birth or geniture.

33. But seeing *all* is corrupted, therefore must the upper water in the wrath of God come to help the astringent, bitter and hot quality of the earth, and soften the quality and *quench* its fire, so that the life may always be generated, and that the holy birth, between death and the wrath of God, may be generated also.

34. But that also the element of *fire* is, and

doth rule in the deep of the air and water, thou seest in tempests of lightning; also thou perceivest how the light of the *sun* kindleth the element of fire on the earth with its *reflection*, although many times aloft in the upper region towards the *moon* it is very cold.

35. But now God separated the palpable water from the impalpable, and placed the palpable on the earth, and the impalpable remained still in the deep, in its own seat, as it had been from eternity.

36. But seeing the wrath also is in *that* water in the deep above the earth, therefore constantly, through the kindling of the stars, and of the water in the *wrath*, such palpable water genereteth itself, which, with its outermost birth, standeth in death.

37. And which, seeing it qualifieth or *uniteth* with the innermost birth of the astral birth or geniture, cometh to help the *Salitter* of the *corrupted* earth, and quencheth its wrath; whereby, in the astral birth or geniture, all standeth in the life. And so the earth generateth the *life* through the *death*.

The Gate of the Mystery.

38. But that there is a *firmament* between the waters, which firmament is called *heaven*, hath this *understanding* or meaning:

39. The whole deep, from the *moon* to the *earth*, standeth with its whole working in the

wrathful and comprehensible or palpable birth or geniture ; for the *moon* is the goddess of the palpable birth ; so the house of the devil, of death, and of hell, is in the circuit, orb or extent between the moon and the earth.

40. Where, *therefore*, the fierce *wrath* of God, in the outermost birth or geniture in the deep, becometh daily kindled and blown up by the *devils* and *all wicked* men, through the great sins of man, which still qualify, mix, unite or co-operate with the *astral* birth or geniture in the deep.

41. Therefore God hath made the firmament, which is called heaven, *between* the outermost and the innermost birth ; and that is a *partition* or division between the outermost and the innermost birth or geniture.

42. For the outermost birth of the water cannot comprehend the innermost birth of the water which is called heaven, and which is made out of the midst or centre of the water.

["*Heaven is the firmament, viz. the fire-sea, or*
" *sea of fire, out of the seven spirits of nature,*
" *out of which the stars, as a quintessence, were*
" *concreted, incorporated or created by the Word*
" FIAT: *It hath or containeth both fire and*
" *water, and hangeth in itself inwardly on the*
" *first Principle, and will bring its wonders, with*
" *or as to the figure of them, into the eternal ; but*
" *its birth or geniture fadeth or passeth away.*"]

43. Now the innermost birth of heaven *reflects*

strongly upon the earth, and holdeth the outermost water upon the earth strongly captive, together with the earth also.

44. If that were not, then, with the *revolution* of the globe of the earth, the water would be divided or dissolved again; also then would the earth crumble, break and moulder away in the deep (and all would be a *Chaos* again).

45. Therefore that firmament, between the outermost palpable water and the inward, holdeth the *earth* and the *palpable* water captive.

But now thou mayest ask, What kind of firmament of heaven then is that which I can neither see nor apprehend?

Answer.

46. It is the firmament *between* the clear Deity and the corrupt nature, which thou must break through when thou intendest to come to God; and it is that very firmament which doth not *quite* stand in the wrath, neither is it altogether or perfectly pure; concerning which it is written, [1] *The very heavens are not pure in the sight of God.* But at the Last Judgment Day the wrath will be purged from them. For it is written, [2] *Heaven and earth shall pass away, but my words shall not pass away*, saith Christ.

47. Now that *impurity* in that heaven is the *wrath*, but the *purity* is the *word* of God, which he once spake, saying; [3] *Let the water under the*

[1] Job xv. 15.

[2] Matt. xxiv. 35. Mark xiii. 31.

[3] Gen. i. 6.

firmament be separated from the water above the firmament. And that word standeth and is *comprised* in the firmament of the water, and holdeth captive or fixed the outward water, together with the earth.

The Gate of the Deity.

Observe here the hidden Mystery of God.

48. When thou beholdest the deep above the earth, thou oughtest *not* to say that it is *not* the gate of God, where God in his *holiness* dwelleth: No, no, think not so; for the *whole* holy *Trinity*, God |the Father, Son, and Holy Ghost, dwelleth in the centre under the firmament of heaven, though that very firmament cannot comprehend him.

49. Indeed, all is as it were *one* body, the outermost and the innermost birth, together with the firmament of heaven, as also the astral birth *therein*, in and with which the wrath of God also qualifieth, mixeth and uniteth; but yet they are one to another as is the government, frame or constitution in *man*.

[1] Note three sorts of births or genitures in man.

50. [1]The *flesh* signifieth, 1. The outward birth or geniture, which is the house of death. 2. The second birth or geniture in man is the *astral*, in which the *life* standeth, and wherein love and wrath wrestle the one with the other; and *thus far* man himself knoweth himself; for the astral birth generateth the life in the outermost, that

is, in the *dead* flesh.   3. The third birth is
generated between the astral and the outermost,
and that is called the animated or *soulish* birth
or geniture, or the soul, and is as large as the
whole man.

51. And that birth or geniture the outward
man *neither knoweth nor comprehendeth* ; neither
doth the astral comprehend it, for every qualifying or fountain spirit comprehendeth only its
innate or instant *root*, which signifieth or resembleth the heaven.

52. And that animated or soulish man must
press through the firmament of heaven to God,
and *live* with God, else the whole man *cannot*
come into heaven to God.

53. For every man that desireth to be saved,
must, with his innate, instant births or genitures,
be as the *whole* Deity with all the three births
in this world is.

54. Man cannot be absolutely or *wholly pure*,
or devoid of *wrath and sin*, for the births of the
[1] depth in this world are not fully pure before [1] Job xv. 16.
the heart of God; love and wrath always *wrestle*
the one with the other, whence God is called [2] *an* [2] Exod. xx. 5.
Deut. v. 9.
angry zealous God.

55. Now as a man is, in the government or
order of his *nativity*, birth or geniture, just *so*
also is the whole body of God in or of this world ;
but in the *water* standeth the *meek* life.

56. As, I. First in the outward body of God,

in or of this world, there is the congealed, astringent, bitter and hot *death*, in which the palpable water is also congealed and dead.

57. Therein now is the *darkness*, wherein king *Lucifer* and his angels, as also all *fleshly* or carnal wicked men, lie captive, even with or in their *living* bodies, as also the *separated* spirits of *damned* men.

58. This birth can neither see, hear, feel, smell nor comprehend the *heart* of God, but is [1] a foolish virgin, which king *Lucifer* in his pride hath caused so to be.

59. II. The second birth is the astral, which thou must understand to be the *life* of the seven qualifying or fountain spirits, wherein *now* the love and the wrath are against each other; therein standeth the *upper* water, which is a spirit of the life, and therein, or *between*, is the firmament of heaven, which is made out of the midst or centre of the water.

60. Now this birth or geniture presseth through the outward congealed birth *quite through* death, and generateth the astral life in the death, that is, in the congealed earth, water and flesh of the beasts and of men, also of the fowls, fishes and worms or creeping things.

61. The devil can reach *half* into this birth, so far as the wrath comprehendeth or reacheth, but no deeper, and thus far goeth his dwelling, but no deeper. Therefore the devil *cannot*

know how the other part in this birth hath
a root; and so far man is come in his knowledge, from the beginning of the world to this
time, since his fall. But the other *root*, called
the heaven, the spirit hath kept hidden and
concealed from man till this time, lest the devil
should have learned it from man, and should
have strowed poison into it for man before
his *eyes*.

62. This *other part* of the astral birth, which
standeth in the love in the sweet water, is the
firmament of heaven, which holdeth captive the
kindled wrath, together with all the devils, for
they cannot enter thereinto; and in that heaven
dwelleth the *Holy Spirit*, which goeth forth
from the heart of God, and striveth or fighteth
against the fierceness, and generateth to himself
a temple in the *midst*, in the fierceness of the
wrath of God.

63. And in this heaven dwelleth the man that
feareth God, even with and [1] in the living body;
for that heaven is as well in man as in the deep
above the earth. As is the deep above the earth,
so is man also, both in love and wrath, till after
the departure of the soul; but when the soul
departeth from the body, then it *abideth* either
in the heaven of love only, or only in the heaven
of wrath.

[1] Or alive in the body here upon earth.

64. That part, which here it hath comprehended in its *departure*, is now its eternal

and indissoluble dwelling-house, and from thence it can *never* get; for there is a great [1]*cleft**
between them; as Christ speaks of *the rich man.*

65. And in this heaven the holy angels dwell amongst us, and the devils in the other part: and in this heaven man liveth *between* heaven and hell, and must endure and suffer from the fierceness many hard *blows,* temptations, persecutions, and many times torments and squeezings.

66. [2]The wrath is called the *cross,* and the *love-heaven* is called *patience,* and the *spirit* that riseth up *therein* is called *hope* and *faith,* which qualifieth, mixeth or *uniteth* with God, and *wrestleth* with the wrath *till it* [3]*overcometh and getteth the victory.*

[2] †
1. Cross.
2. Patience.
3. Hope.
4. Faith.

[3] 1 John v. 4.

67. And herein lieth the *whole* Christian doctrine: He that teacheth otherwise doth *not* know what he teacheth, for his doctrine hath no foot, ground or foundation, and his heart always tottereth, wavereth and doubteth, and knoweth not what it should do.

68. For his *spirit* always seeketh for *rest,* but findeth it not; for it is impatient, and always seeketh after *novelties,* or some new thing; and when it findeth somewhat, it *tickleth* itself therewith, as if it had found some *new treasure,* and yet there is no steadfastness, stability or certainty

* "cleft" (*Kluft*). See Ch. 19, par. 34.

in him, but he seeketh continually for abstinence or for a diversion.*

69. *O ye theologists! the spirit here openeth a door and gate for you:* If you will not now see, and feed your sheep and lambs on a green meadow, but on a dry, seared heath, you must be *accountable* for it before the severe, earnest and wrathful judgment of God ; therefore look to it.

70. I take heaven to witness that I perform here what I must do ; for the spirit *driveth me* to it, so that I am wholly captivated therewith, and cannot be freed from it, whatever may befall me hereafter, or ensue upon it.

The Holy Gate.

71. III. The third birth or geniture in the body of God, in or of this world, is under the firmament of heaven, hidden or concealed ; and the firmament of heaven qualifieth, mixeth or uniteth therewith, but yet not fully *bodily*, but *creaturely*, as the angels and the souls of men do.

72. And this third birth or geniture is the *almighty* and *holy* heart of God, wherein our King *Jesus Christ*, with his natural body, *sitteth*

* "or for a diversion." These words are an addition by Sparrow ; it is probable, however, that they render the meaning of the original, *Abstinentz*, better than the English "abstinence." St M. has dropped the latter altogether and uses only the word "diversion." Anyone who knows the meaning of the prefix *ab*, in German, will understand why J. B. uses this otherwise unsuitable word.

at the right hand of God, as a King and Lord of the whole body or place of this world, who encompasseth, holdeth and preserveth *all* with his heart.

73. And this firmament of heaven is his [1] throne or footstool, and the qualifying or fountain spirits of his natural body *rule* in the whole body of this world, and all is tied, bound or united with them, all whatsoever that standeth in the astral birth in the part of *love*: The other part of this world is tied, bound and united with the *devil.*

74. Thou must *not think,* as *Johannes Calvus* or *Calvinus* thought, which was, that the body of Christ is *not an almighty* [2] *being,* and that it comprehendeth or reacheth *no farther* than the little circumscribed place wherein it is.

75. No; thou child of man, thou errest, and dost not *rightly* understand the *divine* power: Doth not every man in his astral, qualifying or fountain spirits *comprehend* the whole place or body of this world, and the place *comprehendeth* man? it is all but *one body,* only there are distinct members.

76. Why then should not the qualifying or fountain spirits in the natural body of Christ qualify, mix or unite with the qualifying or fountain spirits of *nature*? Is not his body also out of the qualifying or fountain spirits of nature, and is not his heart animated or become soulish from or out of the *third* birth or geniture, which is

the heart of God, which comprehendeth all angels and the heaven of heavens, even the *whole Father*?

77. Ye Calvinists, desist from your opinion, and do not *torment yourselves* with the comprehensible or palpable being; for [1] *God is a Spirit*; [1] John iv. 24. and in the comprehensibility or palpability standeth *death*.

78. The body of Christ is no more the hard comprehensibility or palpability, but the divine comprehensibility or palpability of nature, like the angels.

79. For our bodies also, at the resurrection, will not consist of such hard flesh and bones, but will be like the angels. And though indeed all *forms* and *powers* will be therein, and all *faculties* and *members*, even to the privy parts, yet these will be in another manner of form, and so also will the entrails and guts; but we shall not have the *hard* comprehensibility or palpability.

80. For Christ, after his resurrection, saith to *Mary Magdalen*, at the sepulchre in *Joseph's* garden, [2] *Touch me not, for I am not yet* [2] John xx. 17. *ascended to my God and to your God.* As if he would say, I have *not* now the *bestial body* any more, although I shew myself to thee in my form or shape which *I had*, otherwise, thou, in thy bestial body, couldst *not see me*.

81. And so during the forty days after his resurrection he did *not* always walk *visibly* among the disciples, but *invisibly*, according to

his heavenly and angelical property; though when he would speak or *talk* with his disciples, then he shewed or presented himself in a comprehensible or *palpable* manner and form, that thereby he might speak natural words with them: for the *corruption* cannot comprehend or apprehend the divine (words or things).

82. Also it sufficiently appeareth that his body was of an angelical kind, in that he went [1] John xx. 19. to his disciples [1] *through* closed *doors*.

83. Thus now thou must know, that his body qualifieth, mixeth or uniteth with all the seven spirits in nature in the astral birth in the part of *love*, and holdeth sin, death and the devil captive in its *wrath part*.

84. Thus thou now understandest what God made on the *second day*, when he separated the water under the firmament from the water above the firmament. Thou seest also, how thou art in this world *everywhere* in heaven, and also in hell, and dwellest between heaven and hell, in great danger.

85. Thou seest, also, *how* heaven is *in* a holy man; and that *everywhere*, wheresoever thou standest, goest or liest, if thy spirit doth but qualify or co-operate with God, then, as to *that part*, thou art in heaven, and thy *soul* is in God. [2] John x. 28, 29. Therefore also saith Christ, [2] *My sheep are in my hands, no man can pull them away from me.*

86. In like manner thou seest, also, how thou

art always in hell among all the devils, as to the *wrath*; if thy eyes were but open, thou wouldst see *wonderful* things; but thou standest between heaven and hell, and canst see neither of them, and walkest upon a very *narrow bridge.*

87. Some men have many times, according to or in the sidereal or astral spirit, entered in thither, and been ravished in an ecstasy, as men call it, and have presently known the gates of heaven and of hell, and have told, shewn and declared how that many men dwell in hell, *with* or *in* their living bodies, or with their bodies alive: Such indeed have been scorned, derided or laughed at, but with great ignorance and indiscretion, for it is just so as *they declare*; which I will also describe more at large in its due place, and shew in what manner and condition it is with them.

88. But the water hath a *twofold* birth, and I will here prove that also, with or by *the language of nature*; for that is the *root* or *mother* of *all* the languages which are in this world; and therein standeth the whole *perfect* knowledge of *all* things.

89. For when *Adam* spake at the first, he gave names to all the creatures, according to their qualities and innate, instant operations, virtues or faculties. And it is the very language of the total, universal nature, but is not known to every one. For it is a hidden secret mystery, which is

imparted to me by the grace of God from the spirit,
which hath a delight and longing towards me.

Now observe:

90. The word 𝔚𝔞𝔣𝔣𝔢𝔯 (*Water*) is thrust forth
from the heart, and *closeth* together the teeth, and
passeth *over* the astringent and bitter qualities,
and toucheth them not, but goeth forth *through*
the teeth, and the tongue contracteth and rouseth
up itself, together with the spirit, and *helpeth* to
hiss, and so qualifieth, mixeth or *uniteth* with the
spirit, and the spirit presseth very forcibly through
the teeth. But when the spirit is *almost* quite
gone forth, then the astringent and bitter spirit
contracteth and rouseth up itself, and afterwards
first qualifieth with the word, but yet sitteth still
in its seat,* and afterwards *jarreth* mightily and
strongly in the syllable 𝔣𝔢𝔯.

91. But now, that the spirit conceiveth itself
at the heart, and cometh forth and closeth
together the teeth, and *hisseth* with the tongue
through the teeth, signifieth that the *heart of
God* hath moved itself, and with its spirit made
a *closure* round about it, which is the *firmament*
of *heaven:* Also, as the teeth do shut and *close*
together, and then the spirit goeth through the
teeth, so also the spirit goeth forth from the
heart into the *astral* birth or geniture.

92. And as the tongue *frameth* itself for the

* "sitteth still in its seat." See Ch. 25, par. 82.

hissing, and qualifieth, mixeth or uniteth with the spirit, and moveth therewith, so the soul of man *co-imageth* or frameth itself with the Holy Spirit, and qualifieth, operateth or uniteth therewith, and presseth together jointly in the power thereof, *through heaven*, and ruleth together also therewith in the *word* of God.

93. But, that afterwards the astringent and bitter qualities awaken *behind*, and co-image afterwards to the framing of the word, signifieth that indeed all is as it were *one* body, but the heaven and the Holy Spirit, together with the heart of God, hath its *proper* seat to itself; and the devil, together with the wrath of God, can comprehend neither the Holy Spirit nor the heaven; but the devil, together with the wrath, *hangeth in* the outward birth in the *word*, and the wrath helpeth to image all in the outermost birth in this world, all whatsoever that standeth in the comprehensibility or palpability; just as the astringent and bitter qualities *afterwards rouse* themselves behind to the framing of the word, and qualify, operate or unite therewith.

94. That the spirit *first* goeth over the astringent and bitter qualities unperceived, signifieth that the *gate of God* is everywhere in this world *all over*, wherein the Holy Ghost ruleth; and that the heaven standeth open everywhere, even in the midst or centre of the earth; and that the devil *nowhere* can either see or

comprehend or apprehend the heaven, but is a *grumbling* and snarling hell-hound, which afterwards, when the Holy Ghost *hath* built or raised to himself a Church and Temple, first cometh out from behind and destroyeth it in the wrath, and *hangeth behind* at the word as an enemy, who will not endure that a Temple of God should be raised or built in his land or country, whereby his kingdom might be *lessened* or diminished.

THE TWENTY-FIRST CHAPTER

Of the Third Day.

1. ALTHOUGH in the writings of *Moses the spirit* hath kept the *deepest* mysteries secret, hidden and concealed in the *letter*, yet all is so very regularly described that there is *no defect* at all in the order thereof.

2. For when God through the Word had created heaven and earth, and had *separated* the light from the darkness, and had given a place to each of them, then *each began* at once its birth or geniture and qualifying or working.

3. On the *first day* God drave together (or compacted) the corrupt *Salitter*, which so came to be in the kindling of his wrath, I say, God then drave it together or created it through the *strong* spirit; for the word Schuff (*created*) signifieth here a driving together (or compaction).

4. In this driving together or *compaction* of the corrupted Wrath-*Salitter*, was king *Lucifer* also, as an impotent prince, together with his angels, *driven* into the hell of the Wrath-*Salitter*,

into that place where the outward *half*-dead comprehensibility is generated, which is the place or space between the nature-goddess, the *moon*, and the dead *earth*.

5. Now when this was done the deep became clear, and with the hidden or concealed heaven the light was *separated* from the darkness, and the globe of the earth in the great *wheel* of nature was rolled or turned *once about*; and accordingly there passed the time of [1] *one revolution*, or of one day, which containeth twenty-four hours.

[1] the diurnal motion of the earth, 24 hours.

6. In the duration of the *second day* began the sharp separation, and the *incomprehensible* cleft * was made between the wrath and the love of the light; and so king *Lucifer* was firmly, strongly or fast *bolted up* into the house of darkness, and was *reserved* to the final Judgment.

7. So also the water of life was *separated* from the water of death, yet in that manner as that, in this time of the world, they *hang* the one to the other, *as body and soul*, and yet neither of them comprehendeth the other. The *heaven* which was made out of the midst or centre of the water is the cleft between them, so that the comprehensible or palpable water is a death, and the incomprehensible or impalpable is the life.

8. Thus now the incomprehensible spirit, which *is God*, ruleth everywhere in this world, and replenisheth or *filleth all*, and the comprehensible

* " cleft " (*Kluft*).   See Ch. 19, par. 34.

hangeth or dependeth on him, and dwelleth in the darkness, and can neither see nor hear nor smell nor feel the incomprehensible one, but seeth the works thereof, and is a *destroyer* of them.

9. Now when God had bound up the devil in the darkness through the *closure* of the heaven, which heaven is everywhere in all places, then he began again his wonderful birth or geniture in the *seventh* nature-spirit, and all generated again as it *had done* from eternity.

10. For *Moses* writeth thus: [1] *And God said, Let the earth send forth grass and herbs that yield a seed, and the fruit tree yielding or bearing fruit after its kind, which hath its own seed in itself, upon the earth, and it was so done. And the earth sent forth grass, and the herb that yieldeth seed, each after its kind, and the tree yielding fruit, which hath its seed in itself, every one according to its kind; and God saw that it was good. And so out of evening and morning the third day came to be.*

[1] Gen. i. 11–13.

11. This indeed is very rightly and properly *described*, but the true ground sticketh *hidden* or concealed in the word, and hath *never* been understood by man. For man since the fall could never comprehend or *apprehend* the inward birth or geniture, to perceive how the heavenly birth or geniture is; but his *reason* lay captivated in the outward comprehensibility or *palpability*, and could not penetrate and press through heaven,

and see the inward birth or geniture of God, which also is in the corrupted earth, and *everywhere*, in all places.

12. Thou must *not* here think that God hath made some *new* thing, which *never* was before; for if that were so, then there had been *another* God, which is not possible to be. For without or *besides* this one only God, nothing is at all, for the gates of hell are *not anywhere* without, beyond or *absent* from this one only God; only, there is a *partition* or distinction between the love in the light, and the kindled wrath in the darkness, so that the one cannot comprehend the other, and yet the one hangeth to the other as *one* body.

13. The *Salitter*, out of which the earth is come to be, *was* from eternity, and stood in the seventh qualifying or fountain spirit, which is the *nature*-spirit, and the other six have generated the seventh continually, and are encompassed or surrounded *therewith*, or lie captivated or enclosed therein, as in their mother, and are the power and life of the seventh, just as is the *astral* birth in the flesh.

14. But when king *Lucifer* had stirred the wrath in this birth or geniture, and had with his *loftiness* brought the poison and death into it, then in the wrathful birth, in the fierceness or *sting* of death, such earth and stones were generated.

15. Upon this now ensued the *spewing out*

thereof;* for the Deity could not endure such a birth or geniture in the love and light of God, but the corrupted *Salitter* must be *driven together* into a lump, and lord *Lucifer* also with it. So then presently the innate light in the corrupted *Salitter* went out or extinguished, and the *closure* of the heaven was made between the wrath and the love, that so such *Salitter* might be generated *no* more, and that heaven might hold the wrath in the outermost birth or geniture in nature captive in the darkness, and be an *eternal* partition or separation between them.†

16. This being accomplished in the two days, then on the *third day* the light rose up in the darkness, and the darkness, together with the prince thereof, could not comprehend it.

17. For out of the earth there sprang up grass and herbs and trees, and now also it standeth written thus: [1] *Each according to its kind.* In ¹ Gen. i. 12. these words lieth hidden or concealed the *kernel* of the eternal birth or geniture, and it cannot be comprehended or apprehended by or with flesh and blood, but the Holy Ghost, through the animated or soulish birth, must kindle the *astral* man, otherwise he is blind *herein*, and understandeth nothing but concerning earth and stones, also grass, herbs and wooden trees.

---

* "the spewing out thereof," *i.e.* the spewing out of the wrathful birth.

† "between them," *i.e.* between the wrath and the love.

18. But now is it written here, *God* ſprach (*said*), *Let the earth bring forth grass, and herbs, and fruitful trees.*

Observe here:

19. The word ſprach (*said*), is an *eternal* word, and *was* before the times of the wrath from eternity *in* this *Salitter*, when the *Salitter* still stood in the heavenly form and life, and now also it is *not quite* dead in its centre, but only in the comprehensibility or *palpability*.

20. But now when the light rose up again in the outward comprehensibility, or in death, then the eternal word stood in its *full* birth, and generated the *life* through and out of death, and the corrupted *Salitter* brought forth fruit again.

21. But seeing the eternal *word* must qualify, mix or unite with the corruption in the wrath, thereupon the *bodies* of the fruits were evil and good. For the outward birth or geniture of the fruits must be out of or from the *earth* which is in death; and the spirit of life must be out of the *astral* birth which standeth in love and wrath.

22. For thus stood the birth or geniture of nature in the time of the *kindling*, and was thus together incorporated in the earth, and must also in such a birth spring up again : For it is written, [1] *That the* dead *earth should let the grass and herbs and trees spring up, each according to its kind*, that is, according to the kind and

[1] Gen. i. 12.

quality that it *had been* in from eternity, and as it had been in the heavenly quality, kind and form. For that is called *its own* kind which is received in the mother's body or womb, and is its *own* by right of nature, as its own peculiar life.

23. Thus the earth brought forth *no* strange life, except that which *had been* in it from eternity: As before the time of the wrath it had brought forth heavenly fruits, which had a *holy*, pure heavenly body, and were the food of angels, so now it brought forth fruits according to its comprehensible, palpable, hard, evil, wrathful, poisonous, venomous, *half*-dead kind; for as the mother was, so were her children.

24. *Not* that the fruits of the earth are thereupon *wholly* in the wrath of God; for the one only, incorporated or compacted word, which is immortal and *incorruptible*, which was from eternity in the *Salitter* of the earth, sprang up again in the body of death, and brought forth fruit out of the *dead* body of the earth; but the earth comprehended *not* the word, though the word comprehended the earth.

25. And now as the whole earth was, together with the word, so was the fruit also; but the word remained in the centre of the *heaven*, which is also in this place hiddenly; and this birth or geniture *caused* the seven qualifying or fountain spirits, out of or from the outermost, corrupt and dead birth or geniture, *to form* the body; and

itself, *viz.* the Word or Heart of God, remained in its heavenly seat, sitting on the throne of *majesty*, and filled the astral and also the mortal birth or geniture, but to them was the holy life *altogether* incomprehensible.

26. Thou must not think that thereupon the outermost dead birth or geniture of the earth hath gotten *such* a life, through the risen word that sprang up, that it is *no more* a death, and that death no longer is in her fruit : No ; that can never be ; for that which is *once* dead in God is really dead, and in its *own power* can never be living again ; but the word, which qualifieth, mixeth or uniteth with the astral birth in the part of the love, generateth the *life* through the astral birth or geniture, through the death.

27. For thou seest plainly how all the fruits of the earth, whatsoever it bringeth forth, must *putrefy* and rot ; also that they are a death.

28. But that the fruits get a body other than the earth is, which body is much fuller of virtue, fairer or more beautiful, also of a better taste, relish and smell, is *because* the astral birth or geniture receiveth power or virtue from the word, and formeth or frameth *another* body, which standeth half in the death and half in the life, and standeth *hidden* between the wrath of God and the love.

29. But, that the fruits upon the body are much pleasanter, more lovely, sweeter and milder, and with a good taste and relish, that is [because

of] the *third birth* out of the earth, according to which the earth shall be *purged* and cleansed at the end of this time, and shall be set or put again into its *first* place; but the wrath will abide in death.

The richly joyful Gate of Man.

30. Behold, thus saith the spirit in the word, which is the very heart of the earth, and which riseth or springeth up in his heaven, in the clear flash of the life, wherewith my spirit in its knowledge qualifieth, mixeth or *uniteth*, and through which I write these words.

31. Man is made out of the seed of the earth, out of an incorporated or compacted mass or lump—

["*Understand, out of the matrix of the "earth, wherein the eye is twofold, the one "in God and the other in this world, out of "three Principles.*"]

—and not out of the wrath, but out of the birth or geniture of the earth, as a king or heart of the earth, and stood in the astral birth or geniture in *the part* of the love; but wrath hung to him, which he should have put forth from himself, as the fruit putteth forth from itself the *bitterness* of the tree.

32. But that, *he did not*, but reached back from the love into the wrath, and *lusted* after his dead or mortal mother, to eat of her, and to suck her breast, and to stand upon her stock.

33. Now according to his wrestling so also it befell him, and so he brought himself with his outermost birth or geniture into the death or *mortality* of his mother, and with his *life* he brought himself out from the love into the part of the *wrathful*, astral birth or geniture.

34. And there he standeth now, between heaven and hell, in the *face* of the devil in his kingdom, against whom the devil *warreth*, fighteth and striveth continually, that he might either banish him out of his country into the earth, or make him a child of wrath in hell. And what is now his hope?

Answer.

35. Behold! thou blind Heathen; behold! thou render, perverter, obscurer and wrester of the *Scriptures*, open thy eyes wide, and be not ashamed at this simple plainness; for God lieth hid in the centre, and is yet much more *simple* and plain; but thou seest him not.

36. Behold! thy spirit or thy soul is generated from or out of thy astral birth or geniture, and is the *third* birth *in thee*, just as an apple upon a tree is the *third* birth or geniture of the *earth*, and hath not its vegetation in, from, or within the earth, but from above the earth; and if it were *a spirit*, as thy soul is, it would not suffer the earth any more to tie or *bind* it to corruption.

37. But thou must know, however, that the apple on its stock or branch, with its innermost

birth or geniture, qualifieth, mixeth or uniteth with *the word of God*, through whose power it is grown out of the earth.

38.* But since the wrath is in the body of the mother of the apple, this same mother cannot get the apple out of the palpable birth, and the apple must remain, *as to* its body, in the palpability, in death.

39. But in its power,† in which its *life* standeth, wherewith it qualifieth, mixeth or uniteth with the word of God, this apple will, in its mother, in the power of the word at the Last Judgment Day, be set or put again into its *heavenly* place, and be *separated* from the wrathful and dead or mortal palpability, and spring up in the heaven of this world, in a heavenly form, and be a *fruit* for men in the other life.

["*Here understand, the power of the Principle,*
"*out of which the* apple *and* all things *grow, will,*
"*in the renovation of the world, spring up again*
"*in paradise with the wonders.*"]

40. But seeing thou art made out of the *seed* of the earth—

["*Red earth is fire and water, conceived*
"*with or by the Word* Fiat *out of the*
"*matrix of the earth: when man imagined*

---

* A new translation of this par. has been substituted for Sparrow's rendering.

† "But in its power," etc. "But in its power (the virtue wherein the apple's life consists) wherewith it qualifieth with the Word of God, this apple will, in its mother," etc.

" *or set his desire into the earth he became*
" *earthly.*"]

—and hast set or put thy body *back* again into
thy mother, therefore thy body also is become a
palpable, dead or mortal body, such as thy
mother is.

41. Thy body hath the same *hope* which thy
mother the earth hath, *viz.* that at the Last
Judgment Day, in the power of the word, it will
be set or put again into its *first* place.

42. But seeing thy astral birth standeth here
on earth in the wrath, and qualifieth, mixeth or
uniteth with the love in the word, (just as the
fruit on the tree doth, for the power of the fruit
qualifieth or uniteth with the word), *therefore thy
hope standeth in God.* For the astral birth or
geniture standeth in love and wrath, and *that*, in
this time, it *cannot* boast of, on account of the
outermost birth or geniture in the *flesh*, which
standeth in death.

43. For the dead or mortal flesh hath encompassed the astral birth, and man's flesh is a dead
carcass, whilst it is yet in the mother's body or
womb, and is encompassed with hell and God's
wrath.

44. But now the astral birth generateth the
animated soulish birth, *viz.* the *third*, which
standeth in the word, wherein the incorporated
or compacted word lieth *hidden* in its heaven.

[" *The* Sulphur *to the (production of the) soul*

" *is the first Principle in the eternal will-spirit,*
" *and cometh to life in the third Principle, and*
" *so liveth between love and wrath, and hangeth*
" *to both.*"]

45. Now, since thou hast thy *reason*, and art
not like the apple on the tree, but art created an
angel and the similitude or image of God, *instead*
of the expulsed devils, and *knowest* how thou
canst with thy astral birth, in the part of love,
qualify or unite with the word of God, *therefore
thou canst*, in the centre of the word, set or *put*
thy animated or *soulish* birth into heaven, and
thou canst with thy soul, even with thy [1] living
body in this dead or mortal palpability, *rule* with
God in heaven.

[1] Or body alive.

46. For the [2] word is in thy heart, and qualifieth or uniteth with the soul, as if it were *one
being*; and if thy soul standeth in the love, then
it also is one being.   And, thou mayest say, that
according to thy soul thou sittest in heaven, and
livest and *reignest* with God.

[2] Deut. xxx. 14.   Rom. x. 8.

[" *Understand, according to the spirit of the*
" *soul, with the image out of the animated or*
" *soulish fire.*"]

47. For the soul, which *apprehendeth* the word,
hath an open gate in heaven, and can be prevented
by nothing; *neither* doth the devil see the soul,
because it is *not* in his country or dominions.

48. But seeing thy astral birth standeth with
the one part in the wrath, and that the flesh

through the wrath standeth in death, *thereupon* the devil, in the part of the wrath, seeth *continually* even *into* thy heart, and if thou lettest him have any room or place there, then he teareth out from the word *that part* of the astral birth which standeth in the love.

49. Then thy heart is a dark valley: And if thou dost not labour and work *quickly* again to the birth of the light, *then* he kindleth the wrath-fire therein, and then shall thy soul be spewed out from the word, and then it qualifieth or uniteth with the wrath of God, and so *afterwards* thou art a devil, and not an angel, and canst not, with thy animated or *soulish* birth, reach the gates of heaven.

50. But if thou fightest and strivest with the devil, and keepest the gate of *love* in thy astral birth, and so departest from hence as to the body, then thy soul remaineth in the word *quite hidden* from the devil, and reigneth with God, even unto the day of the restitution of that which was lost.

51. But if thou standest with thy astral birth in the *wrath*, when thou departest from hence as to the body, and thy soul be not comprehended in the word, *then* thou canst never reach the gates of heaven; but into what part thou hast sown thy seed, that is, thy *soul*, in that very *part* will thy body also rise.

The Gate of the Power.

52. That soul and body will [1] come together again at the Day of the Resurrection thou mayest *perceive* here by the earth. For the Creator said, *Let the earth bring forth grass and herbs, and trees bearing fruit, each according to its kind.* Then *each* sprang up according to its kind, and grew. And as before the time of the wrath it *had* a heavenly body, so it got now an earthly one, *answerable* to its mother.

[1] Or find one another.

53. But it is to be considered how all was comprised in the word at the great tumult and *uproar* of the devil, *so that* all sprang up in its *own being* according to its *power*, virtue and kind, as if it had *never been* destroyed, but only altered.

54. Now if it was thus at *that* time, when there was such murdering and robbing, sure it will be much more *so* at the Last Judgment Day, when the earth shall be *separated* in the kindled wrath-fire, and will be living again or revived. Then, *surely*, it will be comprehended in the word of love, as it hath in the same word here generated its fruit of grass, herbs and trees, as also all manner of mineral ores of silver and gold.

55. But seeing the *astral* birth of the earth standeth in the love, and the outward standeth in death, therefore will each remain in its seat, and so life and death will sever themselves.

56. Where, now, would the soul of man *rather*

¹ Note,
Christ's not
being as-
cended to his
Father.

be at the day of regeneration, than in its ¹ *father*, that is, *in the body* which hath generated it?

57. But seeing the soul, all the *while* the body had been in death, remained *hidden* in the word, and seeing the same word also holdeth the earth in the astral birth in the *love*, therefore it [the soul] qualifieth, mixeth or uniteth through the word, *all* the time of its hiddenness and secrecy, also with its *mother* the body, according or as to the *astral* birth or geniture in the earth, and so *body* and soul in the word were never separated the one from the other, but live *jointly* and equally together in *God*.

58. And though indeed the *bestial* body must putrefy and rot, yet its power and virtue *live*, and in the meanwhile there grow out of its power, in its mother, fair, beautiful roses, blossoms and flowers; and though it were *quite* burnt up and consumed in the fire, yet its power and *virtue* stand in the four elements in the *word*, and the soul qualifieth, mixeth or uniteth there-with; for the soul is in *heaven*, and the same heaven is *everywhere*, even in the midst or centre of the earth.

59. *O, dear man, view thyself for a while in this looking-glass*; thou wilt find it more largely to be read of concerning the creation of man. This I set down *here* for this very cause, that thou mightest *the better* understand the *power* of creation, and that thou mightest the better

conceive and *fit* thyself for this spirit, and so
learn to understand *its language*.

The open Gate of the Earth.

Now it might be asked, From or out of what
matter or power and *virtue*, then, did the grass,
herbs and trees spring forth ? What manner of
substance or condition or constitution hath this
kind of creature ?

Answer.

60. The simple saith, *God made all things out
of nothing*. But he knoweth not that God;
neither doth he know what God is : for when
he beholdeth the *earth*, together with the *deep*
above the earth, he thinketh, verily all this is
not God ; or else he thinketh, God is *not there*.
He always imagineth that God dwelleth only
above the azure heaven of the stars, and ruleth,
as it were, with some spirit which *goeth forth*
from him into this world ; and that *his body* is not
present here upon the earth, nor in the earth.

61. Just such opinions and tenets I also have
read in the books and writings of doctors (ber
Doctoren), and there are also very many *opinions*,
disputations and controversies arisen about this
very thing among the *learned*.

62. But seeing God, in his great love, openeth
to me the gate of his being, and remembereth
the *Covenant* which he hath with man, therefore

I will, according to my gifts, faithfully and earnestly unlock and set wide open *all the gates of God*, so far as God will give me leave.

63. It is *not* so to be understood as that I am *sufficient* enough in these things, but only so far as I am able to comprehend.

64. For the being of God is like a wheel, wherein many wheels are made *one in another*, upwards, downwards, crossways, and yet they continually turn, all of them together.

65. Which, indeed, when a man beholdeth the *wheel*, he highly marvelleth at it, and, in its turning, cannot *at once* learn to conceive and *apprehend* it: But the more he beholdeth the wheel, the more he learneth its form or frame; and the more he learneth, the greater longing he hath to the wheel; for he continually seeth somewhat that is more and more wonderful, so that a man can neither behold it, nor learn it *enough*.

66. Thus I also, what I do not *enough* describe in one place concerning this great Mystery, that you will find in another place; and what I cannot describe in this book, in regard of the largeness *

---

* "in regard of the largeness of the Mystery," etc. (*von wegen der länge*), "on account of length." It does not seem that J. B. here emphasises so much "the largeness *of the Mystery*," as the difficulty of writing at length concerning it, owing to his own incapacity to grasp it, as yet, in its fulness. The sentence containing these words might be rendered as follows: "and what I cannot describe in this book, on account of the

of the Mystery, and my incapacity, that you will find in the *others* following.

67. For *this book* is the first sprouting or vegetation of this twig, which springeth or groweth green in its mother, and is *as a child* that is learning to walk, and is not able to run apace at the *first*.

68. For though the spirit seeth the wheel, and would fain comprehend its form or frame in *every* place, yet it cannot do it exactly enough, because of the turning of the wheel: But when the wheel cometh about again, so that the spirit can again see the first apprehended or conceived form, then *continually* it learneth more and more, and always delighteth in and loveth the wheel, and longeth after it *still* more and more.

Now observe:

69. The earth hath just such qualities and qualifying or fountain spirits as the deep above the earth or as *heaven* hath, and all of them together belong to one only body; and the whole or *universal* God is that one only *body*. But that thou dost not wholly and fully see and know him, *sins are the cause* thereof, with and by which thou, in this great divine body, liest *shut*

---

length of such description, and on account also of my incapacity to give it, that you will find," etc.

See Cont. of this B., par. 39 *et seq.*, and Ch. 10, par. 41 *et seq.*

up in the dead or mortal *flesh*; and the power or virtue of the *Deity* is *hidden* from thee, even as the *marrow* in the bones is hidden from the *flesh*.

70. But if thou, in the spirit, breakest through the death of the flesh, then thou seest the hidden God. For as the marrow in the bones penetrateth, presseth or breaketh through and giveth virtue, power and strength to the *flesh*, and yet the flesh cannot comprehend or apprehend the marrow, but only the power and *virtue* thereof, so no more canst thou see the hidden Deity in thy flesh, but thou receivest its *power*, and understandest *therein* that God dwelleth in thee.

71. For the dead or *mortal* flesh belongeth not [1] to the birth of *life*, and therefore cannot receive or conceive the life of the light as a *propriety*; but the life of the light in God riseth up in the dead or mortal flesh, and generateth to itself, from or out of the dead or mortal flesh, *another* heavenly and living body, which knoweth and *understandeth* the light.

72. For this body is but a *husk*, from which the new body groweth—

> [" *The new body groweth out of the heavenly*
> " *substantiality in the Word, out of the flesh*
> " *and blood of Christ, out of the mystery of*
> " *the old body.*"]

—as it is with a *grain* of wheat in the earth. The husk or shell *will not rise* again, no more

[1] Or into.

than it doth in the wheat, but will remain *for ever* in death and in hell.

73. Therefore man carrieth about with him here upon earth, *in* his body, the devil's eternal dwelling-house. O thou fair excellent goddess ! mayest thou not well prance and trick thyself *therein*, and in the meanwhile *invite* the devil into the new birth for a guest, will it not profit thee very much ? Take heed that thou dost not generate a new devil, who will remain in his *own* house.

74. Behold the mystery of the earth : as that generateth or bringeth forth, so must thou generate or bring forth. The earth *is not* that body which groweth or sprouteth forth, but it is the *mother* of that body ; as also thy flesh is not the spirit, but the *flesh* is the mother of the spirit.

75. But now in both of them, *viz.* in the earth and in thy flesh, there is hidden the *light* of the clear Deity, and it breaketh through, and generateth to itself a body according to the kind of *each* body ; for man according to his body, and for the earth according to its *body* ; for as the mother is, so is the *child* also.

76. Man's child is the *soul*, which is generated out of the astral birth from or out of the flesh ; and the earth's child is the *grass*, the herbs, the trees, silver, gold, and all mineral ores.

Now thou askest, How then shall I do, that I may understand somewhat concerning the *birth* or geniture of the *earth* ?

Answer.

77. Behold! the birth of the earth standeth
in its birth or geniture as the *whole Deity* doth,
and there is no difference at all, but only as to
the *corruption* in the wrath, wherein comprehensibility or palpability standeth; that *only* is
the difference or distinction, and is *the death*
between God and the earth.

78. Thou must know that all the seven spirits
of God are *in* the earth, and generate as they do
in heaven: For the earth is in God, and God
never died; but the outermost birth or geniture is
dead, in which the wrath resteth, and is reserved
for king *Lucifer*, to be a house of death and of
darkness, and to be an eternal prison or dungeon.

Of the seven Spirits of God, and of their Operation in the Earth.

79. The *first* is the astringent spirit, and that
contracteth or draweth together in the astral
birth of the seven qualifying or fountain spirits
a *mass* or lump in the earth, through the kindling
of the superior birth or geniture *above* the earth,
and drieth up that with its sharp *coldness*; just
as it contracteth or draweth the water together
and maketh *ice* thereof, so also it contracteth or
draweth together the *water* in the earth, and
maketh thereof a dry mass or lump.

80. Then next the *bitter* spirit, which existeth
in the fire-flash, is also in the *matter* or mass,

and that cannot endure to be captivated or imprisoned in the dried *exsiccated* matter, but rubs itself against the astringent spirit in the dried mass or lump, so long till it *kindleth* the fire; and so when that is done, then the bitter spirit is terrified, and getteth its life.

Conceive this here aright.

81. In the earth thou canst not trace nor find, besides plants and metals, anything but astringency, bitterness, and water: But the water now therein is *sweet*, opposite to the other two qualities: Also it is thin or transparent, and the other two are hard, rough and bitter, and always the one is *against* the other. Thereupon there is a perpetual struggling, fighting and wrestling, but in the struggling of these *three* the *life* doth not yet stand; but they are a dark valley, and they are three things which can never endure one another, but there is an eternal struggling among them.

83.[1] From hence *mobility* taketh its original; also God's wrath, which resteth in the hidden secrecy, taketh its original from hence; and so also the *original* of the devil, of death and of hell, ariseth from hence; as you may read thereof concerning the fall of the devil.

[1] [The numbers follow Sparrow's text. "82" is absent. —Eds.]

The Depth in the Centre of the Birth or Geniture.

84. Now when these *three*, viz. the astringency, the bitterness, and the sweetness, rub themselves one against another; then the astringent quality

groweth predominant, for it is the strongest, and *forcibly* attracteth or draweth the sweetness together, for the sweetness is *meek* and extensive on account of its *suppleness*, and must yield to be captivated or imprisoned.

85. So when that is done, then the bitterness is also together captivated or imprisoned in the *body* of the sweet water, and becometh also together dried up, and then the astringent, the sweet and the bitter are one in another, and struggle so strongly in the *dried* mass or lump till the mass be quite dry : For the astringent quality always contracteth it together, and drieth it more and more.

86. But when the sweet water can defend itself *no* longer, then *anguish* riseth up in it ; just as in man, when he is *dying*, when the spirit is departing from the body, and so the body yieldeth itself captive as a prisoner to death ; just so the *water* also yieldeth itself captive as a prisoner.

87. And in this anxious rising up an anguishing heat is generated, whereby a [1] *sweat* presseth forth, as it doth in a dying man ; and that sweat qualifieth, mixeth or uniteth with the astringent and bitter qualities, for it is their son, which *they* have generated out of the sweet water, and which they had *killed* and brought to death.

88. Now when that is done, then the astringent and bitter qualities *rejoice* in their son, understand, in the sweat, and both of them give to

[1] humour or moisture.

it their power, virtue and life, and stuff it like a
greedy gormandizing hog, so that it *soon* comes
to grow *full* and swelled: For the astringent
quality, and also the bitter, always draw the sap
out of the earth, and stuff it into *their* young son.

89. But the body, which was *first* contracted
or drawn together out of the sweet water, re-
maineth dead or mortal, and the [1]*sweat* of the [1] Or juice of the body.
body, which qualifieth, mixeth or uniteth with
the astringent and bitter qualities, hath the
house therein, where it spreadeth itself forth,
groweth gross, [2]full and lusty or *wanton*. [2] fat, lusci-ous, lascivi-ous.

90. But now the two qualities, *viz.* the astringent and the bitter, cannot leave their contention
and opposition, or contrary will, but wrestle
continually one with the other: The astringent
is strong, and the bitter is *swift*.

91. So now, when the astringent grappleth
with the bitter, the bitter *leaps* aside, and taketh
the son's sap along with it; and then the astringent everywhere presseth hard after it, and would
fain captivate it. Then the bitter rusheth out from
the body, and extendeth itself as far as it can.

92. But when the body begins to be *too strait*
or narrow for it, that it can extend or stretch it
no more, and that the contention is too great,
then the bitter must yield itself captive. Yet,
for all that, the astringent *cannot kill* the bitter,
but only holds it captive, and so the strife in
them is so great that the bitter *breaks out* of the

body in ¹ strings like *threads*, and taketh some of the son's sap or body along with it. *And this now is the vegetation or growing, and incorporating or embodying of a root in the earth.*

Now thou askest, How can God be in that birth or geniture ?

Answer.

93. Behold! that is the birth or geniture of *nature*; and so, if in these three qualities, *viz.* the astringent, the bitter and the sweet, the wrath-fire were not kindled, then thou wouldst *plainly* see where God is.

94. But now the wrath-fire is in all three; for the astringent is much too cold, and contracteth or draweth the body *too hard* together; and the sweet is much too thick and dark, which the astringent soon catcheth, and holdeth it captive, and drieth it *too much*; and then the bitter is *too stinging*, murderous and raging; and so they cannot be reconciled to agree.

95. Else if the astringent were not so much *kindled* in the cold fire, and the water were not so thick, also the bitter not so *swelling*, rising ² Or that fire. and murderous, then they *might* kindle ² the *fire*, from whence the *light* would exist, and from the light the *love*; and so out of the fire-flash the *tone* would exist. Then thou wouldst *see* plainly whether there would not be a heavenly *body* there, wherein the light of God would *shine*.

96. But seeing the astringent is too cold, and

drieth the water too much, thereupon it captivateth the *hot* fire in its coldness, and killeth or destroyeth the body of the *sweet* water, and so the bitter captivateth it, and drieth it up.*

97. So in this *exsiccation* or drying up, the unctuosness or *fatness* in the sweet water is killed or destroyed, in which the fire kindleth itself, and so out of that unctuosity or fatness **an** astringent and *bitter* spirit comes to be.   For when the unctuosness or fat in the sweet water *dieth*, then it is turned into an *anguishing sweat*, in which the astringent and the bitter qualify, mix or unite.

98. The meaning is not that the water dieth *quite*; no, that cannot be, but the astringent spirit taketh captive in its cold fire the sweetness or the unctuosity and *fatness* of the water, and qualifieth, mixeth or uniteth therewith, and maketh use *thereof* for its spirit: Its own spirit being wholly *benumbed*, and in death, therefore it maketh use of the water for its life, and draweth out the water's unctuosity or *fatness* to itself, and bereaveth the water of its power.

* "and so the bitter captivateth it, and drieth it up" (*auch so nimt sie die Bittere gefangen, und vertrocknet sie mit*), "even so [in the same way] it [the astringent] captivateth the bitter, and drieth it up [as well]." But from the construction of the sentence it is impossible to say whether the meaning is that the astringent captivateth the bitter, or the bitter the astringent, and whether or not either singly or both together bring about the drying up. The pronoun is feminine, and may therefore refer to either of these, but cannot refer to "sweet water." St Martin's French translation shews the same ambiguity.

99. Then the water becometh an *anguishing sweat*, which standeth between death and life, and so the fire of the heat *cannot* kindle itself: For the unctuosity or *fatness* is captivated in the cold fire, and so the *whole* body remaineth a dark valley, which standeth in an anguishing birth or geniture, and cannot comprehend or reach the life. For the *life* which standeth in the light cannot elevate itself in the hard, bitter and astringent body; for it is *captivated* in the cold fire, but *not* quite dead.

100. Thou must see that *all this* is really so. For example, take a root which is of a *hot* quality, put it in *warm* water, or take it into *thy* mouth, and make it warm and supple or moist; then thou wilt soon *perceive* its life, and *active* or operative quality: But so long as it is without or *absent* from the heat, it is captivated in death, and is *cold*, as any other root or piece of *wood* is.

101. Then thou seest that the body upon the root is *dead* also; for when the virtue is gone out of the root, then the body is but a dead *carcass* and can operate or effect nothing at all. And that is *because* the astringent spirit and the bitter have *killed* or destroyed the body of the water and attracted the *fatness* or unctuosity thereof to themselves; and thus they have [1] drawn or sucked up the spirit thereof into the *dead body*.

¹ bred or hatched up their spirit in the dead body.

102. Otherwise, if the sweet water *could* keep its unctuosity or fatness in its own *power*, and

the astringent spirit and the bitter did rub themselves one with another very *gently* in the sweet water, then they would kindle the unctuosity or fatness in the sweet water, and then the *light* would instantly generate itself in the water, and would *enlighten* the astringent and the bitter quality.

103. Whereupon they would get their true life, and would be satisfied by the *light*, and rejoice highly therein, and from that *living joy* love would arise, and then the *tone* would rise up in the fire-flash, through the *rising up* of the bitter quality in the astringent. If that were done there would be a *heavenly* fruit, just as it [the fruit] springeth up in heaven.

104. But thou art to know that the *earth* hath all the qualifying or fountain spirits. For through the devil's kindling the spirits of life were incorporated or compacted together also in *death*, and, as it were, captivated, but *not* quite murdered.

105. The *first three*, viz. the astringent, the sweet, and the bitter, belong to the imaging or forming of the body; and therein standeth the mobility, and the *body* or corporeity. And these now have the comprehensibility or palpability, and are the birth of the *outermost* nature.

106. The *other three*, viz. the heat, the love, and the tone, stand in the incomprehensibility, and are generated out of the first three; and this now is the inward birth, wherewith the Deity qualifieth, mixeth or uniteth.

107. If the first three were *not* congealed or benumbed in death they *could* kindle the heat, and then thou wouldst soon see a bright, shining, heavenly body, and thou wouldst see plainly *where* God is.

108. But seeing the first three qualities of the earth are congealed or benumbed in death, therefore they *remain* also a death, and cannot elevate there life into the *light*, but remain a dark valley, in which there *standeth* God's wrath, death, and hell, as also the eternal prison and source or torment of the devil.

109. *Not that* these three qualities of the outermost birth, in which the wrath-fire standeth, are *rejected* and reprobated of the innermost; no, but only the outward palpable body, and therein the *outward* hellish source, quality or torment.

110. Here thou seest once more how the kingdom of God and the kingdom of hell hang one to the other, as *one* body, and yet the one cannot comprehend the other. For the *second birth*, viz. the heat, light, love, and the sound or tone, is hidden in the outermost, and maketh the outward *moveable*, so that the outward gathereth itself together, and generateth a body.

111. Though the body standeth in the outward palpableness, yet it is formed according to the kind and *manner* of the inward birth, for in the inward birth or geniture standeth the *word*, and the word is the sound or tone,

which riseth up in the light in the fire-flash through the bitter and astringent quality.

112. But seeing the *sound* of God's word must rise up through the astringent bitter death, and generate a body in the half-dead water, thereupon that body is good, and also evil, dead and also living; for it must instantly attract the sap of *fierceness* and the body of death, and stand in such a body and power, as doth the earth, its mother.

113. But that the life lieth *hid* under and in the death of the earth, as also in the children of the earth, I will here demonstrate to you.

114. Behold! man becometh weak, faint and sick, and if *no remedy* be used, then he soon falls into death. The sickness is *caused* either by some bitter and astringent herb which groweth out of the earth, or else is caused by an evil, mortiferous deadly water, or by several mixtures of earthly herbs, or by some evil stinking and rank flesh or meat, and surfeit from thence to *loathing*.

115. Now if a learned physician inquireth of the sick person from what his disease is proceeded, and taketh that which is the *cause* of the disease, whether it be flesh, water or herbs, and *distils* or *burneth* it to powder, according as the *matter* is, and so burneth away the outward poison thereof, which standeth in *death*; then, *in that* distilled water, or burnt powder, the astral birth remaineth in its *seat*, where life and death

wrestle one with the other, and are *both capable* of being raised up; for the *dead body* is gone.

116. So now, if thou minglest with this water or powder some good *treacle* or the like, which holdeth *captive* the rising up and the power of the wrath in the astral birth, and givest it to the sick *party* or patient in a little warm drink, be it beer or wine, then operateth the *innermost* and hidden birth of the thing which, through its outermost dead birth, hath caused the *disease* in man.

117. For when it is put into warm liquor, then the *life* in the *thing* becometh rising, and would fain raise itself, and be kindled in the light; but it cannot, because of the *wrath*, which is opposite to it in the astral birth or geniture.

118. But it can do thus much, *viz.* [1] it can *take away* the disease from a man; for the astral life riseth up through death, and taketh away the *power* from the sting of death: And so when that hath gotten the *victory*, then the party becometh sound again.

119. Thus thou seest how the power or *virtue* of the Word and eternal life in the earth, and in its *children*, lieth hidden in the centre in death, and springeth up through death, incomprehensibly as to the death, and continually travaileth in anguish to the birth of the light, and yet cannot flourish or bud, till the death be severed from it.

120. But it hath its life in its seat, and that *cannot* be taken from it, but death hangeth to

it in the outermost birth or geniture, as also the wrath in death; for the *wrath* is the life of death and of the devil; and in the wrath standeth also the corporeal being, or the *bodies* of the devils, but the dead birth or geniture is their *eternal* dwelling-house.

The Depth in the Circle of the Birth or Geniture.

Now one might ask, What manner of substance hath it, or what is the condition thereof, that the astral birth of the *earth* did begin its qualifying, operating and generating one day *sooner* than the astral in the *deep* above the earth; seeing the *fire* in the deep *above* the earth is much sharper and easier to be kindled, than the fire *in* the earth; and seeing also that the earth must be kindled by the fire in the deep *above* the earth, else it can bear no fruit?

Answer.

121. Behold, thou understanding spirit: The spirit speaketh to *thee*, and *not* to the dead spirit of the flesh: Open wide the door of thy astral birth, and elevate that one part of the astral birth in the *light*, and let the other in the *wrath* stand still, and take heed also that thy animated or soulish spirit do *wholly* unite with the light.

122. So when thou standest in such a *form*, then thou art as heaven and earth are, or as the whole Deity is with its births or genitures *in this world*.

123. But now if thou art *not thus*, then thou

art blind herein, though thou were the wittiest and wisest doctor that *ever* could be found in the world.

124. But if thou art thus, then raise up thy spirit and see: through thy astrological art, thy deep sense and thy measuring of circles thou canst not apprehend it; *it must be born* IN THEE, else thou gettest neither grace nor art.

125. If the eyes of thy spirit are to stand open, then thou must generate *thus*, else thy comprehensibility is a foolish virgin, and it befalls thee, as if a *limner**** should offer to *pourtray* the Deity on a table, and tell thee, It is made right, the Deity is just so.

126. Then the *believer* and the limner are both alike, both of them see nothing but wood and colours only, and the one, blind, leadeth the other: *Surely* thou art not to fight there with beasts, but with gods.

Now observe:

127. When the *whole* Deity in this world moved itself to the *creation*, then, not only the *one* part did move, and the other rest, but all stood jointly in the *mobility*, even the whole deep, so far as lord *Lucifer* was king, and so far as the place of his kingdom *reached*, and so far as the *Salitter* in the wrath-fire was *kindled*.

128. The motion of the three births lasted the length of *six days and nights*, wherein all the *seven* spirits of God stood in a *full* moving birth

* "limner" (*Mahler* [*Maler*]), a painter.

or geniture, as also the *heart* of the spirits ; and the *Salitter* of the earth *turned about* in that while *six times* in the great wheel; which wheel is the seven qualifying or fountain spirits of God. At each turning about or diurnal revolution there was generated a several special *work* or production, according to the *innate*, instant qualifying or fountain spirits.

129. For the *first* qualifying or fountain *spirit* is the astringent, cold, sharp and hard birth or geniture, and that *belongeth* to the *first day* ; in the astral birth or geniture the astrologers call it the *Saturnine*, which was performed on the first day. For therein the hard, dry, sharp earth and stones came to be, and were incorporated or compacted together ; moreover, then also was generated the *strong* firmament of heaven, and the heart of the seven spirits of God stood hidden in the hard sharpness.

130. Astrologers appropriate or attribute the *second day* to *Sol* or the sun, but it belongeth to *Jupiter*, to speak astrologically ; for on the *second* day the light brake forth out of the *heart* of the seven qualifying or fountain spirits, through the hard quality of heaven, and caused a mitigation, or an allaying in the hard water of the heaven, and the light became *shining* in that meekness and allaying.

131. Then the meekness and the hard water *separated* themselves asunder, and the hardness

remained in its hard place, as a hard death, and the meekness or softness penetrated through the hardness in the power of the light.

132. And this now is the *water of life*, which is generated in the light of God out of the hard death. And thus the light of God in the *sweet water* of heaven brake through the astringent and hard, dark death; and *thus* the heaven is made out of the midst or centre of the water.

133. The hard firmament is the astringent quality, and the *gentle*, mild or meek firmament is the water, in which the light of life riseth up, which is *the clarity or bright light of the Son of God*. In this manner or form also the *knowledge*, and the light of life, riseth up in man, and the whole light of God in this world standeth in *such* a form, birth, and rising up.

134. The *third day* is very rightly attributed to *Mars*, because Mars is a bitter, and a *furious* raging and stirring spirit. It the *third* revolution of the earth the bitter quality rubbed itself with the astringent.

Understand this Thing rightly.

135. When the light in the sweet water did *penetrate* through the astringent spirit, then the fire-*flash*, terror or crack of the light, when it kindled itself in the water, rose up in the astringent and hard, dead quality, and made all *stirring*: from thence existed the mobility.

136. Now I speak here not *only* of the heaven above the earth, but this stirring and birth or geniture was also *in* the earth, and *everywhere*.

137. But seeing the heavenly fruits, before the time of the wrath, sprang up only in this stirring of the seven qualifying or fountain spirits, and vanished and passed away again by their stirring, and so changed or altered themselves, therefore on the third day of the birth or geniture of the creation they sprang up also through the stirring of the fire-flash in the astringent quality of the earth.

138. Though indeed the *whole Deity* is in the centre of the earth, *hidden*, yet the earth could not, for all that, bring forth heavenly fruit, for the astringent quality had *shut* and barred the hard bolt of death upon it, and so the heart of the Deity, in all the births, *remained* hidden in its meek and light heaven.

139. For the outermost birth is *nature*, and that ought not to reach *back* into the heart of God, neither can it, but it is the body, in which the qualifying or fountain spirits generate themselves, and shew forth and manifest their birth or geniture *by their fruits*.

140.* Therefore on the third day the earth began to spring, just as the qualifying or fountain spirits stood in the crack of the word or fire-flash.

* This par. does not appear in Sparrow's translation, though it is in all the German editions.

THE TWENTY-SECOND CHAPTER

*Of the Birth or Geniture of the Stars, and
Creation of the Fourth Day.*

1. HERE now is begun the describing of the
astral birth. It ought well to be
observed what the *first title* of this book meaneth,
which is thus expressed: *The Day-Spring or
Dawning in the East,* or *Morning-Redness in
the Rising.* For here will a *very simple* man be
able to see and comprehend or apprehend the being
of God.

2. The Reader should not make himself blind
through his *unbelief* and dull apprehension; for
here I bring in the whole or total nature, with all
her children, for a *witness* and a demonstration.
If thou art rational, then look round about thee,
and view thyself; also consider thyself aright,
and then thou wilt *soon find* from or out of what
spirit I write.

3. For my part, I will obediently perform the
command of the spirit, only, have thou a care,
and suffer not thyself to be shut out by an open

door; * for here the gates of knowledge stand open to thee.

4. Though the spirit will indeed go against the current of some astrologers, that is no great matter to me, for I am bound to *obey God rather than men*; men are blind in or concerning the spirit, and if they will not see, then they may remain blind still.

Now observe:

5. Now when upon the *third day* the fire-flash rose up out of the light, which was shining in the sweet water, which flash is the bitter quality which generateth itself out of the kindled *terror* or crack of fire in the water:

6. Then the whole nature of this world became springing, boiling and moving *in* the earth, as well as above the earth, and everywhere, and began to generate itself again in all things.

7. Out of the earth *sprang up* grass, herbs and trees; and in the earth, silver, gold, and all manner of ores came to be; and in the deep above the earth sprang up the *wonderful forming* of power and virtue.

8. But that thou mayest understand what manner of *substance* and condition all these things and births or genitures have, I will describe all in order one after another, that thou mayest

* "shut out by an open door." That is, the door is open, do not imagine that it is shut.

rightly understand the *ground* of this Mystery.
I will treat,

    1. Of the *earth.*

    2. Of the *deep* above the earth.

    3. Of the incorporating or compacting of the bodies of the *stars.*

    4. Of the seven chief qualities of the *planets*, and of their heart, which is the *sun.*

    5. Of the *four elements.*

    6. Of the outward comprehensible or palpable birth or geniture, which existeth out of this *whole regimen* or dominion.

    7. Of the *wonderful proportion* and fitness or dexterity of the whole wheel of nature.

    9. Before this looking-glass I will now *invite* all lovers of the holy and highly-to-be-esteemed arts of *philosophy*, *astrology*, and *theology*, wherein I will lay open the root and *ground* of them.

    10. Though I have not studied nor learned *their* arts, neither do I know how to go about to measure their circles; I take no great care about that. However, they will have *so much* to learn from hence, that many will not comprehend the ground thereof *all* the days of their lives.

    11. I have no use for their tables, formulæ or schemes, rules and ways, for I have *not learned* from them, but I have another teacher or schoolmaster, which is the whole or total N A T U R E.

    12. From that *whole nature*, together with its

innate, instant birth or geniture, have I studied and learned my *philosophy, astrology*, and *theology*, and not from men, or by men.

13. But seeing men *are gods*, and have the knowledge of God the only Father, from whom they are proceeded or descended, and in whom they live, therefore I *despise not* the canons, rules and formulæ of *their* philosophy, astrology, and theology : For I find, that for the most part they [the philosophers, etc.] stand upon a *right ground*, and I will diligently *endeavour* to go according to their rules and formulæ.

14.* For I must needs say that their scheme of formulation is my master ; from it I have the first elements of my knowledge, and it is not my purpose to controvert or amend their formulæ (for I cannot do it, neither have I learned them), but rather leave them where they are.

15. I will *not*, however, build upon their ground, but as a laborious, careful servant I will *dig* away the earth from the root, that thereby men may see the whole tree, with its root, stock, branches, twigs and fruits ; and they may also see that my writing is *no new* thing, but that *their* philosophy and *my* philosophy are *one* body, one tree, bearing one and the *same* sort of fruit.

16. Neither have I any *command* to bring in complaints against them, to condemn them for

* A new translation of this par. has been substituted for Sparrow's rendering.

anything, except for their wickedness and abominations, as pride, covetousness, envy and wrath, *against* which the spirit of nature complaineth very exceedingly, and *not I*: For what can I do, that am *poor dust and ashes*, also very weak, simple, and altogether unable?

17. Only the spirit sheweth thus much: that *to them* is delivered and entrusted the *weighty* talent, and the key; and they are *drowned* in the pleasures of the flesh, and have *buried* their weighty talent in the earth, and have *lost* the key in their proud drunkenness.

18. The spirit hath a long time waited on them, and *importuned* them that they would once open the door, for the *clear day* is at hand; yet they walk up and down in their drunkenness, seeking for the key, when they have it about them, though they *know it not*; and so they go up and down in their proud and covetous drunkenness, always seeking about like the country man for his horse, who all the while he went seeking for him was riding upon the *back* of *that very* horse he looked for.

19. *Thereupon*, saith the spirit of nature, *seeing they will not awake from sleep and open the door, I will therefore do it myself.*

20. What could I, poor, simple *layman*, teach or write of their high art, if it were not given to me by the *spirit* of nature, in whom I live and ¹ am? I am in the condition or state of a vulgar

¹ subsist or have my being.

or layman, and have no *salary*, wages or pay for this writing : Should I, then, oppose the spirit, that he should not *begin* to open where, and in whom, he pleaseth ? *I am not the door*, but an ordinary wooden bolt upon it : Now if the spirit should pluck me out from thence, and fling me into the fire, could I hinder it ?

21. But if I should be an *unprofitable* bolt, which would stubbornly resist to be pulled out, and would bolt up and *hinder* the spirit in the opening, *would* not the spirit be angry with me, tear me off, and cast me away, and provide a more profitable and a *fitter* bolt ? Then should I lie on the ground and be trampled under foot, whereas formerly I made so fair a show upon the door : What would be the use of the bolt, except as firewood ?

22. Behold ! I tell thee a Mystery : so soon as the door is set *wide* open to its angle,* all useless, fastnailed, sticking bolts or bars will be *cast away*, for the door will *never* be shut any more at all, but standeth open, and then the *four winds* will go in and out at it.

23. But the *sorcerer* sitteth in the way, and will make many *so* blind that they will not see the door ; and then they return home and *say*, There is no door at all, it is a mere fiction. And so they go *thither* no more.

* "to its angle," lit., "upon its hinges," *i.e.* as wide as the hinges will allow.

24. Thus men suffer themselves easily to be turned away, and so live in their *drunkenness*.

25. Now when this is done, then the spirit which hath opened the gates is angry, because none will go OUT and IN at its doors any more, and then it flings the door-posts into the abyss, and then there is *no more time* at all. Those that are *within*, remain within; and those that are *without*, remain without. AMEN.

Now it may be asked, What are the stars?

Answer.

[1] Gen. i. 14-19.

26. *Moses* writeth concerning them thus: [1] *And God said; Let there be lights in the firmament of heaven, to divide or distinguish the day from the night; and let them give signs and seasons, days and years; and let them be lights in the firmament of heaven to shine or give light upon the earth; and it was so done. And God made two great lights; the greater light to rule the day, and the lesser light to rule the night; as also the stars. And God set them in the firmament of the heaven, to shine or give light upon the earth; and to rule day and night; also to divide or distinguish the light from the darkness; and God saw that it was good, so out of the evening and the morning the fourth day came to be.*

27. This description sheweth sufficiently that the dear man *Moses* was not the original author thereof; for the first writer did *not* know either

the true God, or the stars, what they were. It is very *likely* that the creation, before the flood, was *not described in writing*, but was kept as a dark word in men's memories, and so delivered from one generation to another, till *after* the flood, and till people began to lead epicurean lives in all *voluptuousness*.

28. Then the *holy patriarchs*, when they saw *that*, *described* the creation, that it should not be quite forgotten, and that the *swinish*, epicurean world might have a looking-glass in the creation, wherein they *might see* that there is a God, and that this being of the world did not *so* stand from eternity ; whereby they might have a glass to look into, and so *fear the hidden God.*

29.* This was the chief teaching and doctrine of the patriarchs, both before and after the flood, [namely] to direct men [*i.e.* men's attention] to the creation, which [object] the whole book of *Job* also driveth at.

30. After these patriarchs came the *wise Heathen*, who went somewhat *deeper* into the knowledge of nature. And I must needs say, according to the ground of the truth, that they, in their philosophy and knowledge, did come even before the face or countenance of God, and yet could *neither* see nor know him.

* A new translation of this par. has been substituted for Sparrow's rendering.

31. Man was so altogether *dead* in death,* and so bolted up in the outermost birth or geniture in the dead palpability; or else they could have thought, that in this palpability there must *needs be a divine power* hidden in the centre, which had *so* created this palpability, and moreover preserveth, upholdeth and ruleth the same.

32. Indeed they honoured, prayed to, or *worshipped* the sun and stars for gods, but knew not how these were created or came to be, nor out of what they came to be : For they might well have thought that that which proceeded from somewhat, and that *that* which created this, must needs be older and higher or greater than *all the stars.*

33. Besides, they had the stones and the earth for an example, to shew that these *must proceed* from somewhat, as also men, and all the creatures upon the earth. For all *give testimony* that there must needs be in these things a mightier and greater *power* at hand, which had so created all these things, in that manner as they are.

34. But, indeed, why should I write much of the *blindness* of the Heathen ; are not *our* doctors, in their crowned ornaments of hoods and cornered caps, *as blind as they*? Our doctors know indeed that there is a God, who hath created all

* "Man was so altogether dead in death," etc. The first clause of this par. is really a completion of the foregoing par. That is, "they . . . did come . . . and yet could neither see nor know him, so entirely torpid in death was man, and so bolted up in the outermost . . . else they [the heathen]," etc.

this, but they know not *where* that God is, nor *how* he is.

35. When they would write of God, then they seek for him *without,* and *absent* from, this world, above only, in a kind of heaven, *as if* he were some image that may be likened to *somewhat.* Indeed they *grant* that that God ruleth all in this world with a spirit; but his corporeal propriety or *habitation* they will needs have in a certain heaven aloft, *many thousand* miles off.

36. *Come on ye doctors! if you are in the right, then give answer to the spirit: I will ask you a few questions.* 1. What do you think stood in the *place* of this world before the time of the world? Or, 2. *Out of what* do you think the earth and stars came to be? Or, 3. *What* do you think there is in the *deep* above the earth? Or, 4. From *whence* did the deep exist? Or, 5. *How* do you think *man* is the image of God, wherein God dwelleth? Or, 6. What do you suppose *God's wrath* to be? Or, 7. What is *that* in man which displeaseth God so much, that he tormenteth and afflicteth man so, seeing *he* hath *created* him? And 8. That he *imputeth sin* to man, and condemneth him to eternal punishment? 9. Why hath he created *that* wherein or wherewith man committeth sin? Surely *that thing* must be far *worse.* 10. Wherefore, and *out of what,* is that come to be? Or, 11. What is the cause or beginning, or the birth or geniture of

God's fierce wrath, out of or from which hell and
the devil are come to be? Or, 12. *How comes
it* that all the creatures in this world do bite,
scratch, strike, beat and worry one another, and
yet sin is imputed *to man alone*? Or, 13. *Out of
what* are poisonous and venomous beasts and
worms and all manner of vermin come to be?
Or, 14. *Out of what* are the holy angels come to
be? And 15. *What* is the *soul* of man? And
lastly, 16. *What is the great God himself*?

37. Give your direct and *fundamental* answer
to all this, and demonstrate what you say, and
leave off your verbal contentions.

Now if you can demonstrate out of *all* your
books and writings, 1. That *you know* the true
and only God; and, 2. *How he is* in love and
wrath: Also, 3. *What* that God is. And 4. If
you can demonstrate that God is *not in* the stars,
elements, earth, men, beasts, worms, leaves, herbs
and grass, nor in heaven and earth; also that *all*
this is not God himself, and that *my* spirit is
false and *wicked*; then *I* will be the first that
will *burn* my book in the fire, and recall and
recant *all* whatsoever I have written, and will
accurse it, and in all obedience *willingly* submit
myself to be instructed by *you*.

38. I do not say that I cannot err at all. For
there are some things which are not *sufficiently*
explained, but are described, as it were, from a
glimpse of the great God, when the wheel of

nature whirled about *too swiftly*, so that man, with his half-dead and dull capacity or apprehension, cannot sufficiently comprehend it; though what thou *findest not sufficiently* explained in one place thou wilt find it done in another; if not in this book, then in the others.

Now thou wilt say, It doth not become me to ask *such* questions; for the *Deity* is a Mystery, which no man can search into.

Answer.

39. Hearken: If it doth not become *me* to ask, then it doth not become *thee* to *judge me*. Dost thou boast in the knowledge of the light, and art a *leader* of the blind, and yet art *blind* thyself? How wilt thou shew the way to the blind? In your blindness must you *not both* fall?

But you will say, We are not blind; for we well see the way of the light. Why then do you contend or dispute about the way of the light, if *none* can see it rightly?

40. You teach others the way, and you are *always* seeking after it yourselves, and so you *grope in the dark*, and discern it not. Or do you *suppose* that it is sin for any man to ask after the way?

41. *O ye blind men! leave off your contentions, and shed not innocent blood; also do not lay waste countries and cities, to fulfil the devil's will; but put on the helmet of peace, gird yourselves with*

love one to another, and practise meekness : Leave off pride and covetousness, grudge not the different forms of one another, also suffer not the wrath-fire to kindle in you; but live in meekness, chastity, friendliness and purity, and then you are and live ALL *in God.*

42. For thou needest *not* to ask, *Where is God?* [1] Hearken, thou blind man; thou livest in God, and *God is in thee*; and if thou livest holily, then *therein* thou thyself art God. For wheresoever thou lookest, there, is God.

[1] See Ch. 14, par. 127.

43. When thou beholdest the *deep* between the stars and the earth, *canst* thou say, That is *not* God, or, There God is *not*? O, thou miserable corrupted man! be instructed; for in the deep above the earth, where thou seest and knowest *nothing*, and sayest there is *nothing*, yet even *there* is the light-holy God in his Trinity, and he is generating *there*, as well as in the high heaven aloft above this world.

44 Or dost thou think that in or at the time of the creation of this world he *departed* and went away from his seat wherein he did sit from eternity? O no; that *cannot* be, for though he *would* himself do so, *he* cannot do it, for he himself is All: As little as a member of the body can be rent off from itself, so little also can God be *divided*, rent or *separated* from being *everywhere.*

45. But that there are so many formings,

figurings or framings in him, is caused by his eternal birth or geniture, which first is threefold, and out of or from that Trinity or Ternary it generateth itself *infinitely*, immeasurably or inconceiveably.

46. Of these births or genitures I will here write, and shew to the children of the last world *what God is*; *not* out of any boasting or pride, thereby to disgrace or reproach anybody! No; the spirit will instruct thee, meekly and *friendly*, as a father doth his children; for the work is not from [1]*my* fleshly reason, but *the Holy Ghost's dear revelation*, or *breaking through* in the flesh. [1] Or the reason of my flesh.

47. In my *own* faculties or powers I am *as blind a man* as ever was, and am able to do nothing; but in the spirit of God *my* [2]*innate spirit seeth through* ALL, though not always with long stay or continuance; but only when the spirit of *God's love* breaketh through my spirit, then is the animated or *soulish* birth or geniture and the Deity one being, one comprehensibility, and one light. [2] Or the spirit that is generated, or rather regenerated, in me.

48. Am I *alone* only so? No, *but all men are so*, be they Christians, Jews, Turks, or Heathen. In *whomsoever* love and meekness is, in *them* is also the light of God. *If thou sayest*, No, this is not so; *consider*:

49. Do not the Turks, Jews, and Heathen *live* in the same body or corporeity wherein thou livest, and do they not make use of that same

power and *virtue* of body which thou usest; moreover, they have even the same body which thou hast, and the *same God* which is thy God is *their God* also?

But thou wilt say, They know him not; also they honour him not.

50. Yes, dear man, now boast thyself that thou hast hit it well! Indeed *thou*, above others, *knowest* God! Behold, thou blind man, wherever love riseth up in meekness, there the *heart of God* riseth up. For the heart of God is generated in the meek water of the kindled light, be it in man, or anywhere else without man; it is *everywhere* generated in the centre, between the outermost and the innermost birth or geniture.

51. Whatsoever thou dost but look upon, *there*, is God, but in this world the *comprehensibility* standeth in the wrath, which the devil hath kindled; and in the hidden kernel, in the midst or centre of the wrath, the light or heart of God is generated, *incomprehensibly* as to the wrath; and so *each* of them remaineth in its seat.

52. Yet, for all that, I do *no way* approve or excuse the *unbelief* of the Jews, Turks, and Heathen, nor their stiff-necked stubbornness, nor their fierce wrath, furious malice and *hatred* against the Christians. No; these things are *mere* snares of the devil, whereby he *allureth*

men to pride, covetousness, envy and hatred, that *he* may kindle in them the hellish fire: Neither can I say that these four sons of the devil are *not* domineering in *Christendom*, and, *indeed*, in every man.

Now thou sayest, What then is the *difference* between Christians, Jews, Turks, and Heathen?

Answer.

53. *Here the spirit openeth both door and gate*; * *if thou wilt not see, then be blind.*

54. I. The *first* difference, which God hath always held and maintained for all *those* who *know* what God is, and how they should serve him, is that they should be *able* by their knowledge to *press through* the wrath into God's love, and *overcome* the devil: But if they do it not, then they are *no better* than those that know it *not*.

55. But if he that knoweth *not* the way *presseth through* the wrath into the love, then is he *like* the man who pressed through *by* his knowledge.   But those that persevere in the wrath, and *wholly* kindle it in themselves, they are *all alike*, one and other, be they Christians, Jews, Turks, or Heathen.

Or *what* dost thou suppose it is, wherewith man *can* serve God?

* "both door and gate" (*Thür und Thor*), that is, both small and great avenues of perception.   The German *Thür* describes, principally, an ordinary door, while *Thor* means nearly always a large entrance, like city gates, etc.

56. If thou wilt *dissemble* with God, and adorn or magnify thy birth, then I suppose thee to be a very fine angel indeed! He that hath *love* in his heart, and leadeth a *merciful*, meek, and lowly-minded life, and *fighteth* against malice and hatred, and *presseth through* the wrath of God into the light, he liveth with God, and is *one spirit* with God.

57. For God needeth no other service, but that his creature, which is in *his* body, do not slide back from *him, but be holy, as he is.*

58. Therefore also God gave the Law to the Jews, that they should diligently study and endeavour after *meek* holiness and love, that thereby all the world might have them for their *looking-glass* or mirror. But when the Jews grew proud, and boasted in their birth, *instead* of entering into love, they turned the law of love into sharpness of wrath; then God *removed* their candlestick, and *went* to the Heathen.

59. II. *Secondly,* There is this difference between the Christians, Jews, Turks, and Heathen: the *Christians know* the Tree of Life, which is CHRISTUS, CHRIST, who is the Prince of our heaven and of this world, and ruleth in all births or genitures as a *King* in God his Father, and men are *his* members.

60. Now Christians know how they can, *by the power* of this Tree, press out from their death, through his death, to him into his life, and reign

and live with him, wherein they also, with their *pressing through* with their *new birth* out from *this dead body*, can be with him in heaven.

61. And though the dead body is in the *midst* or centre of hell among all the devils, yet, for all that, the *new man* reigneth with God in heaven, and the Tree of Life is to *them* a strong gate, through which they do enter into life : But of this thou wilt find more largely in its proper place.

Now observe:

62. *Moses* writeth, that God said, *Let there be lights in the firmament of heaven, which should therein give a light to the earth, and divide or distinguish day and night; also make years and times or seasons.*

63. This description sheweth that the first writer did *not* know what the stars are, though he was capable of understanding the right or law of God, and hath taken hold on the Deity *at the heart*, and looked upon or had respect to the heart, to consider *what* the heart and kernel of this creation is ; though the spirit kept the astral and outermost dead birth or geniture *hidden from him*, and did only drive him in *faith* to the heart of the Deity.

64. Which is also the principal point most necessary for man : For when he layeth hold on *true faith*, then he presseth through the wrath of God, through death into life, and reigneth with God.

65. *But seeing men now, at the end of this time, do listen and long very much after the root of the tree, through which nature sheweth that the time of the discovery of the tree is at hand, therefore the spirit will shew it to them.*   *And the whole Deity will reveal itself, which is the Day-spring, Dawning,* or Morning-redness, *and the breaking-forth of the great day of God, in which whatsoever is generated from death to the regeneration of life shall be restored and rise again.*

66. Behold, when God said, Let there be light, *then* the light in the *powers* of nature, or the seven spirits of God, rose up, and the firmament of heaven, which standeth in the *Word*, in the heart of the water, between the astral and the outermost birth or geniture, was *closed* or shut up by or with the Word and heart of the water, and the astral birth is the place of the *parting-mark* or limit, which standeth half in heaven and half in the wrath.

67. For from or out of that half part of the *wrath* the dead birth generateth itself continually, and out of the other half part, which reacheth with its innermost degree even into the innermost heart and *light* of God, the life generateth itself now continually through death, and yet the astral birth or geniture is *not two* bodies, but *one* body.

68. But when, in these *two days*, the creation

of heaven and of earth was completed, and the heaven was made in the heart of the water, for a difference or *distinction* between the light of God and the wrath of God, then, on the *third day*, through the terror or crack of the fire-flash, which rose up in the heart of the water, and presseth through death, incomprehensibly as to death, there *sprang up* all manner of ideas, forms and figures, as was done *before* the time of the kindled wrath.

69. But seeing the water, which is *the spirit* of the astral life, stood in the midst or centre of wrath, and also in death, thereupon also every body formed itself as was the birth or geniture to life and mobility.

Of the Earth.

70. But now the earth was the *Salitter*, which was cast up out of the innermost birth and stood in death: But when the fire-flash, through the word, rose up in the water, then it was a terror or *crack*, from which existed the *mobility* in death; and that mobility, in all the seven spirits, is now the *astral* birth or geniture.

The Depth. Understand this aright.

71. Now when, on the *third day*, the fire-flash in the water of death had kindled itself, then the life pressed forth *quite through* the dead body of the water and of the earth.

72. But yet the dead water and earth comprehend *no more* than the flash or terror or crack of the *fire*, through which their mobility existeth : But the light that riseth up very softly, gently or meekly in the fire-flash *neither* the earth nor the dead water *can* comprehend.

73. But it retaineth its *seat* in the kernel, which is the unctuosity or *fatness*, or the water of life, or the heaven; for it is the body of life, which the death *cannot* comprehend, and yet it riseth up in the death.

74. Neither can the wrath take hold of it or apprehend it, but the wrath remaineth in the terror or crack of the fire-flash, and maketh the *mobility* in the dead body of the earth and the water.

75. But the light presseth in very gently after, and formeth the birth, which birth, through the terror or crack of the fire-flash, hath gotten its [the birth's] *compacted* body.

Of the Growths or Vegetables of the Earth.

76. When now the *wrathful* fire-flash awakened, and roused up the spirits of nature, which stand in death in the earth, and made them moveable by its fierce terror or crack, then the spirits began, according to their peculiar *divine* right, to generate themselves, as they *had done* from eternity, and form, figure or frame a body together, according to the innate, instant qualities of *that* place.

77. Now, that kind of *Salitter* which, in the

time of the kindling of the wrath, did become
torpid in death, as it did qualify or operate at
that time, in the innate, [1] instant life of the [1] Or instanding.
seven spirits of God, that also *did* rise again
in the time of the regeneration in the fire-flash,
and is not become any *new* thing, but only
another form of the body, which standeth in the
comprehensibility or *palpability* in death.

78. But now *the Salitter* of the earth and of
the water is *no more* able to change or alter itself
in its dead being, and shew forth itself infinitely,
as it did in the heavenly place or seat; but when
the qualifying or fountain spirits form the body, then
it riseth up in the power and virtue of the *light*.

79. And the *life* of the light breaketh through
the death, and generateth to it another body out
of death, which is not *conformable* to, or of the
condition of, the water and the dead earth; also
it doth not get *their* taste and smell; but the
power of the light presseth through, and tempereth
or mixeth itself with the power of the earth, and
taketh from death its *sting*, and from the wrath
its poisonous, venomous power, and presseth forth
up together in the midst or centre of the body,
in the growth or vegetation, as a *heart* thereof.

80. *And herein sticketh now the kernel of the
Deity in the centre in its heaven, which standeth
hidden in the water of life, if thou canst now
apprehend or lay hold of it.*

Of the Metals in the Earth.

81. The *metals* have the same substance, condition and birth or geniture as the *vegetables* upon the earth. For the metals or mineral ores, at the time of the kindling of the wrath in the innate, instant wheel of the seventh nature-spirit, stood in the fabric, *work* or operation of the love, wherein the meek beneficence or well-doing generateth itself *behind* the fire-flash; wherein the holy heaven standeth, which in this birth or geniture, when the *love* is predominant, presents or sheweth forth itself in such a gracious, amiable and blessed clarity or brightness, and in such beauteous colours, like gold, silver and precious stones.

82. But silver and gold in the dead palpability or tangibility are but as a dark stone, in comparison with the root of the heavenly generating; but I set it down here * only that thou mayest know from *whence* it hath its original.

83. But seeing it hath been the most excellent rising up and generating in the holy heavenly nature, therefore also it is loved by man above all other things in this world. For nature hath indeed *written* in man's heart *that it is* better than other stones and earth; but nature could *not* reveal or manifest to him the ground thereof, from whence

---

* "I set it down here," *i.e.* I make mention of the dark stone here.

it is come or proceeded, *whereby* now thou mayest observe the Day-spring or Morning-redness.

84. There are many several sorts of mineral ores, according as the *Salitter* in nature's heaven was *predominant* at its rising up in the light of love: For every qualifying or *radical* spirit in the heavenly nature containeth the property or kind of *all* the qualifying or fountain spirits, for it is ever infected or affected with the other,* from whence the life and the unsearchable birth or geniture of the Deity existeth: But yet it is predominant as to its own power, and that is its own body, from whence it hath the name,

85. But now every qualifying or fountain spirit hath the property of the whole or total nature, and its fabric or *work*, at the time of the kindling of the wrath, was together also incorporated in death; and out of every spirit's fabric or work, earth, stones, mineral ores, and *water* came to be.

86. There also in the earth there are *found*, according to the quality of each spirit, mineral ores, stones, water and earth; and therefore it is that the earth is of so many *various* qualities, all as each qualifying or fountain spirit, with its innate, instant birth or geniture, was at the *time* of the kindling.

---

* "for it is ever infected or affected with the other" (*inficiret*). See Ch. 8, par. 65. A freer rendering, but perfectly accurate as to the meaning, would be, "and each is ever infected with the others."

87. Nature hath likewise manifested or *revealed* so much to man, that he knoweth how he may melt away the strange or heterogene matter from every qualifying or fountain spirit's strange infected innate birth or geniture; whereby that qualifying or fountain spirit might remain chief in its own primacy. ·

88. You have an *example* of this in gold, and in silver, which you cannot make to be pure or fine gold or silver, unless [1] *it be melted seven times in the fire.* But when that is done, then it remaineth in the middle or *central seat* in the heart of nature, which is the water, sitting * in its own quality and *colour*.

89. I. First, the *astringent* quality, which holdeth the *Salitter* captive in the hard death, must be melted away, which is the gross stony *dross*.

90. II. Then secondly, the astringent death of the water is to be separated, from which proceeds a poisonous venomous water of separation, or *aquafortis*, which standeth in the rising up of the *fire-flash* in death, and which is the evil, malignant, even the very worst, source of all in death, even the astringent and bitter *death* itself; for this is the place where the life, which existeth in the sweet water, [2] died in death: And that separateth itself now in the *second* melting.

[2] Or died the death.

91. III. Thirdly, the *bitter* quality, which existeth in the kindling of the water in the fire-flash,

* "remaineth ... sitting." See Ch. 25, par. 82.

is melted away, for that is a rager, raver, tyrant and destroyer.   Also no silver nor gold *can* subsist, if that be not *killed* or mortified ; for it maketh all dry and brittle, and presenteth or sheweth forth itself in several colours ; for it rideth through all spirits, *assuming* the colours of all spirits.

92. IV. Fourthly, the *fire*-spirit, which standeth in the horrible anguish and pangs of life, must be also melted away, for it is a continued father of the *wrath*, and out of or from that is generated the *hellish* woe.

93. Now when the wrath of these four spirits is *killed*, then the mineral orey *Salitter* standeth in the water, like a tough matter, and looketh like that spirit which is predominant in the mineral ore ; and the light which standeth in the *fire* [1] coloureth it according to its own quality, be it silver or gold.

[1] Or tinctureth.

94. And now this matter in the fourth melting looks like silver or gold, but it is not yet [2] *fixed*, nor is it tough or malleable and pure enough ; its body indeed is *subsistent*, but not the spirit.

[2] subsistent.

95. V. Now when it is melted a fifth time, then the *love*-spirit riseth up in the water through the *light*, and maketh the dead body living again, so that the matter, which remained in the first four meltings, getteth power or *strength* again, which was the proper own of that qualifying or fountain spirit which was predominant in this mineral ore.

96. VI. Now when it is melted the sixth time,

then it groweth somewhat *harder*, and then the *life*, which is risen up in the love, moveth and stirreth itself. From this stirring existeth the *tone* in the hardness, and the mineral ore gets a clear *sound*, for the hard and dead beating * or noise of the bitter fiery matter is gone away.

97. In this sixth melting I hold to be the *greatest* danger for [1] chymists about the [2]*preparing* of their silver and gold. For there belongeth to it, and is required for it, a very subtile fire, and it may soon be burnt or made dead or deaf; and it becometh very dim or blind † if the fire be *too* cold.

[1] den Alchymisten.
[2] Or making.

98. For it must be a middle or mild fire; to keep the spirit in the heart from rising it must be gently simmering, then it getteth a very sweet and meek ringing sound, and continually rejoiceth, *as if* it would now be kindled again in the light of God.

99. But if the fire be *too hot* in the fifth and sixth meltings, then the new life, which hath generated itself in the love in the rising up of the light's power out of the water, is kindled again in the *fierceness* in the wrath-fire, and the mineral ore becomes a burnt scum and *dross*, and the alchymist hath *dirt* instead of gold.

* "hard and dead beating" (*Pochen*). See Ch. 10, par. 119.
† "very dim or blind." The editions of 1656 and 1730 have, "*viel zu blind*," "much too blind"; while the editions of 1682 and 1715 have, "*viel zu lind*," "much too soft." St M. prints, "*trop molle*," "too soft." Schiebler prints, "*viel zu gelind*."

100. VII. Now when it is melted the seventh time, then there belongeth to, and is required for, the process, a yet *more* subtile fire, for therein the life riseth up and *rejoiceth* in the love, and will shew forth itself in infinity, as it hath done in heaven *before* the time of the wrath.

101. And in this motion it groweth *unctuous* or fat, and luscious or luxuriant; it increaseth and spreadeth itself, and the highest depth generateth itself very joyfully out of or from the *heart* of the spirit, just as if it would begin an *angelical triumph*, and present or shew forth itself infinitely in *divine* power and form, according to the right of the Deity: and thereby the body getteth its greatest strength and power, and the body coloureth or tinctureth itself with the *highest degree*, and getteth its true beauty, excellency and virtue.

102. And now, when it is *almost* made, then it hath its true virtue and colour, and there is nothing wanting except in this, that the spirit cannot elevate itself with its *body* into the light, but must remain to be a dead stone; and though indeed it be of *greater* virtue than other stones, yet the *body* remaineth in death.

103. *And this now is the earthly god of blind men*, which they love and honour, and *leave* the living God, who standeth hidden in the centre, sitting in his seat. For the dead flesh comprehendeth only a *dead god*, and longeth also only

after such a dead god. *But it is such a god as hath thrown many men headlong into hell.*

104. Do not take me for an alchymist, for I write only in the *knowledge* of the spirit, and not from experience. Though indeed I could here shew *something* else, *viz.* in *how many* days, and in *what hours*, these things must be prepared; for gold cannot be made in one day, but a whole month is requisite for it.

105. But it is not my purpose to make *any* trial at all of it, because I know not how to *manage* the fire; neither do I know the colours or tinctures of the qualifying or fountain spirits in their outermost birth or geniture, which are *two* great defects; but I know them according to (another or) the regenerate man, which standeth *not* in the palpability.

106. At the description of the *SUN* you will find more and deeper things concerning it: My intention is only to describe the whole or *total Deity*, as far as I am capable in my weakness to apprehend [it], *viz.* how *that* is, in love and in wrath, and how it doth generate itself now at present *in this* world. *You will find more concerning jewels and precious stones at the description of the seven planets.*

THE TWENTY-THIRD CHAPTER

Of the Deep above the Earth.

1. WHEN man beholdeth the *deep* above the earth he seeth nothing but *stars*, and *clouds* of water, and then he thinketh, Sure there must be another place, where the Deity presenteth or sheweth forth itself, together with the *heavenly* and *angelical* government: man will needs have the deep, together with its regimen or dominion, *severed* from the Deity; for there he seeth nothing but *stars*; and the regimen or dominion *between*, is fire, air, and water.

2. Then presently he thinketh, God hath made this thus, out of or from his *predestinate purpose, out of nothing*: How then *can* God be in this being? Or, how could that be God himself? He continually imagineth that this is only a *house*, wherein God dwelleth and ruleth by his *spirit*. God cannot be such a God, whose being consisteth in the power of *this* government or dominion.

3. Many will dare to say, What *manner of God* would that be, whose body, being, and

power or virtue, standeth or consisteth in fire, air, water and earth?

4. Behold! thou unapprehensive man, I will shew thee the true *ground* of the Deity. *If* this whole or universal being be not God, *then* thou art not God's image. If he be any other or strange God, then thou hast *no part* in him: For thou art created out of this God, and livest *in* this very God, and this very God continually giveth thee power or virtue, and blessing, also meat and drink, *out of himself*; also all thy knowledge standeth in this God, and when thou *a..st*, then thou art *buried* in this God.

5. Now, if there be any *other* or strange God, without and besides this God, who then shall make *thee* living again out of this God, in whom thou shalt be when thou art departed and turned to *dust*? How shall that strange God, out of whom thou art *not* created, and in whom thou didst *never* live, bring thy body and spirit *together again*?

6. Now if thou art [1] of any *other* matter than God himself, *how* then canst thou be his child? Or *how* can the *man* and *king* Christ be *God's* bodily or corporeal Son, whom God hath generated or begotten out of his *heart*?

7. Now, if his Deity be *another* being, substance or thing than his body, then there must be a twofold Deity in him; his body *would* be of or from the god of this world, and his heart would be of or from the *unknown God*.

[1] Or of any other materials.

8. *O, thou child of man! open the eyes of thy spirit, for I will here shew thee the right and real proper gate of the Deity, as indeed that very one only God will have it.*

9. Behold! *that* is the true one only God, out of whom thou art created, and *in whom thou livest*; and when thou beholdest the deep, and the stars, and the earth, then thou beholdest thy God, and in that same thou livest, and also art, or *hast thy being* therein; and that same God also governeth or ruleth thee, and also out of or from that same God thou hast *thy senses*, and thou art a creature out of or from him and in him; else thou hadst been *nothing*, or wouldst never have been.

10. Now perhaps thou wilt say that I write in a heathenish manner. Hearken and behold! observe the distinct understanding, *how* all this is so; for I write *not* heathenishly or barbarously, but philosophically; neither am I a Heathen, but I have the *deep* and *true* knowledge of the one only great God, who is ALL.

11. When thou beholdest the deep, the stars, the elements, and the earth, then thou *comprehendest not* with thy eyes the bright and clear Deity, though indeed it is *there* and *in them*; but thou seest and comprehendest with thy eyes, first death, and then the wrath of God and the hellish fire.

12. But if thou raisest thy *thoughts*, and con-

siderest *where* God is, then thou apprehendest
the astral birth or geniture, where love and
wrath move one against the other. But when
thou drawest up the *faith* in God, who ruleth
in *holiness* in this government or dominion, then
thou breakest through heaven, and apprehendest
or layest hold on God at his *holy* heart.

13. Now when this is done, then thou art as
the whole or *total* God, who *himself* is heaven,
earth, stars, and the elements, and hast also such a
regimen or dominion in thee, and art also such a
person, as the *whole God* in the place of this world.

Now thou sayest, How shall I *understand* this?
For the kingdom of God and the kingdom of
hell and of the devil are *distinct* one from the
other, and *cannot* be one body. Also the earth
and stones are *not* God; nor the heaven, stars
and elements; *much less* can a man be God;
for if so, he could not be *rejected* by God. Here
I will, by degrees, tell thee the ground of all,
one thing after another; therefore keep the
question in mind.

Of the astral Birth or Geniture, and of the Birth or Geniture of God.

14. *Before* the times of the created heavens,
the stars, and the elements, and before the
creation of *angels*, there was *no* such wrath of
God, no death, no devil, no earth nor stones,
neither were there any stars. But the Deity

generated itself very *meekly* and lovingly, and
formed, framed and figured itself in ideas,
shapes, and images, which were incorporated
according to the qualifying or fountain spirits
in their generating, *wrestling*, and rising up,
and *passed away again* also through their
wrestling, and figured or framed themselves
into another form or condition, all according to
the primacy or *predominancy* of each qualifying or fountain spirit, as you may read before.

15. *But observe here rightly* the earnest and
severe birth or geniture, out of which the wrath
of God, hell, and death, are come to be, which
indeed have *been* from eternity in God, but [1] not [1] not kindled
liable to be kindled or to become predominant.   or domineering.

16. For the whole or total *God* standeth in
seven species or kinds, or in a sevenfold form or
generating ; and if these births or genitures were
not, then there would be neither God, nor life,
nor angel, nor any creature.

17. And *these* births or genitures have *no
beginning*, but have so generated themselves
from eternity ; and as to this depth, *God himself
knoweth not what he is : For he knoweth no
beginning of himself, also he knoweth not anything that is like himself, as also he knoweth no
end of himself.*

18. *These seven* generatings *in all* are *none
of them* the first, the second, or the third, or
last, but they are all seven, every one of them,

both the first, second, third, fourth, and last.
Yet I must set them down one after another,
according to a *creaturely* way and manner, otherwise thou couldst not understand it: For the
Deity is as a wheel with seven wheels made one in
another, wherein a man seeth *neither* beginning
nor end.

Now observe:

19. I. *First*, there is the *astringent* quality,
which is *always* generated from the other six
spirits, which in *itself* is hard, cold, sharp like
salt, and yet *far* sharper.   For a creature cannot
sufficiently apprehend its sharpness, seeing the
sharpness is not *singly* and alone *in* a creature;
but according to the manner and kind of the
kindled hellish quality I know *how* it is: This
astringent sharp quality attracteth or draweth
together, and in the divine love holdeth or
retaineth the forms and images, and so *drieth*
them that they subsist or are *fixed*.

20. II. The *second* generating is the *sweet
water*, which is *also* generated out of all the six
spirits; for it is the meekness, which is generated
out of the other six, and presseth itself forth
in the astringent birth or geniture, and *always*
kindleth again the astringent, and then quencheth
and *mitigateth* it, that it be not too much astringent, as it might be in its own sharpness, if it
were *not* for the water.

21. III. The *third* generating is the *bitterness,*

which existeth out of the fire *in* the water; for it rubbeth and vexeth itself in the astringent and sharp coldness, and maketh the coldness moveable, from whence *mobility* existeth.

22. IV. The *fourth* generating is the fire, which existeth from the mobility or rubbing in the astringent spirit, and that is now a sharp *burning*, and the bitter is a stinging and raging. But when the fire-spirit rubbeth itself thus ragingly in the astringent coldness, then there is an anxious *horrible* quaking, a trembling, and a sharp, opposite, contentious generating.

Observe here the Depth.

23. *I speak here as to the kind and manner of the devil, as if the light of God had not yet kindled itself in these four kinds; and as if the Deity had a beginning; I can no other or nearer way offer it to your judgment, that you may understand it.*

24. In this fourth rubbing is a very hard, and most horrible, sharp and *fierce* coldness, like a refined, melted, and very cold salt-water, which yet is *not* water, but such a hard kind of power and virtue that is like stones.

25. There is also *therein* a raging, raving, stinging and burning, and that water is continually as a dying man, when body and soul are parting asunder, a most *horrible anxiety*, a woeful, painful birth or geniture.

26. *O Man! here consider thyself, here thou seest from whence the devil and his fierce, wrathful malice hath its original, as also God's wrath, and the hellish fire, also death and hell, and eternal damnation.* Ye philosophers, observe that!

27. Now when *these four* generatings rub themselves one upon another, then *heat* gets the primacy and predominancy, and kindleth itself in the sweet water, and then instantly the light riseth up.

Understand this rightly.

28. When the light kindleth itself, then the fire-terror or *crack* cometh forth *first*. As when you strike upon a stone the fire-crack is first, and then the light first conceiveth itself from the fire-crack.

29. Now the *fire-crack* in the water goeth through the astringent quality, and maketh it moveable, but the light generateth itself in the *water*, and becomes *a shining* light, and is an impalpable, meek, and most richly loving being, of which neither I nor any other creature can sufficiently write or speak, but I only *stammer*, like a child which would fain learn to speak.

30. That same light is generated in the midst or *centre*, out of these four *species*, out of the unctuosity or fatness of the sweet water, and replenisheth the whole body of this generating. But it is such a meek, pleasing, *well-doing*, good-

smelling and well-tasting relish, that I know *no similitude* to liken it to, but where life is generated in the midst or centre of death; or as if a man did sit in a huge, scorching, hot, flaming fire, and were suddenly snatched out from thence, and set in such a very exceeding easy place of refreshment, where instantly all the smarting, scalding pains, which he felt afore by the *burning* of the fire, should suddenly pass away, and he be put into such a pleasing temper and *soundness*. Just so the generating of the four kinds or species are set or put into such a *soft* and meek welldoing and refreshment, *as soon* as the light riseth up in them. *Thou must understand me here aright.*

31. I write, and mean it, in a creaturely kind and manner, as if a man had been the devil's prisoner, and were *suddenly* removed out of the hellish *fire* into the *light* of God.

32. For the light hath had no beginning in the generating of God, but hath shone or given light from eternity in the generating, and God *himself* knoweth no beginning therein.

33. *Only, the spirit here setteth open for thee the gates of hell*, that thou mayest see what is the condition of the devils and of hell, and what is the condition of man, when the divine light *extinguisheth* in him, so that he sitteth in the wrath of God and *liveth* in such a generating, in such an anguish, in such smarting pains, in such woe and misery.

34. Neither can I declare it unto thee in any other manner; for I must write *as if the generating or geniture of God had or took a beginning when things came to be thus; but I write here very, really true and precious dear words, which the spirit alone understandeth.*

Now observe the Gates of God.

35. The *light*, which generateth itself from the fire and becometh shining in the water, and replenisheth or filleth the whole geniture and enlighteneth it, and mitigates it, *that light is the true Heart of God, or Son of God*; for he is *continually* generated out of the Father, and is a *Person* other than the qualities and geniture of the Father.

36. For the generating or geniture of the Father *cannot* catch or comprehend the light, and use it to its generating, but the light *standeth* by itself, and is not comprehended by any geniture, and it replenisheth and enlighteneth the whole geniture, *viz.* [1] *the only begotten Son of the Father. This light I call, in the human birth or geniture, the animated or soulish birth—*

[" *Understand, the image which budded* " *forth out of the essences of the soul, accord-* " *ing to the similitude of God.*"]

—or the soul's birth or geniture which qualifieth, mixeth or uniteth with this animated or soulish birth or geniture of God; and *herein* is man's

[1] John i. 14.

soul *one heart* with God: but *that is* when it standeth in this *light*.

37. V. The *fifth* generating in God is when this *light* thus very gently, mildly and amiably presseth through the first four births or generatings, and then it bringeth along with it the heart, and most pleasant *lovely* power and virtue of the sweet water, and so when the sharp births or genitures taste of it, then are they very meek, and *richly full* of love, and it is as if the life did continually rise up in and from death.

38. *There* each spirit tasteth of the others, and getteth mere *new* strength and power, for the astringent quality groweth now very pliable and yielding, because it is mitigated by the power of the light that springeth out of the sweet water, and in the fire the meek love riseth up, for it *warmeth* the coldness, and the sweet water maketh the *sharp* taste very pleasant, lovely, and mild.

39. And so in the sharp and fiery births or generatings there is nothing but a mere *longing* of *love*, a tasting, friendly affecting, gracious, amiable and blessed generating; there is nothing but mere love, and all wrath and bitterness in the centre are *bolted up* as in a strong hold. This generating is a very meek, beneficial welldoing, and the bitter spirit is now the *living* mobility.

40. VI. Now the *sixth* generating in God is *when* the *spirits*, in their birth or geniture, thus *taste* one of another, for then they become very full

of *joy:* For the fire-flash, or the sharpness out of or from the birth or geniture, riseth up aloft, and moveth as the air in this world doth.

41. For when one power or virtue *toucheth* another, then they taste one another, and become very full of joy; for the light becometh generated out of all the powers, and presseth again through all the powers; whereby and wherein the *rising joy* generateth itself, from whence the *tone* or [1] *tune* existeth.

42. For from the touching and moving the living spirit generateth itself, and that same spirit presseth through all births or generatings, very *inconceiveably* and incomprehensibly to the birth or geniture, and is a very richly joyful, pleasant, lovely sharpness, like melodious, sweet music.

43. And now when the birth generateth, then it *conceiveth* or apprehendeth the light, and speaketh or inspireth the light again into the birth or geniture through the moving spirit. *This moving spirit is the third Person in the birth or geniture of God, and is called God the Holy Ghost.*

44. VII. The *seventh* generating is, and keepeth its birth or geniture and *forming* in, the Holy Ghost; and so when that goeth through the sharp births or genitures, then it goeth forth with the tone, and so formeth and *imageth* all manner of figures, all according to the wrestling of the sharp births or genitures one with another.

45. For they wrestle in the birth or geniture

continually one with another, like a loving play or scene, and according as the birth or geniture is with the *colours* and taste in the rising up, so also are the *figures* imaged.

46. *And this birth or geniture now is called* GOD *the Father, Son, and Holy Ghost*: Not one of them is the first, and not one of them is the last: though *I make* a distinction, and set the one after the other, yet not one of them is the first or the last, but they have all been from eternity thus seated in the same *equality* of being.

47. I must write *thus* by way of *distinction*, that the Reader may understand it; for I cannot write mere heavenly words, but must write human words. Indeed all is rightly, truly and faithfully described: *But the being of God consisteth only in power, and only the spirit comprehendeth it, and not the dead or mortal flesh.*

48. *Thus thou mayest understand what manner of being the* Deity *is, and how the three Persons in the Deity are. Thou must not liken the Deity to any image; for the Deity is the birth or geniture of all things.* If, in the first four species or kinds, there were not the sharp birth or generating, then there would be no mobility, neither could the light kindle itself and generate the life.

49. But now this sharp birth or geniture is the *original* of mobility and of life, as also of the light, from whence existeth the *living and*

rational spirit, which distinguisheth, formeth and imageth all in this generating.

50. For the astringent cold birth or geniture is the *beginning* of all things, which quality is astringent, severe, contracting and retentive, and formeth and contracteth together the birth, and maketh the birth thick or solid, so that out of it *nature* cometh to *be*; hence nature and comprehensibility hath its original in the whole body of God.

51. Now *this nature* is as a *dead*, unintellectual being, and standeth or consisteth not in the power of the birth or geniture, but is a body, wherein the power generateth.

52. But it is the body of God, and hath all power as the whole geniture hath, and the generating spirits take their strength and power out of or from the *body* of nature, and continually generate again, and the astringent spirit continually compacteth or draweth together again, and drieth up; and thus the body subsisteth, and the generating spirits also.

53. Now the other birth or geniture is *the water*, which taketh its original in the body of *nature*.

Observe:

54. Now when the light shineth *through* the astringent, contracted body of nature, and mitigateth it, then the mild, beneficent *well-doing* generateth itself in the body, and then the hard

power groweth very mild, and melteth, as ice in the heat of the *sun*, and is *extenuated* or rarefied, as water is in the air; and yet the stock of nature, as to the heavenly comprehensibility, *remaineth* the same.

55. For the astringent and fire-spirit ·holdeth it fast, and the meek water, which melteth from the body of nature in the kindling of the light, goeth through the *severe*, earnest, cold and fiery birth or geniture, and is very sweet, pleasant and lovely.

56. Whereby now the earnest and *austere* birth or geniture is refreshed; and when it tasteth thereof it groweth capable to be raised up, and *rejoiceth*, and also is a joyful rising up, wherein the life of meekness generateth itself.

57. For *this is the water of life*, wherein the love, in God as also in angels and in men, generateth itself: For it is all of one sort of power, virtue and birth or geniture.

58. And now when the births or genitures of the powers taste the water of life, then they quake or tremble for very love-joy, and that trembling or moving, which riseth up in the midst or centre of the birth or geniture, is *bitter*. For it riseth up swiftly out of the birth, when the water of life cometh into the birth or geniture, like a joyful leaping or springing up of the birth.

59. But seeing it riseth up so swiftly, that the birth elevateth itself so suddenly, *before* it be

fully affected with the water of life, thereupon that terror or crack keepeth its bitterness which it hath out of or from the *austere* birth; for the beginning or inceptive birth or geniture is very austere, cold, fiery and astringent.

60. Therefore also is the terror or crack now so *swelling* and trembling; for it moveth the whole birth, and rubbeth itself therein, till it kindleth the fire in the hard fierceness, from whence the light taketh its original. Then the trembling crack becometh enlightened with the *meekness* of the light, and goeth in the birth or geniture up and down, and crossways, both upwards and downwards, like a wheel made with *seven* wheels one in another.

61. In this pressing through and turning about existeth the *tone*, according to the quality of each spirit; and always one power affecteth another, for the powers are as *loving brethren* in one body; and the meekness riseth up; and the spirit generateth and sheweth itself infinitely.

62. For that power which in the *turning about* sheweth itself the strongest in the generating, according to that power, manner and colour, the *Holy Ghost* also imageth, shapeth or frameth the figures in the body of *nature*.

63. *Thus thou seest* that *none* of the powers is the first, also none the second, third, fourth or last; but the last generateth the first, as well as the first the last, and the middlemost taketh

its original from the last, as also from the first, as well as from the second, third, or any of the rest.

64. Thou seest also that nature cannot be *distinguished* from the powers of God, but is all one body.

65. The Deity, that is, the holy power of the heart of God, is generated *in nature*, and so also the Holy Ghost existeth or goeth forth out of the heart of the light *continually*, through all the powers of the Father, and figureth all, and imageth or frameth all.

66. This birth or geniture is now in *three* distinct *parts*, every part being several and *total*,* and yet *not one* of them is divided asunder from the others.

The Gate of the Holy Trinity.

67. *The whole birth or geniture*, which is the heaven of all heavens, as also this world, which is *in* the body of the whole, as also the *place* of the earth and of all creatures, and whatever thou canst think on, *all that together is God the Father*, who hath neither beginning nor end; and wheresoever and upon whatsoever thou thinkest, even in the smallest circle that can be imagined, is the *whole* birth or geniture of God, perfectly, incessantly and irresistibly.

68. But if in a creature, or in any place, the

---

* "several and total" (*ein sonderliches und ganzes*), "a particular [one] and a whole [in itself]."

light be *extinguished*, then in that place is the austere birth or geniture, which lieth hid in the light in the innermost kernel: *And this now is one part.*

69. *The second part, or the second Person, is the light*, which is continually generated from or out of all powers, and enlighteneth again all the powers of the *Father*, and hath the fountain of all powers; but it is therein distinguished from the Father as a *singular Person*, in that it cannot comprehend the birth or geniture of the Father, and yet is the Father's *Son*, which is always generated from or out of the Father: An instance whereof you have in all the kindled *fires* in this world; do but consider of it.

70. Therefore the *Father* loveth this his only begotten or innate *Son* so heartily, *because* he is the light and the meek beneficent well-doing in *his body*, through whose power the Father's *joy* and delight riseth up.

71. *Now these are two Persons*, and neither of them can apprehend, retain, or comprehend the other, and the one is *as great* as the other; and if either of them were not, the other could not be.

72. *Observe here, ye Jews, Turks, and Heathen, for it concerneth you; to you here are opened the gates of God*, harden not yourselves, for now is the acceptable time.

73. You are *not* forgotten of God at all, but if

you convert, then the light and heart of God will rise up *in you*, as the bright sun at noonday.

74. *This I write in the power and perfect knowledge of the great God, and I understand his will herein very well.* For I live and [1] *am* in him, and spring up with this work and labour out of his root and stock; and it must be so: Only, take thou heed, if thou blindest thyself, then there is *no* remedy more; neither canst thou say thou knewest *not* of it, therefore arise, for the day breaketh!

[1] Or have my being in him.

75. *The third diversity, or the third Person in the being of God, is the moving spirit*, which existeth from the rising up in the terror or crack, where *life* is generated, which now moveth in all powers, and is the spirit of life; and the *powers* can no more comprehend him, or apprehend him; but he kindleth the powers, and by his moving maketh figures and *images*, and formeth them according to that kind and manner as the wrestling birth standeth in *every* place.

76. And if thou art not *wilfully* blind, thou mayest know that the *air* is that very spirit; but in the place of this world nature is *kindled* therein very swelling in the wrath-fire, which lord *Lucifer* effected, and the Holy Ghost, who is the spirit of meekness, lieth *hidden* therein in his heaven.

77. Thou needest not to ask where that heaven is. It is in *thy* heart, do but open thy heart, the *key* is here shewn to thee.

78. *Thus there is one God, and three distinct Persons one in another*, and not one of them can comprehend, or withhold, or fathom the original of the others, but the *Father* generateth the Son, and the *Son* is the Father's heart, and his love and his light, and is an original of joy, and the *beginning* of all life.

79. And the *Holy Ghost* is the spirit of life, and a former, framer and creator of all things, and a *performer* of the will in God; that hath formed and created out of or from the body, and in the body of the Father, all angels and creatures, and holdeth and formeth all *still*, daily, and is the sharpness and the living spirit of God: *As the Father speaketh or expresseth the Word, out of or from his powers, so the spirit formeth or frameth them.*

Of the great Simplicity of God.

80. Come on, brave Sir, upon thy brown nag! thou who *ridest* from heaven into hell, and from hell into death, and therein the sting of the devil lieth. *View thyself* here, thou worldly-wise man, that art full of *base* wit, cunning, and subtle policy.

81. Take notice, ye worldly-wise *lawyers*, if you will not come before this looking-glass, even before the *bright* and clear face of God, and view yourselves *therein*, then the spirit presenteth to you the birth or geniture in the innermost astrin-

gent circle; where wit, cunning and prudence are generated, where the *sharpness* of the anxious birth or geniture of God is, for *there* your prudence, cunning and deep-reaching wit are *generated*.

82. Now if you will be gods, and not devils, then make use of the *holy* and *meek law* of God; if not, then you shall for ever eternally generate in the *austere* and severe birth or geniture of God. *Thus saith the spirit, as the word of God, and not of my dead or mortal flesh.*

83. Thou must know that I do not suck it out from the dead or mortal *reason*, but my spirit qualifieth, mixeth or uniteth with God, and proveth or searcheth the *Deity*, how it is in all its births or genitures in its taste and smell: And I find that the Deity is a very simple, *pure*, meek, loving and quiet being; and that the birth of the *Ternary* of God generateth itself very meekly, friendly, lovingly and unanimously, and the *sharpness* of the innermost birth *can never* elevate or swell itself into the meekness of the *Ternary*, but remaineth *hidden* in the deep.

84. And the sharpness in the hidden secrecy is called God's WRATH; and the being of meekness in the *Ternary* or *Trinity* is called GOD. Here nothing goeth out of, or forth from, the sharpness which *perisheth*, or which doth kindle the wrath, but the spirits play very *gently* one with another, like little children when they rejoice one with another, where every one

hath his work, and so they *play* one with another, and lovingly caress one another.

85. In such a work also the holy angels *exercise* themselves; and in the *Ternary* of God there is a very meek, pleasant, and sweet being, where the spirit always elevateth itself in the [1]tone; and one power moveth the other, as if there were a rising up of lovely song, and play upon stringed instruments.

86. And as is the rising up of the spirits in every place, so the tone also formeth itself, but very *meekly*, and incomprehensibly to the *bodies* of the angels, but very comprehensibly to the animated or soulish birth or geniture of angels: and as the Deity presenteth itself in each place, so the angels also present themselves: For the angels were created out of *this being*, and have among them their princes of the qualifying or fountain spirits of God, as these princes are in the birth or geniture of God.

87. Therefore as the being of God presents or sheweth forth itself in the birth or geniture, so do the angels also; and whatsoever be the power which at any time is predominant in the birth of God, and rejoiceth out of the heart of God in the Holy Ghost, the prince of that power in the angels beginneth his hymn of praise before all the others, and jubilateth with his host; now it is one, then the other; for the birth or geniture of God is like a wheel.

88. But when the *heart* of God sheweth forth itself with its clarity or brightness, then there riseth up the whole host or army of *all* the *three* kingdoms of the angels; and in this rising up of the heart of God the *Man* JESUS CHRIST *is King and Chief.* He leadeth the royal *chorus* or choir, with all the holy souls of men, till the Last Judgment Day. And then the holy men are *perfect* angels, and the wicked, *perfect* devils, and that in its eternity.

89. *Here view thyself, thou witty, subtle world, and consider from whence thy prudence, subtlety and wit proceed.*

Now thou wilt say to me:

90. *Dost not thou seek after deeper subtlety than we? Thou wilt [wishest to] climb into the most hidden secrets of God, which is not fit for any man to go about. We seek only after human prudence and subtlety, but thou wouldst be equal with God, and know all; how God is in every thing, both in heaven and in hell, in devils, angels and men. Therefore, sure it is not unlawful to seek for a cunning, sharp wit, and after crafty designs, which bring honour, power or authority, and riches.*

A Reply.

91. If thou climbest up *this ladder* on which I climb up into the deep of God, as I have done, then thou hast climbed well: I am not come to

this meaning, or to this work and *knowledge*, through my *own* reason, or through my *own* will and purpose; neither have I sought this knowledge, nor so much as knew anything concerning it. I sought only for the *Heart* of God, *therein* to hide myself from the tempestuous storms of the *devil*.

92. But when I gat in thither, then this great, weighty and hard labour was laid upon me, which is, to manifest and *reveal* to the world, and to make known, *the great day of the* LORD; and, seeing men seek and long so eagerly after the *root* of the tree, to reveal to them what the whole tree is, thereby to intimate that it [the present time] is *the Dawning, or Morning-Redness of the Day*, which God hath long ago *decreed* in his council. AMEN.

93. Thus thou seest *what God is*, and *how his love and wrath* have been from *eternity*, also how his birth or geniture is: And now thou canst *not* say that thou art *not* in God, or dost *not* live in God, or that God is any *strange* thing which thou canst not come *at*, but must confess, that where thou art, *there* is the gate of God.

94. Now if thou art *holy*, then, as to thy *soul*, thou art with God in heaven; but if thou art *wicked*, then, as to thy *soul*, thou art in hell-fire.

Now observe further:

95. When God created the angels, all of them were created wholly out of this birth or geniture of God; their body was *compacted* or incorporated out of nature, therein their *spirit* and *light* generated themselves, as the Deity generated itself. And, as the qualifying or fountain spirits of God always took their power and strength out of or from the *body* of nature, so the angels also took their power and strength always out of or from the nature of God.

96. And as the Holy Ghost in nature formeth and imageth or frameth *all*, so the spirit of the angels also qualified or united with the Holy Ghost, and did *help* to form, frame and image *all*, that all might be one heart and will, and a mere delight and joy: For the angels are the children of the great God, whom he hath generated in his body of *nature* for the multiplying of the divine joy.

97. But here thou must know that the *bodies* of angels cannot apprehend the birth or geniture of God, neither doth their body *understand* it, their *spirit* alone understandeth it, but the body holdeth still, as the *nature* in God doth, and lets the spirit co-work and labour with God, and play lovingly.

98. For the angels play before and in God, as little children play before their *parents*, whereby the divine joy is increased.

99. But when the mighty, potent prince and king *Lucifer* was created, he would *not* do so, but elevated and swelled himself, and would alone be God, and kindled the wrath-fire in himself, and so did all *his* angels also.

100. Now when that was done he roared with his kindled fire-spirit abroad into the *nature* of God, and then the whole body in the nature of God, as far as Lucifer's kingdom and dominion *reached,* was kindled. But seeing his light was *instantly* extinguished, he could no more qualify or unite with his spirit in the *two* births or genitures, *viz.* of the Son of God, and of the Holy Spirit of God, but remained fixed in the *sharp* birth or geniture of God.

101. For the light of God, and the spirit of God, *cannot* comprehend the sharp birth or geniture, and *therefore* they are *two distinct Persons*; and so lord *Lucifer* could no more touch, see, feel or taste the Heart of God and the Holy Spirit of God, with his *austere*, cold and hard fire-birth, but was *spewed* out with his fire-spirit into the outermost nature, wherein he *had kindled* the wrath-fire.

102. This same nature is, indeed, the body of God, wherein the Deity generateth itself; but the devils cannot apprehend the *meek birth* of God which riseth up in the light. For their body is *dead* to the light, and liveth in the outermost and austere birth or geniture of God, wherein the light *never* kindleth itself again any more.

103. For their unctuosness or fatness in the sweet water is *burnt* up, and that water is turned into a sour *stink*, wherein the light of God can no more kindle itself, and the light of God can no more enter into it.

104. For the qualifying or fountain spirits of the *devils* are shut up in the hard wrath; their bodies are a hard *death*, and their spirits are a fierce *sting* of the wrath of God, and their qualifying or fountain spirits generate themselves continually in the innermost sharpness, according to the sharp [1] law of the Deity.

[1] right or order.

105. For otherwise they cannot generate themselves; neither can they die, nor pass away and vanish, and be no more; but they *stand* in the most anguishing birth or geniture, and there is nothing in them but mere *fierceness*, wrath and malice; the kindled fire-source riseth from eternity to eternity, and they can never touch nor see nor apprehend the *sweet* and *light* birth or geniture of God any more.

Of the kindled Nature.

106. Now God hath *therefore* kindled nature so much and so hard, and did so kindle the burning in his wrath therein, that he might *thereby* build a dwelling-house for the devils, and keep them *prisoners* therein, in that they were the children of wrath, in whom he ruleth, with his fierce *zeal* or jealousy, and they rule in the wrath.

THE TWENTY-FOURTH CHAPTER

Of the Incorporating or Compaction
of the Stars.

1. NOW when the *whole body* of nature in the extent, space or circumference of this world was benumbed or *deadened*, as in the hard death, and yet that the life was *hid* therein, thereupon God moved the whole body of the nature of this world on the *fourth day*, and generated the stars from or out of nature, out of the risen light. For the wheel of God's birth or geniture *moved* itself *again*, as it *had done* from eternity.

2. Indeed it had moved on the *first day*, and had begun the birth or geniture in the body of the *corrupt* nature; for on the *first* day the life *separated* itself from the death, and on the *second* day a firmament was created *between*, and on the *third* day the life *brake forth* through death. For there the light brake *forth* through the darkness, and made the dead body of nature to spring, to flourish, and to be stirring and agile.

3. For on the *third day* the body of nature did

travail *so* hard in anxiety till the *love-fire* had kindled itself in the death, and till the light of life was broken forth through the *congealed* body of death, and had sprung up out of death; but on the third day it stood only in the *fire-crack*, from whence mobility existed.

4. On the *fourth day* the light rose up, and made its seat in the house of death, and yet *death* could not, and cannot, comprehend it. As *little* as the austere birth of God, (which standeth in the innermost kernel from whence life existeth), can apprehend the meekness, and the light of the meekness together with the spirit in the meek-ness, *so little* also can the dead darkness of this world comprehend the light of nature: *no more* can the devils either.

5. But the light shineth through death, and hath made its *royal* seat in the midst or centre in the house of death and of God's wrath, and generateth to itself a *new* [1] *body* of God out of the house of wrath, which new body subsisteth eternally in the love of God, incomprehensibly to the *old* kindled body in the *outmost* birth or geniture.

Now thou wilt ask, How shall I understand this?

Answer.

6. I *cannot* at all write it in thy heart, for it is not for every man's capacity, understanding and apprehension, especially where the spirit standeth

[1] Or divine body.

in the *house of wrath*, and doth *not* qualify, operate or unite with the light of God. But I will shew it to thee in an earthly *similitude*, that thou mightest, if possible, get a little into the *deep* sense.

7. Behold and consider a *tree*: On the outside it hath a hard, gross *rind* or *bark*, which is dead, benumbed, and without vegetation—yet not *quite* dead, but in the impotence; and there is a great difference between the bark and the body that groweth next under the rind or bark. The body hath its living power, and breaketh forth through the *withered* rind, and generateth many fair *young* bodies or *twigs*, all which stand in the *old body*.

8. But the *rind is* as a death, and cannot comprehend the *life* of the tree, but only hangeth to it, and is a *cover* to the tree, in which worms do harbour, which in the end destroy the tree.

9. *Thus* also is the whole house of this world. The *outward* darkness is the house of God's wrath, wherein the devils dwell, and it is rightly the house of death, for the holy light of God hath therein *died*.

[" *Understand, the light stepped into its Princi-* " *ple, and is the outward substantiality in God,* " *as it were dead in our esteem, whereas it liveth* " in God, *but in another source or quality.*"]

10. But the body of this great house, which lieth hid under the *shell* or rind of darkness, incomprehensibly to the darkness, *that* body is

the house of life, wherein love and wrath *wrestle* the one with the other.

11. Now the love always breaketh *through* the house of death, and generateth *holy*, heavenly twigs in the great tree; which twigs stand in the light. For they spring up through the shell or *skin* of darkness, as the twigs do through the shell or bark of the tree, and are *one life* with God.

12. And the wrath also springeth up in the house of darkness, and holdeth many a noble twig *captive* in death, through its infection in the house of *fierceness*.

13. This now is the *sum* or the contents of the astral birth or geniture, of which I here intend to write.

Now it may be asked, What are the stars? or out of what are they come to be?

14. They are the *power* of the seven spirits of God; for when in this world the wrath of God was kindled by the devil, then the *whole house* of this world in nature, or the outermost birth or geniture, was as it were benumbed or *chilled* in death; from whence the *earth* and *stones* are come to be. But when this hard dross or *scum* was driven together into a lump or heap, then the *deep* was cleared. But the deep was very dark, for the light therein was dead in the *wrath*.

15. Now the body of God, as to this world, could not *remain* in death, so God moved himself

with his seven qualifying or fountain spirits to the *birth* or geniture.

But thou must understand this high thing rightly.

16. The *light* of God, which is the *Son* of God, and also the Holy Ghost, *died* not; but the light, which hath gone forth from or out of the heart of God *from eternity*, and hath enlightened nature, ([the nature] which is generated out of the seven spirits), that [light] is *departed* or gone away from the hard *corrupted* nature. From whence it is that the nature of this world, with its comprehensibility or palpability, hath *remained* in death, and cannot apprehend the light of God, but is a dark house of devils.

17. Upon this, on the *fourth* day of the creation, God *regenerated* anew the whole house of this world, with the qualities thereof, and hath *placed* or set the qualifying or fountain spirits in the house of darkness, that he might generate to himself again out of that a *new body*, to his praise, honour and glory.

18. For his purpose was to create *another* angelical host or army out of this house, which was to be done thus: He would create an angel, namely *Adam*, who should generate out of himself creatures *like* himself, who should possess the house of the new birth; and in the middle of time *their king* should be generated or born out of a human body, and possess the new-born

kingdom as a king of these creatures, in place of the *corrupted* and expelled Lucifer.

19. Further, at the *fulness* or accomplishment of this time, God would adorn and trim this house with its qualities, as a royal government, and let those very qualifying or fountain spirits *possess* the whole house, that they might, in that house of darkness and of death, bring forth creatures and images again, as they *had done* from eternity, till the accomplishment or fulfilling of the whole host or army of the new created angels, namely men.   *Then* God would bolt and bar up the devil in the house of darkness in a narrow hell, and then kindle the whole house in its own light again, *all but* the very hole, hell or dungeon of the devils.

Now it may be asked, Why did not God bolt him up instantly, and then he had *not* done so much mischief.

Answer.

20. Behold! this was God's purpose, which [purpose] must stand: that he would re-edify out of the corrupted nature of the earth, or build again to himself an angelical host or army: Understand, a new body, which should *subsist* eternally in God.

21. It was not at all God's intention to let the devil *have* the whole earth for an eternal dwelling-house, but to let him have only the death and *fierceness* of the earth, which he had brought into it.

22. For *what* sin had the *Salitter* committed against God, that it should stand totally in *eternal* shame? None: It was only a body, which must remain still, when the devil elevated or swelled himself therein.

23. Now if God should have instantly *left* it to the devil for an eternal dwelling-house, then out of *that* place a new body could *not* have been built. Now what sin had that space, place or *room* committed against God, that it should stand in eternal shame? None; and therefore that were an injustice.

24. Now the purpose of God was to make a beautiful, excellent, angelical host or army out of the *earth*, and [also] all manner of ideas, forms or images. For in and upon that [earth] all should spring and generate themselves *anew*, as we see in mineral ores, stones, trees, herbs and grass, and in all manner of beasts after a *heavenly* image or form.

25. And though those imagings were *transitory*, seeing they were not pure before God, yet God would, at the end of this time, *extract* and draw forth the heart and the kernel out of the new birth or geniture, and *separate* it from death and wrath; and the new birth should eternally spring up in God, without, *distinct* from this place, and bear heavenly fruits *again*.

26. But the death of the earth, and the wrath therein, should be lord *Lucifer's* eternal house, after the accomplishing of the new birth or geni-

ture. In the meanwhile lord *Lucifer* should lie *captive* in the darkness in the deep above the earth ; and there he now is, and may very shortly expect his portion.

27. That this new birth or geniture might be accomplished, whether the devil will or *no*, the Creator hath therefore, in the body of this world, generated himself, as it were *creaturely*, in his qualifying or fountain spirits ; and all the stars are nothing else but God's *powers*, and the whole body of this world consisteth in the seven qualifying or fountain spirits.

28. But that there are so many stars of so manifold different effects and operations is from the *infiniteness*, which is in the [1] efficiency of the seven spirits of God, in one another, which generate themselves infinitely.

[1] infection or affecting.

29. But that the birth, or the *body* of the stars in their seat, doth not change or alter (but lo as they did from eternity), signifieth that there shall be a *constant*, continued birth or geniture, whereby, in one *uniform* operation, which yet standeth in the infiniteness, the *benumbed* body of the earth should continually and *constantly* be kindled again, and generate itself anew, and so also should the house of darkness of the deep above the earth ; whereby the new body might continually and constantly be generated out of death, till time should be accomplished, and the whole new-born body [perfected].

Now thou wilt object and say, Then sure the stars are God, and they must be honoured and worshipped as God.

30. The wise Heathen also came to this [conclusion], who, indeed, in their sharp or acute understandings, far *excelled* our philosophers; but the *right* door of knowledge hath yet remained *hidden* from them.

31. Behold! the stars are plainly incorporated or *compacted* out of or from God; but thou must understand the difference between the stars and God, for the stars are *not* the heart and the meek pure Deity, which man *is to honour* and worship as God; but they are the innermost and sharpest birth or geniture, wherein all things stand in a wrestling and a *fighting*, wherein the heart of God always generateth itself, and wherein the Holy Ghost *continually* riseth up from the rising of the life.

32. But the sharp birth or geniture of the stars *cannot* again apprehend the heart of God, nor the Holy Ghost; but the light of God, which riseth up in the *anxiety*, together with the moving of the Holy Ghost, remaineth *free* to itself as the heart, and ruleth in the midst or centre of the *closure* of the hidden heaven, which is from or out of the water of life.

33. For from the heaven the stars have their *first kindling*, and are only as an *instrument*, which God useth to the birth or geniture.

34. It is just such a birth as is in *man* ; the body is even the *father* of the soul, for the soul is generated out of the power of the body, and when the body standeth in the anguishing birth or geniture of God, as the stars do, and not in the fierce hellish birth, then the soul of man qualifieth, mixeth or *uniteth* with the pure Deity, as a member in or of his body.

35. Thus also is the heart or light of God always generated in the body of this world, and that generated heart is *one heart* with the eternal, unbeginning, infinite heart of God, which is in and above all heavens.

36. It is *not* generated in and from the stars *only*, but in the *whole* body of this world ; but the stars always kindle the body of this world, that the birth or geniture may subsist everywhere.

But here thou must well observe this.

37. The light or the heart of *God* taketh *not* its original barely from the wild rough stars, where, indeed, love and wrath are in each other, but out of or from the *seat* where the meek water of life is continually generated.

38. For that water, at or in the kindling of the wrath, was not apprehended by *death*, but subsisteth from eternity to eternity, and reacheth to all the ends and parts of or in this world, and is *the water of life*, which breaketh through death, out of which is built the new body of God in this world.

39. And it is *in* the stars, as well as in all ends, corners and places, but not in any place comprehensible or *palpable*, and it at once filleth or replenisheth all alike. It is also in the body of man, and he that thirsteth after this water, and *drinketh* thereof, *in him the light of life kindleth itself*, which is the heart of God ; and there [in that place] presently springeth forth the Holy Ghost.

Now thou askest, How then do the stars subsist in love and wrath ?

Answer.

40. Behold ! the stars are risen or proceeded out of the *kindled house* of God's wrath, as the [1] mobility or stirring of a *child* in the mother's body or womb in three [2] months. But now they have attained their kindling from the eternal, benumbed, not quite dead, water of life, for in nature that water was *never* dead.

[1] first inward stirring of life in the child.

[2] As Gen. xxxviii. 24.

41. But when God moved himself in the body of this world, then on the *third day* the anxiety, in the birth of this world, rubbed itself, from whence the fire-flash existed, and the light of the stars kindled itself in the water of life.

42. For till the *third* day from the time of the kindling of God's wrath in this world, nature, in the anxiety, was a *dark* valley, and stood in death ; but on the third day the life brake through death, and the *new birth* began.

43. For so long, and not an hour longer, *the*

new-born King and grand Prince of this world,
JESUS CHRIST, *rested in death,* and hath
regenerated the *first three* days of the creation
of nature, and that very time [which was] in
death, to light again; that this time might
again be *one* time with the *eternal* time, and
that no day of death might be *between*; and
that the eternal love, and the new-born or
regenerated love out of the new body of nature,
might be one eternal love; and that there might
be *no* difference between the eternal love, and
the new-born or regenerated love, but that the
new-born love might reach into the being or
substance which was from eternity, and *itself*
also be in eternity.

44. Thus the new-born love, which rose out of
the water of life in the light *in* the stars, and *in*
the whole body of this world, is wholly bound
and united with the eternal, unbeginning, infinite
love, so that they are *one* heart and *one* spirit,
which supporteth and preserveth all.

45. In this kindling of the light, in the stars
and elements, the birth of nature did not thereupon *wholly transmute* or change itself into the
holy meekness, as it was before the time of the
wrath, *so that* the birth of nature be now altogether holy and *pure*: No, but it standeth in
its sharpest, most austere, and most anxious
birth, wherein the wrath of God *incessantly*
springeth up like hellish fire.

46. For if, with its sharp birth, nature had *fully* changed itself into love, according to the heavenly right, law or manner, then were the devils again in the *seat* of God.

47. And this thou mayest very well perceive and understand, in *extreme* heat and cold, as also by the poison, bitterness and sourness in this world; all which stand in the birth or geniture of the *stars*, wherein the devil lieth *captive*.

48. The stars are only the kindling of the great house; for the whole house is benumbed in death, as the earth is; for the outermost birth or geniture is *dead* and benumbed, as the rind, shell or bark of a tree. But the astral birth is the *body* in which the life riseth up.

49. But the astral birth is in its body very sharp; yet the new birth, which riseth up in the water of life, and presseth through death, *mitigateth* it. But the new birth cannot *alter* the *kernel* of the sharp birth, but is generated out of it, and *keeps* its own holy new life to itself, and presseth through the angry death, and the angry death comprehendeth it *not*.

50. Now this love and this wrath are indeed one body, but the water of life is the heaven of *partition* between them, so that the love doth not receive or comprehend the wrath, nor the wrath the love, but the love *riseth up* in the water of life, and receiveth into itself, from the first and austere birth, the *power* which is in the

light, and which is generated out of the wrath; so that the new body is born out of the old.

51. For the *old* body, which standeth in the *austere* birth, belongeth to the devil for a house, and the *new* belongeth to the kingdom of Christ.

Now it may be asked, Are not all the three Persons of the Deity in the birth or geniture of meekness in this world?

Answer.

52. *Yes*, they are all three in this world in the *full* birth or geniture of love, meekness, holiness and purity, and they are always generated in such a substance and being, as *was done* from eternity.

53. Behold! God the Father spake to the People of *Israel* on mount *Sinai*, when he gave the Law to them, saying; [1] *I am an angry, zealous or jealous God to those that hate me.*

[1] Exod. xx. 5. Deut. v. 9.

54. Now, of this *one* only Father, who is both angry and also full of love, thou canst not make *two* persons; but he is one only *Father*, who continually generateth his heartily beloved *Son*, and from both these the *Holy Ghost* goeth forth continually.

Observe the Depth in the Centre.

55. The *Father* is the one only being, who himself is A L L, who from eternity continually generateth his heartily beloved *Son*; and *in both* of them the *Holy Ghost* is continually standing in the flash, wherein the life is generated.

56. But now, from the austere and *earnest* birth or geniture of the qualifying or fountain spirits of the Father, wherein the zeal or jealousy and the wrath standeth, the *body* of nature always cometh to be, wherein the *light* of the Son, *viz.* of the Father's heart standeth, incomprehensibly as to nature.

57. For the light is in the midst or centre of the birth or geniture, and is the place of *life* wherein the meek life of God is generated from or out of *all* the powers of the Father, and in the same place the *Holy Ghost* goeth forth from the Father and the Son.

58. Now those powers of the Father which stand in the kindling of the light are *the holy Father, and the meek Father, and the pure birth or geniture of God*; and the spirit which riseth therein is the Holy Spirit. But the sharp birth or geniture is the body, wherein this *holy life* is continually generated.

59. But when the light of God shineth through this sharp birth or geniture, then it becometh very meek, and is as it were like a man that is asleep, in whom the life *still moveth*; and the body is in a sweet, quiet rest.

60. In this body of nature the *kindling* was now made, for out of this body the angels also were created; and if *they had not* elevated and kindled themselves in their highmindedness, then their body would have stood eternally in

a *stillness*, and in an incomprehensible meekness, as it is in the *other* principalities of angels that are without, distinct from this world; and their spirit would have generated itself eternally in *their* body of meekness, as the Holy *Trinity* doth in the body or corporeity of God; and their inborn or *innate* spirit would have been one heart, one will, and one love with or in the Holy Trinity: For to *that end* they were created in the body of God, to be a *joy* to the Deity.

61. But lord *Lucifer* would *himself* be the mighty God, and kindled his body, and excited or stirred up therein the *sharp* birth of God, and opposed the light or bright heart of God, intending to rule therein with his sharpness, which was a thing impossible to be done.

62. But seeing he elevated and kindled himself *against* the right of the Deity, thereupon the sharp birth in the body of the Father *rose up* against him, and took him, as an angry son, prisoner or captive in the sharpest birth, and therein now is his eternal *dominion*.

63. But now when the Father kindled himself in the body of the sharpness, he did *not* for all-that *kindle* the holy source, wherein his most loving heart generateth itself, that thereupon his heart should sit in the source of wrath. No! that is impossible; for the sharp birth *cannot* apprehend the holy and pure birth, but the holy and pure presseth *quite* through the

sharp, and generateth to itself a new body, which standeth again in meekness.

64. And that new body is *the water of life*, which is generated when the light presseth *through* the wrath; and the Holy Ghost is the former or framer therein. But *heaven* is the partition between love and wrath, and is the seat wherein the wrath is transmuted or changed into love.

65. Now when thou beholdest the sun and stars, thou must *not* think that they are the *holy* and pure God, and thou must *not offer* to pray to them, or ask anything of them, for they are not the holy God, but are the kindled, *austere* birth or geniture of *his* body, wherein love and wrath *wrestle* the one with the other.

66. But the holy God is *hidden* in the *centre* of all these things in his heaven, and thou canst neither see nor comprehend him; but the *soul* comprehendeth him, and the astral birth comprehendeth but half; for the heaven is the partition between love and wrath. That heaven is everywhere, even in thyself.

67. Now when thou worshippest or prayest to the *holy God* in his heaven, then thou worshippest or prayest to *him* in *that* heaven which is *in* thee, and that same God breaketh through in *thy* heart with his light; and in his light the Holy Ghost *breaketh* through, and generateth thy *soul* to be a [1] new body of God,

[1] Or new divine body.

which ruleth and reigneth with God in *his* heaven.

68. For the earthly body which thou bearest is one body with the whole kindled body of this world, and thy body qualifieth, mixeth or uniteth with the whole body of this world; and there is no difference between the stars and the deep, as also between the earth and thy body; it is all one body. This is the only difference, thy body is a *son* of the whole, and is in itself as the whole being itself is.

69. Now as the new body of this world generateth itself in *its* heaven, so the new man also generateth himself in *his heaven*; for it is all but *one* heaven, wherein God dwelleth, and therein thy new man dwelleth, and they *cannot* be divided asunder.

70. But if thou art wicked, then thy birth or geniture is *not capable* of heaven, but of the wrath, and remaineth in the other part of the astral birth or geniture, wherein the earnest and *austere* fire-source riseth up, and bolts it up into *death*, so long till thou breakest through heaven, and *livest* with God.

71. For instead of thy heaven thou hast the wrath-devil sitting there; but if thou breakest through, then *he* must get him gone, and the Holy Ghost ruleth and reigneth in *that seat*; and in the other part, *viz.* the fierceness, the devil *tempteth thee*, for it is his nest; and the Holy

Ghost *opposeth* him, and the new man lieth in his own heaven, *hidden* under the protection of the Holy Ghost, and the devil knoweth not the new man, for he is not in *the devil's* house, but in heaven, in the firmament of God.

72. *This I write as a word which is generated in its heaven, where the holy Deity always generateth itself, and where the moving spirit riseth up in the flash of life; even there this word and this knowledge is generated, and risen up in the love-fire through the zealous spirit of God.*

73. I know very well what the devil intendeth; for *that part* of the earnest and austere birth or geniture, wherein love and wrath are set opposite the one to the other, *seeth* into *his* very heart. For when he cometh with his fierce and hellish temptation, like a *fawning* dog, then he setteth upon us with his wrath, in that part wherein the austere birth and geniture standeth, and *therein* the heaven is set in opposition to him, and there the fair *bride* is known.

74. For he stingeth through the *old* man, with an intent to spoil or destroy the *new*; but when the new riseth against him, then the hell-hound retireth, and then the new man *feeleth* very well what advice or counsel the hell-hound hath darted or spit into the astral birth, and then is it time for a clean sweep.

75. But I find that the most cunning devil is set against me; he will raise scorners and

mockers, who will say that I intend by mine *own conceit* to grope, dig deep, and search out the *Deity*. Yes, Mr Scorner, thou art an *obedient* son to the devil, thou hast great cause to mock God's children. *As if I* were able, in mine *own* power, to fathom the depth of the Deity! No! but the Deity searcheth the ground *in me* : Or, dost thou think that I am strong enough to stand against it?

76. Indeed, thou *proud* man, the Deity is a very meek, simple and quiet still being, and gropeth not in the bottom of hell and death, but *in his* heaven,* where there is nothing but a unanimous meekness ; therefore it is not *meet* for me to stand against it.

77. But behold! it is *not* I that have made way for this, but thy desire and highly raised lofty lust hath moved the *Deity* to *reveal* to thee the desire of thy heart, in the highest *simplicity* in the *greatest depth*, that it may be a witness against thee, and a denunciation of the earnest severe day of God.

78. *This I speak to thee as a word of the earnest severity of God, which is generated or born in the flash of life.*

---

* "the Deity . . . gropeth not in the bottom of hell and death, but in his heaven." Gropeth (*grübelt*), "rake into, rummage, hypercritically search into," and also "brood." A free though not inadequate rendering of this clause would be, "the Deity . . . doth not grope or bestir himself anxiously in the bottom of hell and death, but broodeth in his heaven."

THE TWENTY-FIFTH CHAPTER

Of the whole Body of the Stars and of their Birth or Geniture; that is, the whole Astrology, or the whole Body of this World.

1. THE learned and highly experienced *masters* of astrology, or the starry art, are come so high and deep in their understanding, that they know the *course* and *effects* of the stars, what their conjunction, [1] influence, and breaking through of their powers and virtues denoteth and produceth ; and how *thereby* wind, rain, snow, and heat are caused ;* also good and evil, [2] prosperity and adversity, life and death, and all the drivings and *agitations* in this world.

2. Indeed it hath a *true* foundation, which, in the spirit, I know to be *so* ; but their knowledge standeth only in the house of death, in the outward comprehensibility or palpability, and in the beholding with the eyes of the *body* ; but the root of *this tree* hath hitherto remained hidden *from them.*

[1] infection.

[2] good hap, bad hap ; good luck, and mischance or mischief.

* "are caused"—*empöret* (*gebäret*).   See Ch. 3, par. 67.

3. Neither is it my purpose to write of the *branches* of the tree, and to invert or disprove their knowledge; neither do I build upon *their* ground, but I leave their knowledge to *sit* in its own seat, seeing I have not studied it. But, in the spirit of *my knowledge*, I write concerning the root, stock, branches and fruits of the tree, as an industrious and laborious servant to *his* master, in discovering the *whole* tree of this world.

4. *Not* with an intent to set on foot any new thing, for I have *no* command to do so; but my knowledge standeth in this birth or geniture of the stars, in the midst or centre, where the *life* is generated, and breaketh through death, and where the *moving spirit* existeth and breaketh through; and in the impulse or moving *thereof* I also write.

5. Also I know very well that the children of the flesh will *scorn* and mock at me, and say I should *look* to my own *calling*, and not trouble my head about these things; but rather be diligent to bring in *food* for my family and myself, and let those meddle with *philosophy* that have studied it, and are *called* and appointed to it.

6. With such an attempt the devil hath given me so many assaults, and hath so *wearied* me, that I have *often* resolved to let it alone; but my former purpose was too hard for me. For when I took care for the *belly*, and to get my *living*, and resolved to *give over* this business in hand, then the gate of heaven in my knowledge was bolted up.

7. Then my soul was so *afflicted* in anxiety, as if it were captivated by the devil, whereby *reason* gat so many checks and assaults, as if the body were presently to be destroyed or ruined, and the [my] spirit would *not* give over, till it brake through again, through the dead or *mortal* reason, and so hath burst open the *door of darkness*, and hath gotten its seat again in the stead thereof, whereby it gat new life and power again.

8. Whereby I understand that the *spirit* must be *tried* through the *cross* and *affliction*, and I have not failed of bodily temptation, but was fain always to stand *ready* for an encounter, so much hath the devil set himself against *this*.*

9.† But since I perceive that my eternal salvation hangeth upon this [*i.e.* the getting of new life and power] and that through my negligence [in case I were negligent], the gates of the light would be closed against me, which [light] is yet the firmament of my heaven wherein my soul hideth from the stormings of the devil, and which [light and heaven] also I won with great toil and hard assaults, through the love of God and by the breaking-through of my Redeemer and King, Jesus Christ, therefore am I willing to let God have his way and take captive my fleshy reason.

* "against this." The word "this" refers to the last clause of the preceding par., "whereby it [my spirit] gat new life," etc.

† A new translation of this par. has been substituted for Sparrow's rendering.

10. And I have chosen the gate of knowledge of the light, and will follow after the impulse and knowledge of the spirit, though my *bestial body* should be brought to beggary, or be destroyed or ruined. I regard none of these things, but will say with the royal prophet David, [1] *Though my body and soul should faint and fail, yet thou, O God, art my salvation, my comfort, and the refuge of my heart.* [1] Psalm lxxiii. 26.

11. In *thy* name I will venture it, and will not strive against *thy* spirit; though it may hurt the flesh, yet *faith* in the knowledge of the light must move and soar *above* reason.

12. I know also very well, that it is not fit for the disciple to fight against *his Master.* And I know that the high experienced masters of astrology do *far exceed* me in *their* way. But I labour in *my* calling, and they in *theirs*, lest I should be found a lazy idle servant to my Lord, at his coming, when he will demand the *talent* he hath entrusted me withal; but that I may present it to him with usury or profit and gain.

13. Therefore I will not *bury his talent in the earth*, but lend it *out upon usury or interest, lest he should say to me at that time of his requiring it of me, Thou wicked, slothful servant, why hast thou hid my talent in the darkness, and didst not put it out upon use, and so now I might have received it with usury, gain, and profit? For then he would take it quite away from me, and*

give it to another, who hath gained many talents with his one. Therefore I will sow, let him water it, I leave the care to him.

Now observe:

14. The whole house of this world, which standeth in a visible and comprehensible or *palpable* being, is the *old house of God*, or the old body, which stood before the time of wrath in a *heavenly* clarity and *brightness*. But when the devil stirred up the wrath therein, then it became a house of darkness and of *death*.

15. Therefore then also the holy birth or geniture of God, as a special body of itself, *separated* itself from the wrath, and made the firmament of heaven, between the love and the wrath, so that the birth or geniture of the stars standeth in the *middle*. Understand it thus; *viz.* with its outward comprehensibility and *visibility* it standeth in the wrath of death; and with the new birth rising up therein, which standeth in the middle or central seat, where the *closure* of heaven is, it standeth in the meekness of the life.

16. For meekness moveth against the wrath, and the wrath against the meekness, and so *both* are *distinct* kingdoms in the *one* only body of this world.

17. But seeing the love and meekness of God would not leave the body or place of this kindled wrath - world sticking in eternal wrath and ignominy, *therefore* he generated the whole old

body of this world *again* into a rectified reformed body, wherein life did rule in a *divine* manner and way; *though* it be in the kindled wrath, yet it must subsist according to the [1]right of the Deity, so *that* out of it a new body might be generated, which should subsist in holiness and purity *in eternity.*

[1] law and order.

18. For which cause there is appointed in God a *day of separation*, on which love and wrath shall be separated *asunder.*

19. Now when thou beholdest the stars, and the deep, together with the earth, then thou seest with thy bodily eyes nothing else but the *old* body in the wrathful death; thou canst not see heaven with *thy bodily* eyes, for the blue or azure sphere which thou seest above is *not the heaven*, but is only the old body, which may be justly called *the corrupted nature.*

20. There *seemeth* to be a blue or azure sphere *above* the stars, whereby the place of this world is closed and shut out from the *holy* heaven, as men have thought. *hitherto*; yet it is *not so*, but it is *the superior water of nature*, which is much brighter than the water below the *moon.* And now when the *sun* shineth through the deep, then it is as it were of a light-blue or azure colour.

21. But how deep or how large the place of this world is, *no man* knoweth, though some physicists or astrologers *have* undertaken to measure the deep with their measures of circles;

their measuring is but conjectural, or a measuring of somewhat that is *comprehensible* or palpable; as if a man would grasp the wind in his fist.

22. But the true heaven is everywhere all over, to this very time, and till the Last Judgment Day; and the wrath-house of hell and of death is also in this world *everywhere*, even to the Last Judgment Day.

23. But the dwelling of the devils is *now* from the moon to the earth, and in the earth, in the deep caves and holes thereof; especially in wildernesses and desert places, and where the earth is full of stones and bitterness.

24. But their kingly regimen or government is in the deep, in the four coasts or quarters of the equinoctial line or circle, of which I will write in *another* place.

25. But here I will shew thee: 1. How the *body* of this world came to be; and 2. How *it is* at present; and then, 3. How the regimen or *government therein* is.

26. The whole body of this world is as a man's body, for it is surrounded in its utmost circle with the stars and risen powers of *nature*; and in that body the *seven* spirits of nature govern, and the heart of nature standeth in the midst or centre.

27. But the *stars* in general are, and signify, the wonderful proportion or changing *variety* of God. For when God created the stars, he created

them out of the rising up of the *infinity*, out of the old body of God *then* further * kindled.

28. For as the seven spirits of God had, *before* the time of the wrath, generated themselves infinitely by their rising up and by their influences, (whence rose up so many several varieties of figures and heavenly ideas or vegetations), so also the holy God figured his old body of *this corrupted nature* into as many and *various* powers as ever stood in the birth or geniture in the holiness.

Understand this high Thing rightly.

29. Every star hath a several peculiar property, which thou mayest perceive by the curious *ornament* of the budding, blossoming earth. And the Creator hath *therefore* rebuilt and revived again the old kindled body into so many and *various* powers, that *through* this old life, in the wrath, such a new life might generate itself therein, through the *closure* of heaven, that that *new life* might have all the powers and operations that ever the old had before the times of wrath, that it might qualify, mix or unite with the *pure* Deity, distinct from this world, and that *it* might be *one* holy God, together with the Deity without, distinct from this world.

30. Also the *new birth* blossomed in the time of the creation, when man *had not* spoiled or

* "then further" (*nunmehr*), "henceforth."

corrupted it; but by him nature was still *more* corrupted; and so God cursed the ground. But seeing man took hold of the *fruit* of the *old* body, thereupon the *fruit* of the *new* body was hidden in its heaven, and man must now behold it *with* the new body, and cannot partake of it with the natural body.

31. Of which I have a great longing to eat, but I *cannot reach* to it, for heaven is the closure or *firmament* between the old body and the new. And therefore I must let it alone, till I come into the *other life*, and must give my bestial body *mother Eve's wrath-apples to eat*.

Concerning the Kindling of the Heart or Life of this World.

32. When, in *two days*, God had brought the body of this world into a right form, and had made the heaven for a *partition* between the love and the wrath, then, on the *third* day, *the love* pressed through the heaven and through the wrath, and instantly the old body in death stirred and *moved itself* to the birth or geniture.

33. For the *love* is *hot*, and that kindled the fire-source or quality, and that rubbed itself in the astringent and cold quality of the benumbed death, till the astringent quality was *heated* on the *third* day, whereby the mobility or the astringent earth became moveable.

34. For all stood in the fire-crack till the

fourth day, and then the light of the [1]*sun* [1]SOL.
kindled itself; for the whole body stood in anguish or *pain* in the birth, as a woman in travail.

35. The astringent quality was the encompasser or *encloser* of the life; therein * was the heat now anxious, which was kindled through the love of God, and did drive out the astringent quality as a dead body; but the heat retained its seat in the midst or centre of the body, and so pressed through.

36. But when the light of the *sun* kindled itself, then the *next* circle or orb above the *sun* stood in the fire-crack, (for the sun or the light was shining in the water), and the bitterness ascended also in the *fire-crack* out of the water. But the light made very great *haste* after it, and laid hold on the fire-crack; and there it remained as a *captive*, and became corporeal.

37. In this revolution the planet [2]*Mars* came [2]MARS. to be, whose power standeth in the *bitter* fire-crack, for Mars is a tyrant, rager, raver and stormer, like a *fire-crack*; moreover it is *hot*, and a poisonous, venomous enemy of nature; through whose rising up and birth or geniture in the earth all manner of poisonous, venomous, evil worms and *vermin* are come to be.

38. But seeing the heat in the middle point or centre of the body was *so mighty* great, thereupon it extended itself so very largely, and opened

* "therein" = in the astringent quality.

the chamber of death so wide before its kindling of the light, that it (the SUN) is the greatest star.

39. But as soon as the light kindled itself in the heat, so instantly was that hot place *caught* in the light, and then the body of the *sun* could grow *no* bigger. For the light mitigated the heat, and so the body of the *sun* remained there in the midst or centre as a *heart*; for the light is the heart of nature, *not* the heat.

But here thou must observe exactly,

40. As far as the middle point or centre hath kindled itself, *just* so big is the *sun*; for the *sun* is nothing else but a kindled *point* in the body of nature.

41. Thou must not think that there is any other power or virtue in it, or belonging to it, than there is in the whole deep of the *body* everywhere, all over.

42. For should the love of God, through its heaven, kindle the whole body of this world *through the heat*, it would be everywhere all over as light as it now is in the sun.

43. Now if the *great heat* were taken away from the *sun*, then it would be *one* light with God; but seeing in this time that cannot be, therefore it remaineth a *king* and regent in the *old* corrupted and kindled body of nature; and the clear Deity remaineth hidden in the meek heaven.

44. But the light of the meekness of the sun
qualifieth, mixeth or *uniteth* with the pure Deity;
but the *heat* cannot comprehend the light, and
therefore also the place of the sun remaineth in
the body of *God's wrath*, and thou must *not*
worship, nor pray to nor honour the *sun* as God,
for its place or body *cannot* apprehend the water
of life, because of the *fierceness* in the sun.

The highest Ground of the SUN, and of ALL the PLANETS.

45. Here I shall have *adversaries* enough who
will be ready to censure me, for they will not
have regard to consider *the spirit*, but will mind
their *old rules*, and say, Astrologers, who have
written of such matters, understand it better; and
my adversaries will look on *the great open gate*
as a cow looks on a new barn door.

46. Dear Reader, I understand the *astrologers'*
meanings and sayings full well, and I have *per-
used* their writings also, and taken notice how
they describe the course of the *sun* and *stars*,
neither do I despise it, but, for the *most part*,
hold that to be good and *right*.

47. But that in *some* things I write otherwise
than they, I do it not out of self-will or conceit
and *supposition*, doubting whether it be so or *no*.
I dare not make any *doubt herein, neither* can
any man instruct me herein.

48. I have *not* my knowledge by *study*; indeed

I have read the order and *position* of the *seven planets* in the books of astrologers, and find them * to be *very* right; but the root, how the planets came to be, and from what they are proceeded, I cannot learn from *any* man; for they know it *not*, neither was I present when God created the planets.

49. But seeing the doors of the deep, and the gates of wrath, and the *chambers* of death also, are, through the love of God, set open *in my* spirit, *therefore* the spirit must needs look through them.

50. Accordingly I find, that the birth or geniture of nature standeth to this day, and generateth itself, just so as it did when it first took its beginning; and *whatsoever riseth* up in this world, whether men, beasts, trees, herbs, grass, mineral ores, or be it what it will, all riseth up in such a *quality*, manner and form as it first did; also every life, be it good or bad, taketh its original thus [as it did from the beginning].

51. For this is the *right* or law of the Deity: that every life in the body of God should generate itself in *one* manner or uniform way; though it be done through many *various* imagings, yet the *life hath* one uniform way and original in all.

52. I see not this knowledge with my *fleshly* eyes, but with those eyes wherein life generateth

* "find them," *i.e.* find the order and position of the seven planets.

itself *in me*; in that seat the gates of heaven and hell stand open to me, and the *new man* speculateth * into the midst or centre of the astral birth or geniture, and to him the inner and outermost gate standeth *open*.

53. While he yet sticketh in the *old* man of wrath and death, and sitteth also in his heaven, he seeth through *both*; in such a manner also he seeth the stars and elements. For *in God* there is no place of hindrance; *for the eye of the* LORD *beholdeth all*.

54. Now if my spirit did not see through *his* spirit, then I were but a blind stock; but seeing I see the *gates* of God in *my* spirit, and have the impulse to do it, I will therefore write *directly* according as I have *seen* it, and will not regard any *man's authority*.

55. Thou must not conceive it so, as if *my old* man were a *living saint* or angel. *No*, Friend, he sitteth with all men in the house of wrath and of death, and is a *constant* enemy to God, and sticketh in his sins, wickedness and malice, as all men do, and is full of faults, defects and *infirmities*.

56. But thou must know this, that he sticketh in a continual, *anxious* birth or geniture, but would fain be rid of the wrath and wickedness, and *yet cannot*. For he is as the whole house of this world, wherein love and wrath always

* "speculateth" (*speculiret*).   See Ch. 10, par. 33.

wrestle the one with the other, and the new body always generateth itself in the midst or centre of the *anguish.* For so it must be, if thou wilt be born anew, otherwise no man *can reach* the regeneration.

57. In this world man is *always* seeking for soft days of ease for the flesh, and after riches, beauty and bravery, and knoweth *not* that he sitteth therewith in the *chamber* of death, where the sting of wrath darteth into him.

58. *Behold! I tell this to thee, as a word of life, which I receive in the knowledge of the spirit, in the midst or centre in the birth or geniture of the new body of this world, over which the Man JESUS CHRIST is Ruler and King, together with his eternal Father.*

59. Also, I receive it from *before* the seat of his throne, where all holy souls of men stand before him, and rejoice before him; [and I tell thee] *that the desire of the flesh in soft pleasingness, to be rich, to be handsome, beautiful and fair, or to be mighty or potent, is a very bath or lake of hellish wrath,* into which thou crowdest and runnest, as if thou wert drawn in with cart-ropes; for there is very great danger therein.

60. But if thou wouldst know how it is, behold, I will tell thee in a parable or similitude: When thou art pressed, according to the desire of thy heart, into riches and power, then it is with thee as if thou stoodst in a deep water, where the

water always standeth up to thy very mouth, and thou feelest no ground under thy feet, but thou swimmest with thy hands and strugglest to protect or save thyself; now thou art in deep water, now above water again, yet always in a great terror and danger, expecting to sink down to the bottom, the water often coming into thy mouth, and always expecting death.

61. Just in this manner, and no other, thou sittest, when thou art in the *pleasures* of the flesh; if thou *wilt not fight*, thou canst not look for any victory, but thou wilt be *murdered* in thy soft bed of down. For man hath a continual host or *army* before him, which fight with him continually; if he will not *defend* himself, then he is taken captive and slain.

62. But how can he that *swimmeth* in a deep water defend himself? He hath enough to do to protect himself from the water; and yet nevertheless he is assaulted by the devils.

63. *O danger upon danger!* as our King Christ also saith; [1] *It is very hard for a rich man to enter into the kingdom of heaven. A camel will easier go through the eye of a needle, than a rich man enter into the kingdom of heaven.*

[1] Matth. xix. 24.
Mark x. 25.

64. But if any will be new born again, he must *not yield* himself to be a servant to covetousness, pride, state and self-power, to take *delight* in the will or desires of his flesh; but he must struggle and fight against *himself*, against the devil, and

43

against all the *lusts* of the flesh; and he must
think and consider that he is but a *servant* and
pilgrim on earth, who must wander through many
miserable seas of danger into another world; and
there he will be a *lord*, and his dominion will
consist in power, and in perfect delight, beauty
and brightness; *this I tell as the word of the spirit.*

Now observe:

1 *Sol.*

65. The [1]SUN hath its own royal place to
itself, and *doth not go away* from that place
where it came to be at the first. *Some suppose*
that it runneth round about the globe of the
earth in a day and a night; and *some* of the
astrologers also *write so*; and some have undertaken to measure how far its orb and circumference of its *supposed* motion is.

66. This opinion or supposition is *not right*,
but the *earth rolleth* itself about; and *runneth*
with the other planets, as in a wheel, *round* about
the *sun*. The earth doth *not* remain *staying* in
one place, but in a year runneth round *once* about

2 *Venus, Mer-*
cury.

3 *Saturn, Ju-*
piter, Mars.

the *sun*, as the [2]other planets next the sun, but
[3]Saturn and Jupiter, as also Mars, by reason of
their great orb, circumference, and great height,
cannot do it [in a year], because they stand so

4 *Sol.*

high above, and far distant from the [4]SUN.

Now it may be asked, What is the SUN, and
what are the other PLANETS? Or how are
they come to be?

67. Behold! the *other planets* are peculiar bodies of their own, which have a corporeal propriety of themselves, and are *not bound* to any settled or fixed place, but only to their *circle*, orb or sphere wherein they run their course. But the SUN is not such a body, but is only a place or locality kindled by the *light* of God.

Understand it aright.

68. The place where the SUN is, is such a place as you may choose or suppose *anywhere* above the earth; and if God should kindle the light by the heat, then the *whole* world would be such a mere SUN; for that same power wherein the *sun* standeth *is everywhere* all over; and *before* the time of wrath it was everywhere all over in the place of *this world* as light as the *sun* now is, but not *so* intolerable.

69. For that heat was not so *great* as in the *sun*, and therefore the light was also very *meek*; and thus, in respect of the horrible fierceness of the *sun*, the *sun* is differenced or distinguished from the meekness of God. So that man should *not dare* to say that the *sun* is an open gate of the light of God; but it is as the light in a *man's eye*, whereas also the place of the eye belongeth to the body, but the light is different or *distinct* from the body.

70. Though indeed the light existeth by the *heat* in the water of the body, yet it is a peculiar,

distinct thing, which the body *cannot* compre-hend; and such a distinct difference there is *also* between God the Father and God the Son.

71. Thus on the *fourth day*, in the anxious birth or geniture of this world, in the middle point or centre of this world, the S U N is sprung up, and *standeth still** in its eternal, *corporeal* place; for it *cannot* rise up in *one* place, and set in *another*.

72. For it is the only and *sole* natural light of this world, and besides it there is *no more* any true light in the house of death; and though it seemeth as if the other stars did *shine* bright and give *light* also, yet it is *not so*, but they take all their lustre and shining light from the *sun*; as hereafter presently followeth.

The true Birth or Geniture and Descent of the Sun and Planets is just thus, as followeth.

73. Now when the heaven was made for a *distinction* or partition between the light of God and the *kindled corruption* of the body of this world, then was the body of this world a dark valley, and had no light besides the heaven that could have shone forth in the *outward* body; all powers stood as it were captivated in death, and were in great *anguish*, till they had heated themselves in the midst or centre of the body.

---

* "standeth still" (*stehet . . . stille*). St M. has, "*reste fixe*," "remaineth fixed."

74. But when this was *done*, so that the anxious birth or geniture stood so severely in the *heat*, then the love in the light of God brake through the heaven of the *partition*, and kindled the heat.

75. And there rose up the shining light in the heat in the water, or in the fat or oiliness of the water, and the heart of the water kindled itself, and this was done in the *twinkling* of an eye.

76. For as soon as the light had rightly laid hold on the body, the body was captivated in the *light*; and the heat was captivated, and was changed into a moderate, tolerable or suitable meekness, and could stand or extend *no* longer in such anguish.

77. But seeing the heat was so terrified by the light, thereupon its horrible fire-source was *allayed*, and so could kindle itself no further; and so also the breaking through of the love in the light of God through the heaven at this time, with its breaking through, extended or stretched itself *no* further out of, or from God's predestinated purpose; therefore also the *SUN* came to be no bigger.

Of the Planet Mars.

78. But when the *sun* was kindled, then the horrible fire-crack went forth *upwards* from the place of the *sun*, beyond the place of the sun, as a horrible tempestuous *flash*, and in its

corporeal being took along with it the fierceness of the fire, *whereby* the water became very bitter, and the water is the kernel or stock of the *crack*.

79. Now the astrologers write, that the planet *Mars* standeth aloft about 15,750 miles off from the *sun*; which I contradict *not*, because I meddle *not* with the measuring of circles. And so far the swift fire-crack went forth [travelled] from its own place till the light also laid hold on it, and *then* it also was captivated by the light, and stayed and took possession of that place.

80. But that the light could not lay hold of it sooner, was caused by the earnest fierceness and sudden flash, for it was not taken hold of by the *light before* the light had wholly or thoroughly affected or possessed it.

81. And there it is now, as a tyrant, rager and stirrer of the whole body of *this* world; for that is its very office, that with its *revolution* in the wheel of nature it moveth and stirreth all, from whence every life taketh its original.

Of the Planet Jupiter.

82. Now when the bitter fire-crack was captivated by the *light*, then the light in its own power pressed yet *higher* in the deep, till it reached into the *hard* and cold seat of nature. And there the power of the first going *forth* or rising up from the *sun* could not get higher, but sitting, stayed

there corporeally,* and took possession of that *place* for a habitation.

But thou must understand this Thing aright.

83. It was the power of the light which *stayed* in this place, and which is a very meek, friendly, gracious, amiable, blessed and sweet being. The astrologers write, that *this* planet is distant aloft above Mars about 7875 miles. But it is the *mitigator* of the destroying, furious, raging, raving *Mars*, and an original of the meekness in every life ; an original also of the water, from which the life generateth itself, as I shall mention hereafter.

84. Thus far the power of the life *reached* forth from the *sun*, and *not* higher ; but the lustre or *shining* thereof, which hath its power also, reacheth even to the *stars*, and through the whole body of this world.

But thou must understand this exactly, from whence these two Planets are come to be.

85. When the power of the heart of God pressed forth out of the eternal *inexhaustible* fountain of the water of life, through the heaven of the partition, and kindled the water in the place of the sun, then the flash, understand the fire-flash, did shoot forth or went forth out of the water, which

---

* "but sitting, stayed there corporeally" (*und blieb alda corporlich sitzen*). An idiomatic construction which implies no "sitting" at all, but staying behind, standing still, stopping short. Lit., "remained there corporeally."

was very terrible and bitter, and out of which Mars came to be.

86. After this flash the power of the light *shot nimbly* after it, like a meek elevated life, and overtook the fire-crack, and mitigated it, so that it became somewhat *weaker*, and could break no farther through the deep, but stayed trembling.

87. But the power that was gone forth in the light had *more* strength than the fire-crack, and so it rose up higher than the fire-crack, *Mars*, till it came very deep into nature's austereness, and there it became *feeble* also, and *stayed* there.

88. From or out of this power the planet *Jupiter* came to be, and not out of or from that *place* where he is, but it [Jupiter] always kindleth that very place with its power ; but it is as one of the *household* servants in that place, who must always walk about in the place of its office and service.   But the *sun* hath a house of its own ; but *no other* planet hath any house of its own.

89. *If we would rightly search into the original of the birth and geniture of the stars, or into their beginning, then we must exactly know the birth or geniture of the life,* viz. *how the life generateth itself in a body; for all these are one kind of birth or geniture.*

90. He that doth not know nor understand this, he doth not at all know the birth of the stars, for all, concreted together, is one body.   When once life is generated in any creature, the creature's

life standeth or subsisteth afterwards in the creature's own body, as the birth or geniture of the natural body of this world standeth or subsisteth in its own body; for every life must be generated according to the right, law or ordinance of the Deity, as the Deity* generateth itself continually.

91. If this be rightly considered, which, indeed, cannot be done without a *special illumination* of the holy God, then, before he finds anything else, a man findeth the astringent, cold and austere birth or geniture, which is the cause of the *corporeal* nature, or of the imaging, fashioning or *framing* of a thing.

92. Now if it were not for this severe, and cold sharp contracting, compacting power, there would be *no natural* or corporeal being, neither could the birth or geniture of *God* subsist, and all would be unsearchable.

93. But in this hard, severe and cold power standeth [*i.e.* consisteth] the corporeal essence or the body, wherein the spirit of life generateth itself; and out of that same spirit the light and the understanding [generate themselves]; and then through these the senses and the trial or testing of all powers ariseth.

94. For when the *light* is generated, it is generated in the midst or *centre* of the body, as a heart or spirit out of all powers; and there it standeth

* "as the Deity" = in the same way that the Deity.

and remaineth in the place where it had its beginning, and goeth forth *through* all the powers.

95. For as it is generated out of all powers, and
hath the *fountain* of all powers, so with its shining lustre it also bringeth the fountain of all
powers *into* each power; from *whence* then
existeth the taste and smell, also seeing, feeling
and hearing; as also reason and understanding.

96. Now, as the original and beginning of the
life is, in a creature, so is the *first regeneration*
of the nature of the *new* life in the *corrupted*
body of this world. He that *denieth* it hath *not*
the true understanding, nor any knowledge of
nature; and so his knowledge is not generated
in God, but he is a *mocker* of God.

97. I. For behold! thou *canst not* deny that
the life in a creature existeth in the *heat* of the
heart; and in that life also standeth the light of
the animated or *soulish* birth or geniture.

98. Now the heart signifieth the *sun*, which is
the beginning of life in the outward body of this
world. Now, whilst the body standeth in the
mobility or *life*, thou canst not say that the
animated or soulish birth goeth away or *departeth*
from the *heart*.

99. No more doth the *sun* go away or depart
from *its seat*, but retains and keeps its own place
to itself, as a heart; and shineth forth as a light,
or as a spirit of the *whole* body of this world, in
all powers of the body.

100. For its birth also hath a beginning out of all powers, and therefore with its light and heat it is again *one spirit* and heart in the *whole* body of this world.

101. II. Further, thou canst not deny, either, that the *gall* in a creature is *not* existed from the heart, and yet it is the *mobility* or stirring of the heart, by a *vein* that goeth from the gall to the heart; from whence the *heat* existeth. But it hath its first original from the *flash* of life, and so when the life generateth itself in the heart, and the light riseth up in the water, then the *fire-crack* goeth before, which riseth up out of the anxiety of the water in the heat.

102. For when the heat is so *anxious* in the cold in the astringent quality, that the light kindleth itself through the *hidden heaven* of the heart in the corporeity, then the anxious death in the wrath of God is terrified, and *departeth* as a crack or flash from the light, and climbeth upwards very terribly, trembling, and timorously; and the light of the heart *hasteneth* after it, and affecteth or possesseth it, and then it remaineth at a standstill.

103. This is, and signifieth, the planet *Mars*, for thus is [or hath] *Mars* come into being; and its *own quality* is nothing else but a poisonous, *venomous*, bitter fire-crack, which is risen up from the place of the *sun*.

104. But now it is always a kindler of the *sun*,

just as the gall is a kindler of the heart; whence the *heat*, both in the *sun* and in the heart, existeth, and whence the life taketh its original in *all things.*

105. III. Thirdly, thou canst not deny that the *brain* in the head in a creature is the *power* of the heart; for from the heart all powers rise up into the brain, from whence, in the brain, the *senses* of the heart exist.   The *brain* in the *head* taketh its original from the power of the heart.

Now observe:

106. After the fire-crack of the gall, or *Mars*, was departed from the light of life, then the power pressed out of the heart *after it*, through the light of life, even into the head, into the *austere* quality; and when the power can rise up no higher, then it is stayed or captivated by the austere birth, and is *dried* up by the cold.

107. Now here it stayeth, and qualifieth, mixeth or uniteth with the spirit of life in the heart, and is a *royal seat* of the spirit of the heart; for thus far the spirit of the heart's power presseth forth, and there is it *approved.*

108. For the brain sitteth in the severe birth or geniture, and in its *own body* it is the meek power of the heart, and signifieth the *new birth,* which is new regenerated in the midst or centre of the austereness of death and wrath, in *its* heaven, and presseth forth through death into life.

109. For there the spirit or the *thoughts* become a whole creaturely person again, through the affecting or proving of all powers, which in man I call the animated or *soulish* birth.

110. For when the new spirit in the brain is well settled, then it goeth to its *mother* again, into the heart; and then it standeth as a perfect spirit or will, or as a new-born person, which, in man, is called the *soul*.

111. Now behold! as the brain in man is a being and *product*, so also is the planet *Jupiter* a being and product; for it hath its original from the rising up of life, from the power which is risen up out of the *water* of life, out of the *place* of the *sun*, through the light.

112. And that power is risen up so high, that it is *caught* or captivated again in or by the austere, hard and cold power; and there it remaineth *at a stand*; and by the first *revolution* or going forth is become corporeal, and became exsiccated or dried by the austere and cold power.

113. And it is rightly the brain in the *corporeal* government of this world, from whence the senses and the reason are generated, also all meekness and *wisdom* in natural things; but the right and holy spirit in man is generated in the *hidden* heaven in *the water of life*.

114. The outward *Jupiter* is only the meekness and understanding in the outward comprehensi-

bility or *palpable* things; but the *holy* fountain or well-spring is incomprehensible and unsearchable or unfathomable to *outward* reason. For the astral birth or geniture stands only as to its root in the holy heavens, and as to its corporeity [it standeth] in the wrath.

THE TWENTY-SIXTH CHAPTER

Of the Planet Saturnus

1. *S*/*ATURN*, that cold, sharp, austere and astringent regent, taketh its beginning and original *not* from the *sun*; for Saturn hath in its power the *chamber* of death, and is a drier up of all powers, from whence *corporeity* existeth.

2. For as the *sun* is the heart of the life, and an original of all spirits in the body of this world, so *Saturn* is a beginner of all corporeity and comprehensibility or palpability. In the power of *these two* planets standeth the whole body of this world; and there cannot be any creature, nor any imaging, in the natural body of this world, nor any mobility, without the power of *these two*.

3. But *Saturn's* original is the earnest, *astringent* and austere anxiety of the whole *body* of this world; for as, in the time of the kindling of the wrath, the light in the outermost birth or geniture of this world was *extinct*, (which birth or geniture is the [1] *nature* or comprehensibility, or the rising up of the birth of all qualifying or

[1] Ratürlich-
feit.
Naturalness.

fountain spirits), so also the *astringent quality* stood in its sharpness and severest birth or geniture, and attracted or contracted most *strongly* and eagerly the whole work or effect* of the qualifying or fountain spirits.

4. From whence the *earth* and *stones* then came to be, and were very rightly the house of death, or the enclosing or shutting up of the life, wherein king *Lucifer* was captivated.

5. But when, on the first day, the light *somewhat* brake forth again, through the Word or Heart of God in the root of the nature of the body of this world, as a *choosing* or appropriating of the *day*, or as a beginning of the mobility of life, then the severe and astringent birth or geniture again obtained a *glimpse* or rising up of the life in the birth or geniture.

6. From that time the astringent birth stood as it were in an *anxious* death, till *after* the third day, when the love of God pressed through the heaven of the partition, and kindled the *light* of the *sun*.

7. But seeing the heart or *power* of the sun could *not open* the anxious birth or quality of fierceness and wrath, and *temper* the same, especially as it could not do so aloft in that height above *Jupiter*, thereupon that whole

---

* "work or effect" (*Gewirke*), "web, or texture." The word implies not so much what is effected or done as that which is in process of being done.

circumference or sphere stood in a *horrible* anxiety, just as a woman in travail; and yet could not awaken or raise the heat, because of the horrible coldness and astringency.

8. But, nevertheless, seeing the *mobility* was risen up through the power of the *hidden* heaven, therefore nature could *not rest*, but was in anguish to the birth, and generated out of or from the spirit of sharpness an astringent, cold and austere sun or star, which is *Saturn*.

9. For the spirit of heat whence the light ariseth (and out of the light, through the water, the love and meekness), could not kindle itself; but there was a birth or geniture of an austere, cold and severe fierceness, which is a drier, a spoiler and an enemy of meekness, and which in the creatures generateth the hard bones.

10. But *Saturn* was *not* bound to its place, as the *sun is*, for it is not a corporeal place or space in the *room* of the deep; but *Saturn* is a son which is born or generated out of the chamber of death, out of the kindled, hard and cold anxiety, and is only one of the household or family in that *space* or room in which it hath its course and *revolution*. For it hath its corporeal propriety to itself, as a *child*, when the child is born or generated from the mother.

["Saturn, *indeed, was created together with the* "*wheel, when the F I A T created the wheel; but* "*it doth not go forth or proceed from* Sol."]

44

11. But *why* it did rise up thus from God out of the *austere* birth, and what its *office* is, I will mention hereafter, concerning the driving about, or revolution, of the planets.

12. But its height or distance cannot be *exactly* known. But I am fully persuaded that it is in the midst, in the deep between *Jupiter* and the general sphere of the fixed stars or constellations, for it is the heart of the *corporeity* in nature.

13. For as the *sun* is the heart of life, and a cause of the *spirits* of nature, so *Saturn* is the heart and the cause of all *bodies* and imagings, formings and framings in the earth, and upon the earth, as also in the whole body of this world.

14. And as in man the *skull* is a container or encloser of the brain, wherein the *thoughts* are generated, so the *Saturnine* power is an environer, drier and container of all corporeity and comprehensibility or *palpability*.

15. And as the planet *Jupiter*, which is an unlocker and generator of meekness, is *between* the fierce *Mars* and the austere *Saturn*, and generateth the meekness and wisdom in the creatures, so the life and the senses of all creatures are generated *between* these two *qualities*; especially the *new body* of this world, as also the *new man*; of which thou wilt find more concerning the description of man.

Of the Planet Venus.

16. *Venus*, that gracious, amiable and blessed planet, or the kindler of *love* in nature, hath also its original and descent or proceeding from the springing up of the *sun*; but its condition, quality, being and proceeding or descent is *thus*:

Here observe this rightly and exactly.

17. When the *love of God* kindled the place of the *sun*, or the SUN, then, out of the anxiety, out of the place of the *sun*, out of the seven qualifying or fountain spirits of nature, there sprang up, first, the terrible, *fierce*, bitter fire-crack, whose birth and principal or first original is the *kindled bitter wrath* of God, in the astringent quality, through the water.

18. That sprang up *first*, in the kindling of the *sun* out of the chamber of death, and was an awakener or rouser of death, and a beginner of life, and climbed up aloft very fiercely, and trembling, till the light of the *sun* laid hold on it, and affected or possessed it; and there it was caught or captivated by the meekness of the light, and *stayed*; from which the *planet* Mars *came to be*.

19. After that fire-crack had taken place the power of the light, which at the beginning had generated itself out of the unctuosity or *fatness* of the water behind the fire-crack, instantly *shot forth* after it, like a mighty potency or power,

and took the fierce fire-crack captive, and highly elevated itself aloft *beyond* it, as a prince and subduer of the fierceness, from whence now arose the sensibility of nature, or the *planet* Jupiter.

The Gate of Love.

20. But when the *two* spirits, the spirit of the mobility and the spirit of the life, were risen up out of the place of the *sun*, through the kindling of the water, then the meekness, as a *seed* of the water, pressed downward in the chamber of death, with the power of light, with a very gentle and friendly *affection* or influence; from whence existed the love of life, or the *planet* Venus.

But thou must here understand this high Thing.

21. The birth, or the rising or springing up of the seven planets, and of all the stars, is *no otherwise* than *as* the life, and wonderful proportion, variety and harmony of the *Deity*, hath generated itself from *eternity*.

22. For when king *Lucifer* had caused this place of the world to be appointed as a house of wrath for himself, and supposed thus fiercely and powerfully to rule therein, then instantly the light in nature went out, wherein he supposed to be lord; and the whole nature was *benumbed* and congealed as a body of death, wherein was no mobility; and he must remain there in *darkness*, as an eternal, captive prisoner.

23. But now the holy God would *not let* this place of his body (understand *the space or room of this world*) stand in eternal *darkness* and ignominy, and *leave* it to the devils for their proper own, but generated a *new* regimen or dominion of light, and of all the seven qualifying or fountain spirits of the *Deity*; which the devil could *neither* apprehend, *nor* lay hold on, nor touch; neither was it useful or profitable to him at all.

24. But he can no more see in the light of the *sun*, for he can see in the darkness alone; for he is not become a creature in this light, and therefore it is *not* profitable or useful to him.

25. But seeing there must be a new government or dominion, it must needs be *such* a one as the devil could not touch nor lay hold on, nor make use of as his corporeal *proper* own.

Now that Government or Dominion is thus constituted.

26. The Love, or *Word*, or Heart, that is, the innate or *only begotten Son* of the Father, who is the light and meekness, and the love and joy of the Deity (*as he himself said, when he had assumed the humanity*, [1] *I am the light of the world*), he himself took the place of this world by the heart, and sat in the midst or centre of this space or room, in *that* place where the mighty prince and king *Lucifer* did sit before his fall, and there the only begotten Son was *new born* to be a creature.

[1] John viii. 12.

27. And so out of this kindled place of the *sun* there existed and were chiefly generated *six* sorts of qualities, all according to the right, law or order of the *divine* birth or geniture.*

28. I. First, there arose the *fire-crack*, or the mobility in the heat; and that is the beginning of life in the chamber of death.

II. After this, secondly, the light in the unctuosity or *fatness* of the water became shining in the heat; and that is now the *sun*.

III. Thirdly, when now the light of the *sun* had affected or possessed the whole *body* of the *sun*, then the power of life, which rose up out of the first affecting or possessing, *ascended*, as when wood is kindled, or when fire is struck out of a stone.

29. Then first is discerned the *glance* or splendour, and out of the splendour the fire-crack, and after the fire-crack the *power* of the kindled body; and the light, with the power of the body, elevateth itself instantly above the crack, and ruleth or reigneth *much higher*, deeper and more powerfully than the fire-crack.

30. Also the power of the kindled body, in the outgone power without and beyond the fire,

---

* "And out of this kindled place of the sun six distinct (*sonderlich sechserley*) qualities arose and were generated, all according to the law of the divine birth." St M. has, "six kinds of distinct (*particulières*) qualities." The two German words, "sonderlich sechserley" (very quaint, and pure Böhmese), mean that the qualities are six, that they are separate, and that each has its own peculiar character.

qualifieth, mixeth or *uniteth* gently, pleasantly, and very sensibly; and herein rightly is understood the *divine being*.

31. In the same manner also is the *existency* of the *sun*, and of the two planets, *Mars* and *Jupiter*.

32. But since the place of the sun (that is, the sun) had in itself (as also had all other places) all qualities according to the right of the Deity, thereupon instantly, in the first kindling, *all* the qualities went upwards and downwards, and generated themselves according to the eternal, beginningless, infinite law and right.

33. For the power of the light, which did mitigate the astringent and bitter quality in the place of the sun, and made it thin like water, or like the love of life, that power lowered itself, according to the nature of humility.

34. Out of *this* the planet *Venus* existed;[*] for in the house of death Venus is an *opener* of meekness, or a kindler of the water, and a soft penetrator into the hardness, a kindler of the love, in [1] which the upper regimen or *dominion*, viz., the bitter heat, is desirous or longing after *Mars*, and the hearty sensibility is desirous or longing after *Jupiter*.

[1] Venus.

35. From whence the affections or *insinuations* exist; for the power of *Venus* maketh fierce *Mars*

---

[*] "Out of this the planet Venus existed" = out of this descent of the power of the light the planet Venus has arisen, or, has come into being (lit., "is become").

or the fire-crack mild, and mitigateth it, and
maketh *Jupiter* humble, else the power of *Jupiter*
would break through the hard chamber, *Saturn*;
and in men and beasts would break through the
skull or brain-pan; and so the sensibility would
transmute itself into high-mindedness above the
birth-right, or right, law or order of the geniture
of the Deity, in the manner and way of the *proud*
devil.

Of the Planet Mercurius.

36. If we would exactly and *fundamentally*
know how, in the deep of this world, the birth
or *beginning* is of the planets and stars, and of
the essence of all beings, we must accurately
consider the instant or *innate* birth, or the
beginning of *life*, in man.

37. For *that* life taketh such a beginning and
rising, and standeth also in such an order, as doth
the birth or geniture of *the essence of all beings* in
the body of this world.

38. For the instant or innate wheel of the stars
and planets is *no* otherwise than as the birth of
the seventh spirit of nature, before the time of
the world rose up, wherein were formed images
and figures, forms, shapes or ideas, as also *heavenly
fruits*, according to the eternal right, law or order
of the *Deity*.

39. Thus, because man is created according to
the qualifying or fountain spirits of God, and also
out of the *divine* essence, *therefore* hath man's

life such a beginning and rising up as that of the planets and stars hath been.

40. For the beginning, instant or innate state and *being* of the planets and stars is not otherwise than *as* the beginning and impulse or government and dominion *in man*.

41. Now in the same way that the human life riseth up, so also in that way hath the birth of the seven planets and stars risen and sprung up; and *therein* there is no difference at all.

The Centre or Circle of the Birth of Life.
The great Depth.

42. The spirit citeth the physicians to come before this looking-glass; especially anatomists and dissectors of men, who by their *anatomy* would learn the birth and rising or springing up of *man's life*, and who have murdered many *innocent* men, against the right and law of God and of nature, *hoping* thereby to find out the wonderful proportion, harmony and form of nature, that they might thereby be *useful* in restoring the health of others.

43. But seeing in nature they are found to be *murderers*, and malefactors against the law and right of God and nature, therefore the spirit, which qualifieth, mixeth or uniteth with God, doth *not* justify them in their murderous way.

44. They might have had a *nearer* and *surer* way to learn the wonderful birth or geniture of

nature, if their *lofty* high-mindedness, and devilish, murderous curiosity had given them leave, but these have perverted their true *divine* senses or understandings.

45. Their intent was only to *fight* with men, and *not* with gods, therefore it is just they should receive such a reward of their error.

46. Come on, ye crowned ornaments of caps and hoods, etc. Let us see whether a simple layman may be able, in the knowledge of God, to search into the birth or geniture of man's life. If it be *amiss*, then reject it; if it be right, then let it *stand*.

47. I here set down this *description* of the birth or geniture of man's life, to the end that the original of the stars and planets may be the better conceived. In the description of the creation of man thou wilt find all, more fundamentally and *deeply*, what the beginning of man is.

Now observe:

48. The *seed* of man is generated in such a manner as the wonderful proportion, harmony or form of nature in its wrestling and rising up is generated, from eternity.

49. For the *human* flesh is and resembleth nature in the body of God, which is generated from the other six qualifying or fountain spirits, wherein the qualifying or fountain spirits generate themselves again, and shew forth them-

selves *infinitely*, wherein forms and images rise up, and wherein the heart of God, or the holy clear Deity in the middle or central *seat*, generateth itself *above* nature, in that centre wherein the light of life riseth up.

50. But now in man's *body*, in the government or dominion of the birth or geniture, there are *three* several things, each of them being *distinct*, and yet they are not divided *asunder* one from another; but all three together are one only man, after the kind and manner of the *Ternary* or Trinity in the divine being [or essence].

51. The *flesh* is not the life, but is a dead, inanimate being, which, when the government or dominion of the spirit *ceaseth* to qualify or operate therein, soon becometh a dead *carcass*, and putrefieth and turneth to dust or ashes.

52. But now no *spirit* can subsist in its perfection without a body, for as soon as it departeth from the body it loseth its government or *dominion*. For the body is the mother of the spirit, in which the spirit is generated, and in which it *receiveth* its strength and power. The spirit is and remaineth a spirit when it is separated and departed from the body, but it loseth its *rule*, dominion or government.

53. These three dominions or regimens are the whole man, together with flesh and spirit; and they have severally, for their beginning and

dominion or government, a *sevenfold* form, after the kind and manner of the seven spirits of God, or of the seven planets.

54. Now as the dominion or government of God's eternal, beginningless, infinite birth or geniture is, so also is the beginning and rising or springing up of the seven planets and the stars; and just so also is the rising or springing up of *man's life*.

Now observe:

55. When thou mindest, thinkest and considerest what there is in this world, and what there is without, besides or distinct from this world, or what the essence of all beings is, then thou speculatest, contemplatest, meditatest in the whole body of God, who is the essence of all beings; and that is a beginningless, *infinite* being.

56. But it hath in its own seat no mobility, rationality or comprehensibility, but is a *dark* deep, which hath neither beginning nor end. In the dark deep is neither thick nor thin, opaque nor transparent, but it is a dark chamber of death, where nothing is *perceived*, neither cold nor warmth, for it is the *end* of all things.

57. This, now, is the body of the deep, or the very real chamber of death.

58. But in this dark valley there are the *seven* spirits of God, which have neither beginning nor

end, and the one is neither the first, second, third
or last.

59. In these *seven* dominions or regimens the
regimen divideth itself into *three* distinct beings,
where the one is not without the other, nor can
they be divided the one from the other. But
those seven spirits do each of them generate one
another, from eternity to eternity.

60. The *first* dominion or regimen standeth or
consisteth in the [1]body of all things, that is, in   [1] Corpus
the whole deep, or the being or essence of all
beings or essences, which hath, in all corners and
places thereof, in itself the *seven* spirits in possession, or in propriety indivisibly, or irresistibly, for
its proper own.

61. Now if these seven spirits in any one
place *wrestle not* triumphingly, then in that
place there is no mobility, but a deep *darkness*;
and although the spirits are perfect in that
place, yet that place is a dark house; as you
may perceive and understand by a dark cave
or room close shut up, in which the kindled
spirits of the planets and stars *cannot* kindle
the elements.

62. But now the *root* of the seven spirits is
everywhere all over, but when there is no wrestling, then it standeth still and quiet, and *no*
mobility is *perceived*.

63. And such a house is the whole deep without,
within, and above all heavens; which house is

called the *Eternity*. And such a house also is the *house of flesh* in man, and in all creatures.

64. And this being, together,* comprehendeth the eternity, which is *not called* God, but the un-almighty body of nature, wherein, indeed, the Deity is immortal or not dead, but standing hidden in the kernel of the seven spirits; and yet not comprehended or understood.†

65. And such a house also the *whole space* or extent of this world came to be, when the Deity, in the seven spirits, had *hidden* itself from the horrible devils.

66. And the whole space had so *continued*, if the seven planets and stars had not risen or sprung up from God's spirits, which seven planets opened again and kindled the chambers of death in the dark house of this world, in all places everywhere; from whence existeth the regimen or *dominion* of the elements.

67. Moreover, thou art to know also, that the regimen or dominion of the seven spirits of God in the house of this world is not on that account exsiccated or dried up in *death*, that all must needs receive its life and beginning from the planets and stars.

* "And this being, together." "Together" is a literal rendering of the German. St M. has used, "*entier*," "in its wholeness."

† "and yet not comprehended or understood." The idea is that the "kernel of the seven spirits" does not comprehend the being, in its wholeness.

68. *No!* for the clear Deity standeth everywhere hidden in the circle in the *heart* of the whole deep; and the seven spirits stand in the body of the deep in anxiety and great longing, and are still kindled by the planets and stars; from whence existeth the *mobility*, and the birth or geniture in the whole deep.

69. But as long as the heart of the Deity, which [heart] is the corporeity, hideth itself in the body of this world in the outermost birth, the corporeity is a dark house; all standeth in great anguish and needeth a light, which is the sun, to shine in the chamber of darkness, until the heart of God doth move itself again in the seven spirits of God in the house of this world, and kindle the seven spirits.

70. Then the *sun* and stars will return again to their first place, and will *pass away* in such a form or manner; for the Heart and Light of God will give light and shine again in the *corporeity*, that is, in the body of this world, and replenish or fill all.

71. Then the anxiety *ceaseth*; for when the anxiety in the dominion of the geniture or birth-regimen tasteth of the *sweetness* of the light of God, so that the heart of God *triumpheth* together in the birth-regimen, then all is richly full of joy, and the whole body *triumpheth*.

72. Which at present in this time, in the house of this world, *cannot* be, because of the fierce, *captive* devil, who keepeth house in the outermost

birth or geniture in the body of this world, till the *judgment* of God.

73. *Now here thou mayest understand how the heart of God hath the fan or casting-shovel in its hand, and will one day cleanse his floor: which I herewith earnestly declare to you as in the knowledge in the light of life, where the heart, in the light of life, breaketh through, and proclaimeth the bright, clear day.*

Of Man and the Stars.

74. Now, as the *deep*, or the house of this world, is a dark house, where the whole corporeity generateth itself, and is very thick, dark, anxious and half dead, and taketh its moving from the *planets* and *stars* which kindle the body in the outermost birth or geniture, from whence existeth the mobility of the *elements*, as also the figured and *creaturely* being, so also the human house of flesh is a *dark valley*, wherein is indeed the *anxiety* to the birth of life, and it always highly endeavoureth, intending to elevate itself into the light, from whence the *life* might kindle itself.

75. But seeing the heart of God did hide itself in the centre or kernel, *therefore* it [this elevation] cannot be; and *thereupon* [on that account] the anxiety generateth no more but *ONE* seed. The house of the flesh generateth a *seed* of its likeness to the propagating of a man again; and the house of the spirit, in the instant or innate state of the

seven spirits, generateth *in the seed* another *spirit* after its likeness, to the propagating of the *spirit of man* again.

76. And the house of the *hidden* heart generateth also such a spirit as standeth *hidden*, in the body, to the spirit of the house of flesh, as also to the spirit of the astral birth or geniture; just as the *heart of God* in the seven spirits of God standeth hidden in the spirits in the deep of this world, and doth *not kindle* them, till after *this* enumeration or account of *time* is out.

77. This *third* spirit is the soul in man, and qualifieth, mixeth or *uniteth* with the heart of God, as a son or *little* god in the great, *immense or immeasurable God*.

78. Now these three distinct dominions or regimens are generated *in the seed*, which taketh its original in the flesh, as I have mentioned before, within three leaves from this.

Now observe this hidden secret hidden Mystery.   Ye
[1] *Naturalists, observe.   The Gate of the great Mystery.*   [1] Phisici, Natural Philosophers.

79. Out of the *anguishing* chamber in the body of this world, out of the seven spirits of God, are risen or sprung forth the stars, which *kindle* the body of this world; and out of or from the body the *fruit* or *seed* generateth itself, which is the water, fire, air and earth.

80. *The earth is the fruit of the seventh spirit of God, which is nature or corporeity,* wherein

the other six spirits generate themselves again, and figure or frame the *Salitter* of the seventh spirit into *infinite sorts* of forms or shapes; so that the earth also generateth its seed, which is the fruit of *vegetation*, as is apparent to the eye.

81. Now *man's* house of flesh is also such a house as the *dark* deep of this world is, wherein the seven spirits of God generate themselves.

82. But seeing man's body is its proper own, and is a *son of the whole* body of God, *therefore* it generateth also a proper seed of its own, according to the government or dominion of his corporeal, qualifying or fountain spirits.*

83. The body taketh its *food* from the seed of the seven spirits of God in the body of the great deep, which [body] is fire, air, water and earth.

84. Of or from the earth it taketh the birth of the earth, or the fruit, for it is much more noble than the earth. *It is an extracted* mass *out of the* Salitter, *out of the seventh nature spirit.*

85. For when the body of nature was *kindled* by the devil, then the *word* or the heart of God drew together the *mass* [for man's body], before the corrupted *Salitter* was pressed together, which now is called the earth, because of the hard fierceness or corruption.

86. But when the earth was *pressed* together,

---

* "his corporeal . . . spirits." Presumably "man's corporeal . . . spirits." St M. has, "the corporeal fountain-spirits."

then the *mass* stood in the dark deep in the created heaven, *between* the anxious birth or geniture and the love of the Heart of God, till the *sixth day* ; and then the Heart of God breathed the light of life out of or from his Heart into the innermost or *third* birth or geniture in the *mass*.

87. Now when this was done, then in the *mass* the seven spirits of the qualities *began* to qualify or operate ; and in the *mass* the *seed* of the seven qualifying or fountain spirits generated itself, as fire, air and water, *as* it did in the body of the deep.

88. *Thus* MAN *became a living soul*, in that kind and manner as the *sun* is risen or sprung forth, and out of that the seven *planets*.

89. The *light* in man, which the Heart of God *had breathed in*, signifieth or resembleth the *sun* which shineth in the whole deep ; concerning which you will find more clearly about the creation of man.

90. Now behold ! As in the deep of this world, through the *kindling* of the stars, a *seed* is generated out of the body of the dark deep, like the *creaturely* body, so also in like manner, in *man's* house of flesh there is generated a seed, according to the eternal birth-right of the *seven* qualifying or fountain spirits.

91. And in the *seed* there are *three distinct* things, whereof the one cannot fathom the others, and yet the others are in that *one* only seed, and they all qualify, mix or unite one with

another, as one [1] being; and they are also *one* [1] *being*, and yet also *three distinct things*, according to the kind and manner of the *Ternary* or Trinity in the Deity.

92. *First* there is the whole *body* of man, which is a dark house, and hath no mobility besides, or *without*, or distinct from the qualifying or operation of the seven spirits, but is a dark valley, as the body of the deep of this world is.

93. Now in the dark body of man there is also such a regimen or dominion, as to the *seven* spirits, as there is in the body of the deep. And when the seven spirits qualify or operate according to the *birth-right* of the Deity, then, out of the *wrestling* of the seven spirits, a *seed* generateth itself, according to *their* likeness.

94. Now that seed hath first a *mother*, which is the dark *chamber* of the house of flesh. Secondly, it hath a mother, which is the *wheel* of the seven spirits, according to the kind and manner of the seven planets. Thirdly, it hath a mother that is generated in the circle of the seven spirits in the centre, which mother is the *heart* of the seven spirits.

95. And this now is the *mother of the soul*, which shineth through the seven spirits, and maketh them living; and in their stead the seed qualifieth, mixeth or *uniteth* with the Heart of God. But the seed which so qualifieth is *that*

[1] Wesen.

seed alone in which the light is kindled : in that in which the wrath-fire burneth, there this third mother remaineth *captive* in the dark chamber.

96. And though indeed it is the *third* mother,* yet it remaineth but a foolish virgin, if the light be not kindled in it. Just as the deep of this world is a foolish virgin before the Heart of God, in which deep of this world the wheel of the seven spirits standeth in such anxiety, in so much *corruption* and *redemption*, in heat and in cold, as is apparent.

97. But when the *third* mother is kindled in the *light*, then it standeth in the created heaven of the *holy* life, and shineth through the *second* mother, the seven spirits, whereby the seven spirits get a friendly, courteous will, which is the love of the life, as you may read in the eighth chapter of this book, *concerning the love-birth or geniture of God.*

98. But through the *third* mother they cannot constantly or *permanently* shine, for the third mother standeth in the house of darkness ; but they often cast a *glimpse* upon the third mother, even as if it lightened, whereby the third mother *many times* becometh very longing, and rejoiceth highly, but is soon bolted up again by the *fierceness of God's wrath.*

99. The devil also danceth at this gate, for it

---

* "And though indeed it is the third mother"—in the sense of, "In spite of being the third mother."

is the prison wherein the *new* man lieth hid, and wherein the devil lieth captive.

100. I mean, in the house of the deep of this world. Though indeed [in] the house of *flesh* and the deep all [things or parts] qualify with one another as one body, and are one body, only [with] distinct parts or members.

The Deep in the Centre.

101. Now behold! When the *seed* is generated, it standeth in the centre or midst of the body in the *heart*; for there the *mother* catcheth the *Ternary* or Trinity.

102. *First*, the astringent spirit catcheth hold, and that draweth together a mass or *lump* out of the *sweet* water, that is, out of or from the unctuosity or fatness of the *blood* of the heart, or from the sap or *oil* of the heart.

103. Now that oil hath clearly the *root* of the *Ternary* or Trinity in it, *viz.* the *whole man*; for it is just as when kindled tinder is cast into straw.

Now it may be asked, How comes this to pass?

104. *Here now is the true ground of man; observe it exactly, for it is the looking-glass of the great Mystery, the deep secret of the humanity, about which all the learned, since the beginning of the world, have danced, and have sought after this door, but they have not found it.*

105. *But I must once mention, that now is*

the Dawning *or* Morning Redness *of the* Day, *as
the Door-keeper will have me do.*

Now observe:

106. Just as was the first *mass*, out of which
Adam became a living man, so also in like
manner is every *mass* or *seed* of the *Ternary* or
Trinity *in every* man.

Observe:

107. When the *Salitter* or fabric* of the six
qualifying or fountain spirits (which Salitter is
the seventh nature-spirit in the *space* or room of
this world) was kindled, then the *Word* or Heart
of God stood everywhere in the centre or midst
of the circle of the seven spirits, as a *heart*, which
[heart] at once replenished all, *viz.* the whole
space or room of this world.

108. But seeing the deep, that is, the whole
space of this world, was the body of the Father,
(understand the Father of the Heart of God),
understand the Father's *body*, and the Heart in
the whole body did shine forth, *viz.* the Father's
lustre or brightness, then the corrupted *Salitter*
was affected or possessed everywhere with the
light; and the Heart of God could *not fly* out
from it, but did *hide* its lustre and shining light
in the body of the whole deep, *from* the horrid
kindled spirits of devils.

109. When this was done, then the qualifying

* "fabric" (*Gewirke*).   See Ch. 26, par. 3.

or fountain spirits became very fierce and *vehemently* struggling, and the astringent spirit, as the strongest, drew very terribly together in the seventh nature-spirit the fabric and effects * of the other *five*; from whence the bitter earth and stones came to be, but [they] were *not yet* driven together, but moved in the whole deep.

110. In this hour the *mass* was drawn together; for when the Heart of God did hide itself in the *Salitter*, then it cast a *glance* again on the whole space or body, and thought how it might be *remedied* again, whereby another angelical kingdom might be in the deep of this world.

111. *But the glance was the love-spirit in the Heart of God, which in that place of the glance affected or possessed the oil of the water, where previously the light was risen up.*

[1] Luke xxii. 61.

112. *Here consider* [1] *Saint Peter's glance, that was cast upon him in the house of Caiphas: it is the very same.*

113.† And the spirit of the man, (understand the root of the love which, in the rising up of the life out of the water, riseth up through the fire), and also the spirit of the woman, both catch one another in that oil of the heart, where presently a mass, seed, or driving will or desire to the propagating of a man again arises in the mass.

* " fabric and effects " (*Gewirke*). See Ch. 26, par. 3.
† A new translation of this par. has been substituted for Sparrow's rendering.

114. Just in such a way and manner the *first mass* also came to be, for the love-spirit in the Heart of God cast a glance, in the *body* of the kindled wrathful Father, on the *water of life*, whereby, and out of which, the *love* in the fire-flash arose or sprang up *before* the time of the wrath.

115. In this casting of the glance the one spirit caught the other; the unctuous *oil* or water in the wrath *conceived* from the love-spirit in the Heart of God, and qualified, mixed or united with the same, and the astringent spirit drew the *mass together*; and there was clearly a birth, or a will or desire to the *producing* of a whole creature; just as the seed in man is.

116. But now the firmament of heaven, that is *between* the Heart of God and the kindled, hard chamber of death, was closed or shut up; else the *life* in the *mass* had suddenly kindled itself.

117. For the firmament was *within* in the *mass*, as well as *without*, distinct from the *mass*, which is the parting mark or limit of *separation* between the Heart of God and the fierce devils.

118. *Therefore* the *Word* or Heart of God *must* blow up the moving spirit in the *mass*, which was first done but on the *sixth day*, for very assured causes.

119. For if heaven had not, as a firmament, been *shut up* in the *mass*, between the Heart of God and the corporeal, qualifying or fountain

spirits of the *mass*, then the *mass* might have *kindled* the *soul* from or by its *own* power; as it happened with the holy angels.

120. But it was to be *feared* that it would come to pass as it did with that fair little son *Lucifer*, seeing the corporeal, qualifying or fountain spirits in the *mass* were kindled in the *wrath-fire*.

121. Therefore heaven *must* be a firmament between the sparkle which had conceived from the Heart of God in the *first* glance; that though the body *might happen* to perish, yet the *holy seed* might remain, which is the *soul*, which qualifieth, mixeth or uniteth with the Heart of God, out of which a *new body* might come to be, when the whole God should *kindle again* the deep of this world in the light of the Heart of God; and just so it is come to be with the *body*. *The love of God have mercy*, and *take pity on it!*

122. The dear man *Moses* writeth, *That God made man out of a clod of earth*, as the learned have rendered it. But *Moses* was *not* present when it was done.

123. But this I must needs say, that *Moses* hath written very *rightly*, though the true understanding or meaning, out of what the earth proceeded, remained hidden to *Moses*, and to them that have come after him in the *letter*, for the spirit hath kept it hidden to *this* very time.

124. It was also hidden from *Adam*, while he

was yet *in Paradise*; but *now* it will be *fully*
revealed. For the Heart of God hath set upon
or assaulted the chamber of death, and will *shortly*
break quite through.

125. And therefore, in these our present times,
some *beams* of the day will more and more break
through in the hearts of *some* men, and make
known the day.

126. *But when the* Dawning *or* Morning Redness
*shall shine from the east to the west, or from the
rising to the setting, then, assuredly, time will be
no more; but the* SUN *of the Heart of God
riseth or springeth forth, and,* [1] RA. RA. R. P. will
be pressed in the winepress without the city, and
therewith to R. P.*

[1] See *Epistles
of Jacob
Behmen*
(1649), Ep.
23, v. 12.

127. *These are hidden, mystical words, and
are understood only in the language of nature.*

128. *Moses* writeth very *rightly*, that man was
created out of the earth; but at *that* time, when
the *mass* was held by the Word, then the *mass*
was *not* earth. But if it had *not* been held or
kept by the Word, then at that very hour it had
become *black* earth, but the cold wrath-fire was
in it already.

129. For at the very *hour* when *Lucifer*
elevated himself the Father was moved to *wrath*
in the qualifying or fountain spirits against the
legions of *Lucifer*; and the Heart of God hid
itself in the firmament of heaven, where the

---

* " and therewith to R. P.," lit., " and therewith AM. R. P."

Salitter, effect, product or fabric * of the corporeity was *burning* already; for without or distinct from the light is the *dark* chamber of death.

130. But the *mass* was held or kept in the firmament of heaven that it might *not* be congealed; for when the Heart of God *glanced* on the *mass* with its hot love, then the unctuosity or oil in the *mass*, which rose up out of the water through the fire, out of which the light riseth up, and out of which the love-spirit riseth up, caught hold of *the Heart of God*, and was *impregnated* with a *young son*.

131. And that was the *seed of love*; for one love embraced the other; the love of the *mass* embraced and conceived from the love out of the *glance* of the Heart of God, and was thereby impregnated; and this is the birth or geniture of the *soul*; and as to *this son*, man is the image of God.

132. But the qualifying or fountain spirits in the *mass* could not presently be kindled thereby from the soul; for the soul stood only in the seed in the *mass*, hidden with the Heart of God in its heaven, till the Creator *breathed* upon the *mass*; and then the qualifying or fountain spirits kindled the *soul* also, and then both body and soul lived equally together.

133. Indeed the soul had its *life* before the body, but it stood in the Heart of God, hidden in the *mass* in heaven, and was a kind of holy seed,

* "effect, product or fabric" (*Gewirke*). See Ch. 26, par. 3.

qualifying, mixing or uniting with God, which seed is *eternal*, incorruptible and indestructible; for it was a *new* and pure seed for an angel and image of God.

134. But the fabric, effect or product * of the whole *mass* was an extract or attraction of the *Word* of God, out of the fabric or effect of the qualifying or fountain spirits, or of the *Salitter*, out of which the earth came to be.

135. This extract was *not yet* become earth, though it was the *Salitter* of the earth, but was held or kept by the *Word*.

136. For when the love-spirit out of the Heart of God glanced on the *Salitter* of the *mass*, then the *Salitter* did catch hold of it and conceived from it, and was *impregnated* in the centre of the soul, and the *Word* stood in the *mass* in the *sound*; but the *light* abode in the centre of the *mass*, in the firmament of heaven, remaining hidden in the unctuous oil of the heart, and did *not* move itself forth out of the firmament of heaven, in the birth of the qualifying or fountain spirits.

137. Else, if the *light* had kindled itself in the birth or geniture of the soul, then all the seven qualifying or fountain spirits, according to the eternal birthright of the Deity, had triumphed and qualified, mixed or *united* in and with the light, and had been a *living* angel; but seeing the wrath had

* "fabric, effect or product" (*Gewirke*).   See Ch. 26, par. 3.

clearly already infected the Salitter, therefore that danger was to be *feared* that befell *Lucifer*.

Now it may be asked:

138. *Why were not* many masses *created at this time, out of which, instantly at once, there might have been a whole angelical host or army, instead of fallen* Lucifer?

139. *Why should there be so long a time of staying in the wrath?*

140. *And why should the whole host or army be generated out of that one* mass, *in so very long a time?*

141. *Or did not the Creator at this time see and know of the fall of man?*

Answer.

142. *This now is the very door of the hidden, secret Mystery of the Deity.* Concerning which the Reader is to conceive, that it is not in the power or capacity of any man to discern or to know it, if the *Dawning* or *Morning-Redness* doth not break forth in the centre in the soul.

143. For these things are *divine* Mysteries, which no man can search into by his *own* Reason. I also esteem myself most unworthy of such a gift; and besides, I shall have many scorners and mockers against me; for the *corrupted* nature is horribly *ashamed* before the light.

144. But for all that, I cannot forbear; for

when the divine light breaketh forth in the circle or birth of life, then the qualifying or fountain spirits *rejoice*, and in the circle of the life reflect or look back into their mother, into the *eternity*; and they also look forwards into the eternity.

145. It [the breaking forth of the light] is not, however, a permanent essence, nor a constant illumination of the qualifying or fountain spirits, much *less* of the *bestial* body; but it is the *ray* of the breaking through of the *light* of God with a fiery impulse, which riseth up through the meek water of life in the love, and remaineth, abiding in *its* heaven.

146. Therefore I can bring it no further than from the *heart* into the *brain*, before the princely throne of the senses, and there it is *shut up* in the firmament of heaven; and it goeth *not back* again through the qualifying or fountain spirits into the mother of the heart, that it might come on to the *tongue*, for if that were done I would tell it with my *mouth*, and make it known to the *world*.

147. But for that cause I will let it stand in *its heaven*, and write according to my gifts, and with wonder and *admiration* expect what will become of it. For in the qualifying or fountain spirits I cannot *sufficiently* comprehend or apprehend it, because they stand in the *anxious* chamber.

148. With or through the *soul*, I see it *very well*; but the firmament of the heaven is between,

in which the soul *hideth* itself, and there receiveth its *rays* from the light of God; and in that respect it goeth *through* the firmament of heaven as a tempest of *lightning*, but very gently, in a most amiable and pleasant delight and joy.

149. So that I *cannot*, in the comprehensibility, in my *innate*, instant or present qualifying or fountain spirits, or in the circle of life, discern or know it *otherwise*, for *the day breaketh forth apace*.

150. For that cause I will *write* according to this knowledge, though the devil should offer to assault and storm the world; which, however, he cannot do.   But his hour-glass is shewn to him, and set before him.

¹ that con-
tend about
Election and
Predestina-
tion.

151. Now come on, you Electionists, ¹ and contenders about the Election of Grace, you that suppose *you alone* are in the right, and esteem a simple faith to be but a *foolish* thing; you have danced long enough before this door, and have made your *boast* of the Scriptures, that they maintain that God hath of grace *chosen some* men in their mother's womb to the kingdom of heaven, and reprobated or rejected *others*.

152. Here make to yourselves many *masses*, out of which there may proceed other manner of men of other qualities, and *then* you may be in the right.   But out of the *one* only *mass* you can make no more than *one* only *love* of God, which presseth forth through the first man, and so presseth through and upon *all*. If God should

have permitted *Peter* or *Paul* to have written otherwise, then look to the ground, to the *heart.*

153. If you lay hold on the Heart of God, then you have ground *enough.*

154. If God give me life a little while longer, I will shew you Saint *Paul's* Election of Grace.

THE TWENTY-SEVENTH CHAPTER

*   *   *   *   *   *   *